THE TWO TRUTHS
in the Mādhyamika Philosophy
of the Ge-luk-ba Order of Tibetan Buddhism

This book has been approved for inclusion in *Studies in Indo-Tibetan Buddhism*. The editorial board for this series includes:

THE TWO TRUTHS

in the Mādhyamika Philosophy
of the Ge-luk-ba Order of Tibetan Buddhism

by Guy Newland

Snow Lion Publications
Ithaca, New York USA

Snow Lion Publications
P.O. Box 6483
Ithaca, New York 14851

Printed in the USA

ISBN 0-937938-79-3 (paper)
ISBN 0-937938-80-7 (cloth)

Studies in Indo-Tibetan Buddhism Series ISBN 1-55939-000-X

Library of Congress Cataloging-in-Publication Data

Newland, Guy.
The two truths in the madhyamika philosophy of the Ge-luk-ba order of Tibetan Buddhism / by Guy Newland. — 1st ed. U.S.A.
p. cm — (Studies in Indo-Tibetan Buddhism)
Includes bibliographical references and index.
ISBN 0-937938-80-7 (cloth) — ISBN 0-937938-79-3 (paper)
1. Dge-lugs-pa (Sect)—Doctrines. 2. Truth (Buddhism) 3. Mādhyamika (Buddhism) I. Title. II. Series.
BQ7640.N48 1992
294.3'923—dc20 90-27701
CIP

Contents

Note on Transliteration

Except in the bibliography, transliterated words are underlined and (unless the foreign word itself is under discussion) set off by parentheses. The transliteration of Tibetan words into roman letters follows the system set out by Turrell Wylie, with the modification that no letters are capitalized.[1] Transliteration of Sanskrit words follows standard practice. A few words (e.g., "Bodhisattva," "Buddha," "karma," "tantra," and "yogi") of Sanskrit origin are treated as English words.

When not marked as transliterations, Tibetan proper nouns are presented according to a modified version of a phoneticization system devised by Jeffrey Hopkins.[2] In the following table, the transliterated Tibetan root letters appear on the left and their phonetic equivalents on the right.

Table 1

ka = ḡa	kha = ka	ga = ga	nga = nga or n̄ga
ca = j̄a	cha = cha	ja = ja	nya = nya or n̄ya
ta = d̄a	tha = ta	da = da	na = na or n̄a
pa = b̄a	pha = pa	ba = ba	ma = ma or m̄a
tsa = d̄za	tsha = tsa	dza = dza	wa = wa
zha = sha	za = sa	'a = a	ya = ya
ra = ra	la = la	sha = s̄ha	sa = s̄a
ha = ha	a = a		

The macron above a consonant indicates a "high" tone, the pronunciation of which Hopkins describes as "not deep in the throat, but higher or more forward and tending to be sharp and short."[3] Nasals in the root position take on this high tone only when affected by a prefixed or superscribed letter. In order to better reflect actual pronunciation (Lhasa dialect), this system substitutes *k* and *p* for Wylie's *g* and *b*, as in the name Dak-tsang (*stag tshang*). A subjoined *la* causes a syllable to be pronounced "l̄a," except in the case of *zla*, which is pronounced "da." *dbang* is phoneticized as *w̄ang* and *dbyang* is pronounced "ȳang."

Some examples of the correct phonetic forms of a few of the Tibetan names used frequently in this book may be found on the left side of the following list. Transliteration appears on the right.

Table 2

B̄el-den-chö-jay	dpal ldan chos rje
Jam-ȳang-shay-b̄a	'jam dbyangs bzhad pa
J̄ang-ḡya	lcang kya
Jay-d̄zun Chö-ḡyi-gyel-tsen	rje btsun chos kyi rgyal mtshan
S̄ö-nam-drak-b̄a	bsod nams grags pa

However, in the present modified version of the Hopkins system, macrons indicating high tones will not appear in the text. In deference to common usage, a few further deviations from the system are allowed: the title Geshe (which would be Ge-shay), the names Tsong-ka-pa (which would be Dzong-ka-ba), and Lhasa (which is pronounced Hla-sa); also, the names of Tibetans who have lived in the West which are spelled as they are spelled by those Tibetans.

Introduction

SCOPE

When I met with the Dalai Lama at his residence in September of 1984, I described to him the scope of the research that has resulted in this work. His response was to point out that there would be enormous value in a broader comparative study of the two truths as they are treated in the four orders (*chos lugs*) of Tibetan Buddhism (i.e., Ge-luk, Sa-gya, Nying-ma, and Ga-gyu). He also suggested that it would be profoundly helpful to study the relationship between the meanings of the two truths in tantric systems vis-à-vis non-tantric systems. In fact, I had originally planned this work along those very lines; I still think such a book should and will be written. Perhaps this study of the Ge-luk (*dge lugs*) treatment of the two truths in the Mādhyamika phase of their monastic curriculum will be part of the foundation for a more encompassing understanding of the two truths in Tibetan Buddhism.

Systematic consideration of the extrinsic adequacy of the Ge-luk system also falls beyond the scope of this study. That is, while sometimes touching on these issues, my *primary* concerns here include neither the question, "Are the Ge-luk-bas right about what the Indian sources mean?" nor the question, "Is the Ge-luk rendering of Mādhyamika cogent in the context of contemporary philosophy?" Elizabeth Napper and Jeffrey Hopkins have given us a starting point for study of the former question, while Georges Dreyfus and Robert Thurman are among the many scholars working on the latter problem.[1]

This work instead focuses on the *internal* workings of the Ge-luk reading of the two truths doctrine in Prāsaṅgika-Mādhyamika. What textual or doctrinal problems does it solve for those who adopt it? How does it generate in its advocates a sense of a rationally coherent and well-ordered Buddhist world? Where are the fault-lines in the system and how are they handled by successive generations of Ge-luk-ba authors? By probing these questions, we will show how the Ge-luk philosophical treatment of the two truths works as part of a religious system.

THE TWO TRUTHS

Nāgārjuna argued that the meaning of Buddha's teaching of emptiness (*stong pa nyid, śūnyatā*) as ultimate truth (*don dam bden pa, paramārthasatya*) is that when one analytically searches for phenomena that have been assumed to exist, they cannot be found. Nāgārjuna's commentators, Buddhapālita (c.470-540?) and Candrakīrti (seventh century), elaborated what came to be regarded as the Prāsaṅgika branch of Mādhyamika, holding that there is nothing that inherently exists even in a conventional sense. Tsong-ka-pa Lo-sang-drak-ba (*tsong kha pa blo bzang grags pa*, 1357-1419), founder of the Ge-luk-ba order, wrote extensively on Prāsaṅgika-Mādhyamika, asserting that Candrakīrti's radical negation of inherent existence even conventionally *is* compatible with the mere existence of validly established phenomena. Jam-yang-shay-ba (*'jam dbyang bzhad pa*, 1648-1721), Jay-dzun Chö-gyi-gyel-tsen (*rje brtsun chos kyi rgyal mtshan*, 1469-1546), Paṇ-chen Sö-nam-drak-ba (*paṇ chen bsod nams grags pa*, 1478-1554) and others composed textbooks (*yig cha*) on Mādhyamika, interpreting and analyzing Tsong-ka-pa's view in a format conditioned by the pedagogical requirements of the Ge-luk-ba monastic colleges (*grwa tshang*). These textbooks are primarily based on Tsong-ka-pa's *Illumination of the Thought*, which is a commentary on Candrakīrti's *Supplement to (Nāgārjuna's) "Treatise on the Middle Way" (Madhyamakāvatāra)*.

Ge-luk-bas rank Prāsaṅgika-Mādhyamika as the most profound of all thought-systems, and Nāgārjuna (second century), the founder of Mādhyamika, unequivocally declares the importance of the two truths in his *Treatise on the Middle Way*:[2]

> Doctrines taught by the Buddha
> Rely wholly on the two truths:
> Worldly concealer-truths
> And truths that are ultimate.

An ultimate truth is an emptiness—that is, an absence of inherent existence (*rang bzhin gyis grub pa, svabhāvasiddha*). Concealer-truths (*kun rdzob bden pa, saṃvṛtisatya*) are the bases of emptinesses—that is, the phenomena that have the quality of being devoid of inherent existence.

The fundamentals of Tsong-ka-pa's interpretation of the two truths in Prāsaṅgika are intact in every Ge-luk-ba textbook on Mādhyamika:

(1) The two truths are mutually exclusive (*'gal ba*). They are a dichotomous division of objects of knowledge (*shes bya, jñeya*), i.e., all existents.
(2) The two truths, although mutually exclusive, are a single entity (*ngo bo gcig*) because emptiness (ultimate truth) is the mode of subsistence of conventional phenomena (concealer-truths).
(3) The term "concealer-truth," (*kun rdzob bden pa, saṃvṛtisatya*) indicates that conventional phenomena are truths only for the perspective of an ignorant consciousness that conceals reality. In fact, conventional phenomena are not truths, but are falsities (*rdzun pa, mṛṣā*) because they do not exist as they appear.
(4) Nonetheless, concealer-truths are objects found by conventional valid cognition (*tha snyad pa'i tshad ma*), while ultimate truths are objects found by ultimate valid cognition (*don dam pa'i tshad ma*). Conventional valid cognition is not superceded or invalidated by ultimate valid cognition.
(5) Concealer-truths cannot be divided into real (*yang dag, tathya*) and unreal (*log pa, mithyā*) because they are all unreal and false. However, they can be divided into those that are real in relation to a worldly perspective and those that are unreal in relation to a worldly perspective.
(6) Buddha Superiors are omniscient; they simultaneously, explicitly, and without confusion know all concealer-truths and all ultimate truths.

We will investigate each of these positions in some detail, showing how they place Ge-luk-ba at odds with many non-Ge-luk-ba interpreters of Mādhyamika, how they are justified by the Ge-luk-bas, and how they function as critical elements of the Ge-luk effort to construct a rational and coherent Mādhyamika system.

GE-LUK SCHOLASTICISM

As we explore Ge-luk doctrine, we will also gain access to the inner dynamics of Ge-luk scholasticism. As described by D.S. Ruegg, the scholastic period of Tibetan philosophy began in the sixteenth century and has been characterized by "interpretation (often epigonal) comprising continued exegetical and hermeneutical activity largely within the bounds of the different *chos lugs* [religious orders]."[3] Within Ge-luk-ba, it is *de rigueur* to presume that the universe is open to interpretations that are at once logical and consistent with Buddha's teaching. In his five major works on Mādhyamika, Tsong-ka-pa provides not only the general outline for such a philosophy, but many of the fine points as well. Utilizing this "hermeneutic of consistency and coherence"[4] inherited from their founder, each Ge-luk-ba author seeks to follow through on his delineation of a paradox-free Mādhyamika.

Nevertheless, Tsong-ka-pa's scholastic successors find much to disagree about. Ge-luk writers have devoted the greater portion of their enthusiasm and dialectic creativity to internal controversies. Though it has seldom been noted by outside scholars, the rivalries between monastic colleges *within the same Ge-luk monastery* are usually more immediate and more intensely felt than rivalries with other monasteries or with other orders. Behind the prevailing agreement on most important points lies a bewildering maze of clashing rhetoric and opinion on subtleties of doctrine and grammar; there are also conflicts about the degree of pious deference to be accorded Tsong-ka-pa's immediate followers. Accordingly, in addition to elaborating on the six basic points of agreement listed above, we give special attention to issues on which the textbook authors disagree—for example, the problem of defining the "worldly perspective" (*'jig rten shes ngo*) in terms of which concealer-truths are divided into real and unreal. We aim not only to trace the logic of such arguments in detail, but also to demonstrate how they emerge from a dialectic between the authority of traditional scriptural sources and the authority of the individual author's own powers of reason and creative reading.

SOURCES AND RESEARCH PROCEDURES

Sources for this work fall into four main categories: (1) books in Tibetan from which the main sections on the two truths in Prāsaṅgika-Mādhyamika were carefully translated and annotated (for future publication), (2) books in Tibetan from which information has been drawn without translation of a major excerpt, (3) oral teachings on the two truths by Tibetan scholars, and (4) works in Western languages (see bibliography). Three books in the first category are:

(a) Candrakīrti's *Commentary on the "Supplement to (Nāgārjuna's) 'Treatise on the Middle Way'"* along with Candrakīrti's *Supplement Commentary*,
(b) *A Good Explanation Adorning the Throats of the Fortunate, General Meaning Commentary Clarifying Difficult Points in (Tsong-ka-pa's) "Illumination of the Thought"* by Jay-dzun Chö-gyi-gyel-tsen (*rje btsun chos kyi rgyal mtshan*, 1469-1546), and
(c) *Great Exposition of the Middle Way* by Jam-yang-shay-ba (*'jam dbyang bzhad pa*, 1648-1721).

Candrakīrti's *Supplement* is the primary root text for the study of Prāsaṅgika in the monastic educational system. Jay-dzun Chö-gyi-gyel-tsen's work is a required textbook at the Jay (*byes*) college of Se-ra (*se ra*) Monastery and the Jang-dzay (*byang rtse*) college of Gan-den (*dga' ldan*) Monastery. Jam-yang-shay-ba's *Great Exposition of the Middle Way* is a lengthy and detailed treatise that is the focal point for Mādhyamika studies in the Go-mang (*sgo mang*) college of Dre-bung (*'bras spungs*). I also prepared complete but unpolished translations of relevant sections from two other books: *General Meaning Commentary on the Middle Way* by Paṇ-chen Sö-nam-drak-ba (*paṇ chen bsod nams grags pa*, 1478-1554), and *Presentation of Tenets* by Jang-gya Rol-bay-dor-jay (*lcang skya rol pa'i rdo rje*, 1717-1786). Paṇ-chen Sö-nam-drak-ba's book is required reading for the study of Mādhyamika at the Lo-sel-ling (*blo gsal gling*) college of Dre-bung Monastery and the Shar-dzay (*shar rtse*) college of Gan-den Monastery. Jang-gya's well-known treatise on tenet systems also represents a Go-mang perspective.

Among works in the second category, those from which I have gathered important information without translating large sections, there are many sūtras and śāstras, especially Nāgārjuna's *Treatise* on the Middle Way, and Candrakīrti's *Clear Words.* From among Tsong-ka-pa's writings I have referred mainly to his *Illumination of the Thought, Ocean of Reasoning, Great Exposition of the Stages of the Path*, and *Intermediate Exposition of the Stages of the Path.* Tsong-ka-pa's *Illumination of the Thought* is especially important because it explains the meaning of Candrakīrti's *Supplement Commentary*. Of works by Tsong-ka-pa's immediate disciples, I have relied most heavily upon Kay-drup's (*mkhas grub*, 1385-1438) *Thousand Doses* and Gyel-tsap's (*rgyal tshap*, 1364-1432) *Explanation of (Śāntideva's) "Engaging in the Bodhisattva Deeds".* Paṇ-chen Sö-nam-drak-ba's *Disputation and Reply Regarding (Candrakīrti's) "Supplement"* (*dbu ma la 'jug pa'i brgal lan*) and Jam-yang-shay-ba's *Great Exposition of Tenets* have also been essential sources. I have also consulted *Annotations on (Jam-yang-shay-ba's) "Great Exposition of Tenets"*, and *Explanation of the Meaning of the Ultimate and the Conventional in the Four Tenet Systems* by the Mongolian scholar Ngak-wang-bel-den (*ngag dbang dpal ldan*, b. 1779), also known as Bel-den-chö-jay, to resolve difficult points in Jam-yang-shay-ba's interpretation. In order to represent the opinions of modern Tibetan scholars on the two truths, I refer to more recent works including *Instructions on the Profound Meaning* by Kensur Padma-gyel-tsen (*mkhan zur padma rgyal mtshan*, 1908-1985), *Beautiful Ornament for Faith* by Geshe Bel-den-drak-ba (*dpal ldan grags pa*), former head librarian of Tibet House in New Delhi, and *Illumination of Difficult Points* by the contemporary Go-mang scholar Tsul-tim-gya-tso (*tshul khrims rgya mtsho*).

As for the third source category, oral teachings, I received teachings on Jam-yang-shay-ba's *Great Exposition of the Middle Way* and Jang-gya's *Exposition of Tenets* from the eminent Lo-sel-ling scholar Yeshay Tupden (*ye shes thub bstan*), former abbot of Lo-sel-ling, while he was a visiting scholar at the University of Virginia in 1982. During June and July of 1985 I studied Paṇ-chen Sö-nam-drak-ba's *General Meaning Commentary on the Middle Way* with Lo-sang-gya-tso (*blo bzang rgya mthso*), principal of the School of Dialectics in Dharamsala, India. During August and September of 1985, I studied Ngak-wang-bel-den's *Explanation of the Meaning of the Ultimate and the Conventional in the Four Tenet Systems* with Geshe Bel-den-drak-ba. In September of 1985, His Holiness the Fourteenth Dalai Lama, Tenzin Gyatso, met with me once and answered a series of questions about the two truths. During the spring semester of 1987, Geshe Bel-den-drak-ba was a visiting scholar at the

University of Virginia; I met him regularly during that period to ask questions about the two truths. Georges Dreyfus, who as the Venerable Sang-gyay-sam-drup (*sang rgyas bsam grub*) attained the rank of geshe in 1985, also gave me very kind assistance, answering numerous questions about the assertions of the Se-ra and Lo-sel-ling monastic colleges in the course of informal discussions during the fall of 1986 and the spring of 1987. Finally, in June of 1987, through the kindness of Joshua Cutler, I met and questioned Kensur Den-ba-den-dzin (*mkhan zur bstan pa bden 'dzin*), former abbot of Go-mang, at the Tibetan Buddhist Learning Center in Washington, New Jersey.

The research procedures applied to these four classes of material are as follows: (1) I read chapters on the two truths from several of the Tibetan books listed above. In many cases, I prepared draft translations. I made lists of questions about the interpretation of difficult points in the text. (2) From Tibetan scholars I received line-by-line explanations of the meanings of several of these texts with special attention to my pre-formulated questions. Their comments were tape-recorded and, in some cases, transcribed. (3) I analyzed this data and organized it into a coherent presentation of the two truths according to Ge-luk-ba. (4) I compared these conclusions with those of other contemporary Buddhologists working with Sanskrit and Tibetan materials.

ACKNOWLEDGEMENTS

Thanks go foremost to Professor Jeffrey Hopkins of the University of Virginia, through whom I came to study Mādhyamika and Tibetan language. He spent countless hours helping me in this research. Others at the University of Virginia who advised me and assisted me in innumerable ways during the course of this project include Professor Paul Groner and Harvey Aronson. I wish to thank Professor Karen Lang, Professor Julian Hartt, and Professor Benjamin Ray for their suggestions. Professor Richard Martin, South Asia Bibliographer for Alderman Library, has been an invaluable guide.

Still, this would have been a hollow enterprise without the teachings I received, both in the U.S. and in India, from Tibetan scholars who kindly answered my questions, sharing their time and insight without reserve. As described above, my primary Tibetan informants were Kensur Yeshay Tupden, Gen Lo-sang-gya-tso, and Geshe Bel-den-drak-ba; I also received valuable information from

His Holiness, the Dalai Lama, and from Kensur Den-ba-den-dzin.

While I was in India, I enjoyed much-needed hospitality, practical advice, companionship, introductions, and other assistance from several generous individuals. My stay in India could hardly have been worthwhile without the help of Gareth Sparham (Ven. Tup-den-tan-dö), Ven. Lo-sang-tap-kay, Ven. Tup-den-dra-shi, Rin-zin-wang-mo, Gordon Aston (Ven. Lo-sang-tar-chin) and Geshe Ye-shay-tap-kay.

I also thank John Powers, who shared important information from his research on the *Sūtra Unravelling the Thought* (*Saṃdhinirmocana*) and Professor Daniel Cozort, who shared with me his notes on a conversation, pertaining to the two truths, between himself and Geshe Sö-nam-rin-chen.

Finally, I want to thank the friends and family members who have given me the generous financial and emotional support that I needed to complete this work. Although I was chosen to receive a Fulbright-Hays Doctoral Dissertation Abroad Training Grant for a year's research in India in 1984, the Government of India (on the heels of the assassination of Prime Minister Indira Gandhi) denied me the academic visa necessary to use this grant. I thank Mr. Dwight Cossitt for coming forward to provide funds for fieldwork in India. Later he also made suggestions for improvements in a draft of the first chapter.

I thank my wife, Valerie Stephens, for her love and support. While I wrote a first draft in 1986, she supported me by working at a job she disliked. I thankfully remember the generosity of my grandparents, Mr. and Mrs. E. C. Lombard, who continuously and unselfishly shared their resources in furtherance of my goals. Finally, I thank my parents, Elaine and Ross Newland, to whom I am measurelessly indebted.

It has amazed me that almost everyone who has helped me has apparently done so with the wish that I might produce something of some benefit to others. I hope that this work, despite its limitations, may answer those wishes.

1 *Contradiction and Context*

CONTRADICTION AND DEFENSE

Robert Carroll writes that "dissonance gives rise to hermeneutic."[1] The unwillingness to suffer contradiction is among the main forces driving the making and re-making of religion at all levels. Both the *doctrine* of the two truths itself and the *process* through which it is reformulated and presented by the Ge-luk-ba textbook authors can be understood as attempts to resolve contradiction in order to create/discover a coherent world.

As Claude Lévi-Strauss has argued, myths mediate diadic tensions—such as life/death and nature/culture—by tying the opposing fundamentals into a network of metaphoric relationships.[2] When circumstances change, the web of myth must shift in order to diffuse the tension of new contradictions. This process also applies to religious doctrines as they evolve from and in tandem with myth. According to Joachim Wach, "What is expressed by the primitive mind as myth is conceived of in terms of doctrine at a more advanced level of civilization."[3] Wach describes a process by which myths are gradually organized, standardized, and unified, stripped of narrative form, and re-coded as doctrine.[4] Without endorsing the progressivism this might imply, we can affirm a continuity and partial homology between myth and religious doctrine. When myth systems become doctrinal systems, the problems of contradiction and dissonance are certainly not ended; they may be exacerbated. Although potentially inimical to the tradition, cognitive dissonance interacts with faith in a complex dynamic that can produce powerful religious energy. The community's authorities attempt to control and channel this force so as to sustain the enthusiasm and creativity of adherents without altering what they perceive to be the essentials of their faith.

Perhaps we can provisionally include contradictions in three very broad classes: (1) circumstantial, (2) fundamental, and (3) internal. Circumstantial contradiction arises when doctrine requires that certain events occur, but they do not in fact occur, or vice versa. This may lead some members of the community into disaffection from the tradition, but—as Leon Festinger has suggested—in some situations it may revitalize a core group of committed believers and intensify proselytizing activity.[5]

Unlike circumstantial contradictions, fundamental contradictions regularly arise from our experience as cultured animals. A simple example: Here we have the corpse of our friend. What should we do with it? How should we think about our friend now that his body no longer moves? Furthermore, why should this happen to him while our enemy still lives happily? Life presents myriad perplexing circumstances: drought, flood, plague, famine, volcanic eruptions, hail storms, bizarre dreams, trances and fugue states, seizures and so forth. Clifford Geertz writes:[6]

> [S]ome men—in all probability, most men—are unable to leave unclarified problems of analysis merely unclarified, just to look at the stranger features of the world's landscape in dumb astonishment or bland apathy, without trying to develop, however fantastic, inconsistent or simple-minded, some notions as to how such features might be reconciled with the more ordinary deliverances of experience. Any chronic failure of one's explanatory apparatus. . .leads to deep disquiet. . .

One of the functions of myth and doctrine is to fill the gap when our expectations (based on the "ordinary deliverances of experience") are shocked by reality. We see our friend every day and since he always lives and breathes we implicitly expect that he will continue to do so. When confronted with the contradiction of his corpse, doctrines about afterlife tell us that in some way our expectations were realistic—but with a twist.

This pattern (see diagram below) is aptly illustrated in the legendary accounts of Buddha's life found in the *Jātaka* stories and in

Aśvaghoṣa's *Acts of the Buddha*.[7] Leading an idyllic life behind the walls of his father's palace, the young prince Gautama Siddhārtha has no thought that youth and and pleasure will end. This naïveté is shattered when he first encounters the painful realities of aging, sickness and death during his chariot rides through the city. His heroic quest to understand and to overcome suffering begins with renunciation, but eventually leads to a blissful and everlasting nirvāṇa. Thus, the doctrine of the Bodhisattva path mediates the clash between our childish hopes and the scandalous facts. It tells that unending, perfect happiness is possible after all—though not to be had so easily as we had assumed.

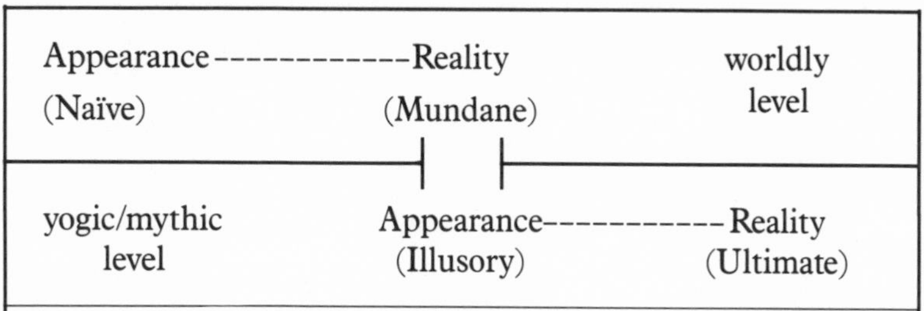

Chart 1: Appearance and Reality

Religions describe new, ultimate realities in relation to which the supposed "hard facts" of the mundane world stand in a new light. They may seem less real; in any case, they are no longer absolute or final in their ordinariness. Their intrinsic significance reduced or eliminated, mundane facts must be revalued in terms of their relationship to the ultimate. If myths provide us with such hidden messages about appearance and reality and if doctrines are attempts to make myth-messages explicit, then it is not surprising to find appearance/reality distinctions enunciated in many cultures. Christian Lindtner speculates that such a differentiation must be as ancient as human reflection.[8] In Buddhism, this idea has its mythic ground in the story that Gautama, sitting beneath a *pīpal* tree at the end of long quest, at last penetrated the dream-like veil of ordinary appearance and woke up to the way things really are. The illusoriness of ordinary appearances is implied in the very title "Buddha," which means means "one who has awakened." Doctrinally, the elaboration of this distinction became associated with the two truths, as we will explain below.

Another species of contradiction, internal contradiction, occurs when two authorities within the same tradition are seen to give conflicting testimony—or when a single authority appears self-contradictory. In mediating the community's fundamental contradictions, a root myth or doctrine shifts the point of tension and temporarily conceals it in a "forest of symbols." Many internal contradictions, especially those that energize the makers of myth and doctrine in later generations, occur at the hidden stress-points of the original formula. Just as the clash between naïve expectations and mundane realities creates the basic problem, tension between the mediating pair, illusory appearance and ultimate truth, gives rise to a new set of philosophical difficulties that must concern all who propound doctrines differentiating appearance and reality. Louis de la Vallée Poussin is among scholars who see the two truths as an "answer" that is at the same time a philosophical *problem*:[9]

> L'importance du problème des deux vérités, vérité de *saṃvṛti* ou d'apparence, vérité de *paramārtha* ou vérité absolue, est grande dans le Grande Véhicule, dan le Vedānta, dans la spéculation indienne en général, et, on peut dire, dans la philosphie universelle.

The problem of the two truths is a second generation problem, a philosophical descendent of existential contradictions and their mytho-doctrinal "solutions."

When members of the community sense a conflict, they search for relief. As Festinger puts it, "Dissonance produces discomfort," and gives rise to "pressures to reduce or eliminate the dissonance."[10] If representatives of the established tradition fail to dampen and channel cognitive dissonance within the tradition, some individuals may minimize their discomfort by weakening their ties to the tradition or diverging from orthodoxy. Therefore, the tradition, as embodied in the authority figures of orthodoxy, seeks to preserve its continuity and wholeness by limiting the sense of contradiction felt by its adherents. To this end, each system relies upon an array of "defense mechanisms"—strategies for controlling cognitive dissonance. I divide these strategies into two types: (1) those that utilize analysis in the defense of faith, and (2) those that reduce analysis in order to sustain faith. It seems that all systems use at least some methods of each type.

There are many different ways to minimize analysis. At the crudest level, authorities punish those who pursue analysis contrary to their direction. Coercive action against those who cross the boundaries of orthodoxy may range from mild rebuke to torture and death. Most systems probably use this method in at least a limited way. Also, the populace can be isolated from alien contacts. As practiced at various times in Tibet, China, Japan, and many other countries, institutionally backed xenophobia insulates society from contradictions that could arise when interaction with aliens leads to events and experiences inexplicable to traditional authorities.

Another commonly used method is to minimize the perception of internal contradiction by creating social pressure for loyalty and cohesion in the face of a real or imagined enemy. This may involve scapegoating and persecuting a minority or attacking a rival faction. It may also be used by minority factions facing such persecution.

The practice of inculcating adherents with unquestioning reverence for the tradition and its representatives is a highly effective method, and is certainly practiced in some measure by every tradition. By investing itself and its representatives (teachers, priests, etc.) with an aura of numinous infallibility, the tradition inhibits the analytical processes that uncover and evaluate evidence of internal contradiction. Faced with evidence of contradiction, the unquestioningly reverent are quick to blame their own ignorance in order to exculpate the sacred authorities.

Finally, the system confronted with solutionless contradiction can insist that it is impossible for humans to comprehend this "mystery." Sacralizing its own incoherence, the tradition rescues itself by disavowing any responsibility for explaining that which it designates as unexplainable, i.e., transcending the limited sphere of human understanding. If a system provides enough satisfying answers, it can well afford to leave a few mysteries—in fact, it may benefit from the numinous aura of the trans-rational thereby established.

INTERNAL CONTRADICTION IN BUDDHISM

In Buddhism, ethical norms are supported by doctrines of karma and rebirth shared in large measure with Hinduism. However, when Buddha combined this ethical bedrock with a metaphysic of momentary impermanence (*anitya*) and selflessness (*nairātmya*), root contradiction was an incipient danger.[11] If in reality there is no self, who is the agent of good and evil? How is the person who commits an action related to the person who experiences its moral effect? Where do karmic potentialities reside between the time of an action and its effect? What is it that moves from one rebirth to the next? The persistent problem of Buddhist philosophy has been to find the middle way: an ontology with enough substance to support the conventional presentations of the ethical system without betraying Buddha's original vision of the ultimate truth of no-self. Too much "substance," and one falls to the extreme of eternalism; negate too much, and one falls to the extreme of nihilism.

Buddhist doctrines on the relationship between conventional appearances and ultimate realities are set forth in terms of two truths. In the *Questions of King Milinda*, Nāgasena applies this distinction to the problem of identity and selflessness. He tells the king that the aggregates (*skandha*) alone are ultimately real, while "Nāgasena" and "I" are merely conventions.[12] Similarly, the *Great Detailed Exposition* (*Mahāvibhāṣa*) states:[13]

> Agents, like the person who is born and who dies, exist conventionally (*saṃvṛti-sat*); the law of birth and death exists ultimately (*paramārtha-sat*). . . . The agent of action and the receiver of the consequences of that action exist conventionally; but action, its ripening and fruit exist ultimately. . . . [A] person is an imputation, while the five aggregates are substantial entities.

As Stcherbatsky has pointed out, this implies an ontology in three parts:[14]

1. Ultimate truth (e.g., the aggregates)
2. Conventional truth (e.g., persons, pots, etc.)
3. Non-existents (e.g., the horns of a rabbit)

On the one hand, since only ultimate truths are found under analytic scrutiny, there must be some sense in which conventional truths do not really exist. On the other hand, if ethical norms, etc. are to be upheld, then conventional truths must have a legitimate status in Buddha's teaching. Paul Williams describes the problem succinctly:[15]

> The distinction between the satyas [truths] reflects. . .the logical requirements of resolving a tension between two epistemological and ontological positions; firstly, that all intentional objects of consciousness including pots and persons are given existential status, and secondly, that the requirements of analytical certainty necessitate a more fun-

> damental ontological status for some existents than for others.

But tension remains because, as John Buescher has noted, "it is untenable to speak of degrees of existence"; something must either exist or not exist.[16]

The "requirements of analytical certainty" become more stringent in Mahāyāna systems; the aggregates (*phung po, skandha*) and even subtle atomic particles (*rdul 'phran, paramānu*) lose any claim to status as ultimate truths. In Mādhyamika, even emptiness itself is empty of ultimate existence, and thus there is nothing whatsoever that exists in an ultimate sense (*don dam du yod, paramārthataḥ*). Consequently, anything that exists at all must exist only in conventional terms (*tha snyad tsam du yod*), as a mere imputation by thought (*rtog pas btags tsam*). Nevertheless, emptiness is designated as the ultimate truth, while all other phenomena are concealer-truths (*kun rdzob bden, saṃvṛtisatya*), that is to say, conventional truths (*tha snyad bden pa, vyavahārasatya*). Ontologically, the two truths now stand on equal footing since both exist conventionally and neither exists ultimately. However, they can still be distinguished epistemologically: Concealer-truths present themselves deceptively, while ultimate truths exist just as they appear to the mind directly realizing them.

However, this new approach does not solve the question of where to ground ethical teachings. Discussing the difficulties that a radical vision of emptiness raises for the Mahāyāna ethical ideal, Edward Conze sees a paradox. Citing a passage from the *Diamond Sūtra*—"And yet, although innumerable beings have thus been led to nirvāṇa, no being at all has been led to nirvāṇa,"—Conze concludes:[17]

> A Bodhisattva is a being compounded of the two contradictory forces of wisdom and compassion. In his wisdom, he sees no persons; in his compassion he is resolved to save them.

Western scholarship on Mādhyamika has changed in many ways in the years since Conze made this statement, but the majority of scholars still agree that, as David Eckel writes, "the element of paradox is essential."[18]

THE GE-LUK-BA MIDDLE WAY

In dramatic contrast to the approach just described, the project of Tsong-ka-pa's (1357-1419) "hermeneutic of consistency and coherence" is to make the Mahāyāna sūtras and the Mādhyamika śāstras the foundation of an edifice of rational theology, a theology without recourse to the defensive maneuvers of "mystery" or transcendental paradox.[19] For Tsong-ka-pa, the works of Candrakīrti (600-650?) led the way—yet earlier generations of Tibetans had already studied these commentaries without reaching Tsong-ka-pa's conclusions. One of the most critical and controversial cornerstones of Tsong-ka-pa's interpretation of Prāsaṅgika is the notion that ordinary conventional consciousnesses can be valid cognizers (*tshad ma, pramāṇa*) despite being tainted by the effects of ignorance. As detailed by Jeffrey Hopkins, Elizabeth Napper, Anne Klein, Georges Dreyfus and others, Tsong-ka-pa and his followers borrowed and adapted an epistemology derived from the works of Dignāga and Dharmakīrti, attempting to synthesize it with the anti-essentialist Prāsaṅgika-Mādhyamika dialectic of Candrakīrti.[20] Critics, both traditional (e.g., Dak-tsang) and academic (e.g., Michael Broido, 1988) have regarded this project as philosophically untenable.[21] My aim here is not to enter this controversy, but to show how the Ge-luk-ba synthesis works for Ge-luk-bas as a mytho-doctrinal resolution of the "problem of the two truths."

Consider, for example, an eye consciousness directly apprehending a patch of blue. Such a consciousness is mistaken because the blue appears to it as something that is inherently existent, i.e., something able to set itself up and exist by way of its own nature. Nevertheless, Ge-luk-bas claim that it is completely authoritative and incontrovertible (*mi slu ba*) regarding the mere existence of blue. While our ordinary sense of existence (*yod pa, bhava*) is thoroughly entangled with our sense of things as inherently existent (*rang bzhin gyis grub pa, svabhāvasiddha*), the two can be differentiated via training in logic and meditation.

Thus, in a similar way, Ge-luk-bas claim that the conventional elements of the path—ethical cause/effect relationships, compassion, the beings for whom the Bodhisattva has compassion, etc.—can exist and operate. They exist only conventionally, but *to exist conventionally is to exist*. Because they are devoid of the intrinsic reality that they appear to have, they are likened to dreams, a magician's illusions, mirages, and so forth. They are "falsities" (*rdzun pa, mṛṣā*). However, unlike the objects that appear in dreams, they do exist and actions taken with regard to them have karmic consequences. To dream of committing murder is one thing; to commit murder is another.

In meditative equipoise on emptiness, all conventional phenomena utterly vanish. However, this does *not* mean that the existence of conventionalities is refuted by a yogi's ultimate realization. The ultimate valid cognizers of non-Buddhas are simply unable to realize ordinary phenomena directly at the same time that they realize emptiness directly. Only Buddha can simultaneously maintain explicit and direct cognition of both ultimate truths and conventional truths. Among sentient beings, there are two distinct types of valid cognizers—ultimate and conventional. Each incontrovertibly certifies one of the two truths without discrediting the other. Tsong-ka-pa sees the compatibility of the two truths—that is, the non-contradiction between conventional reality and profound emptiness—as the key to Mādhyamika. He writes:[22]

> It is a distinguishing feature of Mādhyamika that one can assert all the presentations of cyclic existence and nirvāṇa (that is, production, proof, etc.) without even a particle of inherent existence (i.e., something's being established by way of its own entity).

Expounding what they regard as a non-paradoxical resolution of the problem of the two truths, Tsong-ka-pa and his followers are quite often at odds with the mainstream of twentieth-century academic scholarship on Indian Mādhyamika. In fact, Hopkins lists thirty-two points in the Ge-luk interpretation of Prāsaṅgika that place them at odds with "almost all contemporary academic" views.[23] In the following pages, the peculiar distinctions of the Ge-luk-ba system will be set in relief against a sampling of views from today's secular academy. Again, however, our concern does *not* center on the question of who is right about what Nāgārjuna or Buddha "really intended," nor on the question of whose view more convincingly describes the world as it is. Certainly some readings of a text (or a world) are more persuasive than others, and that I do not focus on these problems here does not mean I think them unimportant. My purpose here is to offer an alternative, and to show some of the details of how that alternative works for those who choose it. Doctrinaire adherence to any single interpretive formula can impoverish reading, closing the text prematurely. When "trans-rational paradox'' becomes a pat answer, as it has for some Buddhists and non-Buddhist interpreters of Buddhism, familiarity with the Ge-luk-ba system may revitalize our reading of Candrakīrti, Nāgārjuna, and sūtra. With Tsong-ka-pa's key, the classical treatises open in surprising ways, ways that may be surprisingly persuasive.

On the other hand, it is clear that ''Tsong-ka-pa's system,'' as institutionalized in the monastic textbooks (*yig cha*), supplies pat answers to many Ge-luk-bas and closes down their reading of Nāgārjuna, Candrakīrti, and even Tsong-ka-pa himself. At worst, the result is a defanged Mādhyamika whose insistence upon the valid establishment (*tshad grub*) of conventional reality serves only to confirm the samsaric (and socio-political) status quo. Cutting against this tendency, and thus revealing it, Jang-gya, Den-dar-hla-ram-ba (b. 1759), and other Ge-luk-ba writers warn their fellows against taking ''these concrete appearances as givens.''[24] Inherent existence, they say, is not some horn-like or hat-like protruberance ready to be lopped off, leaving our world unscathed. The mistaken appearance of inherent existence is interwoven with and infused into everything we see, and thus a thorough refutation of inherent existence should, at first, seem to demolish the only universe we know.

Ideally, the Ge-luk doctrine of the two truths seeks not to preserve the world just as we see it now, but to allow the coexistence of emptiness with a fresh, radically transformed vision of conventional reality. We are not wrong to think that fences and houses and rivers and persons exist; our knowledge of these things is authoritative and incontrovertible. At the same time, we are profoundly deluded about *how* things exist because they appear to us only through the distorting masks of ignorance, masks which make the existence of things seem inseparable from substantiality, permanence, independence, and intrinsic reality.

INTERNAL CONTRADICTION IN GE-LUK-BA

Satisfied that Tsong-ka-pa had established the correct view, later Ge-luk-bas seek mainly to restate and amplify his positions. Here we see new levels of internal contradiction as each author finds a slightly different reading for the works of Tsong-ka-pa and his prominent contemporary disciples, Gyel-tsap and Kay-drup. Although Tsong-ka-pa writes clearly and rarely contradicts what he has written elsewhere in his mature work, there are inevitable ambiguities and implicit tensions.[25]

The Ge-luk-ba study of Mādhyamika centers on Candrakīrti's *Supplement to (Nāgārjuna's) "Treatise on the Middle Way"* as explicated by Tsong-ka-pa in his *Illumination of the Thought*. Students in the monastic colleges (*grwa tshang*) approach these treatises through textbooks (*yig cha*) that explain Mādhyamika along the outlines of the *Supplement* and *Illumination of the Thought*.[26] The textbooks, or substantial portions from them, are memorized by the students and serve as the basis for (1) oral commentary by the teacher during class and (2) debate among the students in the monastery courtyard after class. Thus, they create a shared universe for discourse both between teacher and student and among students of the same college. Intellectual mastery of the textbook and its source-texts is essential for advancement within the monastic academy.

Public debate is vigorous and loud, but usually good-natured. Arguments must be framed as syllogisms, and the respondent must either challenge the reason (i.e., the minor premise) or the pervasion (i.e., the major premise), or else accept his opponent's point. Large sections of every monastic textbook are cast in this same "debate format." Debates are used both to refute opposing systems and to dispel objections that a hypothetical opponent might pose with regard to one's own system. The debate format allows authors to sharpen their arguments while creating texts that their debate-trained readers find accessible and relatively easy to memorize. It seems certain that textbook authors derive at least some of their written debates from oral debates current in their respective colleges and generations. Thus, textbook literature is a critical link between the Mādhyamika of the classical treatises and the living Mādhyamika of courtyard debate. Monastic textbooks bridge both a diachronic gap (classical period/scholastic period) and a synchronic gap (written text/oral debate) because they are written texts following the topical outlines of the original treatises, but using a language roughly patterned after and readily (re)assimilated to the oral debate tradition.

Between sections devoted to debate, a textbook author advances his own system. Here, the author always provides formal definitions of the key concepts under discussion. Usually, subdivisions of the general category are put forth, and each of these may be defined and/or instantiated. This gives the reader a summary-overview of the general interpretation that underlies and is elaborated in the debate sections. The viewpoints thus advanced represent, in some measure, the "orthodox" view of that monastic college. In public debate with other colleges (during the winter session and at the New Year's Festival, *smon lam*), a monk is expected to uphold, insofar as he is able, the arguments advanced by the textbook authors for his college. This insures a certain continuity: members of each generation work through the problems and test the solutions left by their predecessors, all within the context of their shared textbook tradition. However, outside the special context of debate with other colleges, Ge-luk-ba monks differ greatly in their attitudes toward "textbook orthodoxy." Georges Dreyfus notes that many regard their teachers and textbooks as sources of unassailable truth, using textbook definitions as absolutely secure reference points. On the other hand, there are others who "consider the knowledge imparted to them as a tool...accepted provisionally in order to advance" on a quest that is at once philosophical and spiritual.[27]

The authors of the major Ge-luk-ba textbooks on Mādhyamika—Jam-yang-shay-ba, Paṇ-chen Sö-nam-drak-ba, and Jay-dzun-ba—disagree on many fine points. Each attempts to present a cogent and internally consistent account of how Tsong-ka-pa's system works. When their analyses reveal an apparent internal contradiction, they have recourse to three main strategies: (1) reverential deference to sacred authorities, (2) reconciling exegesis, and (3) faith in the ongoing process of exegesis and analysis.

The most revered figures include Buddha, Nāgārjuna, Candrakīrti, Śāntideva, and Tsong-ka-pa. These teachers made no errors in their writings. Kay-drup and Gyel-tsap, Tsong-ka-pa's chief disciples, are also very highly revered but are not always regarded as infallible. For individual Ge-luk-bas, any list of traditional authorities also would have to include the authors of the main textbooks for their monastic college as well as their own lamas. In the so-called "lamaist" ethos of Buddhist Tibet, it is a violation of the norm to deprecate one's teacher or others spiritually senior to oneself—even when there is justification. Trained in faith for these authorities, later scholars usually insist that regardless of what a literal reading of their works might suggest, there is no internal contradiction in their intended teaching. As Kensur Yeshay Tupden has said, great scholars may differ about the words, but never about the meaning.

If faith requires the presumption of innocence—or at least, the *façade* of such a presumption—reason is brought forward to prove the case. Following Tsong-ka-pa's methods, some Ge-luk-ba scholars construct apologetic exegeses reconciling the meanings of apparently contradictory passages of authoritative texts. They argue that careful examination of context and the dictates of reason demonstrate that certain problematic passages demand readings that are far from apparent to the casual reader. Even passages in which word-by-word literal reading (*sgras zin*) clearly contradicts the system can still be accepted as having explicit teachings (*dngos bstan*) that are "literally" (*sgra ji bzhin pa*) acceptable. This is achieved by carrying over the qualifying force of phrases used in other portions of the work.

The analytic process, although begun in the service of tradition, inevitably uncovers new complications and potential contradictions. Occasionally, finding themselves unable to clear away their own doubts on a particular point, Ge-luk-ba authors invoke what we might call the "ongoing quest" model. Indicating that the problem requires further analysis, they express an implicit faith that (1) the system itself has no defect and that (2) the continued application of reason is an appropriate method of truth-seeking, even though it has not yet resolved every point of philosophical difficulty.

Most Ge-luk-ba scholars scrupulously avoid any use of the "mystery" defence. Although the functioning of Buddha's consciousness is described as "inconceivable," Ge-luk-bas invest great energy in wrestling with this and every other doctrinal connundrum they encounter. The tradition is built on the principle that truth is not only knowable, but accessible to reason as well. This stance is reflected both in the teaching that emptiness must be initially realized via inference (*rjes dpag, anumāna*) and in the rigorous training in debate that characterizes the Ge-luk-ba educational system. Buddha said:

> Monks, my words are to be accepted by scholars
> Not [merely] out of respect
> But upon having analyzed them, just as
> Gold is accepted after scorching, cutting, and rubbing.[28]

In this spirit, monks are encouraged to become deeply conversant with the complications of doctrine in private reflection and vigorous public debate rather than blandly parroting the "party line."

Where is the balance between the individual's freedom to pursue analysis and the social pressure for faithful acceptance of the teachings of traditional authorities? Without a doubt, reason is allowed a wider berth in Ge-luk-ba than in many other religious traditions. However, it is possible to push this point too far. When the textbook authors raise a qualm about Tsong-ka-pa's view, in the vast majority of cases their intention is to prepare for a rebuttal—not to question Tsong-ka-pa's authority. Occasionally a problem will be raised and discussed without finding a final resolution. However, this never leads to a negative conclusion about the validity of Tsong-ka-pa's system. The most difficult questions can be left open, with the view that continued analysis by other scholars will turn up a satisfactory answer.

As for courtyard debate, monks are encouraged to attack and defend a wide spectrum of views on every topic in the curriculum. Sometimes, when studying the critiques of Tsong-ka-pa launched by non-Ge-luk-ba scholars, monks will attack Tsong-ka-pa's positions quite vigorously. However, with instructors close at hand to shore up the defense as need be, this can be understood as part of the process of coming into genuine, rather than formulaic, comprehension of the system's soundness. In general, each party tries to show that his or her position is in line with both the dictates of reason and the writings of traditional authorities. If an opponent makes a statement contrary to Tsong-ka-pa's teaching, the quickest rebuttal is to cite Tsong-ka-pa's own words. This sets up the syllogism:

> If Tsong-ka-pa said (X), then your position is wrong.
> Tsong-ka-pa said (X).
> Therefore, your position is wrong.

If one has misquoted, then the opponent can challenge the minor premise. Otherwise, the major premise will probably be challenged. However, as a Ge-luk-ba, the opponent implicitly accepts Tsong-ka-pa's authority. In challenging the major, he commits to a demonstration that his position is actually not contradicted by Tsong-ka-pa's statement. If requested to do so, he must attempt to provide an alternative interpretation of the passage. In other words, no Ge-luk-ba publicly proclaims, "This is what I believe regardless of what Tsong-ka-pa taught." Rather, he or she always seeks some means to reconcile the products of personal reflection with the words of Tsong-ka-pa. In practical terms, I understand a Ge-luk-ba to be someone who not only relies upon Tsong-ka-pa's teachings in general, but feels pressed to seek some type of accommodation between his or her opinions and the statements of Tsong-ka-pa on any specific point.[29]

Each individual scholar finds the balance between faith and analysis at a slightly different point, according to personal inclination and the circumstances of the era. In their textbooks on Mādhyamika, Paṇ-chen Sö-nam-drak-ba, Jay-dzun Chö-gyi-gyel-tsen, and Jam-yang-shay-ba share three main goals: (1) to provide a basis for instruction in the fundamentals of Mādhyamika philosophy, (2) to confirm the fundamental coherence of Tsong-ka-pa's system, and (3) to refute and rebut contrary interpretations. Jam-yang-shay-ba has at least two additional concerns: (1) to demonstrate Tsong-ka-pa's fidelity to his Indian sources, and (2) to reconcile apparent contradictions among Tsong-ka-pa, Kay-drup, and Gyel-tsap. Paṇ-chen Sö-nam-drak-ba (1478-1554) and Jay-dzun Chö-gyi-gyel-tsen (1469-1546) wrote during the ascendancy of the second Dalai Lama, Ge-dun-gya-tso (*dge 'dun rgya mtsho*, b. 1475).[30] At this time, the order was growing in numbers and earning respect throughout the country, but, as D. Snellgrove and H. Richardson put it, "was still untarnished by temporal power."[31] Born in the same century during which Tsong-ka-pa and his immediate disciples died, and flourishing prior to the sect's attainment of political supremacy, Paṇ-chen and Jay-dzun-ba see the founder and his followers in the light of a charisma less magnificent than that appreciated by later generations. Both criticize certain views of Kay-drup and Gyel-tsap. Paṇ-chen Sö-nam-drak-ba is much the bolder of the two, faulting Kay-drup and Gyel-tsap by name and even suggesting that Tsong-ka-pa's writing may require interpretation on certain points.

Jam-yang-shay-ba (1648-1721), textbook author for the Go-mang college of Dre-bung, displays in his work a command of Tsong-ka-pa's Indian sources that the authors of the earlier textbooks do not approach.[32] In long, elaborate arguments he tirelessly unravels doctrinal complications—making Jay-dzun-ba and especially Paṇ-chen Sö-nam-drak-ba seem terse by comparison. Thriving in the heyday of Ge-luk-ba power, Jam-yang-shay-ba also exhibits a very different attitude toward Kay-drup and Gyel-tsap. Relying on Kay-drup especially, Jam-yang-shay-ba seeks common ground with Tsong-ka-pa's "spiritual sons" whenever possible. When he finds an apparently irreconcilable difference between his reading of Tsong-ka-pa and the teachings of Kay-drup or Gyel-tsap, he faults them only to the extent of saying that certain passages should not be read literally. Another important Go-mang-influenced scholar, Jang-gya (1717-1786), rebukes those (such as Paṇ-chen Sö-nam-drak-ba) who (allegedly) show disrespect for Kay-drup by giving unfair refutations based on too-literal readings of Kay-drup's explanations. Go-mang Geshe Den-ba-den-dzin told me that, in his opinion, the thrust of Go-mang scholarship is to reconcile and harmonize the thought of Tsong-ka-pa and his two principal disciples; he contrasted this to the rather more critical approach of Paṇ-chen Sö-nam-drak-ba (Lo-sel-ling) and the Mongolian scholar Ngak-wang-bel-den.[33]

INTELLECTUAL CONTEXT

In their efforts to refute alternative interpretations of Prāsaṅgika-Mādhyamika, the authors of the Ge-luk textbooks on Mādhyamika disclose key landmarks on their intellectual horizons. In most cases, the names of the scholars whose views are criticized remain unmentioned; thus, the *yig cha* present many "wrong views" whose proponents have yet to be identified. The philosophical opponents in relation to whom the authors of the Ge-luk Mādhyamika *yig cha* define their positions on the two truths fall into four categories: (1) the scholars of rival colleges within Ge-luk, (2) Indian scholars, (3) Tsong-ka-pa's Tibetan predecessors, (4) non-Ge-luk critics of Tsong-ka-pa's system.

Contrary to the image of Ge-luk-ba as a monolithic orthodoxy, factional rivalries within Ge-luk have been extremely intense. To those involved, these rivalries are felt as immediate concerns—unlike the rivalries with other orders wherein greater spans of time and distance usually separate the antagonists. Factionalism has been fostered by the existence of several different monastic colleges within each of the major Ge-luk monasteries. Imagine the emotional, social, and political fireworks that would be produced by *two* religion departments teaching the same courses next door to one another on a university campus. In such situations, the individual's sense of identity hinges upon magnifying and preserving very subtle differences.[34] Thus, at Dre-bung Monastery for example, disputes on Mādhyamika between scholars of Lo-sel-ling college and Go-mang college often turn on differences so thin that one hesitates to call them "philosophical." Nevertheless, debating and analyzing such differences plays an enormous role in the textbooks and the lives of those who use them.

Although some authors wrote books that were adopted at more than one monastic college, there are internal rivalries between monastic colleges using different textbooks at each of the three big

Ge-luk monasteries near Lhasa. Gan-den (*dga' ldan*), founded by Tsong-ka-pa in 1409, has two colleges: Shar-dzay (*shar rtse*) adopted the literature of Paṇ-chen Sö-nam-drak-ba, while Jang-dzay (*byang rtse*) primarily adopted that of Jay-dzun Chö-gyi-gyel-tsen, along with works by Gom-day Nam-ka-gyel-tsen (*sgom sde shar pa nam mkha' rgyal mtshan*, 1532-1592) and Jam-ba-dra-shi (*khyung phrug byams pa bkra shis*, sixteenth century). Dre-bung (*'bras spungs*) has four monastic colleges, of which the two most important are Lo-sel-ling and Go-mang; Lo-sel-ling follows Paṇ-chen Sö-nam-drak-ba, while Go-mang follows Jam-yang-shay-ba. At Se-ra (*se ra*), the Jay (*byes*) college follows Jay-dzun Chö-gyi-gyel-tsen along with Gom-day Nam-ka-gyel-tsen, while the May (*smad*) college uses the work of Kay-drup Den-ba-dar-gyay (*mkhas sgrub bstan pa dar rgyas*, 1493-1568) and Drak-ba-shay-drup (*co ne rje btsun grags pa bshad sgrub*, 1675-1748). Thus, by studying Paṇ-chen Sö-nam-drak-ba, Jay-dzun Chö-gyi-gyel-tsen and Jam-yang-shay-ba, we can see the differences among five of the six most important monastic colleges at the three big monasteries.

The main Mādhyamika textbooks are, in effect, subcommentaries on Tsong-ka-pa's Illumination of the Thought, which is a commentary on Candrakīrti's *Supplement to (Nāgārjuna's) "Treatise on the Middle Way"*. Tsong-ka-pa's *Illumination of the Thought* regularly attacks the views of Jayānanda, author of the only extant Indian commentary on Candrakīrti's *Supplement*.[35] Near the beginning of the twelfth century Jayānanda came from Kashmir to Sang-pu (*gsang phu*) Monastery and worked with the great Tibetan translator Ba-tsap Nyi-ma-drak (*spa tshab nyi ma grags*, 1055-?) correcting and retranslating a number of important works on tantra and Mādhyamika.[36] Jayānanda's commentary had a powerful influence on the Tibetan understanding of Candrakīrti, and Tsong-ka-pa regarded this influence as deleterious in many ways.[37] For instance, there are at least twelve references to Jayānanda's commentary and its ideas in the sections of Tsong-ka-pa's *Illumination of the Thought* that cover Candrakīrti's *Supplement* up through the first five Bodhisattva grounds. At least eight of these references are occasions for finding fault; at one point Tsong-ka-pa says that Jayānanda's position is "senseless."[38] In the section of *Illumination of the Thought* dealing with the two truths, Tsong-ka-pa[39] attacks Jayānanda's positions that reflections and mirages are mere conventionalities (*kun rdzob tsam, saṃvṛtimātra*) rather than concealer-truths, that enlightened yogis see tables, etc. not as concealer-truths but only as "mere conventionalities," and that Buddhas pass beyond seeing conventional phenomena all together.[40] Tsong-ka-pa works to show that the two truths include *all* existents. Since they exist and are not ultimate truths, mirages, reflections, tables, chairs, etc. all must be concealer-truths. Buddhas and advanced yogis see them for what they are, and thus even enlightened beings see tables as concealer-truths.[41] Even Jayānanda's basic interpretation of emptiness is called into question. In his *Essence of Good Explanations* (*legs shes snying po*), Tsong-ka-pa argues that the position of "a certain pandit" (apparently Jayānanda) is "utterly wrong" and "nothing but empty talk" because, while "constantly declaring that there is no inherent existence even conventionally," he fails to represent the operation of discriminating argument and causality in the face of this emptiness.[42] Thus, Tsong-ka-pa's enormous reverence for Candrakīrti does not extend to his commentator Jayānanda. On the contrary, *Illumination of the Thought* overturns much of Jayānanda's work, and Tsong-ka-pa's refutations of Jayānanda are routinized and often further elaborated in the Ge-luk textbooks.[43]

Jñānagarbha (eighth century) is another Indian Mādhyamika whose views are a significant part of the backdrop for Ge-luk interpretation of the two truths. In his *Distinguishing the Two Truths* (*Satyadvaya-vibhaṅgakārikā*), Jñānagarbha claimed that conventional truths can be subdivided into real conventionalities (*tathyasaṃvṛti*) and unreal conventionalities (*mithyāsaṃvṛti*).[44] Water, for example, is a real conventionality since it is able to perform the functions that it appears to have. A mirage, on the other hand, appears to be water but is unable to function as water; consequently it is an unreal conventionality. Jñānagarbha apparently felt that Candrakīrti's refutation of inherent existence even conventionally led to a nihilistic extreme in which it would be impossible to make distinctions of this sort.[45] As we shall see (chapters seven and eight), Tsong-ka-pa and the authors of the Ge-luk textbooks direct considerable effort to demonstrations of how it is that water and mirage can be distinguished even though neither can be classed as a "real conventionality."

Among Tsong-ka-pa's many Tibetan forerunners in the effort to interpret the two truths in Mādhyamika, we shall limit ourselves to mentioning Ngok Lo-den-shay-rap (*rngog blo ldan shes rab*, 1059-1109), Dö-lung bya-mar (*stod lung rgya dmar*, eleventh-twelfth century), Cha-ba Chö-gyi-seng-gay (*phya pa chos kyi seng ge*, 1109-1169), Tang-sak-ba (*thang sag pa*, fl. twelfth century) and

Shay-rap-gyel-tsen (*shes rab rgyal mthsan*, 1292-1361).

Ngok Lo-den-shay-rap was a renowned Ga-dam-ba (*bka' gdams pa*) scholar who authored several commentaries on Nāgārjuna's *Treatise* and translated a large number of important works, including Candrakīrti's *Clear Words* and *Supplement*.[46] Prior to Ngok, Candrakīrti's work was known in Tibet, but had not been well translated and had not made a great impact. Thus, Ngok is perhaps the first of the many Tibetan philosophers who have wrestled with the problems of formulating Candrakīrti's view of the two truths. Contrary to a key point of the Ge-luk interpretation, Ngok held that ultimate reality is not something knowable. Apparently his position was that if emptiness were something accessible to yogic apprehension, it thereby would be established as a real thing. Since, on the contrary, emptiness is not "some thing," it must be utterly unknowable. This position has been compared to "Kantian transcendentalism" by Robert Thurman.[47] Hopkins reconstruction of Ngok's position seems slightly different:[48]

> [Ngok does] not accept that an emptiness is an object of knowledge because the mere non-finding of an object under [ultimate yogic] analysis is just *called* an emptiness.

Perhaps Ngok's point was that emptiness (or ultimate truth), like everything else, is a mere designation and a mere appearance (*snang tsam*) rather than some real thing that the yogi finally "gets at" after cutting through the flux of illusion and convention.[49] Ngok apparently thought that if a yogi's ultimate realization were a conscious knowledge of emptiness, then emptiness would be established as something that exists in an ultimate sense, i.e., as an object found by a mind analyzing the ultimate nature of reality. How could this be reconciled with the Mādhyamika claim that even emptiness is empty of ultimate existence? Thus, the only way to avoid reifying emptiness is to stress its unknowability. The force of such arguments placed certain demands on later Ge-luk-ba efforts to show that ultimate reality is knowable. Their critique of Ngok's position had to explain how it is that emptiness can be known by an ultimate mind while existing, like all else, only in a conventional sense.[50]

Ngok's claim that the ultimate is unknowable found support in the work of Dö-lung Gya-mar-jang-chup-drak (*stod lung rgya dmar byang chub grags*, eleventh-twelfth century) who had studied with at least two of Ngok's followers.[51] Dö-lung Gya-mar was an important teacher of tantra, logic, and Mādhyamika during the early 12th century; his many students included Tu-sum-kyen-ba (*dus gsum mkhyen pa*, 1110-1193) and Cha-ba Chö-gyi-seng-gay (*phya pa chos kyi seng ge*, 1109-1169).[52] He is credited with authorship of numerous works, including commentaries on Mādhyamika texts such as Jñānagarbha's *Distinguishing the Two Truths* and Śāntideva's *Engaging in the Bodhisattva Deeds* (*Bodhisattvacaryāvatāra*).[53] Śāntideva's *Engaging in the Bodhisattva Deeds* states that "The ultimate is not the province of awareness," and in Dö-lung Gya-mar's interpretation this means that an ultimate truth can never be the object of any consciousness.[54] Thus, to support their claim that the ultimate is knowable, the Ge-luk-bas must solve exegetical problems as well as philosophical problems. They must show why Dö-lung Gya-mar's apparently straightforward reading does not hold up; Jam-yang-shay-ba, in particular, devotes himself to this problem.[55]

Cha-ba Chö-gyi-seng-gay (*phya pa chos kyi seng ge*, 1109-1169) studied not only with Dö-lung Gya-mar, but also with Ngok Loden-shay-rap's main disciple, Dro-lung Lo-drö-jung-nay (*gro lung blo gros 'byung gnas*). Non-sectarian, though most often counted as a Ga-dam-ba (*bka' gsams pa*), Cha-ba served as abbot of Sang-pu from 1152 until the year of his death. He was a prolific author, making contributions especially in the areas of logic and Mādhyamika.[56] Like Ngok, Cha-ba assumed that if emptiness were known by the ultimate mind of a yogi, it would thereby be established as something existing in an ultimate sense. However, while Ngok thus arrived at an unknowable emptiness, Cha-ba (more logician than mystic) insisted that emptiness is an absolute negation (*med par dgag pa*) that is accessed via thorough analysis of the way things exist. Cha-ba apparently concluded that since emptiness is found by a mind that analyzes the ultimate nature of things, it must exist in an ultimate sense. Thus, while Ngok is faulted by Ge-luk for placing emptiness beyond the reach of cognition, Cha-ba is faulted for reifying emptiness. We know that Ngok "wrote many refutations" of Candrakīrti's Prāsaṅgika-Mādhyamika; he seems to have preferred Yogacāra-Svātantrika-Mādhyamika authors such as Śāntarakṣita and Kamalaśīla.[57]

Ge-luk-bas are indirect heirs to Cha-ba in their scholasticism, their emphasis on the study of logic and epistemology as foundations for study of Mādhyamika, and their insistence that emptiness can and should be conceptually apprehended through logical analysis of the way things exist. However, unlike Cha-ba, they follow Candrakīrti, insisting that all phemomena are devoid, even conventionally, of any trace of inherent existence, natural existence, or ultimate existence. Cha-ba could not reconcile Candrakīrti's claim that even emptiness exists only as a convention with the logic and epistemology of valid cognition (*tshad ma, pramāṇa*); this task remained for Tsong-ka-pa and his successors.

Of the "Eight Mighty Lions of Logic" among Cha-ba's students, at least two—Ma-ja Jang-chup-dzön-dru (*rma bya byang chub brtson 'grus*) and Dzang-nag-ba Dzön-dru-seng-gay (*gtsang nag pa brtson 'grus seng ge*)—studied and "preferred the system of Jayānanda" to Cha-ba's refutations of Candrakīrti. Ma-ja Jang-chup-dzön-dru also studied Mādhyamika with the translator Ba-tsap Nyi-ma-drak (*spa tshab nyi ma grags*, 1055-?); in fact, he is known as one of the "Four Sons of Ba-tsap." Also among the four was Tang-sak-ba (*thang sag pa*, fl. twelfth century), a famous scholar of Mādhyamika who wrote several commentaries on works by Nāgārjuna, Candrakīrti, and Āryadeva. Tang-sak-ba established a monastery (Tang-sak) that remained a major center for Mādhyamika teaching at least through the fifteenth century. Tang-sak-ba's lineage was marked by a close reliance upon Candrakīrti's *Clear Words* and *Supplement*.[58]

According to Ge-luk-ba sources, Tang-sak-ba held that all phenomena lack even conventional existence.[59] Generally, Tang-sak-ba's position is represented by Ge-luk-bas as a nihilistic misreading of Candrakīrti, a reading that fails to understand that Candrakīrti is refuting *inherent* existence, not all existence. Elsewhere, Tang-sak-ba is faulted for his position that the basis of division of the two truths is the entities of all phenomena (*chos thams cad kyi ngo bo*).[60] Ge-luk-bas have been insistent that the basis of division of the two truths is objects of knowledge (*shes bya, jñeya*); we will explore their quarrel with Tang-sak-ba's alternative in chapter two.

Tsong-ka-pa and his successors have been especially vehement in their objections to the views of Shay-rap-gyel-tsen (*shes rab rgyal mthsan*, 1292-1361) and his followers. Shay-rap-gyel-tsen, an abbot of Jo-mo-nang, formulated his view in *Ocean of Definitive Meaning* (*nges don rgya mtsho*) and other writings; his followers are called Jo-nang-bas. As Ge-luk political power reached its apogee under the Fifth Dalai Lama in the seventeenth century, the Jo-nang-bas were proscribed and their monasteries and other property were completely confiscated and converted to Ge-luk use. Tibet's intersectarian conflicts were almost always driven by motives more political than "purely philosophical"; indeed, the Jo-nang-bas were allies of the king of Tsang (*gtsang*), the main political and military adversary of Ge-luk in the first half of the seventeenth century. On the other hand, for more than two hundred years before they destroyed the Jo-nang-ba order the Ge-luk-bas had been denouncing Shay-rap-gyel-tsen's philosophy as something utterly beyond the pale of Mahāyāna Buddhism. By comparison, the Karma Ga-gyu-bas (*bka' brgyud pa*), who had been especially powerful and bitter opponents of Ge-luk, suffered confiscation but not proscription. While the immediate occasion for the persecution of Jo-nang was its defeat in a power struggle, proscription suggested itself as a penalty in the context of a long history of substantial and deeply felt philosophical differences. This hostility is reflected in the banning of Shay-rap-gyel-tsen's major books from the premises of Ge-luk monasteries more than 150 years prior to his order's extinction.[61]

Shay-rap-gyel-tsen asserts a doctrine called "other-emptiness" (*gzhan stong*). Emptiness, ultimate truth, is the absolute reality. It alone exists in a true and ultimate sense. Conventional phenomena are empty of their own true existence and they are also empty of being the ultimate truth. The ultimate truth is *not* self-empty (*rang stong*)—that is, it is not empty of its own true existence as in Candrakīrti's system; rather, it is empty in that it is devoid of being any of the conventional phenomena of cyclic existence. In brief, Shay-rap-gyel-tsen holds that conventional truth and ultimate truth are different entities (*ngo bo tha dad*); conventional appearances are erroneous (*'khrul snang*), while the ultimate is a separate, absolutely pure Reality. He bases his theory on the *Sūtra Unravelling the Thought* (*Saṃdhinirmocana*) and the *Kālacakra Tantra*, as well his own experience. In his *Essence of Good Explanation*, Tsong-ka-pa is intent on showing that Shay-rap-gyel-tsen has misinterpreted the *Sūtra Unravelling the Thought* so as to accept as definitive (*nges don*) sūtra passages that were actually non-literal teachings given to *non-Buddhists* for the sake of drawing them into the dharma. Later Ge-luk scholars attack the Jo-nang-ba position by comparing it to the Sāṃkhya doctrine that cyclic existence is driven by the confusion of pure "person" (*puruṣa*) or "principal" (*pradhāna*) with the strands (*guṇa*) of nature (*prakṛti*).[62] Ge-luk-bas very frequently use the Sāṃkhya "principal" as a stock example of something that exists only in bad philosophy; the rhetorical effect of this example against Jo-nang may be part of its appeal. Jo-nang philosophy also seems to be an important target of Ge-luk-ba efforts to demonstrate the absurdity of holding that the two truths are different entities (*ngo bo tha dad*).[63]

The first important critic of Tsong-ka-pa's philosophy was his junior contemporary, the Sa-gya scholar Rong-dön Ma-way-seng-gay (*rong stong smra ba'i seng ge*, 1367-1449).[64] A polymath credited with as many as three hundred works, Rong-dön began a strong Sa-gya tradition of criticizing Tsong-ka-pa's philosophy. Rong-dön's younger students included Go-ram-ba Sö-nam-seng-gay (*go ram pa bsod nams seng ge*, 1429-1489) and Śākya Chok-den (*śākya mchog ldan*, 1428-1507), both of whom became important Sa-gya scholars and critics of Ge-luk-ba.[65] Ge-luk-ba scholars regard Rong-dön's lineage of Mādhyamika commentary as tending toward a nihilistic extreme, especially in its failure to acknowledge that conventional phenomena are validly established (*tshad grub, pramāṇasiddha*).[66] In chapter two we will note Rong-dön's position that the basis of division of the two truths is "mere phenomena" (*chos tsam*). Although Ge-luk-bas consider object of knowledge (*shes bya*), existent (*yod pa*), established base (*gzhi grub*), and phenomenon (*chos*) equivalents, they posit *objects of knowledge*, rather than any equivalent, as the basis of division into the two truths.

Certainly one of the most vigorous critics of Ge-luk interpretations of Mādhyamika was the Sa-gya-ba Dak-tsang Shay-rap-rin-chen (*stag tshang shes rab rin chen*, b. 1405). He argued that Tsong-ka-pa, through addiction to logic, had deviated from Candrakīrti's view that phenomena exist "only for the world, without analysis."[67] He enumerated eighteen alleged contradictions within Tsong-ka-pa's work. These direct accusations of internal contradiction against their founder were particularly galling to later Ge-luk writers. If Shay-rap-gyel-tsen is especially prominent among Ge-luk's "prior antagonists" (i.e., the pre-Tsong-ka-pa intellectual adversaries), then Dak-tsang holds a similar position among later critics. Jang-gya Rol-bay-dor-jay (*lcang skya rol pa'i rdo rje*, 1717-1786) sees good reason for this parallel:

> With the exception of the Jo-nang system and, later, the system of the view of the translator Dak-tsang Shay-rap-rin-chen, the instructions on the [Mādhyamika] view of most of the early scholars and adepts each had an Indian scholar or adept as their source.[68]

One of the main purposes of Jam-yang-shay-ba's massive *Great Exposition of Tenets* (*grub mtha' chen mo*) was the refutation of Dak-tsang's *Freedom From Extremes Through Knowing All Tenets* (*grub *mtha' kun shes nas mtha' bral grub pa*). Forty folios of the *Great Exposition of Tenets* are devoted exclusively to that task, while the remainder teems with briefer rebuttals. At times, Jam-yang-shay-ba resorts even to name-calling. For example, Dak-tsang's treatment of Candrakīrti's refutation of "production from other" leads Jam-yang-shay-ba to call Dak-tsang "one who wishes to do a dance having cut off the head of a crazy, dancing peacock and hung it on his behind."[69]

Among the many points of contention between Dak-tsang and Ge-luk-ba authors, there are four issues of disagreement closely related to our discussion of the two truths: (1) the basis of division of the two truths, (2) the divisibility of emptiness, (3) the nature of a Buddha, and (4) the status of conventional phenomena. While Ge-luk-bas held that the basis of division is objects of knowledge, Dak-tsang argued that it is *uninvestigated and unanalyzed* objects of knowledge, in order to emphasize his belief that if the two truths were found under thorough yogic analysis of how things exist, then they would have to be inherently and naturally existent. While Ge-luk-bas argue that it is meaningful to make a conceptual distinction between "this *table*'s emptiness of inherent existence" and "this *chair*'s emptiness of inherent existence," Dak-tsang argues that this is impossible. While Ge-luk-bas envision a Buddha as a being who simultaneously knows all conventional phenomena and all emptinesses, Dak-tsang (following Jayānanda) seems to regard a Buddha as having transcended all cognition and all consciousness. Most importantly, while Ge-luk-bas insist that ordinary conventional phenomena (tables and chairs, etc.) exist insofar as they are apprehended by valid (*tshad ma, pramāṇa*) consciousnesses, Dak-tsang scoffs at this claim and maintains that ordinary conventional phenomena are merely posited by ignorance (*ma rig pa, avidyā*). Conventional valid cognition, the keystone of the Ge-luk system, is the focus of Dak-tsang's attack. He argues:

> Those [pretending] to follow Candrakīrti who assert *through analysis with many reasons* that impure mistaken appearances are validly established have a great burden of contradictions.

and,

> [T]he presentation of valid cognition that is well known in the world. . . [may be] asserted *in a way that indulges the*

> *perspective of the world*. However, a so-called "valid cognizer comprehending conventionalities" is only non-existent *in the perspective of slight analysis* of our own system.[70]

As suggested by the parts I have emphasized in these passages, Dak-tsang leaves open a possible role for conventional valid cognition as a concession to the psychological and spiritual needs of ordinary, worldly beings. However, this indulgence is granted on a strictly non-analytical basis, i.e., prior even to superficial investigation of how ordinary phenomena exist and function.

Tsong-ka-pa and his defenders, on the other hand, insist that there is room at the level of worldly convention for a reasonable and analytical description of how logic, causation, cognition, and other ordinary processes operate. As long as one follows the general contours of worldly language and thought, without trying to say, "This is how things *really* exist," "This is the irreducible building block of nature," etc., one *can* do analysis and reach conclusions about what kinds of things exist and how they work. The bases for such investigations, as well as their termini, are conventional valid cognitions—that is, authoritative (uncontradicted) knowledge about conventional objects.

THE POLITICAL DIMENSION

This philosophical position has distinct political implications. Governments and other institutions do not enhance their prestige or authority by emphasizing their provisional and temporary nature. Rather, they find ways to stress the enduring and legitimate, i.e., *valid*, establishment of their regime. Tibet is the only country that has been governed by Mādhyamika philosophers. It can hardly be coincidental that Tibet is also the very country where Mādhyamika began to stress the *valid establishment* (*tshad grub, pramāṇasiddha*) of the ethical and hierarchical distinctions of the conventional world. To say this much is easy; to specify the precise nature of the relationship between Ge-luk political power and Ge-luk philosophy is a more difficult and delicate problem. Certainly no one can imagine that Tsong-ka-pa concocted his reading of Candrakīrti as a political device. On the other hand, it is inescapable that Ge-luk doctrine emerged in political contexts and had political ramifications. Thus, our story has a political dimension which must be acknowledged even if it cannot be explored in this work.

Michael Broido attributes enormous political significance to Ge-luk philosophy, arguing that the Ge-luk interpretation of the two truths is the basis "of their reform of Tibetan Buddhism, and so even [the basis] of their claims of geopolitical hegemony (insofar as these rested on anything other than naked force)."[71] Broido's basic insight into the political importance of religious philosophy is correct, but we must note that Tsong-ka-pa's system was in place and known to other Tibetan philosphers for two centuries before the Ge-luk-bas, with the help of Mongol allies, achieved anything approaching "geopolitical hegemony". Furthermore, the subtleties of Tsong-ka-pa's interpretation of the two truths have never been known to the average Tibetan. Consequently, the *direct* impact of Ge-luk Mādhyamika doctrine on Ge-luk authority over the populace must always have been rather narrow.

Rather than Mādhyamika doctrine, it is the institutional ideology surrounding the office of the Dalai Lama that has been the front line in the effort to legitimate Ge-luk power. Both political history and spiritual ideology point to the office of the Dalai Lama as the point at which power from beyond blesses and sanctions Ge-luk rule. In 1578 the title *Dalai Lama* (which means "Ocean Lama") was accorded by the Tümät Mongol Altan Khan to Sö-nam-gya-tso (*bdod nams rgya mtsho*, 1543-1588), the second reincarnation of the founder of the important Ge-luk monastery Tra-shi-lun-bo (*bkra shis lhun po*). Thus, Sö-nam-gya-tso became the third Dalai Lama, and his previous incarnations were posthumously designated the first and second Dalai Lamas. The fourth Dalai Lama, Yön-den-gya-tso, (*yon dan rgya mtsho*, 1589-1617) was actually the great grandson of Altan Khan. The close relationship between the fifth Dalai Lama, Ngak-wang Lo-sang-gya-tso (*ngag dbang blo bzang rgya mthso*, 1617-1682), and the Qośot Mongol Gushri Khan led to the defeat of the Tsang rulers who stood in the way of Ge-luk efforts to unite Tibet.

In religious terms, the Dalai Lama is not only the reincarnation of earlier charismatic figure(s), but the living incarnation of Avalokiteśvara, the celestial Bodhisattva of compassion. It is well known that most Tibetans, even many well-educated and otherwise Westernized Tibetans, regard the Dalai Lama as a god. They address him, speak of him, and write about him in the very highest honorific language, often using forms reserved for him alone; he receives the fervent prayers and offerings of clerics and laity from all stations. Ge-luk-ba officials successfully attached to the office of Dalai Lama a sacred authority that echoes the divine power of the Tibetan kings of the seventh through ninth centuries.[72] The political implications of this are clear to the communist Chinese who, in defiance of justice and international law, now occupy Tibet.[73] In recent years, a very few monasteries in Tibet have been allowed to hold small classes on Mādhyamika doctrine. However, importation to Tibet of photographs of the exiled Dalai Lama is strictly forbidden.[74]

The preeminence of other factors not withstanding, certainly Ge-luk Mādhyamika doctrine has had a complex relationship with Ge-luk political fortunes. The problem of where to ground (i.e., how to rationalize) ethical injunctions is not only a philosophical and religious problem; it is also a problem of political ideology for those who see their interest in the maintenance of a well-regulated social order. Perhaps the appeal of Ge-luk-ba to its powerful patrons (e.g., the Pak-mo-dru-ba) lay partly in their claim to possess a solution to this problem that is both rationally persuasive and scripturally supportable. The preservation in Ge-luk-ba doctrine of valid hierarchical religious distinctions, e.g., the distinction between saṃsāra and nirvāṇa and the many different levels within saṃsāra, may be (mis)taken as a sanction for ranked socio-ethical distinctions, e.g. the distinction between non-celibate laity and celibate clerics, distinctions between landowner, peasant, and nomad, etc. Perhaps it is a reflection of growing Ge-luk political ambition and investment in temporal matters that Tsong-ka-pa's successors, unlike Tsong-ka-pa himself, define conventional reality mainly in terms of its *validity* rather than in terms of its deceptiveness or illusoriness (see chapter six). As noted above, one of the spiritual dangers of Ge-luk-ba Mādhyamika is its susceptibility to construction as a conservative, i.e., status quo confirming, doctrine. It seems likely that this spiritual liability has been a political strength.

Furthermore, because the Ge-luk-ba version of the two truths doctrine led clerics to regard ethical norms as validly established, rather than as merely provisional expedients, it reinforced the call for strict adherence to monastic vows. While the reformation of Tibetan Buddhism did not begin with Tsong-ka-pa, it was Tsong-ka-pa who philosophically buttressed that reformation in a way that allowed it to win the day. The strict celibacy demanded of Ge-luk clerics identified them as beings who have left the ordinary world for a higher calling, thus enhancing their authority. Ge-luk (which means "the order of virtue") gained a reputation for discipline and piety, and this reputation helped the order attract powerful patrons and allies such as the Pak-mo-dru-ba (*phag mo gru pa*) and several Mongol groups, thereby building its temporal prestige and power.

There are also political implications in the Ge-luk-ba arguments that ultimate truth (i.e., emptiness) is a knowable (*shes bya, jñeya*) that must be *initially* cognized through the careful pursuit of reasoned analysis. Like other Buddhists, Ge-luk-bas seek non-dualistic and non-conceptual insight (*rtog med ye shes, nirvikalpajñāna*) into reality. However, for them this is not a spontaneous, naturally arising, objectless intuition; rather, it something that must be gradually and artificially cultivated, and it has a specific and rationally comprehensible object—emptiness. Although emptiness is the very nature of the mind, non-conceptual realization of this natural emptiness is a hard-won cultural product. The initial stages of creating it include not only training in ethics, but also complete conceptual mastery of what "emptiness" means and how logic can be used to approach it. This philosophical stance strengthens the religious authority (and consequently the political authority) of those who control and have access to educational institutions. The Ge-luk-ba elite was traditionally educated at a few very large monasteries, most of them near Lhasa, and the success of the Ge-luk order was associated with a tendency for prestige and authority to become highly concentrated (by Tibetan standards) in the hierarchies of these large, centrally located institutions. A network of branch monasteries provded both a feeder system for promising students and sinecure for those graduates who were not of the very highest caliber. Without claiming that the resources of such institutions were absolutely necessary for spiritual development, there certainly was an implication that enrollment at these monasteries represented a very rare spiritual opportunity. Likewise it was implied that advancement through the curriculum and academic hierarchy of these institutions reflected, if not growth in wisdom, then at least the mastery of a kind of conceptual knowledge without which non-conceptual wisdom could hardly be expected to arise. The title *geshe* (*dge bshes*) was given to graduates of the several monastic colleges of Dre-bung, Se-ra, and Gan-den; its Sanskrit equivalent, *kalyāṇamitra* (usually translated "spiritual friend"), is often an epithet of a guru, i.e., a spiritual master. The abbots of these monasteries were always geshes, and the Dalai Lamas themselves were expected to become geshes; thus the god-king was also the god-scholar and the scholar-king.

PREVIEW

This work is mainly an exploration of the content of Ge-luk-ba interpretations of the two truths in Mādhyamika. While the attitudes and processes that have shaped those interpretations are of great interest, the complexity of the topic has dictated that the primary focus, in the following chapters, be the actual content of the doctrine. It is hoped that these doctrinal discussions will stand, for the reader, within the framework of this opening chapter.

In this first chapter we have suggested a model in which the evolution of myth and doctrine is propelled by the need to obviate contradiction in order to create and maintain a coherent world. We have depicted the scholastic Ge-luk-ba as one who seeks to overcome contradiction by following Tsong-ka-pa in quest of an understanding of the world that is both logically sound and scripturally defensible. Paradox and mystery are not considered acceptable recourses when faced with apparent internal contradictions. Every attempt is made to find an answer that is both reasonable and somehow reconcilable with scripture. (When no solution can be found, the "ongoing quest" can be invoked.) The works of Nāgārjuna, Śāntideva, Candrakīrti are re-read and construed within the boundaries of Tsong-ka-pa's system. Tsong-ka-pa, Kay-drup, and Gyel-tsap are re-read in attempts to show their internal coherence. Details and examples filling this rough outline of the Ge-luk-ba scholastic process are to be found throughout the following chapters.

The remaining eleven chapters concentrate on the topical substance of the doctrine of the two truths. The sequence of chapters is based, very roughly, on the topical sequence within the relevant sections from Candrakīrti's *Supplement to the Middle Way*, Tsong-ka-pa's *Illumination of the Thought*, and Ge-luk-ba monastic textbooks on Mādhyamika. Chapters two, three, and four answer general questions about the division into the two truths: What is divided? Do the two truths include everything that exists? What is the relationship between the concealer-truths and ultimate truths? Ge-luk-bas agree that the two truths are a dichotomous division of all objects of knowledge and that there is a oneness of entity between them. The meaning and implications of these assertions are explored and contrasted with the views of non-Ge-luk-ba interpreters of Mādhyamika, especially the views of contemporary Western scholars. Chapters five through nine discuss the nature and subdivisions of the two truths individually, while chapters ten, eleven, and twelve consider specific epistemological problems pertaining to the positions set forth in the preceding chapters.

While the remainder of this work focuses on doctrinal content, the processual model outlined in this chapter is not left behind. Chapters two, three, four, five, and eleven discuss issues upon which there is near unanimity within Ge-luk-ba. They show how the Ge-luk-bas attempt to free Mādhyamika from paradox and solve the "problem" of the two truths through a very precise analysis of what the truths are and how they are related to one another. Chapters six, seven, eight, nine, ten, and twelve consider issues upon which there is significant disagreement within Ge-luk-ba, and from time to time we will note how these disputes exemplify the different styles of resolving contradiction among Ge-luk authors.

2 *The Basis of the Division*

THE GE-LUK-BA POSITION

What is divided into the two truths? The precise identification of the basis of division of the two truths is critical to the Ge-luk-ba effort to maintain a non-paradoxical compatibility between emptiness and the conventional distinctions of rational thought and ethics. Jam-yang-shay-ba insists that to expound on the meaning of the two truths without first understanding *what it is that they are two of* is like climbing on the branches of a rootless tree.[1]

Ge-luk-bas unanimously assert that the basis of division of the two truths is objects of knowledge (*shes bya, jñeya*). Tsong-ka-pa's *Illumination of the Thought* states, "Although there indeed are many different ways of asserting what the basis of division of the two truths is, here it is taken to be objects of knowledge."[2] Tsong-ka-pa argues that this is proven by a passage from the *Meeting of the Father and Son Sūtra* (*Pitṛputrasamāgamasūtra*) as cited in Śāntideva's *Compendium of Instructions* (*Śikṣāsamuccaya*):[3]

> It is thus: The Tathāgatas thoroughly understand conventionalities and ultimates. Also, objects of knowledge are exhausted within the two, concealer-truths and ultimate truths.

Ge-luk-bas claim that reasoning as well as scripture establishes that objects of knowledge are the basis of division of the two truths. Candrakīrti's *Supplement Commentary* says:[4]

> [U]ltimates gain their entities through being the objects of certain exalted wisdoms of those who see reality.... Other [objects, i.e., conventionalities] gain their existence through the power of perceivers of falsities...

Taking these characterizations as "given," Ge-luk-bas (such as Ngak-wang-bel-den) argue that the two truths must be two types of object of knowledge.[5] Ultimate truths are objects known by the wisdom that realizes emptiness, while concealer-truths are objects known via conventional valid cognition. Therefore, the basis of division is objects of knowledge.

OTHER ASSERTIONS

However, as Tsong-ka-pa points out, there are many other assertions about the basis of division. In works by various non-Ge-luk-bas, one may read that the basis of division of the two truths is (1) truths, (2) the entities of all phenomena from forms and so forth through omniscient consciousnesses, (3) mere appearances, (4) uninvestigated and unanalyzed objects of knowledge, (5) non-reified objects, (6) phenomena, or (7) perspectives. Let us consider Ge-luk-ba objections to each of these assertions.

(1) *Truths.* Some scholars have assumed (naturally) that the two truths are two types of truth and that truths are therefore the basis of division.[6] The term "truth" refers to something that is non-deceptive (*mi slu ba*). In common parlance, a statement is true if there is concordance between the meaning it expresses and the factual situation to which it refers. It is this correspondence that allows us to judge a statement to be non-deceptive, and therefore true. Similarly, in the context of the two truths, a truth is a phenomenon that *exists as it appears.* It is non-deceptive in that there is agreement between its mode of appearance and its mode of subsistence.

By this standard, Ge-luk-bas hold that no concealer-truths are truths; most Ge-luk-bas also hold that all ultimate truths are truths.[7] Whatever is a concealer-truth is necessarily a falsity (*rdzun pa, mṛṣā*)—that is, something whose mode of appearance is deceptive with regard to its mode of subsistence. Although the word "truth" occurs in the term "concealer-truth", this does not indicate that concealer-truths are a certain type of truth or a level of truth. Rather, it means that concealer-truths are phenomena wrongly perceived to be truths by ignorant, "concealing" consciousnesses.[8]

When Ge-luk-bas says that an elephant (for example) is a not a truth, but a falsity, they mean that it is not a truth even in conventional terms (*tha snyad du*). Once a person has realized emptiness, it is the authority of conventional valid cognition that knows an elephant as a falsity. Only emptiness appears to an ultimate valid cognizer, a mind realizing emptiness; thus, ultimate valid cognition cannot establish that an elephant is a falsity because it is not aware of elephants at all. However, if an elephant is a falsity even for conventional valid cognition, then by what authority do Ge-luk-bas distinguish between an elephant and a magician's illusion that appears to be an elephant? It is necessary to develop criteria and vocabulary to distinguish the coarse falseness of illusions and mirages from the subtle falseness of ordinary objects. We will return to this important question in chapter seven. For now, three points must be clear: (1) the word "truth," in the context of Ge-luk-ba discussions of the two truths, refers to an object that exists as it appears; (2) a concealer-truth is not a truth even conventionally; and therefore (3) truth cannot be the basis of division of the two truths. As Michael Sweet writes:[9]

> The Mādhyamika assertion of two truths should not lead one to assume that this school accepts two different levels or degrees of reality; from earliest times Buddhist texts have denied there is a multiplicity of truths, and the Mādhyamika is in accord with this.

(2) *The entities of all phenomena from forms up through omniscient consciousnesses.* Candrakīrti's *Supplement* states:[10]

> [Buddha] said that all things have two entities—
> Those found by perceivers of reality and of falsities.

In considering the meaning of this passage, Tang-sak-ba[11] (*thang sags pa*) holds that the entities of all phenomena—from forms, sounds, and so forth up through omniscient consciousnesses—are the basis of the division into the two truths. Jam-yang-shay-ba responds by arguing that if the entity of a form, for example, were such a basis of division, both concealer-truths and ultimate truths would be included within the entity of that form.[12] As Hopkins explains Jam-yang-shay-ba's criticism:[13]

> The problem with this position is that since, for instance, a form would be a basis of division into a truth-for-a-

> concealer and an ultimate truth, the ultimate truth which is a division of form would have to be a form in which case it would be composed of material particles.

While this seems to be Jam-yang-shay-ba's meaning, I do not think Tang-sak-ba's position can be dismissed so readily because Tang-sak-ba does not say that form is the basis of division. Rather, he says that the entities of all phenomena are the basis of division. Since Tang-sak-ba's assertion is based on a passage by Candrakīrti in which the word "entity" (*ngo bo*) means "nature" (*rang bzhin*) as glossed by Candrakīrti himself,[14] it is only fair to begin a discussion of Tang-sak-ba's view with the assumption that when he says "the entities of all phenomena" he is referring to the natures of those phenomena. The ultimate nature of form is the emptiness of form—an ultimate truth. The conventional nature of form is form—a concealer-truth. Each phenomenon does have two natures, one of which is an ultimate truth and one of which is a concealer-truth. Thus far, Tang-sak-ba's assertion seems acceptable.

However a question arises: Does Tang-sak-ba mean to assert a single universal division with one basis of division (the entities of all phenomena)? Or is he rather thinking of a separate division into the two truths in relation to every phenomenon individually? The principle to keep in mind is that it must be possible for the basis of division, whatever it is, to serve as a predicate for each of the divisions and their subdivisions. If there were a single universal division into the two truths, with the natures of all phenomena as the basis of division, then every subdivision of the two truths—that is every phenomenon—would individually be a nature (either conventional or ultimate) of all phenomena because "the natures of all phenomena" is the basis of division. For example, we should be able to say, "Form is a nature of all phenomena." On the other hand, if Tang-sak-ba means that the natures of each phenomenon, taken individually, are the basis of division of the two truths in general, then the nature of form, for example, is a basis for the division into the two truths. Since an omniscient consciousness, for example, is a concealer-truth, it would have to be a nature of form. Every phenomenon would be a nature not only of itself but of every other phenomenon and we would arrive at a philosophical position reminiscent of the Hua-yen doctrine of mutual interpenetration.

Rather than either of these alternatives, it is much more likely that what Tang-sak-ba meant is that "natures of form" is the basis of division into the two truths *with regard to form*, "natures of sound" is the basis of division into the two truths *with regard to sound*, and so forth up through omniscience. From the Ge-luk-ba viewpoint this is a reasonable and accurate statement, but it fails to provide a basis of division for the two truths in general. It is important to know that both truths pertain to every phenomenon individually, but this does not answer the general question: If the two truths are not two types of truth, then of what are they two types?

(3) *Mere appearances.* According to Ngok-lo-tsa-wa (*ngog lo tstsha ba blo ldan shes rab*, 1059-1109) and his followers, mere appearance (*snang tsam*) is the basis of division of the two truths.[15] In refuting this, Jam-yang-shay-ba first establishes that the two truths are fully comprehensive of their basis of division.[16] (This will be discussed in the next chapter.) Consequently, if mere appearances were the basis of division, anything that merely appeared to any consciousness would have to be one or the other of the two truths. For example, a mirage being water would have to be either a concealer-truth or an ultimate truth because for a consciousness apprehending the mirage there is the mere appearance of the mirage as water. Since a mirage being water does not exist, the two truths would have to include non-existents if their basis of division were mere appearances.

In positing mere appearances as the basis of division, it is not Ngok's intention to include such false appearances within the two truths. Rather, it is his position that objects of knowledge, posited as the basis of division of the two truths by Ge-luk-bas, is too narrow because ultimate truths—emptinesses—are not objects of knowledge. In his system, the unfindability of an object under analysis is *called* emptiness, but there is no existent or object of knowledge to which "emptiness" refers; if emptiness were cognizable, it would (absurdly) have to be inherently existent. As Hopkins explains:[17]

> Ngok's idea is that if an analytical consciousness cognized an emptiness, then that emptiness would necessarily inherently exist. For, an analytical consciousness is searching to find whether an object inherently exists or not, and if it "finds" or cognizes an emptiness of inherent existence of that object, then it would seem that the emptiness must

inherently exist since, according to him, it would be able to bear ultimate analysis.

The Ge-luk-ba reply is that the unfindability of a table under ultimate analysis is the emptiness of that table and that this emptiness is "found" or cognized by a consciousness analyzing the table.[18] However, because the table, and not the emptiness of the table, is under analysis at that time, the cognition of emptiness does not entail that emptiness is inherently existent. The emptiness of the table is itself unable to bear ultimate analysis, and is therefore empty of inherent existence.

According to Ngak-wang-bel-den,[19] the scriptural evidence upon which Ngok bases his view that emptiness is not an object of knowledge includes a controversial passage from Śāntideva's *Engaging in the Bodhisattva Deeds*:[20]

> Conventionalities and ultimates:
> These are asserted as the two truths.
> The ultimate is not the province of awareness.
> Awareness is asserted to be a conventionality.

Dö-lung Gya-mar's (*stod lung rgya dmar*, fl. early twelfth century) interpretation of this stanza illustrates how it can be used to support the conclusion that ultimate truths are not objects of knowledge. In his view, the fourth line—"Awareness is asserted to be a conventionality"—means that all awarenesses and all objects of awareness must be concealer-truths. The third line—"The ultimate is not the province of awareness"—means that an ultimate truth cannot be the object of *any* consciousness. The fourth line serves as reason proving the thesis of the third line. Therefore, according to Dö-lung Gya-mar, the meaning of these lines is "Ultimate truths cannot be objects of any consciousness because all consciousness and all objects of consciousness are concealer-truths."

Tsong-ka-pa's *Illumination of the Thought*[21] explains that this stanza represents Śāntideva's reflection on a passage from the *Meeting of the Father and Son Sūtra* (cited by Śāntideva in his *Compendium of Instructions*):[22]

> The Tathāgatas see conventionalities as the province of the world. That which is ultimate is inexpressible, is not an object of knowledge, is not an object of consciousness, is not an object of thorough knowledge, and is indemonstrable.

Rather than presenting a thesis and reason, the third and fourth lines of Śāntideva's stanza serve, in the Ge-luk-ba view, to describe ultimate truths and concealer-truths in accordance with the teaching of this sūtra passage. Gyel-tsap's *Explanation of (Śāntideva's) "Engaging in the Bodhisattva Deeds"* further illuminates Śāntideva's intention:[23]

> [The ultimate] does not appear dualistically to the direct valid awareness that explicitly realizes it. From this point of view, it is not the province of that [awareness]. It is an object to be known by the direct valid cognizer that comprehends it.

Conversely, we can understand that those phenomena that appear dualistically to the direct perceivers apprehending them are conventionalities. This interpretation seems to restrict the meaning of "awareness" in this context to direct perceivers. If a direct perceiver has dualistic appearance, then its object is a conventionality. If not, then its object is an ultimate truth.

Although certain complications arise when we examine later Ge-luk-ba commentary on this passage (see chapter six), it must be clear that the system is absolutely steadfast in asserting that *sentient beings can know the ultimate.* Borrowing from Kay-drup-jay's *Thousand Doses,*[24] Jam-yang-shay-ba[25] hurls four *reductio ad absurdum* arguments at those who maintain that emptiness is unknowable:

(a) Śāntideva must have contradicted himself because his *Compendium of Instructions* cites a sūtra indicating that objects of knowledge are the basis of division of the two truths, while his *Engaging in the Bodhisattva Deeds* teaches that the ultimate is unknowable.
(b) Since the ultimate cannot be known, Buddha taught the ultimate without knowing it. Therefore, sūtras that say that the Buddha knows emptiness are incorrect.
(c) Emptiness does not exist because it is not an object of knowledge. Since sūtra and śāstra sources state that if emptiness did not exist there would be no point in making great sacrifices on the path, other sūtras that say that such sacrifice should be made are incorrect.
(d) All sentient beings are already liberated from suffering because the mode of subsistence of phenomena has been clear to them for countless aeons. This must be the case because

> if emptiness is non-existent, phenomena have no mode of subsistence apart from the way that they appear.

(4) *Uninvestigated and unanalyzed objects of knowledge.* The root text of Dak-tsang's (*stag tshang lo tsa ba shes rab rin chen*, 1405-?) *Freedom From Extremes Through Knowing All Tenets* says,[26] "[Sūtra] states that the basis of division of the [two] truths is mere objects of knowledge." His auto-commentary on that work explains that[27]

> . . . mere objects of knowledge in a perspective without investigation or analysis, without differentiation, are the very basis of division of the two truths.

Dak-tsang's point is that nothing can bear analysis. Therefore, one can speak of the two truths only in terms of non-analytical, non-investigative consciousnesses.

Jam-yang-shay-ba rejects this conclusion.[28] While no phenomenon is found when it is itself subjected to ultimate analysis, an analytical consciousness does find the emptiness of whatever it takes as its basis of analysis. Jam-yang-shay-ba points out that even Dak-tsang himself asserts that an ultimate truth is an object found by an ultimate reasoning consciousness. Why, then, should analytical consciousnesses be excluded from those whose objects of knowledge constitute the basis of division?

(5) *Non-reified objects.* Certain Tibetan teachers held the position that non-reified objects (*sgro ma brtags pa'i yul*) are the basis of division of the two truths. To this, Jam-yang-shay-ba objects that illusions and mirages are both reified objects and concealer-truths.[29] They must be considered reified objects because they are reified by the sense consciousnesses which they mislead. Since they exist and are not ultimate truths they must be concealer-truths. Therefore, the proposed basis of division, non-reified objects, is unsuitable because it does not include all concealer-truths.

(6) *Mere phenomena.* Certain Tibetans give an equivalent of objects of knowledge as the basis of division of the two truths. For example, Rong-dön (*rong ston*, 1367-1450), a Sa-gya-ba who founded Nalanda (Nalendra) Monastery in Tibet, posits "mere phenomena" (*chos tsam*).[30] Although object of knowledge (*shes bya*), existent (*yod pa*), established base (*gzhi grub*), and phenomenon (*chos*) are equivalents, Ge-luk-bas posit objects of knowledge, rather than any equivalent, as the basis of division into the two truths. In the first place, this is the term used in the *Meeting of the Father and Son Sūtra*.

Ngak-wang-bel-den gives a further explanation that suggests the soteriological dimension of the division:[31]

> Turning the mind inward, what must be known (*shes par bya dgos*) without fail for the sake of release is precisely the two truths. Therefore, there is an essential point for [religious] practice even in the mere name "objects of knowledge."

(7) *Perspectives.* Many Western scholars hold that the two truths are not two types of object, but rather two viewpoints, perspectives, or types of consciousnesses. Frederick Streng, for example, maintains this position consistently:[32]

> Since there are no intrinsically different objects of knowledge, the distinction between "mundane truth" and "ultimate truth" does not pertain to different objects of knowledge, e.g., the world and ultimate reality. It refers, rather to the manner by which "things" are perceived.

and:[33]

> [T]here are two forms of understanding: world-ensconced truth and the highest truth.... The distinction...is a difference of attitude or awareness about oneself in relation to existence. It is foremost an epistemological difference, which becomes an ontological difference insofar as knowledge determines what one becomes.

Elsewhere Streng states, "Thus, the basic difference between conventional and ultimate truth is...a difference of the perspective...."[34] Reaching a similar conclusion by a very different route, Lindtner writes:[35]

> The two truths cannot be claimed to express different levels of objective reality since all things always equally lack *svabhāva*. They are merely two ways of looking (*darśana*) at things, a provisional and a definite.

Similarly, C.W. Huntington claims that "emptiness is nowhere defined as an object of knowledge (*jñeya*)," but rather is a "perspective" or "mode of seeing."[36]

The definitions and etymologies of the two truths that we will examine in later chapters, as well as the insistence on "objects of *knowledge*" as the basis of division, demonstrate that Ge-luk-bas are sensitive to the epistemological ramifications in the Prāsaṅgika presentation of the two truths. Nevertheless, their assertion that the two truths are *objects* of consciousness stands in clear contrast to the view of the two truths as attitudes, perspectives, modes of understanding, or other species of subjectivity. Streng argues that since objects are not inherently different from subjects, one cannot speak of the two truths as objects. From the Ge-luk-ba viewpoint, this is far from convincing. If we needed an inherently existent difference between subject and object before we could talk about objects, then why would we not also need an inherently existent distinction between one "manner of seeing" and another before we could describe the difference between the two truths? Since nothing inherently exists, there are no distinctions that inherently exist. Nevertheless, we can make distinctions between the two truths conventionally and we can likewise differentiate object and subject conventionally.

On this point there is evidence for the Ge-luk-ba interpretation in the Indian Mādhyamika tradition. For example, Candrakīrti's *Supplement Commentary* states:[37]

> Here [it is explained] that the Supramundane Victor Buddhas, who unerringly know the entities of the two truths, teach a twofold entity for all internal and external things—compositional phenomena, sprouts, and so forth—in this way: conventionalities and ultimates.

Having said that the two truths pertain to external as well as internal things, Candrakīrti repeatedly uses the word object (*yul, viṣaya*) in his definitions of the two truths. For example, his *Supplement Commentary* says:[38]

> Concerning these, ultimates gain their entities through being the objects of certain exalted wisdoms of those who see reality.

And:[39]

> Also, between those two natures, that which is the object of a perceiver of reality is suchness; it is "ultimate truth." That which is the object of a perceiver of the false is a concealer-truth.

Part of the spiritual message embodied in the "two perspectives" interpretation is that enlightened beings and ignorant beings live in the same world, but see it in radically different ways. Ge-luk-bas agree with this, but in stressing that ultimate truths are a special class of objects—rather than a special way of seeing the same objects—they risk being misunderstood to mean that ultimate truths are "a world apart," disconnected from the ordinary things we see around us. Of course, the system maintains that the emptiness of a table is the very *nature* of that table. A table and its emptiness are a single entity. When an ordinary conventional mind takes a table as its object of observation, it sees a table. When a mind of ultimate analysis searches for the table, it finds the emptiness of the table. Hence, the two truths are posited in relation to a single entity by way of the perspectives of the observing consciousnesses. This is as close as Ge-luk-bas will come to defining the two truths as perspectives. They adhere to two important distinctions: (1) The two truths are the objects of two different types of perspective, and not the differing perspectives themselves or some indefinite mixture of object and subject. (2) Although they are one entity, a table and its emptiness are distinct phenomena; there is nothing that is both table and its emptiness. This second point will explored in chapters three and four.

These distinctions are critical to the Ge-luk-ba philosophical project, the preservation of non-paradoxical compatibility between the two truths. The conventional mind that finds a table is not discredited by the ultimate mind that finds the emptiness of the table. The first is valid because a table (a conventional truth) does exist; the second is also valid because the table's real nature is an emptiness of inherent existence (an ultimate truth).

Many Western interpreters (e.g., de Jong, Lindtner, and Crittenden) of Indian Mādhyamika have explicitly rejected such an ontological interpretation of the division.[40] However, if instead the two truths were two ways of looking at precisely the same thing, then the ultimate truth-cognition would supercede and discredit the conventional truth-cognition; both could not be valid. Criticizing this approach, Robert Thurman writes that Ngok's position[41]

> reminds us of contemporary interpreters of the two realities who forget that they are categories of "knowables" (*jñeya*), facts, and by calling them "epistemological" rather than "ontological," end up saying "really there is only one reality."

Thurman recognizes that some modern interpretations of the two truths as antithetical perspectives diverge from the (Ge-luk-ba) middle way by allowing conventional truth to be invalidated and discredited by ultimate truth. Yet it also true that many modern interpreters struggle to maintain the legitimacy of both perspectives—despite claiming that the two truths (as perspectives) yield logically contradictory information about a single phenomenon. This accounts for the prevailing, albeit not unanimous, conclusion that the Mādhyamika *modus operandi* is soteriological paradox, contradiction, and (in the case of David Eckel) irony.[42]

In my opinion, the Ge-luk-ba interpretation of the two truths must be considered an ontology in the sense that it is a doctrine that classifies two types of existent objects—rather than two types of knowledge. However, the *method* of division is not ontological. Phenomena are not divided by way of their manner of existing because all phenomena, including emptinesses, are only conventionally existent; none are ultimately or inherently existent. Lindtner makes precisely this point when he writes, "The two truths cannot be claimed to express different levels of objective reality since all things always equally lack *svabhāva*."[43] Instead, Ge-luk-bas distinguish the two truths by way of a distinction between the types of consciousness that apprehend them. In fact, many of the problems discussed by Ge-luk-bas in the context of the two truths are epistemological in that they concern the validity and nature of the consciousnesses that know the two truths. Insisting at the outset on "*objects* of *knowledge*" as the basis of division, Ge-luk-bas give an important epistemological dimension to their presentation of two truths, while at the same time cutting off any idea that two truths are subjective perspectives.

3 *The Two Truths as a Dichotomy*

THE MEANING OF "PRECISE ENUMERATION"

According to the Ge-luk interpretation, every object of knowledge must be either a concealer-truth or an ultimate truth. No object of knowledge can be both a concealer-truth and an ultimate truth and no object of knowledge can be neither a concealer-truth nor an ultimate truth. Thus, the two truths are a "precise enumeration" (*grangs nges*) that includes every object of knowledge, eliminating the possibility of any further category among objects of knowledge. They are a dichotomy.

Scriptural support for this view begins with the *Meeting of the Father and Son Sūtra*, which says, "Also, objects of knowledge are exhausted within the two, concealer-truths and ultimate truths." Tsong-ka-pa's *Illumination of the Thought*, commenting on this passage, says, "... because [sūtra] says "are exhausted within these," [objects of knowledge] are precisely enumerated as the two truths."[1] Also, the *Meeting of the Father and Son* says:[2]

> He who knows the world, without listening to others,
> Teaches with just these two truths,
> Conventionalities and ultimates.
> There is no third truth.

and Candrakīrti's *Supplement Commentary* says:[3]

> Here, the truths of suffering, origin and path are included within concealer-truths and true cessations are entities of ultimate truths. Similarly, any other truth that exists at all is definitely only included within the two truths.

Besides the four noble truths, Buddhist sūtras refer to many other phenomena using names that include the word "truth." There is, for example, a list of "truths" explained in the *Sūtra on the Ten Grounds* (*Daśabhūmikasūtra*) and cited by Candrakīrti in his *Supplement Commentary*.[4] Although many objects of knowledge are called "truths," each must be either a concealer-truth or an ultimate truth.

The proof through reasoning that the two truths are a precise enumeration eliminating any further category of object of knowledge proceeds from two premises: (1) ultimate truths are non-deceptive (*mi slu ba*), and (2) concealer-truths are deceptive (*slu ba*). As we shall see in the chapter on the realizational sequence (chapter ten), one approaches realization of an object as a concealer-truth by way of understanding it as false and deceptive. An object is non-deceptive if the way it appears to a valid cognizer directly realizing it is in accord with the way it exists.[5] Here, "the way it exists" is a casual way of referring to its final mode of subsistence (*gnas tshul mthar thug pa*) or ultimate nature. If the undisguised final nature of an object is comprehended by the consciousness directly realizing it, then it is an ultimate truth. Otherwise, it is deceptive, a falsity, and a concealer-truth.

Working from these premises, Ngak-wang-bel-den states the argument:[6]

> If something is positively distinguished within the meaning of falsity—that is, the deceptive—then its being a non-deceptive truth must be excluded. Because of this, the deceptive and the non-deceptive are mutually exclusive contradictories (*phan tshun spangs 'gal*). Therefore, those two pervade all objects of knowledge. Because of this, they eliminate further categories that are both or neither.

The *locus classicus* for this argument is Kamalaśīla's *Illumination of the Middle Way*:

> With respect to a pair of phenomena having the character of mutual exclusion, if something's being one is refuted while its being the other is not established, then it does

> not exist. Therefore, a position that is neither [of those phenomena] is unfeasible.

This straightforward statement of the law of the excluded middle by an Indian Mādhyamika is an additional piece of evidence supporting a position held by Ruegg:[7]

> Although it has been alleged that Buddhist philosophers—and, indeed, other Indian thinkers as well—ignore or reject the principles of non-contradiction and excluded middle, this contention certainly cannot be sustained as concerns Nāgārjuna and his school, whose entire reasoning is in fact founded upon them.

THE TWO TRUTHS AS CONTRADICTORIES

Candrakīrti's *Supplement* states, "[Buddha] said that all things have two entities. . . ."[8] For Ge-luk-bas this indicates that all phenomena have two natures. The final nature of a table—its emptiness of inherent existence—is the ultimate truth that exists in relation to the table and the conventional nature of a table is the concealer-truth that exists in relation to the table. When Ge-luk-bas say that the two truths are contradictories, they do not mean that it is paradoxical for one table to have these two natures. They mean that it is impossible for any one thing to be both a concealer-truth and an ultimate truth.

One very influential Ge-luk-ba exposition of the meaning of contradiction is found in a work from the fifteenth century by Jam-yang-chok-hla-ö-ser (*'jam dbyangs phyogs lha 'od zer*), the famous *Collected Topics of Ra Dö*. The "collected topics" literature, the usual starting point in the monastic syllabus, gathers together and systematically introduces technical vocabulary from the works of Dignāga, Dharmakīrti, and the Abhidharma literature. According to Jam-yang-chok-hla-ö-ser, contradictories are best defined as "those that abide discordantly."[9] This means that they are (1) different (*tha dad*), and that (2) it is impossible for anything to be both of them. Although there are two types of contradictories, contradictories that do not abide together (*lhan gcig mi gnas 'gal*) and mutually exclusive contradictories (*phan tshun spang 'gal*), in fact contradictory and mutually exclusive contradictory are equivalents. Sets of contradictories that do not abide together are, for example, hot and cold, light and darkness, the crow and the owl, and the consciousness conceiving that the self is inherently existent and the wisdom realizing that an inherently existent self does not exist.[10] Whenever one member of such a pair is present, it interrupts or displaces the other. As Donald Lopez puts it, "this type of contradiction involves actual displacement of one thing by the other; the two cannot inhabit the same place, be it a consciousness or the limb of a tree."[11]

Jam-yang-chok-hla-ö-ser defines mutually exclusive contradictories as: "those that abide discordantly through being excluded and excluder."[12] The excluder (*yongs gcod*) is that which is brought forward and positively distinguished in the mind. The excluded (*rnam bcad*) can be anything that is thereby negated. For example, when one realizes that a pot is impermanent, impermanent is the excluder and permanent is the excluded. Mutually exclusive contradictories are of two varieties: direct contradictories (*dngos 'gal*) and indirect contradictories (*rgyud 'gal*). The *Ra Dö* definition of direct contradictories is: "those abide in direct and mutual discord."[13] Thing and non-thing, permanent phenomenon and impermanent phenomenon, and the deceptive and the non-deceptive are examples of direct contradictories. Direct contradictories are necessarily dichotomous divisions of all phenomena.

The *Ra Dö* definition of indirect contradictories is: "those that abide in indirect and mutual discord," while a later collected topics work, Pur-bu-jok's *Intermediate Path of Reasoning* makes the same point with a slightly longer definition: "those that are not the damaged and the damager in a direct sense, yet abide discordantly."[14] Indirect contradictories are, for example, blue and yellow, hot and cold, and permanent phenomenon (*rtag pa, nitya*) and functioning thing (*dngos po, bhava*), etc. When one realizes that the color of a chair is blue, yellow is only indirectly or implicitly eliminated by way of the fact that yellow is included within the class of non-blue. Note that many indirect contradictories, such as blue and yellow, are not dichotomous divisions of all objects of knowledge. Therefore, since indirect contradictories are a type of mutually exclusive contradictory, there are many mutually exclusive contradictories that are not dichotomies.

On the other hand, some indirect contradictories *are* dichotomies of all phenomena. Take the example of functioning thing and permanent phenomenon. Functioning thing and impermanent phenomenon are equivalents, and thus every phenomenon is either a functioning thing or a permanent phenomenon. Nevertheless, functioning thing and permanent phenomenon are *indirect* contradictories, rather than direct contradictories, because the meaning of functioning thing—"that which performs its function"—and the meaning of permanent phenomenon—"the non-momentary"—do not stand in direct contradiction. One can realize that a pot is a functioning thing through seeing that it holds water without realizing that it is not permanent. Thus, it is possible for two phenomena to be a dichotomy, yet still to be indirect contradictories because they have meanings that do not explicitly exclude one another.[15]

Conversely, dichotomies are considered direct contradictories when their meanings do directly exclude one another, and this is how concealer-truth and ultimate truth come to be considered direct contradictories. Although the terms "concealer-truth" and "ultimate truth" do not suggest a direct contradiction, their meanings—the deceptive (*slu ba*) and the non-deceptive (*mi slu ba*)—are explicitly and mutually exclusive. Therefore, when one realizes that emptiness is an ultimate truth, one must also realize that it is not a concealer-truth.

As explained above, contradictory and mutually exclusive contradictory are equivalents, i.e., whatever is one is the other. Thus, contradictories that do not abide together are actually, in effect, a subset of mutually exclusive contradictories. The two truths are an example of mutually exclusive contradictories that are *not* part of that subset. In other words, it is impossible for anything to be both a concealer-truth and and ultimate truth, but the two truths do not displace one another. To the contrary, they are everywhere co-existent, as will be explained in the next chapter.

ADDITIONAL CATEGORIES

Jam-yang-shay-ba argues that because the two truths are a precise enumeration that eliminates other categories, one cannot legitimately make a three-way division of objects of knowledge into concealer-truths, ultimate truths, and mere conventionalities (*kun rdzob tsam, saṃvṛtimātra*).[16] The notion that mere conventionalities might be a third category derives from Candrakīrti's *Supplement Commentary*:[17]

> Hearers, Solitary Realizers, and Bodhisattvas who have abandoned afflictive ignorance see compositional phenomena as like mere existents such as reflections. For

> them, they are fabricated natures and not truths because they lack the conceit of true existence. For children, [compositional phenomena] are deceivers; for others, they are mere conventionalities because of being dependent-arisings, like illusions and so forth.

Foe Destroyers[18] (*dgra bcom pa, arhat*) and pure ground Bodhisattvas (i.e., those on the eighth ground or above), have abandoned afflictive ignorance. Free from the concealing ignorance that mistakenly apprehends forms, etc. as truths, they regard phenomena as like illusions—that is, as mere conventionalities. However, Ge-luk-ba interpreters stress that Foe Destroyers and pure ground Bodhisattvas recognize that these mere conventionalities are concealer-truths because they are misunderstood as truths by the ignorant, concealing consciousnesses of *other* sentient beings, those who have not eradicated the afflictions.[19]

As Buddhist practitioners advance on the path, their perspective evolves stage by stage. Since Ge-luk-bas insist that the two truths are a comprehensive division of *objects* of knowledge (rather than levels or viewpoints), they seek to characterize the realizations of each new perspective without resorting to the addition of new "truths" representing those new perspectives. The system does encounter a few complications in describing the functioning of a Buddha's perfectly enlightened mind, wherein all ultimate truths and all concealer-truths, without any diminishment of their diversity, are realized directly and simultaneously. Nevertheless, Ge-luk-ba writers face these difficulties without introducing a further category among objects of knowledge corresponding to the unique subjectivity of perfect enlightenment.

In contrast, some Chinese Buddhists devised a "third truth" to resolve dialectic tension between the existence of phenomena conventionally (concealer-truth) and their non-existence ultimately (ultimate truth). Leon Hurvitz writes:[20]

> Sato...professes to trace the three truths...to an attempt on the part of Chinese Buddhists to answer the question of Existence and Non-existence which so exercised Chinese thinkers during the Six Dynasties.... A solution was found in the invention of a third truth. Whether or not this is correct, the moment two opposites are alleged to be in contradiction to each other, a further term, reconciling them, is automatically implied.

This doctrine of three truths originated in forged sūtras of Chinese composition and reached full development in the writings of Chih-i (538-597). Hurvitz presents his understanding of Chih-i's three truths:[21]

> As long as one dichotomizes. . .one will never come any nearer to Reality. . . . The inaccessibility of Reality to this common approach is designated *k'ung* [emptiness]. Needless to say, this does not constitute a denial of the empirical world, which is considered to be identical with Reality. This non-denial of the empirical world is designated *chia* [provisional existence]. Neither of these terms, however, refers to Reality itself, but rather to the relationship in which it stands in our minds. The designation of Reality, chosen to indicate the complete lack of contradiction between *k'ung* and *chia* is *chung* [middle]. . . . The most important thing to bear in mind, however, is the essential identity of the three terms.

Just as there is an essential identity among the three truths, there is also an essential identity among subject, object, and non-dualism. The three truths may be considered in any of these three ways. Hurvitz writes:[22]

> The cognizing mind and the cognized objects are interdependent, and the sphere in which they exist in a state of interdependence is a third realm transcending both of them. The attainment of Truth or Buddhahood (the two are identical) consists of a transfer of the self to this third realm. . .

Chih-i's doctrine of the middle truth provides a point of unity between the two truths in a transcendent synthesis encompassing them both. Ge-luk-bas, on the other hand, assert that concealer-truth and ultimate truth are direct contradictories: there can never be anything that is both, and there can never be any third truth beyond just these two. However, Ge-luk-bas have other ways to mitigate the sense of an unbridgeable rift between the two truths. As we shall explain in the next chapter, for every object, the two truths must exist together as a single entity. For example, a pot can never occur without its emptiness, nor can the emptiness of a pot occur apart from a pot.

Furthermore, there is an "essential identity" between the two truths in that the final nature of both truths is emptiness. In ontological terms, there is no transcendent synthesis, beyond emptiness, that unites the two truths; however, emptiness is the real nature of both truths. Form is empty of inherent existence and form's emptiness of inherent existence is likewise empty of inherent existence, and the emptiness of emptiness is empty, and so forth. Thus, it seems that in Ge-luk-ba, emptiness itself carries out at least one of philosophical functions of Chih-i's middle truth.

If we look at the question of a third truth in epistemological terms, we find that in Ge-luk-ba: (1) concealer-truths are the realm of conventional valid cognizers, (2) ultimate truths are the realm of ultimate valid cognizers, and (3) a unique feature of a Buddha Superior's consciousness is the ability to manifestly and simultaneously realize the two truths without mixing them into a composite. Insofar as Chih-i's middle truth can be understood as a perspective in which emptiness and dependent-arisings are simultaneously and fully understood, we may propose a Buddha's omniscient mind as the closest Ge-luk homologue. Ge-luk-bas do not posit a third truth corresponding to the unique subjectivity of perfect enlightenment.

4 *The Relationship Between the Two Truths*

NEITHER THE SAME NOR DIFFERENT

Many Buddhist texts describe the two truths as being neither the same nor different. In Ge-luk-ba, some of these scriptures are read to mean that the two truths are neither one isolate (*ldog pa gcig*) nor different entities (*ngo bo tha dad*). Turning this into a positive statement, it is said that the two truths are one entity, but different isolates. This does not mean that every concealer-truth is one entity with every ultimate truth. Rather, it means that for any given phenomenon, there must be a particular concealer-truth and a particular ultimate truth that are inextricably bound together, existing in the same place at the same time. For example, with regard to a table, the table itself is a concealer-truth and the table's emptiness of inherent existence is an ultimate truth. We say that the table is empty (*stong pa, śūnya*) of inherent existence because it has the quality of being devoid of inherent existence, but we cannot say that it is an emptiness (*stong pa nyid, śūnyatā*) of inherent existence. As Ruegg puts it,[1]

> *Śūnya* is an epithet of all *dharmas*. . . *śūnyatā* on the other hand is the fact, or truth, of the emptiness of all *dharmas*.

In the case of a red table, we may say that the table is red because it has the quality of redness. However, we do not conclude that the table *is* redness or that redness *is* the table. Also, even though a red table is both red and a table, there is nothing that is both redness and a table. Analogously, a table's emptiness cannot be predicated to the table, nor can the table be predicated to it, nor can we find anything that is both the table and its emptiness. Still, table and its emptiness are locked together in a single entity, just as a red table must exist together with its redness.

That the two truths are "different isolates" means, for example, that a table and its emptiness can be distinguished in terms of how they are understood by a conceptual consciousness. To say that two things are different isolates is to make only the most minimal distinction between them. Since conceptual consciousnesses often operate under the sway of language, things are different isolates as soon as they are given different names—even if those names refer to the same object.[2] For example, *khyi* (the Tibetan word for dog) and *dog* are different isolates. We even have to say that Guy Newland and Guy Martin Newland are different isolates. Since even equivalent, mutually inclusive phenomena can be different isolates, the assertion that the two truths are different isolates is the very mildest statement of differentiation. However, as we have seen, Ge-luk-bas also hold that the two truths are actually mutually exclusive, and that they cannot be predicated to one another.

Regarding the scriptural evidence for understanding the two truths as one entity but different isolates, Tsong-ka-pa's *Intermediate Exposition of the Stages of the Path* says:[3]

> In several texts there are statements that the two truths are neither one nor different. Some of these refer to inherently existent one and different, and some refer [to the two truths] as being neither different entities nor one isolate.

Ge-luk-bas settle on a passage from the *Sūtra Unravelling the Thought* as the primary scriptural basis for the argument that the two truths are neither one isolate nor different entities. The *Sūtra Unravelling the Thought* says:[4]

> The character of compositional phenomena and the character
> Of the ultimate are free from being one or different.

Demonstrating the relationship between the two truths through reasoning, Tsong-ka-pa's *Illumination of the Thought* says:[5]

> Although there are many different [opinions] regarding the meaning of the division [i.e., the relationship between the two truths], here both [concealer-truths and ultimate truths] have entities, and, since there is nothing that is not either one entity or different entities and since if phenomena were different entities from [their respective] emptinesses of true existence, they would be truly established, [the two truths] are one entity but different isolates [i.e., conceptually isolatable], like product and impermanent thing.

This argument uses the process of elimination to establish that the two truths must be one entity. In order to exist at all, form and the emptiness of form must both have entities. If form and its emptiness were different entities, then one could not say that it is the nature of form to be empty of inherent existence. In that case, form would have to be inherently existent. Since this is absurd (in Prāsaṅgika), the only alternative is to assert that form and its emptiness are one entity. Tsong-ka-pa cites Nāgārjuna's *Essay On the Mind of Enlightenment* (*Bodhicittavivaraṇa*):[6]

> Suchness is not observed
> As a different [entity] from conventionalities,
> Because conventionalities are explained as emptinesses
> [i.e., as empty of inherent existence]
> And just emptinesses are
> [Posited in relation to] conventionalities,
> It being definite that without one, the other does not occur,
> Like product and impermanent thing.

Paṇ-chen Sö-nam-drak-ba suggests that Nāgārjuna is commenting on the famous passage from the *Heart of Wisdom Sūtra* (*Prajñā-hṛdaya*):[7]

> Form is empty; emptiness is form.
> Apart from form there is no emptiness;
> Apart from emptiness there is no form.

Whether or not Paṇ-chen's remark is accurate, in giving the relationship between product and impermanent thing as an example Nāgārjuna clearly indicates that the relationship between a form (concealer-truth) and its emptiness (ultimate truth) is quite close. Product and impermanent thing are equivalents, and they are therefore mutually inclusive: Whatever is a product is necessarily an impermanent thing and whatever is an impermanent thing is necessarily a product. If the two truths were actually and literally equivalent, then all forms would be emptinesses and the emptinesses of forms would themselves be forms. This would entail numerous absurdities. For example, since emptinesses are permanent, forms would have to be permanent; or, if it were held that forms must be impermanent, then their emptinesses would also be impermanent.

Any pair of equivalents must be one entity and different isolates because equivalents represent different ways of looking at the very same things. For example, when one considers tables and so forth in terms of disintegration, one describes them as impermanent things. When one considers tables and so forth in terms of their arising from causes, one describes them as products. In this way, product and impermanent thing can be isolated conceptually, yet remain a single entity.

For Tsong-ka-pa, it is clear that even though the relationship between product and impermanent thing is given as an example, this does not mean that the two truths are equivalents. In his *Illumination of the Thought* Tsong-ka-pa writes,[8]

> [Candrakīrti's teaching that both truths exist with regard to every phenomenon] does not at all indicate that just the single entity of a sprout *is* the two truths in relation to common beings and Superiors.

The two truths are not two names for precisely the same thing; they cannot be the very same thing conceptualized in two different ways. If they were, one would have to say that just as a table is both a product and an impermanent thing, table is also a concealer-truth and an ultimate truth. If table were an ultimate truth, then anyone could effortlessly escape cyclic existence through the ordinary direct perception of a table.

If the two truths are not equivalents, then why does Nāgārjuna compare their relationship to the relationship between product and impermanent thing? Nāgārjuna writes, "It being definite that without one, the other does not occur, like product and impermanent thing," and Tsong-ka-pa comments:[9]

> [Nāgārjuna indicates] that [the two truths] have the definite relationship of indispensability (*med na mi 'byung*) and that since, moreover, this is a relationship of one nature

> (*bdag gcig pa'i 'brel ba*), [the two truths] are the same entity like product and impermanent thing.

If a cause does not exist, then its effect will not occur, and thus a cause is indispensably related to its effect. However, a cause cannot be related within one nature with its effect because a cause does not exist at the time of its effect. Therefore, as Tsong-ka-pa explains, Nāgārjuna's example, "like product and impermanent thing," not only illustrates a relationship in which there is mutual indispensability, but also specifies that the two truths—unlike cause and effect—are a single entity. Although product and impermanent thing are equivalents, and although their relationship is given as an example, equivalence is one aspect of their relationship that cannot be carried over and strictly applied to the exemplified relationship between the two truths.

THE TWO TRUTHS CANNOT BE DIFFERENT ENTITIES

Not everyone agrees that form and its emptiness are one entity. Jam-yang-shay-ba reports that Ngok and his followers assert that the two truths are "different in the sense of negating that they are one."[10] In general, they assert three types of difference; the other two are: (1) being different entities and (2) being one entity but different isolates. Ngok holds that permanent phenomena cannot be one entity with anything. Since an ultimate truth is a permanent phenomenon, it cannot be one entity with a concealer-truth. Avoiding the conclusion that the two truths must be different entities, Ngok assigns the relationship between the two truths to the third category, "different in the sense of negating that they are one."

In his *Illumination of the Thought*, Tsong-ka-pa argues that while no phenomenon has an inherently existent entity, all phenomena must have entities in order to exist.[11] Thus, whether permanent or impermanent, every phenomenon must be either one entity or different entities with each other phenomenon. In support of this view, Tsong-ka-pa finds a passage in Kamalaśīla's *Illumination of the Middle Way* indicating that oneness of entity occurs even among permanent phenomena.[12]

The Jo-nang-bas assert that the two truths are different entities. Jeffrey Hopkins summarizes the contrast between the Jo-nang-ba "emptiness of other" (*gzhan stong*) and the Ge-luk-ba "emptiness of self" (*rang stong*):[13]

> The Jo-nang-bas hold that the two truths are different entities. Theirs is a view of "emptiness of other"—an ultimate truth is empty of being a truth-for-a-concealer and a truth-for-a-concealer is empty of being an ultimate truth. This is said to be similar to the Sāṃkhya teaching that the root of cyclic existence is the confusion of the person [*puruṣa*] and the nature [*prakṛti*] and that liberation is gained by realizing that the person is not the manifesting nature and that the manifesting nature is not the person. Through differentiating the two, a yogi is released from cyclic existence. For a Ge-luk-ba, it is true that an ultimate truth is not a truth-for-a-concealer and vice versa, but this distinction does not constitute emptiness. An emptiness is a phenomenon's own lack of inherent existence; thus, this doctrine is called "emptiness of self" which does not mean that a table is empty of being a table but that a table is empty of its own inherent existence...

Jam-yang-shay-ba sets forth four arguments against those who hold that the two truths are different entities.[14] Hopkins explains the first three as follows:[15]

> [1] If conventional and ultimate truths were different entities, the lack of inherent existence of a form would not be the final mode of existence of the form because it would be completely separate from the form.
> [2] Just so, realization of the non-inherent existence of a form would not overcome the conception of the form as inherently existent.
> [3] Also, a yogi's cultivation of high paths would be senseless because understanding emptiness would not be related with destroying misconception of the objects themselves.

Jam-yang-shay-ba's fourth consequence is that even Buddha would not have escaped bad rebirth or the conception of true existence. Jam-yang-shay-ba apparently formed this list of four consequences by combining ideas from the *Sūtra Unravelling the Thought* with ideas from Prajñāmokṣa's commentary on Atiśa's *Essential Instructions on the Middle Way* (*Mādhyamakopadeśa*).[16] As summarized by Ngak-wang-bel-den, the four arguments from sūtra are:[17]

> If the two truths were different entities, then (1) the mind realizing the emptiness of true existence would not overcome the conception of true existence; (2) the emptiness of true existence of a form would not be the mode of abiding of that form; (3) the non-affirming negative that is the mere excluder (*rnam par bcad tsam*) of the true existence of a form would not be the real nature of that form; and (4) Buddha Superiors would see forms as truly existent and would see the emptiness of true existence separately.

Although emptiness of true existence and emptiness of inherent existence are not equivalents in the *Sūtra Unravelling the Thought*, they are equivalents in Prāsaṅgika. Making that adjustment, we find that Jam-yang-shay-ba's first consequence corresponds to the sūtra's second, and that Jam-yang-shay-ba's second corresponds to the sūtra's first. Jam-yang-shay-ba's fourth consequence corresponds to the sūtra's fourth to the extent that both pertain to Buddhas. His thought may be that if Buddha Superiors saw forms as truly existent while seeing emptiness as a separate entity, then they would be on this account unable to abandon the conception of true existence. Hopkins interprets Jam-yang-shay-ba's fourth consequence in this manner when he writes,[18]

> Similarly, a Buddha would not have forsaken the apprehension of inherent existence because he would have only a powerless apprehension of an emptiness which was entirely separate from objects.

Jam-yang-shay-ba omits the sūtra's third consequence and substitutes an argument based on the third of Prajñāmokśa's three. Prajñāmokśa writes:[19]

> If [ultimate truth and concealer-truth] were different, [1] they would not be the real nature (*chos nyid*) and the possessor of the real nature (*chos can*), and [2] [realization of ultimate truth] would not overcome the signs [that is, the conceptions of inherent existence] of compounded things; [3] even cultivation of the path would be senseless.

Ngak-wang-bel-den hints at a criticism of Jam-yang-shay-ba for confounding the refutations from sūtra with those of Prajñāmokśa.[20] However, since Jam-yang-shay-ba backs up his four consequences by quoting excerpts from both the *Sūtra Unravelling the Thought* and Prajñāmokśa's work, he must have had his sources in mind while he was writing.[21] He apparently *intended* to create a new list of four consequences using these sources for inspiration rather than as an absolute guide.

The sequential logic of the three consequences given by Prajñāmokśa may provide a justification for Jam-yang-shay-ba's approach. First, it is established that if the two truths were different entities, then the emptiness of a form would not be its mode of subsistence, its final and real nature. If realizing the emptiness of a form did not help one to understand the nature of that form, then it would not counteract the already existing misconception of that form as inherently existent. If it is impossible to abandon such a misconception, then it is pointless to make any effort to cultivate the path. Even a Buddha's perfect understanding of emptiness would not damage the conception of inherent existence in the slightest. This sequence of consequences proceeds from an insight about the relationship between the two truths as bases (*gzhi*) to an appreciation of the importance of that insight for the process of abandoning afflictive ignorance. This, in turn, bears implications for the path (*lam*) and its result (*'bras bu*).

Ngak-wang-bel-den seems to find Jam-yang-shay-ba's set of consequences inferior to that of the *Sūtra Unravelling the Thought*.[22] He argues that on Jam-yang-shay-ba's list the fourth consequence (that Buddhas could not abandon the conception of true existence or the assumption of bad rebirth) reiterates a fault already brought to light by the second (that a mind realizing the emptiness of true existence would not overcome the conception of true existence) in that it merely presents a particular case of the general principle that was already indicated in the second. In other words, Buddha Superiors are just one example of persons whose realization of emptiness would not overcome ignorance.

THE TWO TRUTHS AS DIFFERENT ISOLATES

Scriptural support for the position that the two truths are not one isolate is found in the passage from the *Sūtra Unravelling the Thought* cited above:[23]

> The character of compositional phenomena and the character
> Of the ultimate are free from being one or different.

Furthermore, if logical difficulties plague any assertion that the two truths are literally equivalent and mutually inclusive, they completely overwhelm the notion that the two truths are one isolate. While equivalents are one in meaning but different in name, being one isolate entails being one in both name and meaning. The "isolate" of a phenomenon is the opposite of the negative of that which is one with the phenomenon. For example, a conceptual consciousness apprehending a chair gets at its object by eliminating everything other than exactly *chair.* Through this process of double negation it arrives at a generic image (*don spyi, arthasāmānya*) of chair, an image stripped of all the richness of specific detail and varied properties that appear to an eye consciousness directly apprehending a chair. While the operation of conceptuality does not require the use of language, when language is used and understood, conceptual thought seeks its objects along the lines of linguistic distinctions. In this context, the phrases "Guy Newland" and "the author of these words" refer to the same person, but they refer to distinct isolates and thus are approached by conceptuality along different avenues. Similarly, in saying that the two truths are different isolates, the Ge-luk-bas have made the most minimal distinction that can be made between things that have different names.

Seeking an Indian Mādhyamika source to show that "different" can mean different conceptual isolates, Jam-yang-shay-ba finds a passage from Kamalaśīla's *Illumination of the Middle Way:*[24]

> [T]hrough specific points of reference, it is not contradictory for one [phenomenon, a wisdom consciousness in meditative equipoise] to be an entity of both [the ultimate and the conventional]. That is, if one thinks of wisdom in terms of its being an impermanent consciousness, then it clearly falls within the realm of the conventional. However, when one reflects on its non-dualistic cognition of the ultimate object, it appears as an ultimate.

Thus, "through specific points of reference," meditative equipoise as conventional and meditative equipoise as ultimate can be conceptually isolated despite being the very same entity. Since this wisdom consciousness remains a concealer-truth, and is only designated as a concordant ultimate, Jam-yang-shay-ba does not present Kamalaśīla's remark as an example of an Indian Mādhyamika clearly stating that the two truths are different isolates within one entity. However, it does suggest that the idea of distinct conceptual isolates within one entity has authentic roots in Indian Mādhyamika.

Hopkins explains the four consequences that Jam-yang-shay-ba employs against the position that the two truths are one isolate:[25]

> [1] On the other hand, if the two truths were utterly the same, everything true of one would be true of the other. In that case, for every truth-for-a-concealer such as desire and hatred which was overcome on the path, an ultimate truth also would be overcome. [2] Just as truths-for-a-concealer have many dissimilar and different aspects such as color, shape, odor, and taste, so ultimate truths would be dissimilar and different. [3] Just as many truths-for-a-concealer are afflictions, so many ultimate truths would also be afflictions. [4] Just as common individuals directly cognize truths-for-a-concealer such as forms, sounds, odors, and tastes, so they would absurdly directly cognize the emptiness of forms and so forth.

The *Sūtra Unravelling the Thought* gives four consequences, summarized by Ngak-wang-bel-den as follows:[26]

> If the two truths were one isolate, then (1) common beings would directly realize the mode of subsistence, (2) afflictions such as desire would be produced even while one is observing reality, (3) divisions by way of diverse aspect would not exist even among forms, and (4) one would not have to strive to search for the mode of subsistence of form.

Prajñāmokśa gives three consequences:[27]

> If [the two truths] were one, [1] just as conventionalities are abandoned, so the ultimate also would be abandoned; [2] just as conventionalities have differences, so the ultimate also would have differences; [3] just as conventionalities are defiled, so the ultimate also would be defiled.

Again, Jam-yang-shay-ba quotes both sources, making it clear that he has created a hybrid list by intention rather than fault of memory. Jam-yang-shay-ba's first three consequences are based on Prajñāmokśa's consequences Jam-yang-shay-ba's fourth consequence corresponds to the first consequence from the sūtra. I can find no particular reason for the selection or sequencing of these four. Perhaps Jam-yang-shay-ba simply felt that among the seven arguments, these four were the most persuasive. Again, as above,

Ngak-wang-bel-den implies that the list of four consequences given in the *Sūtra Unravelling the Thought* is preferable to Jam-yang-shay-ba's list in that the consequences given in the sūtra are logically distinct.[28] Ngak-wang-bel-den stresses that the sūtra consequences illustrate four quite different faults that are entailed by the position that the two truths are one isolate. These are as follows:

> (1) If common beings directly realized the mode of subsistence, then liberation could be achieved without striving; (2) if afflictions could arise during the direct realization of emptiness, then no amount of striving would lead to liberation; (3) if all conventionalities had the same aspect, then one could not differentiate an eye consciousness from an ear consciousness and so forth; (4) if one did not have to strive to search for the mode of subsistence, then the path to liberation would be beginningless.

In this case Ngak-wang-bel-den does not say that the consequences Jam-yang-shay-ba has borrowed from Prajñāmokṡa are redundant. However, he implies that this is his opinion by presenting these four distinct faults derived from sūtra followed by the statement that Jam-yang-shay-ba's version "requires analysis" in that it diverges from the sūtra and from Gyel-tsap's *Commentary on (Atiśa's) "Introduction to the Two Truths"*.[29] Unlike the sūtra consequences, Prajñāmokṡa's three consequences use a single method to demonstrate the absurdity of holding that the two truths are precisely identical. Each takes a quality properly associated with concealer-truths (being objects of abandonment, having diversity, and being defiled) and attaches it to ultimate truth.

Ngak-wang-bel-den points out that each of the eight consequences found in the *Sūtra Unravelling the Thought* is a correct consequence implying a proof.[30] This means, for example, that one can take the first consequence derived from the sūtra, "It absurdly follows that the the valid cognizer realizing the final nature form does not overcome the awareness apprehending form as truly existent because, according to you, form and the final nature of form are different entities," and reformulate it as a proof statement: "Form and the final nature of form are one entity because the valid cognizer realizing the final nature of form overcomes the awareness apprehending form as truly existent."

Ngak-wang-bel-den stresses that the Prāsaṅgika refutations of the assertions of other philosophical systems regarding the relationship between the two truths are spin-offs from the more fundamental task of refuting innate misconceptions about the two truths.[31] On the one hand, if phenomena existed just as they ordinarily appear, then their final mode of subsistence (an ultimate truth) would be identical to their conventional nature (a concealer-truth). Therefore, reasonings refuting the assertion that the two truths are one isolate undermine the innate misconception that phenomena exist just as they ordinarily appear. On the other hand, there is an innate misconception that emptiness of true existence is incompatible with the capacity to perform actions. If these two were incompatible, then, for example, a seed capable of producing a sprout could not be one entity with its own emptiness of true existence. Therefore, reasonings refuting the idea that the two truths are different entities undermine the innate misconception that emptiness of true existence and the capacity to perform actions are incompatible. In this way, Ngak-wang-bel-den suggests that the greatest value of these arguments about the relationship between the two truths is found not in their role in sectarian controversy, but in their effect on the meditation practice of the individual Buddhist.

THE TWO TRUTHS AS SEEN BY ADVANCED PRACTITIONERS

Ge-luk-ba writers draw sharp philosophical distinctions between the two truths: not only are they different isolates, but they are mutually exclusive and neither can be predicated to the other. However, sometimes these differences are less rigidly maintained in descriptions of the experiences of advanced yogis. It is frequently said that when the ultimate truth is realized directly, emptiness and the mind of the yogi seem utterly undifferentiable, like fresh water poured into fresh water. In Ge-luk-ba, it is vital to make conceptual distinctions between emptiness and the mind realizing emptiness, but those distinctions are not apparent to the yogi in non-conceptual meditation on emptiness and they fail to convey the flavor of the yogi's experience.

Just how closely are the two truths related? As we have seen, Tsong-ka-pa says that Nāgārjuna gave the relationship between product and impermanent thing as an example of the relationship between the two truths in order to show that the two truths are related within one nature. However, there are many non-equivalents that are related within one nature; for example, product and table, or table and the impermanence of table. Perhaps Nāgārjuna chose a pair of equivalents in order to emphasize that the two truths have an especially close relationship that is somehow like equivalence. That is, in Ge-luk-ba the two truths are not actually equivalents, but it is recognized that for certain advanced meditators they seem to work as though they were equivalents: They are not only compatible, but each points toward and reinforces the other.

Ngak-wang-bel-den notes that the position that the two truths are different entities is linked to the innate misconception that emptiness and the capacity to produce effects are incompatible. Under the sway of ignorance, there is a strong inclination to radically separate the two truths and see them as two opposite and conflicting realms. In fact, it is true that concealer-truths are the sphere of conventional valid cognizers and ultimate truths are the sphere of meditative equipoise on emptiness. Among sentient beings, neither valid cognizer crosses into the realm of the other. Moreover, ultimate truth and concealer-truth are direct contradictories; they are mutually exclusive and it is therefore impossible for any one thing to be both. However, that the two truths exclude one another does not mean that realization of one is detrimental to realization of the other. To the contrary, comprehension of conventional existence and comprehension of emptiness must advance together. In the long run, if understanding emptiness does not enhance one's understanding of how things exist conventionally as dependent-arisings, then one has misunderstood emptiness.[32] Nāgārjuna's *Treatise on the Middle Way* says:[33]

> That which is a dependent-arising
> We explain as emptiness.
> This is dependent imputation;
> Just this is the middle path.

Jang-gya elaborates:[34]

> When one thoroughly analyzes with faultless reasoning, one generates increased conviction with respect to how this or that phenomenon lacks inherent existence. To the extent that one does so, the inducement of ascertainment with respect to how those phenomena are merely dependent imputations increases. To the extent that the inducement of conviction with regard to the way that phenomena are only dependent imputations increases, the inducement of ascer-

> tainment with regard to the way phenomena are empty of inherent existence increases.

Realization of the conventional, interdependent nature of phenomena and realization of their emptiness should be mutually reinforcing. Concealer-truths are the bases, or substrata, for ultimate truths. If, when one sees a concealer-truth such as a table, one understands that it is contingent and impermanent, and does not exist as it appears, then this may lead to reflection on its actual mode of subsistence—emptiness. Likewise, when one emerges from meditation on the emptiness of a table, and a table reappears, one readily understands that this appearance is a conventionality, an illusion-like concealer-truth. Therefore, even though the two truths are mutually exclusive, for certain yogis *they are like equivalents insofar as realization of one can induce realization of the other.*

THE TWO TRUTHS AS ATTRIBUTE AND SUBSTRATUM

Candrakīrti says that all phenomena have both truths. Therefore, it must be possible to posit both truths with regard every phenomenon. This means that for everything that exists there is an emptiness and a basis of emptiness included within one entity. Ngakwang-bel-den notes that this leaves a slight problem involving the emptiness of emptiness.[35] How can one posit a *concealer-truth* with regard to an emptiness that is the mere absence of inherent existence in another emptiness? Some propose the existence of emptiness as the concealer-truth in this case.[36] The present Dalai Lama prefers to posit the emptiness that serves as the basis for the second emptiness as the concealer-truth in relation to the emptiness of emptiness. He writes:[37]

> [W]hen that ultimate truth becomes the basis of analysis and when its mode being is posited, then that ultimate truth becomes the basis of qualification in relation to the quality [of lacking inherent existence] that is its mode of being. Thus, there is even an explanation that in these circumstances an emptiness can be viewed as a conventional truth.

For example, having realized the emptiness of a table inferentially, one might turn one's analysis upon that very emptiness, searching for its ultimate nature. In this specific context, the emptiness of the table is called a concealer-truth, while the emptiness of the emptiness of the table is the ultimate truth, because the emptiness of the table is the basis in relation to which inherent existence is eliminated.[38]

This approach coincides with Tsong-ka-pa's statement that emptinesses are posited with regard to the conventionalities that are their bases.[39] For each emptiness, there must be something that possesses the quality of lacking inherent existence. In some loose sense, then, all phenomena are concealer-truths insofar as they are all bases of emptinesses. Of course, this is a special context; in general, no emptiness can be considered a concealer-truth. However, when asked, "What is the concealer-truth that is posited in relation to the emptiness of emptiness?" the Dalai Lama posits the quality-possessing emptiness that is the basis of analysis, thereby drawing attention to a central fact about the relationship between the two truths: Concealer-truths are the quality-possessors, the substrata, and the bases of emptinesses, while ultimate truths are the final and real natures that are possessed by each phenomenon.

In fact, it is only as the real nature (*chos nyid, dharmatā*) and the possessor of that real nature (*chos can, dharmin*) that we can understand how the two truths can be one entity and yet be mutually exclusive. This chapter began with the example of redness and a red table. The *Sūtra Unravelling the Thought* gives many similar examples of attribute/substratum (*khyad chos/khyad gzhi*) relationships, illustrating how the two truths are neither one nor different: a white conch shell and its white color, gold and its yellowness, a *vīṇā* and its melodiousness, pepper and its hot taste, cotton and its softness, a tree and its fragrance, etc.[40] Similarly, Nāgārjuna's *Essay on the Mind of Enlightenment* says:[41]

> Just as sweetness is the nature of sugar
> And hotness the nature of fire
> So [we] assert that the nature
> Of all things is emptiness.

It seems that once we know that two phenomena are mutually exclusive within one entity, they must be related as quality and quality-possessor.[42]

The two truths are unusual in that, unlike most quality and quality-possessor pairs, they are a dichotomy of all objects of knowledge. Redness and red table are mutually exclusive within one entity, but there are innumerable other phenomena; although similarly related, concealer-truth and ultimate truth include all phenomena.[43] Also, emptiness is not an ordinary quality, like red and yellow, that a table may happen to have. It is a quality possessed by all phenomena alike, and it is the real nature and final mode of subsistence of each phenomenon. It is the only thing one finds when one searches for a table among a table's bases of designation, and realization of it leads to liberation.

CONCLUSION

Through careful philosophical investigation, laying out a series of fine distinctions, Ge-luk-bas attempt to resolve the sense of contradiction, paradox, or mystery in the relationship between the two truths. This is very different from the views of almost all non-Ge-luk-ba interpreters of Mādhyamika. Some contemporary interpreters see conventional truth as completely contradicted, repudiated, and transcended by ultimate realization. Sangharakshita, for example, writes:[44]

> [I]n order to give a negative description of [Absolute Truth], it was necessary to have something to negate. The "something" is the conventional truth.

Others see a complete contradiction between the two truths that cannot be resolved in philosophical discourse, but *can* be resolved in mystical, trans-conceptual, yogic realization. Conze, for example, holds that in the Mahāyāna scriptures the contradiction between the two truths is dealt with "as with other contradictions, by merely stating it in an uncompromising form," but that these statements "cease to be paradoxical and absurd when one realizes that they attempt to describe the universe at the level of complete self-extinction."[45] In a sense, this amounts to saying that the two truths are logically incompatible, but soteriologically complementary.

More than thirty years later, writing about Jñānagarbha rather than the perfection of wisdom sūtras, David Eckel seems to point to a similar conclusion. He writes that "the two truths are contradictory perspectives" which lead us into a "disorienting world of paradoxical discourse."[46] The relationship between the two truths is best described as "unstable irony, in which each perspective simultaneously undermines the other."[47] At the same time, Eckel writes that the two truths[48]

> are opposites that complement each other. Each perspective helps to deepen and reinforce the other so that the two together make a balanced system.

For Eckel, the two truths "undermine" each other logically, but somehow, presumably in a soteriological sense, also "reinforce" each other. Ge-luk-bas, on other hand, argue that when properly understood the two truths are not only spiritually compatible, but logically compatible as well. Their argument hinges on a description of the two truths not as contradictory perspectives, but as objects found by two different types of valid knowledge. This makes ultimate truths a specific class of known phenomena—the qualities or properties of being empty of inherent existence. Every phenomenon has such a property, even emptinesses themselves, and thus ultimate truths are infinite in number, yet all of the same taste: empty of inherent existence.

This Ge-luk approach stands in contrast to the views of Western interpreters such as Richard Robinson, who hold that emptiness "has no status as an entity, nor as the property of an existent or an inexistent" because it pertains to a meta-system which is descriptive of, but external to, the primary system.[49] In Ge-luk-ba, there is no "meta-system" or "meta-critical language." There can be no language that is not conventional language. Ultimate truths (emptinesses) are conventionally existent entities,[50] conventionally existent phenomena, conventionally existent properties and, like everything else, they must be accounted for and find their place within the conventional language system of Ge-luk-ba theology. While mutually exclusive of concealer-truths, ultimate truths do not discredit or undermine them. They are the real nature (*chos nyid, dharmatā*) of concealer-truths, and as such they are always and everywhere co-existent with them.

5 *Meanings of* Saṃvṛti *and* Paramārtha

THE MEANINGS OF *SAṂVṚTI*

Concealer-truth is a translation of the Sanskrit *saṃvṛtisatya* and its Tibetan equivalent, *kun rdzob bden pa*. In his *Clear Words* Candrakīrti explains that *saṃvṛti* has three meanings:[1]

> *Saṃvṛti* (*kun rdzob*) means entirely obstructing. That is, ignorance is the concealer (*saṃvṛti*, *kun rdzob*) because it entirely covers up the suchness of all[2] things. Or, *saṃvṛti* (*kun rdzob*) means interdependence; it has the sense of "due to being interdependent." Or, *saṃvṛti* means "term"; it is equivalent with "worldly convention." [In this sense,] it has the character of expression and expressed, consciousness and object of consciousness, etc.

Tsong-ka-pa comments on these three meanings in his *Ocean of Reasoning*:[3]

> [1] The concealer (*kun rdzob*) is nescience or ignorance because it covers up or obstructs the suchness of things. Since this applies to the [Sanskrit] equivalent of *kun rdzob*, it is explained in terms of that; it is not that every *kun rdzob* is an obstructor.
> [2] Or, *kun rdzob* means interdependent. This means that, since it must be interdependent, it is untrue that it has

> a self-instituting nature. The reason for explaining the term in this way exists even among ultimate truths, but the term *kun rdzob* does not apply [to ultimate truths]. For example, the basis for the explanation of the term "lake-born" [a type of lotus] exists among frogs [since frogs are born in lakes], but the term does not apply to them [because they are not a type of lotus].
>
> [3] Or, *kun rdzob* means terms—i.e., worldly conventions. Also, since it is explained as having the character of expresser and expressed, consciousness and object of consciousness, and so forth, it is not held to be merely the object-possessing conventions, consciousnesses and expressions.

Thus, the three "etymologies" (*sgra bshad*) or ways to explain the term *kun rdzob* are: (1) an ignorant consciousness that conceals reality, (2) that which is interdependent (*phan tshun brtan pa, parasparasaṃbhavana*), and (3) worldly conventions (*'jig rten tha snyad, lokavyavahāra*).

In referring to these three meanings as "etymologies" the Geluk-bas are not making a linguistic claim about the history of the term. The point is that these are a set of connotations or "senses" that the word *saṃvṛti* may bear in various contexts. This list of three meanings is not, nor does it seem intended to be, a comprehensive account of the philosophical meanings of the term—even within the limited scope of early Mādhyamika literature.[4] On the other hand, it does seem that in Mādhyamika the word *saṃvṛti* always carries at least one of these three connotations.

TRUTH-FOR-A-CONCEALER

Candrakīrti and Tsong-ka-pa make it clear that the *kun rdzob* in the term "concealer-truth" (*kun rdzob bden pa*) is to be understood in the first sense, as the concealing ignorance. According to traditional etymologies of *saṃvṛti* in its first sense connotation, *saṃ* is an abbreviated form either of *samyak*, meaning "reality," or of *samanta*, meaning "entire." Since *vṛt* means to cover, obstruct, or overturn, *saṃvṛti* means "that which entirely obstructs reality." Candrakīrti's *Clear Words* says:[5]

> Something is a concealer (*kun rdzob, saṃvṛti*) because it entirely obstructs (*kun nas sgrib, samantādvaraṇa*). Igno-

> rance (*mi shes pa, ajñāna*) is called a concealer because it entirely conceals the suchness of things.

The *Descent into Laṅkā Sūtra* says

> That [consciousness] which is mistaken regarding the lack
> of inherent existence
> Is asserted as the concealer (*kun rdzob, saṃvṛti*) of reality.

Referring to this, Candrakīrti's *Supplement* states,[6]

> The Subduer said that an obscuring [consciousness] is the
> concealer (*kun rdzob, saṃvṛti*)
> Because it obstructs the nature...

Candrakīrti's *Supplement Commentary* explains:[7]

> Concerning that, because through this sentient beings are obscured from seeing things as they are, it is called an obscuring [consciousness], an ignorance. This [ignorance] which has an essence of obstructing perception of the nature, superimposing a non-existent entityness of things, is the concealer (*kun rdzob, saṃvṛti*). Those which through that concealing [consciousness] appear as truths and those that, while not inherently existent, individually appear to be inherently existent are truths for a worldly, erroneous, concealing [consciousness].

Concealer-truths are not truths in general; they are misconceived to be truths by the concealing ignorance. Tsong-ka-pa's *Intermediate Exposition of the Stages of the Path* says:[8]

> The concealing consciousness (*shes pa kun rdzob pa*) in whose perspective forms and so forth are posited as true is the first of the three [meanings of *kun rdzob*].

and his *Ocean of Reasoning* says:[9]

> The concealer (*kun rdzob*) in whose perspective form and so forth are posited as truths is an ignorance that superimposes the existence of inherently existent entities on phenomena that lack such entities.

Tables and so forth are falsities and not truths because they appear to be inherently existent, while in fact they are empty of inherent existence. Nevertheless, they are called concealer-truths or truths-for-a-concealer (*kun rdzob bden pa*) because they are mistakenly apprehended as truths by the ignorance conceiving inherent existence. Superimposing inherent existence on phenomena, this ignorance blocks the apprehension of emptiness, and thereby conceals the real nature of phenomena. This concealing ignorance takes phenomena to be non-deceptive truths in that it imagines that phenomena are inherently existent, just as they appear.

While this clearly identifies the *kun rdzob* in *kun rdzob bden pa* as a very specific type of ignorant consciousness, and also explains how this ignorance actively misconceives things as truths, it does not provide an accurate *definition* of concealer-truth (see chapter six), for if concealer-truth were defined as "that which is true in the perspective of the conception of true existence," then even emptiness and non-existents—such as an inherently existent self of persons—would be concealer-truths.[10]

T. R. V. Murti's interpretation of Mādhyamika identifies the *saṃvṛti* in *saṃvṛtisatya* as *avidyā*, but conflicts with the Ge-luk-ba view by explaining *avidyā* not as an innate misconception of inherent existence, but as "Reason," which is "the categorizing function of the mind" that manifests itself in philosophy.[11] Thus, according to Murti the elimination of *avidyā* is the transcendence of "the interminable opposition of philosophical viewpoints."[12] In many ways, Murti's position is virtually antithetical to the Ge-luk-ba view of Mādhyamika, which uses the phrase "reasoning consciousness" (*rigs shes*) to refer not to ignorance but to its opposite, the wisdom realizing emptiness. According to the Ge-luk-bas, the ignorant consciousness that is the *saṃvṛti* in *saṃvṛtisatya* is a fundamentally unreasonable and illogical misconception that things exist inherently. This misconception tinges both the "natural" experience of cowherds and animals and the philosophical constructions of non-Mādhyamika philosophers. In the latter, its influence is detected when those systems break down in self-contradiction. Conversely, Ge-luk-ba Mādhyamikas assume that the refutation of inherent existence clears the way for a coherent and systematic description of the world.

INTERDEPENDENCE

Tsong-ka-pa explains that "interdependent," the second sense of *kun rdzob*, means that it is *untrue* that something has a self-instituting nature. Accordingly, some later Ge-luk-ba interpreters give "falsity" (*rdzun pa*) as the second meaning of *kun rdzob*.[13] However, it must be noted that even ultimate truths, which are not falsities, are devoid of a self-instituting nature. They depend upon their bases of imputation, the conventional valid cognizers that certify their existence, and the concealer-truths that are their substrata. As Candrakīrti's *Supplement Commentary* says:[14]

> [U]ltimates gain their entities through being the objects of certain exalted wisdoms of those who see reality. They are not established by their own natures.

Therefore, Tsong-ka-pa is careful to point out that ultimate truths are not *kun rdzob*, even though they are interdependent phenomena. *Kun rdzob* carries the sense of interdependence, but interdependence is not a definition of *kun rdzob* and it is not the case that all interdependent phenomena are *kun rdzob*.

According to T. R. V. Murti, emptiness is an absolute that transcends the realm of interdependent phenomena. In direct contrast to Tsong-ka-pa, he explains the second etymology of *saṃvṛti* as having a meaning that automatically excludes emptiness:[15]

> [*Saṃvṛti*] may also mean the mutual dependence of things—their relativity. In this sense it is equated with phenomena, and is in direct contrast with the absolute which is by itself, unrelated.

Several other contemporary interpreters have described Mādhyamika as a form of absolutism (e.g., Lindtner and Mehta) or have made statements tending to support that conclusion (e.g., Sprung and Matilal).[16] Thurman, while *not* identifying Mādhyamika as an absolutist philosophy, does use the word "absolute" to refer to emptiness.[17] If emptiness were an absolute, it would transcend the sphere of what exists in a relative way, just as Murti explains. Such an absolute emptiness would be independent of everything else, and would have to be self-instituting, existing by way of its own nature. This is contrary to the Ge-luk-ba interpretation of Mādhyamika, according to which even emptiness, like all other phenomena, exists only in a conventional, interdependent, and relative sense.[18]

CONVENTIONS

Within the third meaning of *kun rdzob*, as worldly convention, we can distinguish two distinct usages. Candrakīrti and Tsong-ka-pa both state that, in this third sense, *kun rdzob* includes both consciousnesses and their objects. At least once, Tsong-ka-pa uses the term *kun rdzob* to refer specifically to conventional consciousnesses.[19] More typically, however, *kun rdzob* as worldly convention (*'jig rten gyi tha snyad, lokavyavahāra*) refers not only to terms and consciousnesses, which are "object-possessors" (*yul can*), but also to the objective referents of terms and consciousnesses. Candrakīrti clearly says that *saṃvṛti* (*kun rdzob*) as worldly convention refers to "expression and object expressed, consciousness and objects of consciousness."[20]

Nevertheless, the notion that *saṃvṛti* does refer to worldly terms and conventions has been taken as a reference point by Western interpreters of Mādhyamika who understand the thrust of Nāgārjuna's *Treatise on the Middle Way* to be an attack on a defective theory of language. Douglas Daye, for example, makes Nāgārjuna's point to be that "the distinctions of language (witness nirvāṇa and saṃsāra) are merely and only internally consistent and are only pragmatically correlated with our perceptions."[21] Nathan Katz elaborates a similar view:[22]

> [T]he claim of Nāgārjuna that things have no intrinsic nature, *svabhāva*, is a grammatical rather than an ontological statement. To say that things have *svabhāva* is to say that one can coherently speak of them apart from their everyday language, that a word has a referent, which is to say that a word is more than a convenient designation. It is precisely this naive conception of language that Nāgārjuna is negating. . . .

For all their fascination, serious problems remain in this and other Wittgenstein-influenced interpretations of Mādhyamika. One critical problem has been noted by Napper in her discussion of Chris Gudmunsen's *Wittgenstein and Buddhism*:[23]

> If "view of language" [is taken as the object of negation and] means a particular philosophical theory about language, then only those holding that theory would be bound in cyclic existence; even if language in general is meant, then only those who use language—i.e., *not* babies and *not*

> most animals—would be caught within the snare of cyclic existence, and this contradicts basic Buddhist cosmology.

In other words, do we really want to say that cows have a "naive conception of language"? If not, do we really want to say that cows are already free of the delusions Nāgārjuna was trying to refute?

Perhaps proponents of the linguistic interpretation of Mādhyamika can brush off such questions because they do not themselves accept a traditional Buddhist cosmology. However, the classical Buddhist philosophers may be presumed to have held traditional cosmologies. If we are attempting to imagine, in so far as it is possible, their views, how can our best account be one that immediately violates their cosmology without a word of justification? As the mutual transformation of world cultures continues, we should gradually pass out of this "matching concepts" stage. As Mādhyamika becomes more and more familiar to Western philosophers, the technique (*upāya*) of making it intelligible and "legitimate" via comparison with Wittgenstein, Derrida, etc., should become obsolete. Lineages of philosophical influence are fast becoming global, and thus comparative philosophy must increasingly focus on and appreciate, without mystifying or absolutizing, nuances of difference.

In any case, it seems clear that for both Candrakīrti and Tsong-ka-pa, conventions (*tha snyad, vyavahāra*) are not confined within the limitations of language. They include consciousnesses and their objects as well as expressions and their conventional referents.

Again, it must be emphasized that this explanation provides the connotation of *kun rdzob* in some contexts rather than its strict denotation or definition. For Ge-luk-bas, even emptiness is an object of a consciousness and an object of a term because it is an object realized by the mind and an object to which the term "emptiness" refers. However, this does not mean that emptiness is a conventionality (*kun rdzob*); the term conventionality is normally a synonym of concealer-truth (*kun rdzob bden pa*). Accordingly, in his *Intermediate Exposition of the Stages of the Path*, Tsong-ka-pa, commenting on this third sense of *kun rdzob*, warns, "Also, [we] do not hold that all objects of consciousnesses and objects of expression are concealer-truths."[24] As with the second meaning of *kun rdzob* (i.e., interdependent), emptiness is included within the third sense, or connotation, of *kun rdzob* but is excluded from what the term strictly denotes.

CONVENTIONAL EXISTENCE

The *Descent into Laṅkā Sūtra* says:

> The production of things [exists] conventionally (*kun rdzob tu, saṃvṛtitaḥ*);
> Ultimately it lacks inherent existence.

Tsong-ka-pa emphasizes that *kun rdzob* here refers to the manner in which the mere production of things does exist.[25] It does *not* refer to the concealing ignorance. If the first line meant that the production of things exists only for the concealing ignorance, then things would not exist at all since the conceived object of the concealing ignorance does not exist even in conventional terms (*tha snyad du yang med*).

This leaves the question: If the *kun rdzob* in the phrase "exist conventionally" (*kun rdzob tu yod*) does not refer to ignorance, then what does it mean? Jang-gya states that it refers to conventional valid cognition.[26] However, one must remember that all phenomena, even emptiness, are only conventionally existent. In support of Jang-gya's position, it might be argued that all existents are conventionally existent in the sense that the existence of every phenomenon, even emptiness, is posited by a conventional valid cognizer. Since the existence of emptiness is not an emptiness, it cannot be an object realized by ultimate valid cognition. Hence, the existence of emptiness, like the existence of all other phenomena, is a concealer-truth and must be established by conventional valid cognition. The problem with this argument is that it only proves that the *existence of emptiness* is conventionally existent; it does not adequately explain why emptiness itself, which is beyond the ken of conventional valid cognition, should be so posited. Jam-yang-shay-ba and Ngak-wang-bel-den avoid this problem by explaining that from among the three meanings of *kun rdzob*, the *kun rdzob* in the first line of the stanza quoted above carries both the sense of interdependence and the sense of worldly convention, but does not refer to the concealing ignorance.[27] Thus, when Ge-luk-bas say that all phenomena are conventionally existent (*kun rdzob tu yod*), they do not at all mean that phenomena exist only from the standpoint of the concealing ignorance. Rather, they mean that phenomena exist interdependently, and that phenomena exist in conventional terms (*tha snyad du yod*).

"Existing in conventional terms" means that something is known to the world (that is, it is found by a valid cognizer) and is not discredited by any other valid cognition, conventional or ultimate. In an important passage from Tsong-ka-pa's *Great Exposition of the Stages of the Path*, he elaborates three criteria for something to exist in conventional terms:[28]

> (1) it must be well known to the world, i.e., to conventional consciousnesses (*tha snyad shes pa la grags pa*),
> (2) it must not be invalidated by conventional valid cognition, and
> (3) it must not be invalidated by a reasoning consciousness analyzing the ultimate.

The second requirement excludes, for example, a mirage being water, because the status of a mirage as water can be discredited by conventional valid cognition. In other words, a mirage may appear to be water, but conventional valid cognition can establish that it is not; thus, a mirage does not exist as water even in conventional terms. The third requirement excludes inherent existence, which must be refuted by ultimate valid cognition, and having been so refuted is thereby established as utterly non-existent.

The precise meaning of the first requirement is problematic. Two questions must be answered: (1) If emptiness exists, it must exist in conventional terms since nothing is ultimately existent. Therefore, emptiness must meet these three qualifications. What does it mean to say that emptiness is "well known to conventional consciousnesses"? (2) What does the clause "well known to conventional consciousnesses" exclude from the class of conventional existents? That is, why is it necessary?

Tsong-ka-pa indicates that the conventional consciousness to which he is referring is a consciousness which, while it may analyze its object, never questions or scrutinizes its object's mode of existence.[29] He stresses that this conventional consciousness exists among all beings, and not only among those who are innocent of philosophy.[30] Perhaps the most important passage for understanding Tsong-ka-pa's point is this:[31]

> [The relationship between] actions and effects, the grounds and paths, and so forth are not well known to the common person. However, when [such things] are taken as objects through hearing and experience, etc., they appear to ordinary minds that do not analyze how [their final] mode

of being exists. Thus, [while it would be] a fault [if such things] were not well known in the world, this is not the case.

Although Tsong-ka-pa's examples of topics unfamiliar to the common person include only concealer-truths, why should we not assume that emptiness is also included in his "and so forth"? Certainly, Buddhists and students of Buddhism frequently hear about emptiness and reflect on emptiness without reaching the point of investigating exactly how emptiness exists. I think this adequately answers the first question of what it means to say that emptiness is well known to conventional consciousnesses.

However, if emptiness is "well known to the world" when people hear about it without questioning it deeply, then must we not say that an omnipotent God, Brahman, the three *guṇas*, *prakṛti*, and so forth are also renowned to the world? In fact, *all* philosophical constructs are "well known to the world" in the sense that Tsong-ka-pa uses the phrase in this context. This brings us to our second question: If the phrase "well known to the world" does not exclude from conventional existence even the philosophical constructs of non-Buddhist systems, then why does Tsong-ka-pa state it at all? Is it not logically unnecessary in the light of the two clauses that follow it? Does it eliminate anything at all? Perhaps it might be construed to eliminate things that even ordinary mature worldly persons would never imagine to exist, i.e., the horns of a rabbit, a tortoise hair cloak, etc.

In any case, it is impossible that this first clause should eliminate anything that is not also eliminated by one or the other of the latter two clauses. Together, conventional valid cognition and ultimate valid cognition comprise all valid knowledge. If either of them discredits something, then that thing does not exist at all. Whatever is discredited by neither of them must exist, and whatever exists must exist only in conventional terms. Thus, it is impossible that anything should be excluded from conventional existence *solely* because it is not renowned to conventional consciousnesses.

Thus, the clause "well known to the world" is not necessary in the logical sense; it is heuristically necessary. In the Ge-luk-ba presentation of Prāsaṅgika, "existence" and "existence in conventional terms" are mutually inclusive—that is, whatever is one is necessarily the other. "Existence" requires that something be established by valid cognition. By including the qualification "well known to the world'' in his explanation of what it means to exist in conventional terms, Tsong-ka-pa conveys how the connotation of ''existence in conventional terms'' differs from that of ''existence.'' Although they are mutually inclusive, their meanings are reached by different conceptual routes and thus bring a different flavor to the mind. Specifically, Tsong-ka-pa indicates that the meaning of ''existent in conventional terms'' is reached not by determining what is established by valid cognition, but by first setting out the very broad class of things that are taken as objects by ordinary, uninvestigating, worldly consciousnesses—and then narrowing that class by eliminating whatever valid cognition discredits.

CONVENTIONAL TRUTH

The term ''conventional truth'' (*tha snyad bden pa, vyavahārasatya*) is often employed as an equivalent for concealer-truth. Without questioning the appropriateness of this usage, Jam-yang-shay-ba stresses that (1) the ''convention'' (*tha snyad, vyavahāra*) in conventional truth is not the same as the *kun rdzob* in concealer-truth, and (2) that the meaning of ''truth'' (*bden pa, satya*) in conventional truth is different from the meaning of ''truth'' (*bden pa, satya*) in concealer-truth.[32] The first point is already clear, since we have seen that, although in general *kun rdzob* can mean ''conventionality,'' in the context of concealer-truth it refers to the concealing ignorance.

As for the second point, in general ''truth'' refers to a phenomenon that is non-deceptive, there being full agreement between the way it exists and the way it appears; however, in the term ''concealer-truth'' it means ''truth for the perspective of ignorance.'' Jam-yang-shay-ba argues that ''truth'' can have neither of those two meanings in the term ''conventional truth.'' Unlike the case of concealer-truth, there is nothing in the term ''conventional truth'' to indicate that truth could mean ''truth for ignorance.'' Why not say, then, that in the term ''conventional truth,'' truth has its general and usual meaning, that which is non-deceptive? Why not say that truth here refers to a concordance between mode of appearance and mode of subsistence? ''Conventional truth'' would then mean ''truth in conventional terms'' or ''that which, in conventional terms, has a concordance between its mode of appearance and its mode of abiding.'' If this were the meaning of ''conventional truth,'' then a conventional truth, such as a form, would have to subsist in the very manner in which it appears to an eye consciousness. Since objects apprehended by the sense consciousnesses of sentient beings appear to be inherently existent, if a form were a truth conventionally in this way, it would have to be inherently existent conventionally. Therefore, since Prāsaṅgikas refute inherent existence even conventionally, conventional truth cannot mean being a truth conventionally. Most Ge-luk-bas hold that emptiness *can* be posited as a truth conventionally because it does not present a deceptive appearance of inherent existence to the wisdom directly realizing emptiness.

According to Jam-yang-shay-ba, "truth" (*bden pa, satya*) in "conventional truth" does not mean "non-deceptive," but simply means "existent."[33] A conventional truth is that which exists as, or is meaningful as, a conventional object. He cites Amarasiṃha's *Immortal Treasury* (*'chi med mdzod, amarakośa*):[34] "*Satya* [means] true, good, existent, praised, and worthy of worship." Nevertheless, existing in terms of conventions (*tha snyad du yod*) and being a conventional truth (*tha snyad bden pa*) have two quite different meanings. Emptinesses are not conventional truths or conventional objects because they are ultimate truths. However, all phenomena including emptinesses exist in conventional terms; there is nothing that exists ultimately.

WORLDLY CONCEALER-TRUTHS

One frequently encounters the phrase "worldly concealer-truths" (*'jig rten kun rdzob bden pa, lokasaṃvṛtisatya*) in literature on the two truths. Candrakīrti's *Clear Words* states that "worldly" is used only as an additional description and does not imply the existence of non-worldly concealer-truths.[35] Worldly concealer-truth means "truth for a worldly concealer"—that is, truth for the concealing ignorance of a world. Candrakīrti's *Clear Words* tells us that "world" in this context refers to a type of person.[36] Later, Candrakīrti adds a further specification:[37]

> In one way, those who abide in the erroneous perceptions of sense powers harmed by eye disease, blue eye-film, jaundice, etc., are *not* worlds.

In considering what Candrakīrti may have meant by this, it is important to remember that:

> (1) a person whose sense powers are affected by disease or optical illusion either may or may not have an ignorant consciousness that assents to the misperceptions that result from those conditions, and
> (2) all worldly persons have ignorance about the final nature of phenomena—regardless of whether their senses are damaged by disease.

Maintaining these distinctions, it becomes easier to understand what Candrakīrti means when he says that people whose perceptions are distorted by disease are, in a certain sense, not worlds. Concealer-truths or truths-for-a-concealer are phenomena that are misapprehended as truths by the *subtlest* ignorance of even ordinary, healthy persons. A person with jaundice who sees a white piece of paper as yellow, may have an ignorant consciousness that believes that the paper is actually yellow, just as it appears. That misconception conceals the white color in the nature of the paper. However, that misconception is not the concealing ignorance in terms of which that paper is a concealer-truth because it is not a conception of inherent existence. As Jam-yang-shay-ba says,[38]

> [S]ince erroneous—that is, false—consciousnesses of one whose sense powers have been damaged by jaundice and so forth are not the worlds in relation to whose perspective something is posited as right, *worldly* concealer-truth is stated in order to make that point.

Therefore, the word worldly helps to specify that, in the context of the explanation of *kun rdzob bden pa* as truth-for-a-concealing-ignorance, the concealing ignorance in whose perspective things are truths is a deep ignorance, found among all unliberated persons, rather than a misconception resulting from occasional or superficial causes.

Accordingly, Jam-yang-shay-ba explains that while the main "worlds" are common beings who have never realized emptiness directly, Superiors on the paths of seeing and meditation can also be considered worlds because the concealing ignorance still occurs in their continuums, albeit in a weakened form.[39] Jam-yang-shay-ba cites Śāntideva's *Engaging in the Bodhisattva Deeds*, "Two types of world are seen: yogis and ordinary beings."[40] There are no non-worldly concealer-truths—that is, no truths-for-*un*worldly-concealers—because concealing ignorances exist only in the continuums of "worlds," i.e., persons within cyclic existence.

While Candrakīrti's *Clear Words* states that the "world" in worldly concealer-truth (*'jig rten kun rdzob bden pa, lokasaṃvṛtisatya*) is a person, Jam-yang-shay-ba is careful to make the point that in Buddhist sūtras and treatises, *lokasaṃvṛti* frequently refers to terminological conventions or conventional consciousnesses rather than to persons.[41] For example, in the passage from the *Meeting of the Father and Son Sūtra*, "The Tathāgata sees conventionalities as the province of the world," the term "world" refers to certain consciousnesses. Also, Candrakīrti uses the term "world" to refer to consciousnesses rather than persons in the two truths section of his *Supplement*. He writes:[42]

> Objects realized by the world [and] apprehended
> By the six unimpaired sense powers are true
> From just [the viewpoint of] the world; the rest
> Are posited as unreal from just [the viewpoint of] the world.

Although there is some disagreement regarding the precise identification of the "world" in this stanza (see chapter eight), Ge-luk-bas follow Tsong-ka-pa in asserting that it is a worldly *consciousness*, rather than a person.[43] The point of these considerations is that, despite a clear and explicit statement in Candrakīrti's *Clear Words* that "world" refers to a person, "world" (*'jig rten, loka*) can mean different things according to context. As is the case with *saṃvṛti*, it is important to identify the particular sense of the word *world* each time it occurs.

THE ULTIMATE (DON DAM)

Ultimate truth is a translation of *paramārthasatya* and its Tibetan equivalent, *don dam bden pa*. Explanations of the term *paramārtha* occur in the context of two distinct questions within the Mādhyamika tradition: (1) What does it mean to exist (or not to exist) ultimately (*don dam du, paramārthataḥ*)? (2) What does it mean to be an ultimate truth (*don dam bden pa, paramārthasatya*)? Tsong-ka-pa suggests that it was failure to distinguish between these two questions that led Ngok Lo-den-shay-rap (1059-1109) to conclude that ultimate truths could not be objects of knowledge because if they were they would have to exist ultimately, as objects found by an ultimate mind. Through the converse of the same conflation,

Cha-ba-chö-gyi-seng-gay (*phya pa chos kyi seng ge*, 1109-1169) concluded that ultimate truths are ultimately existent because they are found by an ultimate mind.[44]

ULTIMATE EXISTENCE

Regarding the first question, the meaning of "ultimate existence," it must be noted that many of the Indian Mādhyamika sources for understanding this term are within the Svātantrika branch, rather than the Prāsaṅgika branch, of the Mādhyamika tradition. The terms *Svātantrika* (*rang rgyud pa*) and *Prāsaṅgika* (*thal 'gyur pa*) were first coined in Tibet, apparently by Ba-tsap Lo-tsa-wa Nyi-ma-drak (*pa tshab lo tsa wa nyi ma grags*, 1055-?) who translated Candrakīrti's *Clear Words* and *Supplement* into Tibetan.[45] Noting Candrakīrti's sharp attack on Bhāvaviveka, he designated Candrakīrti and his followers *Prāsaṅgikas* (i.e., Consequentialists) and called Bhāvaviveka and his supporters *Svātantrikas* (i.e., Autonomists). These names refer to an argument about how Mādhyamikas should frame arguments against their opponents. Bhāvaviveka apparently held that one must use syllogisms (*sbyor ba, prayoga*), or else consequences (*thal 'gyur, prasaṅga*) that will eventually be converted to syllogisms. Bhāvaviveka criticized Buddhapālita's commentary on Nāgārjuna's *Treatise on the Middle Way*, arguing that Buddhapālita's logical method was faulty because he mainly relied upon contradictory consequences–i.e., *reductio ad absurdum* type arguments—that did not convert into appropriate syllogistic demonstrations. Candrakīrti defended Buddhapālita, arguing that a Mādhyamika is not required to construct arguments that conclude in syllogisms.

It was Tsong-ka-pa, in his *Essence of Good Explanations* (*legs shes snying po*), who first adumbrated the Svātantrika/Prāsaṅgika distinction as a difference not only in logical method but in philosophical view as well. Tsong-ka-pa argued that Bhāvaviveka's insistence upon the eventual use of syllogisms implies an acceptance of reference points that appear the same way to both parties. From this, Tsong-ka-pa deduced that Bhāvaviveka, unlike Candrakīrti, accepts that phenomena do exist in accordance with their appearance as inherently existent (*rang bzhin gyis grub pa, svabhāvasiddha*), that is, naturally existent (*rang gi mtshan nyid kyis grub pa, svalakṣaṇasiddha*). While the exact workings of this argument have been controversial, it has had considerable influence (*not* to say universal acceptance) in Tibet, even beyond the Ge-luk-ba order.

Accordingly, Ge-luk-bas define a Svātantrika as someone who refutes ultimate existence (thus avoiding the extreme of permanence) but asserts that all phenomena inherently exist in a conventional sense (thus avoiding the extreme of annihilation). A Prāsaṅgika, on the other hand, denies inherent existence even conventionally (thus avoiding the extreme of permanence), but admits mere existence in a conventional sense (thus avoiding the extreme of annihilation). Prāsaṅgikas see the Svātantrika attempt to separate ultimate existence from inherent existence, denying one while accepting the other, as a philosophical failure. To refute ultimate existence is to refute inherent existence, and vice versa. Thus, only for Prāsaṅgikas, and presumably not for Svātantrikas, can the descriptions of ultimate existence below be considered equivalent to descriptions of inherent existence.

Ultimate existence (*don dam du yod, paramārthasiddha*) has two meanings: (1) existing for the perspective of a conceptual reasoning consciousness analyzing reality, and (2) existing as an objective mode of subsistence without being posited by way of appearing to a non-defective awareness. In the first meaning of ultimate existence, derived from Bhāvaviveka's *Blaze of Reasoning* (*Tarkajvālā*), "ultimate" refers to any awareness (even a conceptual awareness) realizing emptiness.[46] To exist ultimately would mean being able to withstand analysis (*dpyad bzod thub pa*) by an such ultimate mind. An ultimate mind is an consciousness of analytical wisdom that searches out the way that things exist, their final mode of being. If something were ultimately existent, it would exist for and be found by the reasoning consciousness analyzing its final mode of being. That is, if a chair were truly existent, then when I search to see how a chair really exists I should at last find the chair itself. Instead, the mind searching for the final nature of the chair finds the emptiness of the chair. Thus, according to the Ge-luk-ba reading of Bhāvaviveka, ultimate existence would entail that something exist as its own final nature, while the emptiness of a phenomenon points to its inability to hold up under analysis searching for its final nature. However, in his retrospective formulation of the view of the Svātantrika school, Tsong-ka-pa determines that the ignorance imagining that something can sustain ultimate analysis of its nature is *artificial* (*kun btags*) ignorance, an idea not innate but misbegotten from the study of defective philosophies.

In its second meaning, derived from Kamalaśīla's *Illumination of the Middle Way*, ultimately existing means *existing as an objective mode of subsistence, without being posited by way of appearing to a non-defective awareness*. This type of ultimate existence is the main object of negation of Mādhyamika reasoning, as described by Svātantrika.[47] While in fact there is nothing that exists in this way, every unliberated sentient beings has innate ignorant consciousnesses that mistakenly superimpose this kind of ultimate existence. Every phenomenon must rely upon a non-defective valid cognizer in order to be posited as an existent. Nothing, not even emptiness, has its own independent objective mode of subsistence and therefore there is no phenomenon that is ultimately existent in this sense. Since the innate ignorance that misconceives phenomena as existing ultimately in this way is the innate root of cyclic existence, Jang-gya stresses that a yogi seeking to realize emptiness should first identify, within his or her own mental continuum, this conception of ultimate existence and take it as the object of refutation.[48]

ULTIMATE TRUTH

What, then, does "ultimate" mean in the term "ultimate truth" (*don dam bden pa, paramārthasatya*)? Prāsaṅgika and Svātantrika disagree about how to understand the term "ultimate" (*don dam*) in "ultimate truth" (*don dam bden pa*). Neither disputes that in *don dam bden pa*, *don* (*artha*) means object (*yul, viṣaya*) and *dam* means ultimate or supreme. However, Bhāvaviveka's *Blaze of Reasoning* lists three ways that these meanings can be combined:

(1) Since reality is both an object and the ultimate, it is the ultimate object (*don dam, paramārtha*). According to this explanation, paramārtha is a *karmadhārya* compound. Both object (*don, artha*) and ultimate (*dam, parama*) refer to the object (*yul, viṣaya*), an emptiness, as opposed to the subject (*yul can*), the mind realizing emptiness.
(2) Since reality is the object of a supreme mind, the non-conceptual exalted wisdom of meditative equipoise, it is the object of the ultimate (*dam pa'i don, paramasya artha*). According to this explanation, *paramārtha* is a *tatpuruṣa* compound in which *object* (*don, artha*) refers to the object (*yul*), while *ultimate* refers to the subject.
(3) *Paramārtha* (*don dam*) can also be read as a *bahuvṛhi* compound meaning "that having an ultimate object." In this

> sense, *paramārtha* is an adjective that is understood to refer to the consciousnesses realizing emptiness inferentially. Here, both parts of the compound refer to a consciousness, the wisdom directly realizing emptiness. This wisdom is ultimate (*parama*) because it is the supreme mind; it is an object (*artha*) in that it is sought by those who wish to abandon afflictions. Although the parts of the compound individually refer to a direct realization of emptiness, the compound as a whole describes inferential realization of emptiness, which "has the ultimate object" insofar as it is concordant with the ultimate mind, meditative equipoise directly realizing emptiness. Inferential realization of emptiness is concordant with this ultimate mind because they both realize the ultimate truth, emptiness, and they both are objects sought by those seeking liberation.[49]

The second of these explanations holds favor with most Svātantrikas, while Prāsaṅgikas follow the first. Candrakīrti's *Clear Words* says:[50]

> Since it is an object and an ultimate, it is an ultimate object (*paramārtha*). Since just that is a truth, it is an ultimate truth (*paramārthasatya*).

As Jam-yang-shay-ba and other Ge-luk-bas explain the Prāsaṅgika interpretation, emptiness is called "ultimate truth" (*don dam bden pa, paramārthasatya*) because (1) it is an object (*don, artha*) since it is an object found by a wisdom of meditative equipoise, (2) it is ultimate since it is the real mode of subsistence (*gnas lugs*), and (3) it is a truth since its mode of appearance and mode of subsistence are concordant.[51] Therefore, in contrast to the Svātantrika approach (wherein *dam* refers to a mind directly realizing emptiness), the Prāsaṅgikas hold that in the context of explaining the meaning of the term *don dam bden pa* (*paramārthasatya*), both ultimate (*dam, parama*) and object (*don, artha*) refer to ultimate truth itself.

DISTINGUISHING ULTIMATE EXISTENCE AND ULTIMATE TRUTH

Emptiness, as an ultimate truth, is an *ontological* ultimate because, as Jam-yang-shay-ba explains, it is the final mode of being of all phenomena. Nevertheless, emptiness does not ultimately exist because it does not bear analysis by a reasoning consciousness investigating its final nature and because it does not have its own objective mode of subsistence. The distinction between being an ultimate (*don dam yin*) and ultimately existing (*don dam du yod*) is critical in Tsong-ka-pa's system. Emptiness is found, known, and realized by a mind of ultimate analysis, and therefore it is an ultimate truth. However, emptiness is not ultimately existent because it is not found by the ultimate mind analyzing *it*.

For example, when a table is the basis of analysis, the ultimate mind finds not the table but the emptiness of the table. When the emptiness of the table is the basis of analysis, the ultimate mind finds not the emptiness of the table but the emptiness of the emptiness of the table, and so forth. In other words, an emptiness is no more able to bear ultimate analysis than anything else. Every emptiness is the final mode of abiding of some phenomenon (either an ultimate truth or a concealer-truth), but there is no phenomenon, not even an emptiness, that is its *own* final mode of abiding.[52]

Thus, in the Ge-luk-ba reading of Prāsaṅgika, the *plurality* of emptinesses is philosophically significant. If there were only one emptiness, then it would have to be its own mode of abiding, and thus it would be inherently existent. Emptiness is often spoken of, even by Ge-luk-bas, as though it were unitary, and indeed it is said that all things have "one taste" (*ro gcig*), i.e., the taste of no-inherent-existence. On the other hand, the Ge-luk-ba assertion of emptiness*es* (all of which are the final nature of something and none of which is its own ultimate nature) helps maneuver the Ge-luk-bas away from a reifying extreme. An emptiness, i.e., an ultimate truth, is an ontological ultimate insofar as it is the final mode of being of some phenomenon, but it is not a self-instituting monistic ground.

6 *Definitions of the Two Truths*

THE GENERAL DEFINITIONS

Candrakīrti's *Supplement* states:[1]

> [Buddha] said that all things have two entities—
> Those found by perceivers of reality and of falsities—
> That objects of perceivers of reality are suchnesses,
> [And] that objects of perceivers of falsities are concealer-truths.

The Tibetan words translated as "objects of perceivers of falsities" in the last line are *mthong ba brdzun pa*, literally meaning "false perceiver." Since the third line explicitly uses the word "object" (*yul*), we can carry that meaning over into the fourth line. Therefore, it seems that Candrakīrti is saying that objects of false perceivers are concealer-truths. However, commenting on the fourth line of this stanza, Tsong-ka-pa's *Illumination of the Thought says*,[2]

> [An object] found by a conventional valid cognizer perceiving a false object of knowledge is a concealer-truth.

Also, Tsong-ka-pa's *Ocean of Reasoning* defines the concealer-truth of a sprout as,[3]

> the entity of a sprout that is found by a conventional consciousness comprehending an object of knowledge that is a false, deceptive object.

Inverting the natural syntax of Candrakīrti's line, Tsong-ka-pa reads *brdzun pa* (falsity or false) as the *object* of the perceiver rather than as an adjective describing the perceiver. For Tsong-ka-pa, the perceiver is a conventional valid cognizer, incontrovertible or undeceived (*mi slu ba*) with regard to a conventional object. A conventional object is a falsity because it presents the conventional valid cognizer with a deceptive appearance of inherent existence, while in fact it lacks inherent existence.

Based on the third line of that stanza, "Objects of perceivers of reality are suchnesses," Tsong-ka-pa's *Illumination of the Thought* says, "An object that is found by a reasoning consciousness perceiving, i.e., comprehending, the meaning of reality is a suchness, an ultimate truth."[4] Also, in his *Ocean of Reasoning*, Tsong-ka-pa defines the ultimate truth of a sprout as "the entity of a sprout found by a reasoning consciousness perceiving an object of knowledge that is only the real nature."[5]

Ngak-wang-bel-den sets forth brief definitions[6] of the two truths based on these passages. He writes:[7]

> The definition of ultimate truth is: an object found by a reasoning consciousness distinguishing the final [mode of subsistence]. The definition of concealer-truth is: an object found by a reasoning consciousness distinguishing conventions.

Here, "reasoning consciousness" refers to a valid cognizer (*tshad ma, pramāṇa*). It can be either a direct perceiver or an inferential valid cognizer. "Distinguishing the final mode of subsistence" means looking for the ultimate nature of an object. For example, not satisfied with table as a mere conventional imputation, one can search for the table among its parts, the collection of its parts, and so forth. The only object found or realized by such a mind is an ultimate truth. "Distinguishing conventions" means examining falsities without questioning their deceptive appearance as inherently existent.

In effect, these definitions tell us that ultimate truths are realized by valid cognizers that realize the final nature of an object, while concealer-truths are realized by valid cognizers that realize the conventional nature of an object. Sometimes they are presented in a very succinct form. For example, Jang-gya writes,[8]

> Since Candrakīrti's *Supplement Commentary*[9] says "objects of perceivers of falsities are concealer-truths," an object found by a conventional valid cognizer is also stated as a positor of concealer-truth.

Such definitions seem to involve a circular element: A concealer-truth is the object of a conventional valid cognizer; a conventional valid cognizer is incontrovertible with regard to conventional, or false, natures; and such falsities, in turn, are said to be concealer-truths. Are we back where we began? Certainly not, for along the way certain important facts become clear. For Ge-luk-bas, both concealer-truths and ultimate truths are existent objects of knowledge. Moreover, valid sources of knowledge include not only ultimate minds, whose province is emptiness, but conventional minds, whose province is all other phenomena. Since there are valid, or incontrovertible, knowers of both truths, positing emptiness does no harm to conventional presentations of moral cause and effect, the need for compassion, and so forth.

INCLUDING THE EXCEPTION

The "inconceivable" (*bsam gyis mi khyab pa, acintya*) way in which a Buddha knows objects threatens to disrupt the internal consistency of the Ge-luk-ba definition cycle. Among sentient beings, conventional valid cognizers cannot realize emptinesses, and ultimate valid cognizers cannot realize concealer-truths. However, all of a Buddha's consciousnesses are omniscient. Buddha Superiors simultaneously know all aspects of all phenomena. We may speak of a Buddha's mind knowing the mode of subsistence or a Buddha's mind knowing the varieties of conventional phenomena, but every one of a Buddha's consciousnesses, even the sense consciousnesses, knows everything. Since a Buddha's reasoning consciousness distinguishing the ultimate knows not only emptinesses, but also tables and so forth, how can Ge-luk-bas define "ultimate truth" as an object found by a reasoning consciousness distinguishing the ultimate? Is a table an ultimate truth because it is realized by a Buddha's omniscience knowing the mode of subsistence? Is emptiness a concealer-truth because it is seen by a Buddha's eye consciousness? In the face of this problem, Tsong-ka-pa produces a second set of definitions in his *Illumination of the Thought*:[10]

> The definitions explained before refer to the general case. This is because a Buddha's way of knowing is treated as an exception, unlike that on the tenth ground and below. Therefore, when treated so as to include a Buddha's way of knowing as well, the definition of ultimate truth is: (1) an object found by a valid reasoning consciousness that sees reality (*yang dag pa*) and (2) with regard to which [such a valid reasoning consciousness] is a valid reasoning consciousness. Through this, the definition of concealer-truth also should be known.

Also, Kay-drup's *Thousand Doses* says:[11]

> The definition of ultimate truth is: that with regard to which the valid cognizer by which it is found becomes a distinguisher of the ultimate. The definition of concealer-truth is: that with regard to which the valid cognizer by which it is found becomes a distinguisher of conventions. These are faultless definitions for the systems of both Prāsaṅgika and Svātantrika.

Although there are slight variations and refinements in the wording, many Ge-luk-ba scholars posit definitions of the two truths modeled after these. Their advantage is that since they are comprehensive, they allow the system to remain consistent even when describing a Buddha's omniscience. For example, a table is an object found by a Buddha's omniscience realizing the mode of subsistence. It is not, however, that with regard to which such an omniscience becomes a valid cognizer distinguishing the ultimate. Therefore, the table is not an ultimate truth. To take another example, a Buddha's eye consciousness knows both a table and the emptiness of the table, but it becomes a distinguisher of conventions only with regard to table and other conventionalities—not with regard to emptiness. Thus, emptiness is not a concealer-truth.

Should these more comprehensive definitions be posited instead of the shorter definitions that cover only the general case? Or are both sets acceptable? Here we find real differences of opinion among the various monastic colleges. In their textbooks on Mādhyamika, Paṇ-chen Sö-nam-drak-ba and Jay-dzun Chö-gyi-gyel-tsen, posit only comprehensive, exception-including definitions of the two truths. Paṇ-chen offers a general argument for the comprehensive definitions: Omnisciences realizing the mode are reasoning consciousnesses distinguishing the final mode of subsistence, and omnisciences realizing the varieties are reasoning consciousnesses that are distinguishers of conventions.[12] Since an omniscient consciousness is a reasoning consciousness distinguishing the final mode of subsistence only because it realizes emptiness, it becomes such only in relation to emptiness and not in relation to conventional phenomena. Since an omniscient consciousness is a distinguisher of conventions only because it realizes concealer-truths, it becomes a distinguisher of conventions in relation to concealer truths. This argument only explains why the definitions that have the qualifying clauses include the way a Buddha knows objects. Paṇ-chen Sö-nam-drak-ba does not explicitly refute definitions that lack such qualifications. Jay-dzun-ba, on the other hand, opens his two truths exposition with a direct attack on the shorter definitions.[13]

JAY-DZUN-BA'S CRITIQUE OF THE SHORT DEFINITIONS

One of Jay-dzun-ba's arguments is based on two tenets that are unique to Prāsaṅgika.[14] The first is that consciousnesses, even wrong consciousnesses, are direct valid cognizers with regard to their appearing objects. Taking a conceptual consciousness thinking that sound is permanent as an example, Hopkins explains this assertion:[15]

> Its appearing object is merely a generic image of permanent sound and not actual permanent sound because permanent sound does not exist. The consciousness is valid *with respect to its appearing object* because it notices and can induce memory of this generic image, no matter how erroneous it is.

Of course, the conception of sound as permanent is not a valid cognizer because it is not an incontrovertible knower of its main object. However, it is valid with respect to the *appearance* of sound as permanent.

Secondly, Prāsaṅgikas refute the assertions of other systems regarding the existence of self-conscious direct perceivers (*rang rig mngon sum, svasaṃvedanapratyakṣa*). Systems that posit self-consciousness (i.e., Cittamātra, the Reason-Following branch of Sautrāntika, and the Yogācāra-Svātantrika branch of Mādhyamika) do so in order to account for memory of the subjective side of previous experience.[16] Since it is possible to remember the subjective dimension of earlier experiences, and not just its objective content, they argue that there must be a type of consciousness that "knows the knower" at the same time that the knower is apprehending an object. For example, when one remembers having seen something blue, one remembers not only blue, but also the experiencer of blue, the consciousness apprehending blue. While the eye consciousness apprehending blue takes on the aspect of that external apprehended object, the self-consciousness takes on the aspect of the apprehending awareness. Prāsaṅgikas insist that if one needed a knower to know the knower, one would also need a knower to know that knower, etc., and they avoid this absurdity by denying the existence of self-consciousness.

Jay-dzun-ba applies these two principles to a sentient being's (that is, a non-Buddha's) direct realization of emptiness. He argues that this consciousness must appear to itself because there is no self-knower to which it could appear and thereby come to be later remembered. Also, it must realize what appears to it because all consciousnesses are valid cognizers with regard to their appearing objects. Therefore, it must realize itself. Of course, such a consciousness directly realizing emptiness is a reasoning consciousness distinguishing the ultimate. Since it also realizes itself, it itself must be an object found by a reasoning consciousness distinguishing the ultimate. Therefore, if a short definition of ultimate truth (e.g., "an object found by a reasoning consciousness distinguishing the ultimate") were adequate, a sentient being's consciousness directly realizing emptiness would be an ultimate truth. This is absurd since ultimate truths are permanent (*rtag pa, nitya*), negative phenomena (*dgag pa, pratiṣedha*), while consciousnesses are impermanent (*mi rtag pa, anitya*), positive phenomena (*sgrub pa, vidhi*).

One problem with Jay-dzun-ba's argument is that it gives the impression that direct realization is a dualistic mind. It not only sees its main object, emptiness, but must also realize itself as a subject knowing emptiness. This requires that the ultimate wisdom realize two objects, only one of which is an ultimate truth. Jam-yang-shay-ba avoids this problem by insisting that the exalted wisdom consciousness directly realizing emptiness realizes nothing but emptiness.[17] All sense of object and agent vanish, and no object other than emptiness is cognized. He cites Tsong-ka-pa's *Ocean of Reasoning*:[18]

> [E]laboration (*spros pa, prapañca*) is not merely the elaboration of the object of reasoned negation, but also the elaboration of appearance. The mode of transcending that [elaboration of appearance] refers to the vanishing of all elaborations of dualistic appearance in the perspective of [a consciousness] directly realizing suchness.

How can the vanishing of all dualistic appearance be reconciled with the assertion that consciousnesses must be valid cognizers of their appearing objects? The answer is that Jam-yang-shay-ba does not assert that *all* consciousnesses are valid with regard to their appearing objects. He makes an exception for non-mistaken consciousnesses. In Prāsaṅgika, the only non-mistaken awareness found in the continuums of sentient beings is the direct realization of emptiness. This special exception is also made in Lo-sel-ling (which follows Paṇ-chen Sö-nam-drak-ba), but is not admitted by Jay-dzun-ba.

There is another problem with Jay-dzun-ba's argument against the short definitions. Tsong-ka-pa states that he posits the second set of definitions in order to include the way that Buddha Superiors know objects. He specifically contrasts this to the way objects are known on the "tenth ground and below." Since direct realization of emptiness begins on the first ground, Jay-dzun-ba's position implies that Tsong-ka-pa inaccurately stated the lower boundary of consciousnesses that are exceptions to the first set of definitions.

However, Jay-dzun-ba has another, more persuasive argument against the short definitions. If "object found by a reasoning consciousness distinguishing the ultimate" could be posited as the definition of ultimate truth, then a pot would be an ultimate truth because (1) since every omniscience knows all phenomena, a pot is found by a Buddha's omniscience knowing the mode, and (2) a Buddha's omniscient consciousness knowing the mode is a reasoning consciousness distinguishing the ultimate. This must be the case, since if a Buddha's omniscient consciousness knowing the mode were not a reasoning consciousness distinguishing the ultimate, then there would have been no need for Tsong-ka-pa to posit the more comprehensive definitions. In other words, if there had been any way to reconcile the first set of definitions with the way a Buddha knows objects, why would Tsong-ka-pa have bothered to posit the second set? This is the same argument Paṇ-chen Sö-nam-drak-ba uses to support his comprehensive definitions.[19]

JANG-GYA AND JAM-YANG-SHAY-BA

Ngak-wang-bel-den states that Jang-gya and Jam-yang-shay-ba approve both sets of definitions.[20] However, Jang-gya seems to prefer the more comprehensive definitions. He writes that for something to be a concealer-truth means that[21]

> (1) it is an object found by a conventional valid cognizer that comprehends an object of knowledge that is a falsity, a deceiving thing, and (2) it is that with regard to which that valid cognizer comes to be an analyzer of conventions.

Jang-gya continues,

> Also, since Candrakīrti's *Supplement*[22] says "objects of perceivers of falsities are concealer-truths," another way to posit concealer-truth is: "object found by a conventional valid cognizer." However, it is the thought of Tsong-ka-pa's great explanation of Candrakīrti's *Supplement* to posit a definition like that just explained [in two parts] by way of including the manner in which objects are cognized at the time of the fruit [i.e., Buddhahood].

It seems that Jang-gya prefers his comprehensive, two-part definition, but states the briefer form out of deference to Candrakīrti's authority. Later, in the section on ultimate truth, Jang-gya gives *only* a comprehensive definition.[23] Nevertheless, he nowhere attacks the short definitions as Jay-dzun-ba does.

In his textbook on Mādhyamika, Jam-yang-shay-ba neither uses nor refutes the short definitions. For concealer-truth, he gives a typical definition of the second type: "that which is an object found by a conventional valid cognizer which comprehends it and which becomes a conventional valid cognizer with regard to it."[24] His primary definition of ultimate truth belongs to a third type, discussed below.[25] He gives other definitions of ultimate truth that are clear examples of the exception-including type.[26] On the other hand, Jam-yang-shay-ba *does* present short definitions in a later composition, his *Great Exposition of Tenets*.[27] His textbook on Mādhyamika foreshadows this movement to the short definitions, presenting arguments that support their viability. Jam-yang-shay-ba's analysis of this issue clearly moves the discussion a level beyond what earlier textbooks offer. His main points are (1) that adequate definitions need not take account of the inconceivable way that a Buddha knows the world and (2) that it is necessary to have a precise understanding of the meaning of the term "object found" (*rnyed don*).

The first point is that if the definitions of the two truths must remain perfectly consistent and applicable even in the context of discussions of Buddhahood, then other definitions should meet that same criterion. There are a great many definitions that describe their definienda in terms of relationships with consciousnesses. Many of these fail to meet a test for comprehensiveness with regard to the way a Buddha knows objects. For example, the definition of a form sense-sphere (*gzugs kyi skye mched, rupāyatana*) is "an object of apprehension of an eye consciousness." However, a Buddha's eye apprehends all phenomena, including sounds and so forth. Obviously, sounds are not what we would ordinarily consider "visible objects." If we nonetheless posit them as form sense-spheres, on the grounds that they are known by a Buddha's eye consciousness, how will the system differentiate sounds from visible objects? Jam-yang-shay-ba writes:[28]

> [I]f one were to apply whatever is the mode of knowing of a Buddha's exalted wisdom to the mode of knowing of awarenesses and consciousnesses [in general], all worldly conventions would be destroyed.

In support of this view, Jam-yang-shay-ba cites Tsong-ka-pa's prefatory remarks to the second set of definitions:[29]

> The definitions explained before refer to the general case. This is because a Buddha's way of knowing is treated as an exception, unlike that on the tenth ground and below.

Jam-yang-shay-ba presents his comprehensive definition of ultimate truth not as a general definition, but as a definition stated "from the common viewpoint of reasoning consciousnesses in general and an exalted knower of all aspects."[30] It is acceptable to state comprehensive definitions, but one cannot demand that all definitions take into consideration the exceptional aspects of a Buddha's mind. Even though all the objects of a Buddha's eye consciousness are not form sense-spheres, it is acceptable to posit a definition of form sense-sphere without taking this into account. It would seem that, by analogy, "an object found by a reasoning consciousness distinguishing the final mode of subsistence" would be an adequate definition for ultimate truth, despite the exceptional case of a Buddha's omniscience knowing the mode. Likewise, "an object found by a reasoning consciousness distinguishing conventions" should define concealer-truth, despite the exceptional case of a Buddha's omniscience knowing the varieties. Thus, Ngak-wang-bel-den says that Jam-yang-shay-ba accepts both types of definitions.

JAM-YANG-SHAY-BA'S SECOND ARGUMENT

Jam-yang-shay-ba brings up another, quite different reason for holding that qualifications should be added to the definitions of the two truths. As mentioned above, Prāsaṅgikas assert that all mistaken consciousnesses are valid cognizers of their appearing objects and that, therefore, mistaken consciousnesses comprehend their appearing objects. If we were to take "object found (*rnyed don*) by a conventional valid cognizer" and "object comprehended (*gzhal bya, prameya*) by a conventional valid cognizer" as equivalents, then inherent existence would be an object found by a conventional valid cognizer because it appears to all conventional minds and all minds must comprehend what appears to them. In that case, "object found by a conventional valid cognizer" would include inherent existence and hence would be too broad to work as the definition of concealer-truth. Therefore, if "object of comprehension" and "object found" were equivalent, the qualifying clauses would be needed.

In fact, however, Jam-yang-shay-ba holds that in Prāsaṅgika, "object found" and "object comprehended" are not equivalents. He argues that whatever appears to a mistaken consciousness must be comprehended by it, but need not be found by it.[31] For example, there is an appearance of inherent existence to Foe Destroyers in states subsequent to meditative equipoise. Since inherent existence appears to them, it must be an object comprehended by them. However, since Foe Destroyers have eradicated all conceptions of inherent existence, they fully understand that the appearance of inherent existence is deceptive. Even though it appears to them, inherent existence does not exist from their perspective. Therefore, inherent existence is not an object found by the exalted wisdoms of states subsequent to meditative equipoise in the continuums of Foe Destroyers because in order for an object to be found by an awareness, it must exist for the perspective of that awareness.

Because they have no consciousnesses conceiving inherent existence, Foe Destroyers provide the clearest example of how object found and object of comprehension are not equivalents. However, even ordinary beings, who have not abandoned the conception of inherent existence, do not ascertain table as inherently existent every time they see a table. To a conventional valid cognizer of a table, table *appears* inherently existent, but what is realized or found is just table. Therefore, while the addition of qualifying clauses to the definitions of the two truths serves to prevent misinterpretation by those who do not understand the differences between the various types of objects in the Prāsaṅgika, accurate general definitions are possible without such clauses.

Regarding to the meaning of "object found," Jam-yang-shay-ba's *Great Exposition of the Middle Way* and *Great Exposition of Tenets* both state that objects implicitly realized by an awareness are not objects found by that awareness.[32] Jam-yang-shay-ba cites passages by Jñānagarbha, Candrakīrti, and Tsong-ka-pa to support his view that the term "object found" can only be applied when the aspect of that object appears to the consciousness that realizes it. An inferential valid cognizer realizing emptiness explicitly realizes emptiness—that is, it realizes emptiness via the appearance of the aspect of emptiness at that time. It implicitly realizes the existence of emptiness. If the term "object found" were mistakenly understood to include objects realized implicitly, while their aspects are not appearing, then the existence of emptiness would be an object found by a reasoning consciousness distinguishing the ultimate. Again, the addition of qualifying clauses to the short definitions prevents such a misinterpretation, but is not mandatory for someone who properly understands the meaning of the phrase "object found." Another way to avoid such misunderstanding of the short definitions is to add the word "explicit." For example, Jam-yang-shay-ba's short definition of concealer-truth refers to "an object explicitly found (*dngos kyi rnyed don*) by an awareness engaging in the terms or conventions of the world..."[33]

DEFINITIONS BASED ON ŚĀNTIDEVA

Śāntideva's *Engaging in the Bodhisattva Deeds* says:[34]

> Conventionalities and ultimates,
> These are asserted as the two truths.
> The ultimate is not the province of awareness.
> Awareness is asserted to be a conventionality.

Tsong-ka-pa explains that in this stanza from *Engaging in the Bodhisattva Deeds*, Śāntideva gives the meaning of a passage from the

Meeting of the Father and Son Sūtra cited in Śāntideva's *Compendium of Instructions:*[35]

> The Tathāgatas see conventionalities as the province of the world. That which is ultimate is inexpressible, is not an object of knowledge, is not an object of consciousness, is not an object of thorough knowledge, is indemonstrable...

The last two lines of Śāntideva's stanza serve, in the Ge-luk-ba view, to describe ultimate truths and concealer-truths in accordance with the teaching of this sūtra passage. Referring to these two lines, Gyel-tsap's *Explanation of (Śāntideva's) "Engaging in the Bodhisattva Deeds"* further illuminates Śāntideva's intention:[36]

> The first line teaches the definition of ultimate truth and the second line teaches the definition of concealer-truth. "Awareness," in both the former and latter cases, is dualistic awareness and not mere awareness. Also, [they define the two truths] in terms of how they are comprehended.... [The ultimate] does not appear dualistically to the direct valid awareness that explicitly realizes it [and] from this point of view, it is not within the province of that [dualistic awareness]; it is an object known by the direct valid cognizer that comprehends it.... [A concealer-truth] is that realized by way of appearing dualistically to the direct valid awareness that explicitly realizes it.[37]

Many Ge-luk-bas posit definitions of this type in their explanations of Svātantrika-Mādhyamika.[38] For example, Ngak-wang-bel-den writes:[39]

> The definition of ultimate truth is: a phenomenon realized by the direct valid cognizer realizing it by way of the vanishing of dualistic appearance. The definition of concealer-truth is: a phenomenon realized by the direct valid cognizer realizing it by way of an association with dualistic appearance.

While the definitions based on Candrakīrti (explained above) define the two truths in terms of ultimate and conventional valid cognizers (which both may be either conceptual or non-conceptual), these definitions differentiate the two truths specifically from the viewpoint of how they appear to non-conceptual valid cognizers.[40] They do not, of course, deny the existence of conceptual realization of emptiness; they merely define the two truths in terms of the manner in which they are known by direct perceivers.

Although they often occur in presentations of Svātantrika tenets, such definitions can also be asserted in Prāsaṅgika. For example, in his *Presentation of the Two Truths*, Gyel-tsap writes, "The definition of concealer-truth is: that realized from the viewpoint of its appearing dualistically to the valid cognizer that directly realizes it."[41] Also, Jam-yang-shay-ba's main definition of ultimate truth is "that which is realized by the awareness that directly realizes it by way of a vanishing of dualistic appearance."[42]

DUALISTIC APPEARANCE

The meaning of the term "dualistic appearance" (*gnyis snang*) varies widely according to context and author. Frequently, it refers to the appearance of subject and object as different. For example, Tsong-ka-pa's *Ocean of Reasoning* says:[43]

> The *Introduction to the Two Truths Sūtra* states:
>
> > Devaputra, the ultimate truth passes beyond being the object of [any consciousness] ranging right through an exalted wisdom that has the supreme of all aspects; it is not as it is expressed in the phrase 'ultimate truth'.
>
> This explains that [ultimate truth] is not seen by way of the diverse appearance of the two—subject and object—to an awareness when one says, "ultimate truth." Thus, this is a source [proving] the absence of dualistic appearance, and not a source [proving] that a Buddha does not realize the ultimate.

In the same vein, dualistic appearance may refer to the appearance of something as different from the consciousness perceiving it. Gyel-tsap's *Presentation of the Two Truths* says, "[A Buddha's exalted wisdom] realizes concealer-truths from the viewpoint of [their] appearing as different from it."[44] Again, in many contexts, "dualistic appearance" refers to any appearance of the conventional phenomena that are the bases of emptiness. For example, Tsong-ka-pa's *Illumination of the Thought* says:[45]

> *Objection:* Would a nature with such an aspect of the vanishing of dualistic appearance not be imperceptible?

> Therefore, how do Buddhas perceive it?
> *Answer:* It is true that since dualistic appearance has vanished, it is not perceived in a dualistic manner.... Nevertheless, [Candrakīrti] says that they perceive it in the manner of non-perception.... [Non-perception means that] the suchness of the aggregates and so forth must be perceived by way of not perceiving those [aggregates and so forth].

In other contexts, dualistic appearance can refer to the appearance of a conceptual generic image, or the appearance of inherent existence.[46] Jam-yang-shay-ba considers the appearance of something as having parts to be a type of dualistic appearance.[47] At other times, he uses "dualistic appearance" as the equivalent of "mistaken appearance."[48] Candrakīrti's *Supplement Commentary* lists a variety of dualistic elaborations from which the wisdom directly realizing emptiness is free:[49]

> Therefore, in suchness the qualities of things and non-things, one's own and others' things, truth and non-truth, everlasting and annihilated, permanent and impermanent, blissful and suffering, clean and unclean, self and selfless, empty and non-empty, definition and definiendum, sameness and otherness, production and cessation, and so forth do not occur.

If direct perception of ultimate reality transcends *all* types of dualistic distinctions, then how can we even say there is an object, emptiness, realized by an agent, wisdom? Ngak-wang-bel-den writes:[50]

> Although we can posit the exalted wisdom directly perceiving suchness as the ultimate consciousness and ultimate truth as the object known by that [wisdom], the perspective of that exalted wisdom is free from the two, object and agent. There is no contradiction because object and agent are posited only for the perspective of conventional awarenesses.

Any mind that knows its object by way of the vanishing of all types of dualistic appearance must be a wisdom directly realizing emptiness. Also, among sentient beings, any wisdom directly realizing emptiness must be free from all types of dualistic appearance.

On the Buddha ground, however, the exalted wisdom knowing the varieties of conventional phenomena realizes the varieties by way of an association with dualistic appearance, but is still a wisdom realizing emptiness because all Buddha's consciousnesses are omniscient. Gyel-tsap points out this exception in his *Presentation of the Two Truths*:[51]

> Although the exalted wisdom of a Buddha's meditative equipoise comprehends the mode [of being of phenomena, i.e., emptiness] by way of the vanishing of dualistic appearance, it comprehends the varieties in the manner of dualistic appearance. Hence, it is not the case that direct valid cognizers comprehending ultimate truth must have no dualistic appearance.

In chapter twelve, we will return to the special problems of explaining how a Buddha knows objects. Here, it is enough to note that this exception does not limit the comprehensiveness of definitions of the two truths that are derived from Śāntideva's *Engaging in the Bodhisattva Deeds*. For example, consider Ngak-wang-bel-den's Svātantrika definition of ultimate truth, "a phenomenon realized by the direct valid cognizer realizing it by way of a vanishing of dualistic appearance." Even a Buddha's omniscience knowing the varieties, while realizing concealer-truths through an association with dualistic appearance, realizes ultimate truths only by way of a vanishing of dualistic appearance.

CONCLUSION

As we saw in chapter two, the Ge-luk-bas begin their attempt to resolve what La Vallée Poussin called the "problem of the two truths" by holding that the basis of division is objects of knowledge. This is a major step away from the realm of paradox because it cuts off the idea that the two truths are contradictory perspectives on a single sphere of objects. Instead, as we saw in chapters three and four, the Ge-luk-bas present the two truths as two spheres of objects that remain mutually exclusive, even though they are always and everywhere locked together. The definitions of the two truths emphasize this view of the two truths as distinct spheres that are accessed and validated via separate epistemic pathways, pathways that never intersect in a single consciousness until Buddhahood. Neither truth damages the other since each is authenticated by its own type of valid cognition.

Of course Candrakīrti does not use the vocabulary of "valid cognition" in this way. It is brought over by Ge-luk-bas into Prāsaṅgika from the works of Dharmakīrti. Candrakīrti simply says:[52]

> [Conventionalities] gain their existence through the power of perceivers of falsities of common beings, all of whose eyes of awareness are covered by cataract-films of ignorance.

Tsong-ka-pa's *Illumination of the Thought* introduces the emphasis on *validity* when he explains that Candrakīrti means that a concealer-truth is an object "found by a conventional valid cognizer perceiving a false object of knowledge."[53] This definition preserves Candrakīrti's strong emphasis on the deceptiveness of the object, but balances it by asserting the existence of authoritative consciousnesses that cognize, and thus confirm, such objects. Still, Tsong-ka-pa makes it perfectly clear that, in order to realize that something is a concealer-truth, one must first see it as a falsity. The later Ge-luk-ba tradition agrees that all concealer-truths are falsities, but drops words like "falsity" and "deceptive" from its definitions, thus placing even heavier emphasis on the *validity* of concealer-truths as objects found by conventional valid cognizers.

7 *The Divisions of Concealer-Truths*

Candrakīrti approaches the subdivision of concealer-truths by first dividing the consciousnesses perceiving them. He states:[1]

> Also, those that perceive falsities are asserted to be of two types—
> Those with clear sense powers and those having defective sense powers.
> Consciousnesses of those having defective sense powers are asserted
> To be wrong in relation to those having good sense powers.

Candrakīrti then divides the objects of those two types of perceivers:[2]

> Objects realized by the world [and] apprehended
> By the six unimpaired sense powers
> Are true from just [the viewpoint of] the world. The rest
> Are posited as unreal from just [the viewpoint of] the world.

Thus, at first glance, it appears that for Candrakīrti the only criterion for dividing concealer-truths into right and wrong in relation to the world (in the case of consciousnesses) or real and unreal in relation to the world (in the case of their objects) is the absence or presence of sensory impairment in the apprehending awareness. Tsong-ka-pa explains that in this context, sensory impairment is brought about by a superficial (*'phral*) cause of mistakeness.[3] Superficial causes of mistakeness are circumstantial (*glo bur*), non-innate[4] factors which, when present, produce misperception by impairing the physical and/or mental sense powers. Among those that impair the physical sense powers, some exist within the continuum of the sentient being whose consciousness they are affecting. Such internal causes of mistakeness can cause misperception even in the absence of any external condition for error. Candrakīrti mentions eye disease, jaundice, and consumption of the fruit of the thorn-apple.[5] Eye disease can cause one to perceive "falling hairs," while jaundice and the consumption of thorn-apple are said to cause everything to appear yellow and gold respectively. Jam-yang-shay-ba adds spirit-possession and contagious disease to the list.[6]

There are also external factors that impair the physical sense powers even in the absence of any internal superficial cause of mistakeness. For example, a mirror held in front of a face produces a reflection that appears to be a face. Oil and water can also produce deceptive reflections. Shouting into a canyon produces an echo that sounds like another voice. Sunlight on pale sand when the weather is hot produces a mirage that appears to be water. Mantric spells and special substances used by magicians can cause sticks or rocks to appear as horses or elephants.

Mantric spells and substances are also included among causes of mistakeness that impair the *mental* sense power. Other examples are bad tenets, defective reasoning, and dreams. Following someone who teaches the Sāṃkhya system, for example, can cause one to mistakenly believe that there is a permanent, unitary, all-pervasive "nature" (*rang bzhin, prakṛti*) or "principal" (*gtso bo, pradhāna*) that is the agent of all actions.[7]

Generally, consciousnesses arising from sense powers impaired by such a superficial cause of mistakeness, together with their objects, are wrong or unreal in relation to the world, while consciousnesses not impaired by such, together with their objects, are right or real in relation to the world. Complications arise because there are some misconceptions that can arise under the influence of either deep (*phul*), innate conditions or temporary, superficial conditions. For example, the artificial (i.e., tenet-study induced) conception of the person as inherently existent is affected by superficial impairment because it arises under the influence of the circumstance of having been exposed to a defective philosophy. However, the innate conception of the person as inherently existent is a consciousness free from superficial impairment because it arises from a deep cause of mistakeness that has existed beginninglessly. Nevertheless, the conceived objects of these two conceptions are precisely the same. Similarly, the innate and artificial forms of the conception of the person as self-sufficient represent the very same wrong idea, differing only with regard to the presence or absence of a superficial cause of mistakeness. In such cases, how can we determine what is right or wrong in relation to the world?

Tsong-ka-pa supplies a criterion by explaining the meaning of the phrase "right (or real) in relation to the world":[8]

> The positing of a conventional object—apprehended by [any of] the six consciousnesses without such impairment—as real and the positing of an object that is the opposite as unreal is done in relation only to a worldly consciousness because those [respectively] are not subject to invalidation and are subject to invalidation by a worldly consciousness with respect to their existing in accordance with how they appear.

Tsong-ka-pa explains that if there is a consciousness not directed toward emptiness that can realize that something is unreal, then that thing is unreal in relation to the world, and the consciousness apprehending that thing is wrong in relation to the world.[9] If something can be realized as unreal only by consciousnesses directed toward suchness, and not by any others, then it is real in relation to the world, and the consciousness apprehending it is right in relation to the world. Therefore, the artificial conception of inherent existence, for example, is right in relation to the world despite the presence of a superficial cause of mistakeness; also, the innate conception of the person as self-sufficient is wrong in relation to the world despite the absence of a superficial cause of mistakeness.

Jam-yang-shay-ba argues that Candrakīrti must have accepted such exceptions because his *Commentary on (Nāgārjuna's) "Sixty Stanzas of Reasoning"* says, "Those that are wrong apprehend [the body] as blissful and so forth."[10] Jam-yang-shay-ba holds that the misconceptions of the body (exemplifying the first noble truth) as clean (*dag pa*), blissful (*bde ba*), permanent (*rtag pa*), and self (*bdag*) have both artificial and innate forms.[11] "Self" (*bdag*) here refers the opposite of the coarse selflessness, coarse selflessness being the person's emptiness of being self-sufficient and other phenomena's emptiness of being objects used by such a person.[12] By stating that those are "wrong" (*phyin ci log*), Candrakīrti indicates that some misconceptions, despite not being affected by a superficial cause of error, can be discredited without relying on a realization of emptiness.

THERE ARE NO REAL CONVENTIONALITIES

As the Prāsaṅgika and Svātantrika systems differ significantly in the way they present subdivisions of concealer-truths, a very brief look at the Svātantrika approach to this topic is in order. The *locus classicus* for the division of concealer truths in Svātantrika is a statement in Jñānagarbha's *Distinguishing the Two Truths*:[13]

> Since they are [respectively] able and unable
> To perform functions as they appear,
> A division of real and unreal
> Conventionalities is made.

Jang-gya derives Svātantrika definitions of the subdivisions from this passage.[14] He defines an unreal concealer-truth (*log pa'i kun rdzob bden pa, mithyāsaṃvṛtisatya*) as:

> a phenomenon that is an object found by a conventional valid cognizer [and] which is not able to perform a function in accordance with how it appears to the awareness perceiving it.

and his definition of real concealer-truth (*yang dag kun rdzob bden pa, tathyasaṃvṛtisatya*) is:

> a phenomenon that is an object found by a conventional valid cognizer [and] which is able to perform a function in accordance with its appearance to the awareness perceiving it.

For example, water and a face are real concealer-truths, while a mirage and a reflection of a face are unreal concealer-truths.[15]

In contrast, Prāsaṅgikas *do not divide concealer-truths into real and unreal* because *all* concealer-truths are unreal in that they are falsities. Every concealer-truth presents a deceptive appearance of inherent existence to the consciousness of the sentient being apprehending it. Likewise, all consciousnesses perceiving falsities are mistaken because their objects of apprehension appear to be inherently existent. Candrakīrti's *Supplement Commentary* says:[16]

> Therefore, without a condition of impairment to the senses as thus explained, conceptions of objects apprehended by the six sense powers are true for just the world, and not in relation to Superiors.

This might be construed to mean that Candrakīrti asserts the division into real and unreal only conventionally, but not ultimately—that is, not in the perspective of a mind realizing emptiness. Thus, Michael Sweet writes:[17]

> Even though the Prāsaṅgika-Mādhyamika distinguishes between a "true conventional" (*tathyasaṃvṛtiḥ*), defined as the ordinary perception of any object by an inimpaired [*sic*] sense organ, and a "false conventional" (*mithyāsaṃvṛtiḥ*) comprising illusions, mirages and the like, both aspects of conventional truth are regarded as "false from the standpoint of the ultimate."

Sweet holds that Prāsaṅgikas divide conventionalities into real and unreal conventionally, but not ultimately. Ge-luk-bas disagree, arguing that if this were so, then water, table, and so forth would be *real* in a conventional sense. Thus, they would have to exist conventionally in accordance with their appearance as inherently existent. This would contradict the Prāsaṅgika refutation of inherent existence even conventionally.

In order to explain what Candrakīrti means when he says that objects apprehended by the six unimpaired sense powers are "true for just the world, and not in relation to Superiors," Tsong-ka-pa's *Illumination of the Thought* comments, "Here 'superior' and 'Mādhyamika system' have similar meaning."[18] Tsong-ka-pa's *Intermediate Exposition of the Stages of the Path* suggests why these two are equivalent in this context:[19]

> [T]his [Prāsaṅgika-Mādhyamika] system explains that appearances of reflections, etc., and blue, etc., to those who possess ignorance do not differ with respect to whether they are mistaken in relation to their appearing object [because all have a mistaken appearance of inherent existence]. Therefore, [Prāsaṅgika-Mādhyamika] does not divide conventional objects into real and unreal.

Blue, face, pot, table, and so forth cannot be differentiated from reflections, mirages, and so forth in terms of whether they exist as they appear—because none of them do. Among sentient beings, consciousnesses apprehending conventionalities cannot be differentiated as mistaken and non-mistaken—because they are all mistaken. By glossing "in relation to Superiors" as "in our own Mādhyamika system," Tsong-ka-pa shows that Prāsaṅgika-Mādhyamikas do not assert a division of conventionalities into real and unreal *even conventionally* because they hold all conventional objects to be falsities and all perceivers of falsities to be mistaken. Somewhat atypically, Tsong-ka-pa's commentary on Candrakīrti here is not explicitly directed against a nihilistic extreme, but rather is aimed at guiding the reader away from an extreme of over-reification.

Accordingly, Tsong-ka-pa's *Intermediate Exposition* argues that the assertion of real conventionalities in Svātantrika is contingent upon (and thus indicative of) the Svātantrika assertion of inherent existence.[20] This point is echoed by Ngak-wang-bel-den.[21] If phenomena were inherently existent, then one *could* make the distinction that the eye consciousness apprehending a face is not mistaken, while the eye consciousness apprehending a reflection of a face is mistaken. Also, one could posit water as a real concealer-truth because it appears as water and functions as water, and posit a mirage as an unreal concealer-truth because it appears as water but does not function as water. Conversely, the non-assertion of the division of conventionalities into real and unreal in Prāsaṅgika derives from their refutation of inherent existence even conventionally.

Tsong-ka-pa's *Great Exposition of the Stages of the Path* asserts that in order for something to exist conventionally, it must be uncontradicted by both types of valid cognizers, conventional and ultimate.[22] When an ultimate valid cognizer fails to find an object either among that object's bases of designation or elsewhere, it realizes an emptiness that is the mere absence of inherent existence. Thus, without contradicting the mere existence of that object, it does contradict inherent existence. This explains why Tsong-ka-pa equates "our own Mādhyamika system" with the perspective of a Superior in the *Illumination of the Thought* and equates it with the perspective of a reasoning consciousness that accords with a Superior's perception in the *Intermediate Exposition of the Stages of the Path*.[23] Prāsaṅgikas do not assert anything ultimately because nothing can bear ultimate analysis. Therefore, all of the assertions and refutations of Prāsaṅgika are made conventionally. However, in order for something to exist even conventionally, it must be free from contradiction by ultimate valid cognition. It need not be found by an ultimate valid cognizer only emptiness is found by an ultimate valid cognizer. It need not bear analysis by an ultimate valid cognizer; nothing meets this test. Still, it must be free from contradiction or refutation by *all* valid sources of knowledge, including the mind realizing emptiness. The division of conventionalities into real and unreal does not meet this criterion because there are no conventionalities that are real in the sense of existing in accordance with their appearance as inherently existent.

REAL AND UNREAL IN RELATION TO THE WORLD

Inasmuch as a horse and a magician's illusion that appears to be a horse both deceptively appear to be inherently existent, Prāsaṅgikas do not distinguish one as truth and the other as falsity. They are both falsities. However, this does not mean that Prāsaṅgikas are utterly unable to distinguish horse and illusory horse. A horse is true, right, and real in relation to the perspective of the world, while an illusory horse is false, wrong, and unreal in relation to the perspective of the world. Prāsaṅgikas can make this distinction in relation to the world, without making it in terms of the special perspective of their own system. Ge-luk-bas (e.g., Ngak-wang-bel-den) often explain this by referring to a story from the *Buddhapālita Commentary*.[24] While inspecting the paintings on a temple wall, two villagers begin to argue. One identifies the image of a god holding a trident as Kṛṣṇa and that of a god holding a wheel as Īśvara. The other villager ("correctly") holds the opposite opinion, and they appeal to a wandering ascetic to resolve the dispute. To this sage, it was apparent that neither painting is a god. Nonetheless, he satisfies the villagers by answering the question in terms of their assumption, telling them who is right and who is wrong. Although the sage does not reply from the perspective of his personal understanding of the nature of the gods, he does not lie to the villagers because his answer is correct in relation to their shared worldly perspective.

Analogously, Prāsaṅgikas posit conventionalities as real and unreal in relation to the perspective of ordinary conventional valid cognizers—these being, of course, mistaken consciousnesses. The mistakeness of conventional valid cognizers pertains to the factor of inherent existence, and does not prevent them from authoritatively differentiating a horse from an illusory horse. In fact, the mistakeness of a conventional valid cognizer actually contributes to its capacity to make such distinctions because, among sentient beings, non-mistaken consciousnesses do not cognize concealer-truths at all.[25]

There are two different ways to describe how Prāsaṅgikas differentiate horse and illusory horse as true and false respectively. According to one approach, the deciding factor is whether a conventional valid cognizer can posit the existence of a phenomenon consistent with the way the object appears to the world. Tsong-ka-pa's *Great Exposition of the Stages of the Path* says:[26]

> Although sense consciousnesses are alike in being mistaken, from the viewpoint of the existence or non-existence of an object consistent with that appearance in the worldly perspective, sense consciousnesses that see reflections and so forth are wrong conventionalities and other, unimpaired sense consciousnesses are right conventionalities.

When a face is imputed to a nose, forehead, etc., there is a relationship between the bases of imputation and the object imputed. The functions of a face are performed by the collection of objects to which a face is imputed. Although a face deceptively appears to the world as an inherently existent face, and is therefore a falsity, it is "true" in the sense that an object *consistent* with that appearance, a mere face, does exist there. Therefore, Jam-yang-shay-ba explains that although nothing exists just as it appears to worldly consciousnesses, faces are "real" and reflections are unreal from the viewpoint of the presence or absence of an object consistent (*rjes su mthun pa*) with their appearance.[27] This does not prove that faces are real in general, but it shows what it means to say that they are real in relation to the worldly perspective.

There is no contradiction between this and the other explanation of the division of real and unreal in relation to worldly perspective. As mentioned above, if a conventional valid cognizer, uninfluenced by prior experience in ultimate analysis, can realize that something is unreal, then it is unreal in relation to the world; if no such conventional valid cognizer can realize it as unreal, then it is real in relation to the world. For a worldly consciousness to determine that a reflection of a face, for example, is unreal, it must recognize the absence of a face in the face-like appearance of the reflection.

In the context of the division of consciousnesses perceiving falsities into right and wrong in relation to the worldly perspective, realizing that a subject (i.e., a consciousness) is wrong means realizing that it is a wrong consciousness, a consciousness mistaken with regard to its main object of engagement. Jay-dzun-ba writes:[28]

> The definition of *a right subject in relation to the worldly perspective*[29] is: (1) a consciousness, and (2) that which a conventional valid cognizer in the continuum of a person who has not experienced realization of emptiness cannot realize as being a wrong consciousness.
>
> The definition of *a wrong subjective conventionality in relation to the worldly perspective* is: (1) a consciousness, and (2) that which a conventional valid cognizer in the continuum of a person who has not experienced realization of emptiness can realize as being a wrong consciousness.

For example, an ordinary conventional valid cognizer can determine that an eye consciousness apprehending a mirage as water is a wrong consciousness because that eye consciousness misapprehends its object of engagement, a mirage, as water. On the other hand, the eye consciousness apprehending water as water is correct with regard to its object of engagement. Therefore, it is not a wrong consciousness and cannot be cognized as such by any valid mind.

In the context of the division of concealer-truths—the objects of perceivers of falsities—into real and unreal in relation to the world, "unreal" refers to something that is deceptive and false in the sense of not existing as it appears. Jay-dzun-ba gives the following definitions:[30]

> The definition of *a real object in relation to the worldly perspective* is: (1) a conventionality that is an object, and (2) that which a conventional valid cognizer in the continuum of a person who has not experienced realization of emptiness cannot realize as not existing as it appears.
>
> The definition of *an unreal objective conventionality in relation to the worldly perspective* is: (1) a conventionality that is an object, and (2) that which a conventional valid cognizer in the continuum of a person who has not experienced realization of emptiness can realize as not existing as it appears.

No concealer-truths exist as they appear because all have the subtle deceptiveness of an appearance as inherently existent. Without relying on a previous realization of emptiness, conventional valid cognition cannot penetrate this deception. However, some objects, such as reflections, also have coarser types of deceptiveness. Although conventional valid cognizers that are not directed toward emptiness cannot realize the subtle falseness of a reflection's appearance as inherently existent, they can realize that a reflection of a face is deceptive insofar as it appears to be a face but is not.

TRUE/FALSE AND TRUTH/FALSITY

According to Jam-yang-shay-ba and Jay-dzun Chö-gyi-gyel-tsen, although Prāsaṅgikas do not distinguish horse and illusory horse as truth (*bden pa*) and falsity (*rdzun pa*)—since both are falsities—they do distinguish them as true (*bden*) and false (*brdzun*). In the context of their presentations of the two truths, the terms "truth" and "falsity" indicate whether something exists as it appears, while the terms "true" and "false" indicate whether something is real in relation to the world. Jam-yang-shay-ba and Jay-dzun-ba agree that to apprehend something as real or as a truth is to hold that it exists as it appears in all ways. There must be full concordance between its mode of subsistence and its mode of appearance.

Since all concealer-truths falsely appear to be inherently existent, none of them are real. While some concealer-truths, forms and so forth, are real in relation to the worldly perspective, it is not the case that they are so designated by way of the world's misapprehending them as real.[31] In fact, worldly ignorance misapprehends all concealer-truths as real. Rather, they are posited as real in relation to the world because the world—conventional valid cognition not directed toward suchness—is unable to realize them as unreal. There is a crucial difference between (1) seeing something as real and (2) being unable to realize that it is unreal. This point will be taken up again in the next chapter.

One might think that since real means "truth," unreal should mean falsity. However, this is not always the case. Jay-dzun-ba explains that a person who has not realized emptiness can realize that a reflection is unreal through seeing that it appears as a face but does not exist as a face.[32] However, he holds that in order to realize that something is a concealer-truth or falsity, one must first refute its inherent existence.[33] Similarly, Jam-yang-shay-ba and Ngak-wang-bel-den allow that one can realize an object as unreal without refuting its inherent existence.[34] Jam-yang-shay-ba and Jay-dzun-ba both work from the assumption that "real" means that something exists as it appears and "unreal" means it does not exist as it appears. Since concealer-truths appear to be inherently existent, the apprehension that they exist as they appear must involve a conception of inherent existence. However, in order to realize that a reflection is unreal, it is enough to realize that its appearance as a face is deceptive. Can an ordinary adult realize that a reflection of a face does not exist as it appears? Jay-dzun-ba and Jam-yang-shay-ba say, "Yes, because an adult can realize that a reflection does not exist as a face."[35]

PAṆ-CHEN SÖ-NAM-DRAK-BA

Paṇ-chen Sö-nam-drak-ba differs from Jay-dzun-ba and Jam-yang-shay-ba on several of these points. First, he refutes the distinction between "true" and "truth."[36] From the viewpoint of the other authors, this creates a serious problem for Paṇ-chen. For example, Buddha's teachings on cause and effect are falsities because they are concealer-truths. Were Buddha's teaching therefore false? Was Buddha a liar? Despite leading to such difficulties in debate, Paṇ-chen's approach has the virtue of eliminating what seems to be a highly artificial distinction. It is realistic and grammatically accurate to recognize that while the words "true" and "false" may have many different meanings according to context, within any given context "truth" is simply that which has the quality of being true and falsity is that which the quality of being false. As a substitute for the distinction between false and falsity, Kensur Padma-gyel-tsen writes of coarse falseness and subtle falseness.[37] A face has only the subtle falseness, but a reflection of a face has both.

This leads to our second point, the issue of what it means for something to exist as it appears or not exist as it appears. Svātantrikas, Cittamātras, and Sautrāntikas can realize that a generic image of a pot, while not a pot, appears to be a pot for the conceptual consciousness apprehending pot. Is this a realization that the generic image of pot does not exist as it appears? Paṇ-chen answers with an emphatic "No," but Jay-dzun-ba answers, "Yes, but this does not mean that a Sautrāntika can realize that a generic image of a pot is empty of inherent existence."[38] Unlike Jam-yang-shay-ba and Jay-dzun-ba, Paṇ-chen holds that in order to realize that a reflection does not exist as it appears, one must refute its inherent existence. It is not enough just to realize that the reflection of a face is not a face. One must realize that a reflection of a face does not inherently exist as a reflection of a face.[39]

Furthermore, Paṇ-chen asserts that there are *no* phenomena that exist as they appear.[40] He argues that all phenomena, including emptiness, have a discordance between the way they exist and the way they appear because there is a discordance between the way they exist and the way they appear to the *conceptual consciousnesses* apprehending them. For the ascertainment factor of a mind realizing the emptiness of a table inferentially, there is a realization of the non-inherent existence of the table. However, the emptiness of the table appears as though it were itself inherently existent. For Paṇ-chen's followers, this leaves the difficulty of explaining how emptiness can be called "truth" when it does not exist as it appears. In the face of this problem, the contemporary Lo-sel-ling scholar Kensur Yeshay Tupden asserts that even emptiness is a falsity. Others say that emptiness is a truth because it exists as it appears *to an awareness that realizes it in direct perception*.[41] Still, for Paṇ-chen's followers, emptiness (like all other phenomena) does not exist as appears (*snang ba ltar du ma grub*) because this would entail its being truly existent (*bden par grub pa*).

For Jam-yang-shay-ba and Jay-dzun-ba, when one asks whether emptiness exists as it appears, the awareness to which the phrase "exists as it appears" implicitly refers is a *direct valid cognizer*.[42] Emptiness is a truth because it exists as it appears. That is, there is a concordance between the way it exists and the way it appears to the valid cognizer directly realizing it. Of course, Jam-yang-shay-ba cannot assert that emptiness is truly existent because that would entail its being inherently existent. If emptiness is a truth, and exists as it appears, and has a concordance between its mode of subsistence and its mode of appearance, then what does it mean to say that it does not truly exist? Just as Paṇ-chen's followers have to add a qualifying clause to their explanation of "truth," Jam-yang-shay-ba's followers need a qualifier in their explanation of true existence. For example, one scholar has suggested that if something were to truly exist, it would have to exist as it appears to common beings.[43] Alternatively, in order to account for the appearance of true existence to Superiors, one could say that true existence means that something exists as it appears to a mistaken consciousness. Or, to be perfectly clear, one might hold that true existence means existence in accordance with an appearance as inherently existent.[44] It is also explained that true existence can mean something's existing as its own mode of subsistence.

WHAT ARE UNREAL CONVENTIONALITIES?

Tsong-ka-pa's *Illumination of the Thought* says:[45]

> *Question:* Since you do not assert real conventionalities, there is no division [of conventionalities] into real and unreal; but why do you not posit objects and subjects polluted by ignorance as unreal conventionalities (log pa'i *kun rdzob*)?
> *Answer:* Conventionalities must be posited by conventional valid cognizers; therefore, even when on posited unreal conventionalities, they would have to be posited in relation to those [conventional valid cognizers], whereas [objects and subjects] polluted by the predispositions of ignorance are not established as mistaken by conventional valid cognizers.

While the gist of Tsong-ka-pa's passage seems to be that unreal conventionalities do not exist, later Ge-luk-ba interpretations unanimously assert the contrary. The problem is this: If "unreal" in the phrase "unreal conventionality" as used in that passage means falsity in the general sense, then unreal conventionalities exist because *all* conventionalities are unreal conventionalities and can be recognized as such by conventional valid cognizers that arise subsequent to realization of emptiness. This seems to contradict Tsong-ka-pa. On the other hand, "unreal" in that passage could mean "unreal in relation to the worldly perspective." In that case, unreal conventionalities certainly exist since a worldly conventional valid cognizer not directed toward emptiness can realize that a mirage, for example, appears as water but does not exist as water.

Jam-yang-shay-ba advocates the former position. According to him, all conventionalities are unreal conventionalities[46] and all concealer-truths are unreal concealer-truths[47] because there are special conventional valid cognizers—subsequent to and influenced by realizations of emptiness—that realize that forms and so forth falsely appear to be inherently existent. Form and so forth are real in relation to the "worldly perspective" explicitly indicated in Candrakīrti's stanza[48] by the words "true from just [the viewpoint] of the world" because an ordinary conventional valid cognizer, not directed toward suchness, cannot realize that they are unreal. However, they are unreal in general because they are falsities. Furthermore, leaving aside the specific context of Candrakīrti's stanza, they are unreal in relation to the worldly perspective because certain conventional valid cognizers, relying upon previous realizations emptiness, can realize that they are wrong, unreal, falsities.

In Jam-yang-shay-ba's interpretation, Tsong-ka-pa's phrase "objects and subjects polluted by ignorance" refers specifically to the conceptions of an inherently existent self of persons and other phenomena and the conceived objects of such ignorant consciousnesses. Tsong-ka-pa does not mean that these are not unreal conventionalities in general, he means that they are not conventionalities that are unreal in relation to the perspective of the "world" *explicitly indicated in the context of Candrakīrti's stanza*. That is, they cannot be invalidated by ordinary conventional valid cognizers not directed toward emptiness.

Jay-dzun-ba and Paṇ-chen offer the alternative interpretation. They argue that unreal conventionalities exist, but that not all conventionalities are unreal conventionalities. Unreal conventionalities include mirages, illusory horses, and so forth, but exclude water, horses, and so forth. An object is an unreal conventionality only if a conventional valid cognizer in the continuum of a person who has not realized emptiness can realize that it does not exist as it appears. Tsong-ka-pa's statement means that objects and subjects polluted by ignorance, such as an inherently existent self, cannot be posited as unreal conventionalities because conventional valid cognizers in the continuums of those who have not realized emptiness cannot realize them as unreal.

Jam-yang-shay-ba and Jay-dzun-ba agree that "objects and subjects polluted by ignorance," in this context, refers *only* to ignorant consciousnesses and their conceived objects. In a broader sense, pollution by ignorance might be understood to refer to the presence of an appearance of inherent existence. In this broader sense, an eye consciousness of an ordinary sentient being apprehending a face and an eye consciousness misapprehending a reflection as a face are both "polluted by ignorance" in that, through the force of ignorance and its predispositions, their objects *appear* to be inherently existent. In fact, Tsong-ka-pa defines "pollution by ignorance" in this broader sense in another context.[49] Jam-yang-shay-ba and Jay-dzun-ba cannot allow "having an appearance of inherent existence" to be the meaning of "pollution by ignorance" in *this* context because here Tsong-ka-pa states that objects and subjects polluted by ignorance cannot be realized as mistaken via ordinary conventional valid cognition, yet an ordinary conventional valid cognizer can realize that a reflection (an object "polluted by ignorance" insofar as it appears to be inherently existent) is not a face. Therefore, ordinary conventional valid cognition *can* realize the coarse mistakeness of something that also has an appearance of inherent existence. For Jam-yang-shay-ba and Jay-dzun-ba, the realization of such "polluted objects and subjects" as unreal (or wrong) would not, of course, entail a refutation of the inherent existence that appears to a mind apprehending a reflection; it would only involve realizing that a reflection is not a face. Nonetheless, such an interpretation of "pollution by ignorance" in this context would lead to a contradiction of Tsong-ka-pa's statement that objects and subjects polluted by ignorance cannot be realized as mistaken by ordinary conventional valid cognizers.

DEFINITIONS

Jay-dzun-ba gives the following definitions:[50]

> The definition of *a right subject in relation to the worldly perspective* is: (1) a consciousness, and (2) that which a conventional valid cognizer in the continuum of a person who has not experienced realization of emptiness cannot realize as being a wrong consciousness.
>
> The definition of *a wrong subjective conventionality in relation to the worldly perspective* is: (1) a consciousness, and (2) that which a conventional valid cognizer in the continuum of a person who has not experienced realization of emptiness can realize as being a wrong consciousness.
>
> The definition of *a real object in relation to the worldly perspective* is: (1) a conventionality that is an object, and (2) that which a conventional valid cognizer in the continuum of a person who has not experienced realization of emptiness cannot realize as not existing as it appears.
>
> The definition of *an unreal objective conventionality in relation to the worldly perspective* is: (1) a conventionality that is an object, and (2) that which a conventional valid cognizer in the continuum of a person who has not experienced

> realization of emptiness can realize as not existing as it appears.

Note that Jay-dzun-ba is careful to exclude the word "conventionality" from the definitions and definienda that are right or real in relation to the worldly perspective. We will discuss the reason for this below. Also, note that Jay-dzun-ba uses the phrase "not existing as it appears" in the last two definitions; for Paṇ-chen, it is impossible for someone who has not realized emptiness to realize that something does not exist as it appears.

Ngak-wang-bel-den supplies the following definitions:[51]

> The definition of a *conventionality that is real in relation to the worldly perspective* is: that classified as a conventionality that a conventional consciousness alone, without relying on a reasoning consciousness distinguishing the ultimate, cannot posit as either an object or a subject that is unreal.
>
> The definition of a *conventionality that is unreal in relation to the worldly perspective* is: that classified as a conventionality that a conventional consciousness alone, without relying on a reasoning consciousness distinguishing the ultimate, can posit as either an object or a subject that is unreal.

The inclusion of the word "conventionality" in both definienda is in line with Ngak-wang-bel-den's argument (below) that this phraseology is acceptable. Once the word conventionality is included in the definienda, it must be added to the definitions as well because the definition must convey the full meaning of the definiendum.[52]

REAL IN RELATION TO THE WORLD

As we have seen, Candrakīrti approaches the division of concealer-truths indirectly, first dividing consciousnesses apprehending falsities and then setting up a corresponding division of their objects. Candrakīrti says, "Objects of perceivers of falsities are concealer-truths."[53] Thus, when he later divides objects of perceivers of falsities into real and unreal in relation to the world, this must be construed as a division of concealer-truths. However, it is not a "precise enumeration." Whatever is a concealer-truth must be either real or unreal in relation to the world because a conventional valid cognizer not directed toward suchness must either have or not have the ability to realize it as unreal. However, whatever is real or unreal in relation to world is not necessarily a concealer-truth. After dividing concealer-truths in relation to the world, Candrakīrti's next stanza explains:[54]

> Entities as they are imputed by the Forders
> Strongly affected by the sleep of ignorance
> And those imputed to illusions, mirages, and so forth
> Are just non-existent even for the world.

The three *guṇas*, "principal" (*gtso bo, pradhāna*) and so forth do not exist at all. Likewise, a mirage that is water or an illusory horse that is a horse do not exist. These are all unreal in relation to the world because a conventional valid cognizer can contradict them without relying on a preceding realization of emptiness. However, they do not exist at all and therefore they are not concealer-truths. Also, an inherently existent self is an example of something that is real in relation to the world, but is not a concealer-truth. Even emptiness could be considered real in relation to the worldly perspective in the sense that a conventional valid cognizer not directed toward suchness cannot realize it as unreal. Jam-yang-shay-ba excludes emptiness by including the phrase "it appears to a worldly consciousness" in his definition of real in relation to the worldly perspective.[55] Other authors divide concealer-truths into conventionalities that are real in relation to the worldly perspective and conventionalities that are unreal in relation to the worldly perspective. The addition of the word "conventionality" automatically eliminates emptiness and non-existents, but raises another controversy which will be discussed below.

Jam-yang-shay-ba argues that just as real objects in relation to the world ('jig rten shes ngo la ltos te yul yang dag) and unreal objects in relation to the world (*'jig rten shes ngo la ltos te yul log pa*) need not be concealer-truths, so it is with the apprehending subjects. His example is "an eye consciousness that is incontrovertible with regard to the inherent existence of form." He holds that although such an eye consciousness does not exist, it is nevertheless a right subject in relation to the worldly perspective because a conventional valid cognizer not directed toward suchness can neither (1) realize that it does not exist as it appears, nor (2) realize that it is not a subject. That is, although such an eye consciousness is not a consciousness at all, it is a consciousness in relation to the worldly perspective. The justification for this claim that a right subject in relation to the worldly perspective does not have to be a consciousness in general is the word-order of the Tibetan which, like the word-order of the English translation, places the word "subject" (*yul can*) between the word "right" (*yang dag*) and the qualifying phrase "in relation to the worldly perspective." It would be unusual for the qualifier to affect only the word "right" without also modifying the intervening word "subject."

In contrast, Jay-dzun-ba gives definitions that require something actually *to be* a consciousness (and, therefore, an existent) in order to be a conventionality that is a right or wrong subject in relation to the worldly perspective. The best argument in favor of this interpretation is that Candrakīrti's intention appears to have been to divide the consciousnesses perceiving concealer-truths into two categories. Candrakīrti's *Supplement* states:[56]

> Also, those that perceive falsities are asserted to be of two types—
> Those with clear sense powers and those having defective sense powers.
> Consciousnesses of those having defective sense powers are asserted
> To be wrong in relation to those having good sense powers.

There is nothing here or in Candrakīrti's *Supplement Commentary* or in Tsong-ka-pa's *Illumination of the Thought* to suggest that the basis of division is anything other than existent consciousnesses that apprehend concealer-truths. However, Jam-yang-shay-ba can argue that this does not prove that the categories emerging from the division necessarily include only existents.

REAL CONVENTIONALITIES IN RELATION TO THE WORLDLY PERSPECTIVE

In order to construct the division of concealer-truths as a precise enumeration, excluding non-existents and ultimate truths, some authors add the word "conventionality" to each subdivision. This leads to disagreement over the phrase *'jig rten shes ngo la ltos te yang dag kun rdzob*. Depending upon which textbook one follows, this means either "conventionality that is real in relation to the worldly perspective" or "real conventionality in relation to the worldly perspective." The question is one of grammar: Does the word "conventionality" come under the modifying force of the phrase "in relation to the worldly perspective" in that Tibetan phrase?

Jay-dzun-ba and Paṇ-chen refute, while Jang-gya and Ngak-wang-bel-den assert, the existence of conventionalities that are real in relation to the worldly perspective.[57] In brief, the argument against their existence is that a conventionality does not exist as it appears, while something that is "real" does exist as it appears. Therefore, it is impossible for anything to be both a conventionality in relation to the worldly perspective and real in relation to the worldly perspective. Jang-gya agrees with this last statement; however, he holds that "conventionality that is real in relation to the worldly perspective" refers to something that is (1) real in relation to the worldly perspective, and (2) a conventionality *in general.* This is clearly a case in which the scholars agree on the meaning, but disagree on the words. Tsong-ka-pa's *Intermediate Exposition of the Stages of the Path* says:[58]

> [Prāsaṅgikas] posit *real and unreal conventionalities in relation to just the world* or conventional valid cognizers, not in relation to a reasoning consciousness that accords with a Superior's perception.

This has been understood to imply that Tsong-ka-pa accepts that there are real conventionalities in relation to the worldly perspective. Also, Tsong-ka-pa again uses that term in his *Great Exposition of the Stages of the Path.* Arguing for the acceptability of the term "conventionalities that are real in relation to the worldly perspective," Jang-gya refers to these passages:[59]

> Generally in the Prāsaṅgika system, merely positing a pot as a conventionality that is real in the worldly perspective does not have to lead to [its being] both real in the worldly perspective and a conventionality in the worldly perspective. Therefore, those terms [conventionality that is real in relation to the worldly perspective and conventionality that is unreal in relation to the worldly perspective] are permitted because even Tsong-ka-pa's *Great Exposition of the Path* and *Intermediate Exposition of the Path* use each of them. Hence, many convoluted explanations are unnecessary.

Paṇ-chen, though aware that Tsong-ka-pa uses those terms, still maintains that real conventionalities in relation to the worldly perspective do not exist "because it is permissible to comment (*bkral*) that the words of [Tsong-ka-pa's] *Stages of the Path* require interpretation in this context."[60] It is remarkable that Paṇ-chen would use the phrase "requiring interpretation" in reference to a passage by Tsong-ka-pa. In the face of what appears to be the strong evidence of Tsong-ka-pa's words, Paṇ-chen relies on his own reading of the grammar and insists that the term "real conventionalities in relation to the world" is unacceptable. The twentieth-century Lo-sel-ling scholar, Ken-sur Padma-gyel-tsen gives his view of the controversy:[61]

> Since our own textbook states that those words are involved (*'brel*)[62] in a need for interpretation, I think that this means that [consciousnesses unaffected by superficial causes of error and the objects of such consciousnesses] are (1) right [or real] in relation to the worldly perspective, and (2) conventionalities in general. As explained before, this does not mean that real conventionalities are posited; nor does it mean that real conventionalities are posited even in relation to the worldly perspective.

Kensur Padma-gyel-tsen holds that when Tsong-ka-pa refers to real and unreal conventionalities in a worldly perspective, he *intends* that the referent of the qualifying phrase is only the words "real" and "unreal', and not real conventionalities and unreal conventionalities. This is something that everyone can accept. The issue of whether this is grammatically tenable remains in dispute, and Paṇ-chen Sö-nam-drak-ba is convinced that it is not.

Paṇ-chen Sö-nam-drak-ba is content to say that this passage is interpretable (*drang don, neyārtha*). He uses this term not in the strict Prāsaṅgika sense, according to which scriptures teaching emptiness are definitive (*nges don, nītārtha*), while all others are interpretable. Rather, in accordance with its usage in Cittamātra, he employs the term "interpretable" to indicate that a passage cannot be accepted literally. In Cittamātra, strictly speaking, the terms "definitive" and "interpretable" should apply to the teachings of sūtras. In order to class a sūtra as requiring interpretation, it is necessary to explain not only why it cannot be accepted literally, but what Buddha really meant to teach. For example, the sūtra passage that states "father and mother are to be killed," means that existence (*srid pa, bhava*) and attachment (*sred pa, tṛṣṇā*), the tenth and eighth of the twelve links of dependent arising, must be eradicated. Thus, by using the term "interpretable" when he disagrees with Tsong-ka-pa, Paṇ-chen Sö-nam-drak-ba implies that, like sūtras, Tsong-ka-pa's word is accurate when properly understood. However, unlike later Ge-luk-bas such as Kensur Padma-gyel-tsen, Paṇ-chen Sö-nam-drak-ba does not struggle to explain the "true" underlying meaning of this passage. Instead, he seems intent upon refuting its literal meaning. For some readers, this creates the impression that he is using "interpretable" as a euphemism for "wrong."[63]

There is a passage in Kay-drup's *Thousand Doses* that seems to support Paṇ-chen's view:[64]

> Therefore, it is said that there is a twofold division into real and unreal in the worldly perspective. However, the glorious Candrakīrti nowhere says that there is a division into the two, real conventionalities in the worldly perspective and unreal conventionalities in the worldly perspective. My own lama [Tsong-ka-pa] also did not explain that, and it is not at all suitable to assert such because pot, pillar, and so forth are not conventionalities in the perspective of an ordinary worldly awareness and because it would be extremely absurd to posit something as a falsity in relation to the awareness in whose perspective it is posited as true.

I believe that his statement also influenced Jam-yang-shay-ba's position, but in a very different way. When stating the division of conventionalities into those that are real in relation to the world and those that are unreal in relation to the world, Jam-yang-shay-ba, like Jang-gya, exempts the term "conventionality" from the qualifying force of the phrase "in relation to the worldly perspective." For example, he writes:[65]

> It follows that a reflection in a mirror is a conventionality that is unreal in relation to the worldly perspective because (1) it is unreal in relation to the worldly perspective and (2) it is a conventionality.

However, Jam-yang-shay-ba does not follow through on this logic by using the term "conventionality that is real in relation to the perspective of the world" (*'jig rten shes ngo la ltos te yang dag kun rdzob*). He cites Kay-drup and relates some of the pertinent debate, but never actually refutes or approves that phrase.[66] It appears that Jam-yang-shay-ba, "in order to be in agreement with [Kay-drup's] *Thousand Doses*," avoids explicitly asserting his apparent opinion that, just as reflections, mirages, etc. are conventionalities that are unreal in relation to the worldly perspective, so faces, water, etc. are conventionalities that are real in relation to the worldly perspective.[67]

Thus, the contrast between Paṇ-chen and Jam-yang-shay-ba on this topic is not merely a matter of a grammatical disagreement; there is also a marked contrast in how they handle the conflicting evidence in the writings Tsong-ka-pa and Kay-drup. Paṇ-chen works by the light of his own sense that a reasonable reading of the grammar should make the phrase in question unacceptable, and he sticks to that view even in the face of an apparent contradiction with Tsong-ka-pa's own words. Moreover, he never troubles himself to quote or even to refer to the passage by Kay-drup that supports his view. In marked contrast, Jam-yang-shay-ba follows his very different sense of what is reasonable to the brink of open contradiction with Kay-drup—and then stops short. On what amounts to a point of grammar, without a philosophical imperative, Jam-yang-shay-ba balks at writing anything derogatory to the authority of one of Tsong-ka-pa's spiritual sons.

Ngak-wang-bel-den advances the sharpest argument in favor of dividing conventionalities into conventionalities that are real in relation to the worldly perspective and conventionalities that are unreal in relation to the worldly perspective.[68] He points out that Kay-drup's critique of that construction uses the phrase "in the worldly perspective" (*'jig rten pa'i shes ngo na*) rather that the phrase "in relation to the worldly perspective" (*'jig rten shes ngo la ltos te*). I will explain the importance of this distinction in detail in the next chapter; here, it is enough to note that by introducing this distinction, Ngak-wang-bel-den is able to divide conventionalities into (1) conventionalities that are *real in relation to* the worldly perspective, and (2) conventionalities that are *unreal in relation to* the worldly perspective—*without* contradicting Kay-drup's refutation of real and unreal conventionalities *in* the worldly perspective. Ngak-wang-bel-den assumes that Kay-drup must have seen Tsong-ka-pa's *Great Exposition of the Stages of the Path* and *Intermediate Exposition of the Stages of the Path*. Since Tsong-ka-pa asserts real and unreal conventionalities in relation to the worldly perspective in those works, how could Kay-drup claim that his lama did not speak of such? Therefore, Ngak-wang-bel-den claims, Kay-drup's refutation of real and unreal conventionalities *in* the worldly perspective should not be construed to include a refutation of real and unreal conventionalities *in relation to* the worldly perspective.

CONCEALER-TRUTHS IN RELATION TO THE WORLD

As we have seen, the phrase "in relation to the worldly perspective" has the the power to radically alter the meaning, and therefore the acceptability, of various phrases. This is also true in the case of the term "concealer-truth'. Candrakīrti's *Supplement Commentary* says:[69]

> A few dependent-arisings such as reflections, echoes, and so forth, appear to be false even to those who have ignorance...[T]hat which is false even conventionally is not a concealer-truth.

Does this mean that the reflection of a face in a mirror is not a concealer-truth? Tsong-ka-pa's *Intermediate Exposition of the Stages of the Path* says:[70]

> Since a reflection of a face, for instance, is not true as a face for a worldly conventional [consciousness] of someone trained in language, it is not a concealer-truth in relation to [that consciousness]. Nonetheless, because it is an object found by a perceiver of a false object of knowledge—a deceptive object—it is a concealer-truth.

Also, Tsong-ka-pa's *Illumination of the Thought* says:[71]

> Therefore, Candrakīrti's statement that a reflection is not a concealer-truth is made within the consideration that, with respect to a reflection of a face, for instance, its being a face is false for a conventional [consciousness] of a worldly [person] trained in language and hence it is not a concealer-truth in relation to that [consciousness]. How could it be that [a reflection] is not posited as a concealer-truth as described [by Candrakīrti] in [the line from his *Supplement*], "objects of perceivers of falsities are concealer-truths"?

Since objects of knowledge are precisely enumerated as concealer-truths and ultimate truths, it follows that reflections, mirages, echoes, and so forth must all be concealer-truths. Therefore, when Candrakīrti indicates that they are not concealer-truths, he must mean that they are not concealer-truths *in relation to the world*. According to Tsong-ka-pa, the concealing consciousness in the phrase "concealer-truth in relation to the world" is not a consciousness conceiving true existence. Rather, it is a consciousness conceiving that a reflection of a face is a face, or a conception that a mirage is water, or some other, similar, and relatively coarse, misconception.

Tsong-ka-pa argues that Candrakīrti cannot be interpreted in any other way. He writes:[72]

> Otherwise, if it were contradictory for something to be a concealer-truth if it does not exist as a truth conventionally, this would contradict [Candrakīrti's] statements that establishment [of an object] by way of its own character does not exist even conventionally as well as all the presentations that all refutations of true establishment and proofs of no true existence are done conventionally.

This refers directly to Candrakīrti's statement, "That which is false even conventionally is not a concealer-truth." If something had to be a truth conventionally in order to to be a concealer truth, then the true existence of concealer-truths could not be refuted conventionally. Or, to rephrase the problem, if something had to be a truth conventionally in order to be a concealer-truth, then the only concealer-truths would be emptinesses.[73]

CONCLUSION

Because Prāsaṅgikas refute real conventionalities, they do not divide conventionalities into real and unreal. All conventionalities are unreal. Some critics have concluded that Prāsaṅgikas cannot distinguish between conventionalities and non-existents. Murti for example, writes that the Mādhyamika "does not draw any distinction between the false (illusory) and the utterly unreal (*asat*) such as hare's horn."[74] In the Ge-luk-ba interpretation of Prāsaṅgika, there is a difference between non-existents and conventionalities, even though both are deceptive and unreal (*log pa*). A horse and a magician's illusion that appears as a horse are both utterly unreal (*log pa*) because both are misconceived and misperceived as inherently existent, while in fact they are *equally* devoid of the slightest trace of inherent existence. Just as one finds no horse in the illusion, when one searches for a horse among the bases of designation of horse, asking, "Are the legs the horse? Is the tail the horse?" and so forth, one will not find a horse. Therefore, the horse is *like* an illusion, in that it appears one way and exists another. Still, this does not prevent the Ge-luk-ba Prāsaṅgika from noting that a horse can be ridden into town, while an illusion cannot. The Ge-luk-ba Prāsaṅgika also notes that it takes no great wisdom to understand the deceptiveness of the illusion's false appearance as a horse, while it does take great wisdom to understand the deceptiveness of a horse's appearance as inherently existent.

Candrakīrti calls the distinction between horse and illusion of horse a distinction between what is real for the world and what is unreal for the world. He does not precisely identify "the world" in this context, and he certainly does not say that what is real for the world is validly established (*tshad mas grub pa*). On the other hand, his description of the Bodhisattva's activities in his *Supplement* presumes that actions do have moral effects, and that some actions, and not others, lead to liberation. If emptiness precluded the validity of the distinction between an illusion or a dream on the one hand, and an illusion-like conventionality on the other hand, then would not a dream of committing murder effectively condemn one to hell? And would not someone who dreamed of becoming a Buddha actually be a Buddha? Thus, we return to the fundamental problem, described in chapter one: where to ground ethical distinctions in a world of emptiness.

The thrust of the Ge-luk-ba interpretation is to demonstrate that emptiness, when properly understood as the absence of inherent existence, does not undermine or subvert the distinction between a complete illusion and an illusion-like conventional fact. Moreover, the Ge-luk-bas insist that the solution to this "problem of the two truths" is found not only in the yogi's trans-conceptual experience, but also in logic; in fact, yogis must use reasoning to find their way into trans-conceptual experience of ultimate reality. By rejecting a division of concealer-truths into real and unreal even conventionally, the Ge-luk-bas preserve the Prāsaṅgika position that no concealer-truth can be *real* (i.e., existing just as it appears) even in a conventional sense. At the same time, by claiming that Candrakīrti's distinction between real and unreal in relation to the the world involves a test of how things are understood by a type of *valid cognizer*, the Ge-luk-bas attempt to preserve a philosophical foundation for ethics and the path.

8 *The Worldly Perspective*

CANDRAKĪRTI AND TSONG-KA-PA

As we have seen, Candrakīrti divides concealer-truths into (1) real from the viewpoint of the world, and (2) unreal from the viewpoint of the world:[1]

> Objects realized by the world [and] apprehended
> By the six unimpaired sense powers
> Are true from just [the viewpoint of] the world. The rest
> Are posited as unreal from just [the viewpoint of] the world.

Candrakīrti's *Supplement Commentary* says:[2]

> Therefore, without a condition of impairment to the senses as thus explained, conceptions of objects apprehended by the six sense powers are true for just the world, and not in relation to Superiors.

Tsong-ka-pa's *Illumination of the Thought* explains:[3]

> The positing of a conventional object—apprehended by [any of] the six consciousnesses without such impairment—as real, and the positing of an object that is the opposite as unreal is done in relation only to a worldly consciousness because those [respectively] are not subject to invalidation and are subject to invalidation by a worldly

consciousness with respect to their existing in accordance with how they appear.

How do we identify the worldly perspective or worldly consciousness in relation to which concealer-truths are posited as real or unreal and in relation to which consciousnesses apprehending concealer-truths are posited as right or wrong in this context?[4] Most Ge-luk-bas today agree that it must be a conventional valid cognizer not directed toward suchness. This identification is made on the basis of passages such as these from Tsong-ka-pa's *Illumination of the Thought:*[5]

> The rest—that is to say, reflections and so forth—which appear as objects when the sense powers are impaired are posited as being unreal in relation to just the world. The word "just" indicates that without relying on a reasoning consciousness, just a conventional valid cognizer is sufficient to posit those consciousnesses as mistaken.

> Principal and so forth are wrongly imputed by those whose minds have been affected by tenets. Although those are not realized to be erroneous (*phyin ci log pa*) by an ordinary worldly awareness, they are realized to be so by conventional valid cognition that is not directed toward suchness (*de kho na nyid la mngon du ma phyogs pa'i*), in which case they are realized to be wrong by a worldly consciousness.

That is, while ordinary persons can realize that a reflection is not a face, they may be unsure about the "principal" (*gtso bo, pradhāna*) described by the Sāṃkhya system. Nonetheless, Tsong-ka-pa considers principal and so forth to be unreal in relation to the world because there are some conventional valid cognizers that can discredit such superimpositions without being "directed toward suchness." One need not rely upon prior meditation on emptiness in order to refute them. Most Ge-luk-bas have built their interpretations on these passages. For example, Jang-gya writes:[6]

> Accordingly, since it appears that it is the thought of the Foremost [Tsong-ka-pa] to posit as "unreal in the perspective of the world" those objects and subjects that a conventional valid cognizer not directed toward emptiness can realize as unreal and to posit as "real in the perspective

> of the world'' those objects and subjects that [a conventional valid cognizer not directed toward emptiness] cannot realize as unreal, it is clear that the consciousness to which "worldly perspective'' refers must be a single [type of] consciousness that is not directed toward suchness.

The situation has not always been so clear.

KAY-DRUP AND JAM-YANG-SHAY-BA

Confusion and controversy on this point arose from the writings of Kay-drup. Since Kay-drup is revered as one of Tsong-ka-pa's most important disciples, it was inevitable that later generations would have to reckon with his interpretation. How Paṇ-chen, Jam-yang-shay-ba, and other Ge-luk-ba scholars handle the following passage is not only fascinating as a doctrinal issue, but also reveals a great deal about the differences among their interpretive approaches. Kay-drup's *Thousand Doses* says:[7]

> That there is a division into real and unreal in the worldly perspective means that an ordinary, innate, worldly awareness makes a division into real and unreal. It is not at all the case that worldly conventional valid cognizers make a division into real and unreal because it is irrational to propound, "While asserting this as an object established by valid cognition, I do not assert it in my own system.'' This is also because the worldly awareness in the perspective—that is, mode of apprehension—of which form and so forth are established as real is a consciousness conceiving true existence (*bden 'dzin*); thus, it is not suitable to be a conventional valid cognizer.

Kay-drup's procedure is to ask, "What worldly consciousnesses divide objects into real and unreal?'' They cannot be valid cognizers for two reasons. First, if a valid cognizer, which is an authoritative source of knowledge, established such a division into real and unreal, then it would be absurd for Prāsaṅgikas not to assert it. What possible basis could there be for refusing to assert real conventionalities if they were validly established? Second, if valid cognizers made a division into real and unreal, they would apprehend some conventional phenomena as real, as truths, as things that exist as they appear. However, since forms and so forth appear to be inherently existent, the apprehension of them as existing as they appear is a consciousness conceiving true existence. This is a wrong consciousness, not a valid cognizer.

Jam-yang-shay-ba was greatly influenced by this passage. He relates that some scholars understand Kay-drup to mean that both real and unreal are posited by a single, non-valid, ordinary worldly consciousness.[8] Disagreeing, Jam-yang-shay-ba cites Tsong-ka-pa, just as we have above, to show that the worldly perspective in which things are posited as *unreal* must be a conventional valid cognizer that is not directed toward suchness.[9] However, he insists that Kay-drup is correct to exclude valid cognizers from the worldly perspective in which things are real. Jam-yang-shay-ba's interpretation is presented in a chart on the next page.[10]

Among conventional consciousnesses—the apprehenders of concealer-truths—there are valid and non-valid consciousnesses. Non-valid consciousnesses include consciousnesses conceiving true existence, other wrong consciousnesses, and other non-valid consciousnesses such as correctly assuming consciousnesses, and so forth.

Among consciousnesses conceiving true existence, some are consciousnesses conceiving that an object exists by way of its own entity, while others are consciousnesses conceiving that an object exists as it appears. Jam-yang-shay-ba posits *only the latter* as the worldly perspective for which things are real. Since even an ordinary consciousness can realize that a reflection does not exist as it appears, consciousnesses conceiving true existence with regard to reflections, mirages, and so forth cannot be included in the worldly perspective for which things are real.[11] Therefore, Jam-yang-shay-ba limits the worldly perspective for which things are real in this context to consciousnesses conceiving true existence with regard those concealer-truths (such as tables and chairs) that conventional valid cognizers cannot realize as unreal without relying on a realization of suchness.[12]

Conventional valid cognizers are divided into those that are directed toward suchness and those that are not directed toward suchness. Among the latter, there are ordinary, innate valid cognizers—for instance, the eye consciousness apprehending a form—and valid cognizers that are *not* ordinary, innate awarenesses. "Extraordinary" valid cognizers not directed toward suchness realize the coarse selflessness of persons, the non-existence of a prin-

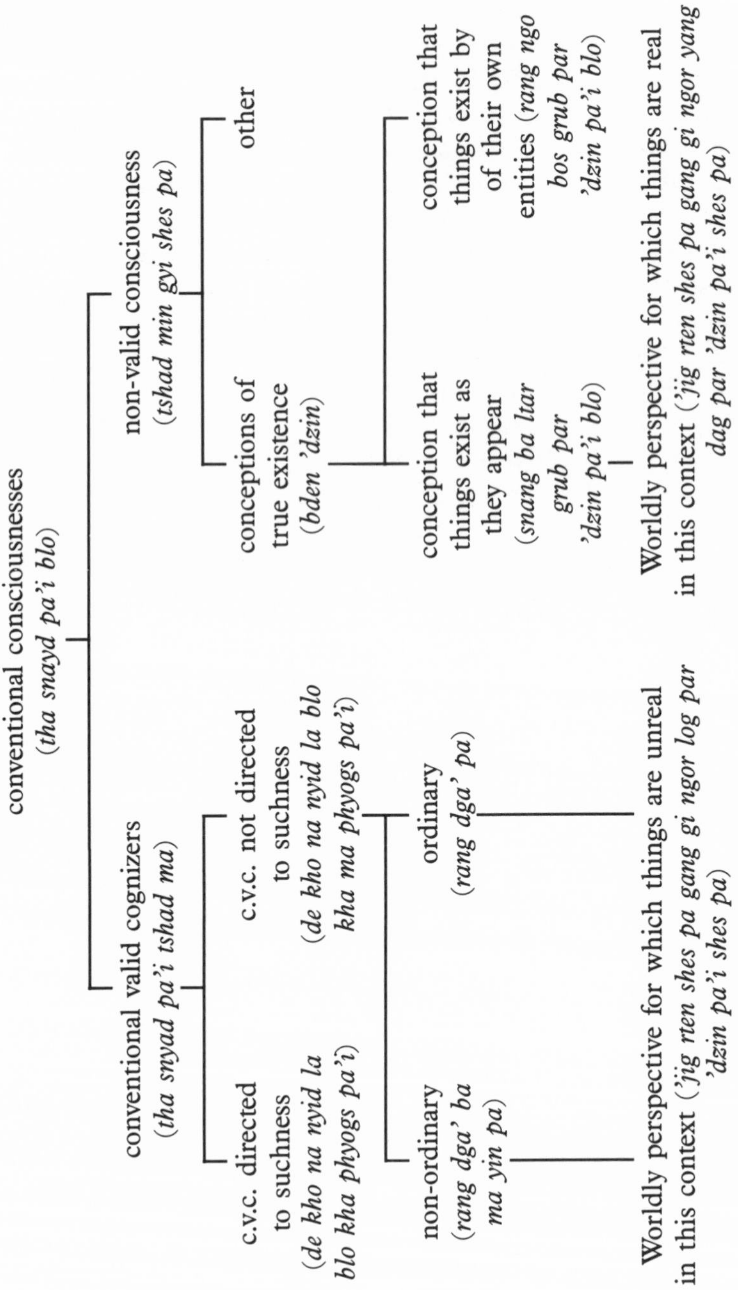

Chart 2: The Worldly Perspectives in this Context according to Jam-yang-shay-ba

cipal as described in Sāṃkhya, and so forth. These are realizations that arise only under the influence of special training, but they can be attained without reflection upon the final mode of subsistence of reality. Jam-yang-shay-ba explains that the worldly perspective for which things are unreal in the context of Candrakīrti's division of concealer-truths comprises all conventional valid cognizers not directed toward suchness. Unlike the worldly perspective for which things are real, which involves only ordinary awarenesses, valid cognizers not directed toward suchness include both ordinary and non-ordinary awarenesses. Therefore, Jam-yang-shay-ba comments that Kay-drup's statement that ordinary, innate awarenesses make the division into real and unreal pertains not to all cases, but to the majority.[13]

The thrust of this interpretation is that when we talk about an object being real for the perspective of an awareness, it is not enough to say that the awareness is unable to see that object as unreal. An awareness for whose perspective an object is real must apprehend that object as something that exists as it appears. Since nothing inherently exists, and all concealer-truths deceptively appear to be inherently existent, a worldly perspective in which something is apprehended as existing as it appears must be a wrong consciousness rather than a valid cognizer.

In his *Great Exposition of Tenets*, Jam-yang-shay-ba explains that "real in the worldly perspective" has two different meanings.[14] Prāsaṅgikas deny that conventional objects can be real in the sense of existing as they appear to the world. However, they admit that conventional objects can be "real or true" in a certain sense. For example, water appears to be inherently existent, and is therefore a falsity, but water also appears to moisten, quench thirst, and so forth. Water is "true" in the sense that it does not deceive a worldly consciousness about the fact of its existence or the fact of its capacity to perform its characteristic functions. The worldly perspective in which water is apprehended to exist *just as it appears* must be a wrong consciousness, but the worldly perspectives in which water is apprehended to exist and to perform its functions are conventional valid cognizers.

If there is a valid cognizer in whose perspective water can be posited as real or true in this latter sense, then why does Jam-yang-shay-ba insist that, in the context of Candrakīrti's division, the worldly perspective for which something is real must be a wrong consciousness? Why not simply say that when Candrakīrti talks about forms being real in the worldly perspective, he means that there are conventionally existent forms that exist and are effective? Why does Jam-yang-shay-ba insist upon taking the word "real" in this context to refer to something's existing just as it appears? I believe it is because Jam-yang-shay-ba took his cue from Kay-drup. Kay-drup had been attacked on this point by Paṇ-chen Sö-nam-drak-ba, and Jam-yang-shay-ba sought to demonstrate the soundness of Kay-drup's teachings.

While it is counter-intuitive and apparently inappropriate in the context of Candrakīrti's division of concealer-truths, this approach does allow Jam-yang-shay-ba to reconcile statements explaining the refutation of inherent existence even conventionally in Tsong-ka-pa's *Great Exposition of the Stages of the Path* with statements in the section on the two truths in Tsong-ka-pa's *Illumination of the Thought*. For example, Tsong-ka-pa's *Great Exposition of the Stages of the Path* says:[15]

> Since it is not suitable ultimately to make [a reasoned refutation of inherent existence, such a refutation] must be made conventionally. For the perspective of such a conventional valid cognizer, sense consciousnesses are mistaken. For the perspective of ordinary conventional consciousnesses other that that, [sense consciousnesses] are not mistaken.

Since the ultimate awareness realizes only emptiness, it does not apprehend inherent existence as false, nor does it apprehend itself as the refuter of inherent existence. The falseness of inherent existence and the mistakeness of awarenesses to which inherent existence appears are concealer-truths that are realized by special conventional valid cognizers that can be attained only by those who have previously realized emptiness. Since these special conventional valid cognizers realize form as a falsity and the eye consciousness apprehending form as mistaken, there cannot be other conventional valid cognizers for which form is real. Although some valid cognizers are directed toward emptiness and others are not, these two types of conventional valid cognizer cannot give contradictory information because they are both valid, authoritative, incontrovertible sources of knowledge.

In his *Illumination of the Thought*, as cited above, Tsong-ka-pa explains that the principal imputed by Sāṃkhyas and similar objects are realized as unreal by a conventional valid cognizer not directed toward suchness. However, he never clearly and explicitly states that a conventional valid cognizer not directed toward suchness *is* the worldly perspective in relation to which things are posited as real. Where is the evidence suggesting that Tsong-ka-pa posits a valid cognizer as the worldly perspective in relation to which things (tables, etc.) are real? There is a passage in his *Intermediate Exposition of the Stages of the Path* that seems to support this interpretation:[16]

> [Prāsaṅgikas] posit real and unreal conventionalities in relation to just the world, or conventional valid cognizers (*'jig rten pa'am tha snyad pa'i tshad ma*), not in relation to a reasoning consciousness that accords with a Superior's perception.

It definitely seems that Tsong-ka-pa is glossing the term "world," as it occurs in Candrakīrti's stanza, as "conventional valid cognizer." However, since Jam-yang-shay-ba follows Kay-drup in not accepting that conventionalities are real in the perspective of any conventional valid cognizers, he offers an alternative interpretation of this passage. Reading the phrase *'jig rten pa'am tha snyad pa'i tshad ma* not as a gloss but as a set of two distinct types of awarenesses, he writes:[17]

> Since Tsong-ka-pa's *Intermediate Exposition of the Stages of the Path* says, "[Prāsaṅgikas] posit real and unreal conventionalities in relation to just the world or a conventional valid cognizer...," real and unreal are explained to be posited respectively by ordinary worldly consciousnesses and conventional valid cognizers; the word "or" (*'am*) indicates that the ordinary worldly consciousness [for whose perspective something] is posited as unreal is a valid cognizer as well.

That is, Jam-yang-shay-ba claims that "world" here refers to ordinary worldly consciousnesses. As Kay-drup explains, the division of most conventionalities into real and unreal is made by ordinary worldly consciousnesses. Worldly consciousnesses conceiving true existence posit things as real. Other worldly consciousnesses (that happen also to be conventional valid cognizers) posit mirages and so forth as unreal.

Jam-yang-shay-ba makes a distinction between, on the one hand, real and unreal in the worldly perspective and, on the other, real and unreal in the worldly perspective *in the context of this stanza by Candrakīrti*. In general, the worldly perspective includes all conventional valid cognizers. No concealer-truths are real in the worldly perspective in general because there are special conventional valid cognizers that realize that concealer-truths do not exist as they appear. Therefore, all concealer-truths are unreal in the worldly perspective in general, but only some, reflections and so forth, are unreal in relation to the worldly perspective in this context—conventional valid cognizers not directed toward suchness.

Jam-yang-shay-ba's and Kay-drup's interpretations run against the grain of Candrakīrti's apparent intention here. Candrakīrti maintains that objects and subjects free from superficial impairment are real in relation to the world, while impaired subjects and their objects are unreal in relation to the world. Since Jam-yang-shay-ba and Kay-drup claim that the worldly perspective for which things are real in this context must be a consciousness conceiving true existence, it would follow that *all* phenomena are real in the worldly perspective in this context because there are consciousnesses conceiving true existence even with regard to mirages, etc.

For Jam-yang-shay-ba, who holds that the worldly perspective for which things are *unreal* is a conventional valid cognizer not directed toward suchness, this would also imply that reflections and so forth are both real and unreal for the worldly perspectives in this context. They are real because a consciousness conceiving true existence apprehends them as existing as they appear; they are unreal because the other worldly perspective, a conventional valid cognizer not directed toward suchness, can realize that they do *not* exist as they appear.

In order to avoid these contradictions of Candrakīrti (contradictions to which Kay-drup's approach would otherwise lead), Jam-yang-shay-ba differentiates *two* types of consciousnesses conceiving true existence. As explained above, some apprehend objects as existing by way of their own entities, while others see objects as existing as they appear. The former pertain to all objects, while the latter pertain only to conventionalities that are real in relation to the worldly perspective, e.g., tables and chairs. That is, Jam-yang-shay-ba defines a specific subclass of consciousnesses conceiving true existence, consciousnesses conceiving that something exists as it appears, that operate only with regard to phenomena (such as tables) that conventional valid cognizers not directed toward suchness are unable to discredit. Of course, there are sentient beings who conceive phenomena such as mirages to exist as they appear—but those ignorant minds are not consciousnesses conceiving true existence in Go-mang. For example, is a consciousness conceiving that a reflection of a face exists as it appears a consciousness conceiving true existence? Jam-yang-shay-ba suggests that it is *not*, because, whereas a consciousness conceiving true existence is refuted only in reliance upon ultimate analysis, even ordinary awarenesses of adults can realize that a reflection does not exist as it appears.

It is through this ingenious (albeit artificial) distinction that Jam-yang-shay-ba maintains the refutation of inherent existence conventionally—by denying that there are any conventional valid cognizers included in the worldly perspective for which things are real in this context—while preserving the main meaning of Candrakīrti's division, that some concealer-truths are real in relation to the world and others are unreal in relation to the world.

NGAK-WANG-BEL-DEN

Ngak-wang-bel-den (b.1797), Jam-yang-shay-ba's annotator and a scholar of considerable insight, devises a better way to reconcile the refutation of inherent existence conventionally with the assertion that some concealer-truths are real in relation to the worldly perspective. He agrees with Jam-yang-shay-ba that an awareness in whose perspective a concealer-truth is real must be a wrong consciousness, but he does not agree that this is what Candrakīrti meant when he explained that objects and subjects free from superficial impairment are real from only the worldly viewpoint. The key to his approach is the distinction between the phrases "in the perspective" (*shes ngo na*) and "for the perspective" (*shes ngor*) on the one hand, and on the other hand, the phrase "in relation to the perspective" (*shes ngo la ltos te*).[18] An awareness in whose perspective an object is real must apprehend that object as real, but an awareness in relation to whose perspective an object is real need not apprehend that object as real. "In relation to" means "in reliance upon." For example, since there are conventional valid cognizers that realize a table as unreal, it is unreal in the perspective of conventional valid cognition. However, this is established in relation to, or in reliance upon, an ultimate valid cognizer realizing emptiness.

Ngak-wang-bel-den explains that Candrakīrti's division of concealer-truths into real and unreal is made in relation to the worldly perspective; it is not made in the worldly perspective. The worldly perspective in relation to which things are posited as real or unreal is the perspective of conventional valid cognition. Reflections are unreal in relation to the perspective of the world because a conventional valid cognizer can realize them as unreal without relying on a realization of emptiness. Forms are real in relation to the perspective of the world because a conventional valid cognizer cannot realize them as unreal without relying on a realization of emptiness. However, form is unreal in the worldly perspective because there are some conventional valid cognizers that apprehend form as unreal.

Ngak-wang-bel-den writes:[19]

> Accordingly, although real and unreal are differentiated in relation to conventional valid cognition, they are not differentiated in the perspective of conventional valid cognition. It should also be known that although conventional phenomena are posited as unreal in relation to reasoning consciousnesses, they are not posited as unreal in the perspective of reasoning consciousnesses.

Thus, the "in/in relation to" distinction also applies to the mind realizing emptiness. For the mind realizing emptiness, elaborations such as "real" and "unreal" vanish and only emptiness itself is apprehended. Therefore, nothing is real or unreal in the perspective of a mind realizing emptiness. However, concealer-truths are unreal *in relation to* a mind realizing emptiness because the non-existence of inherent existence contradicts concealer-truths' existing as they appear.

With these examples before us, we can see how "real/unreal in the perspective" differs from "real/unreal in relation to the perspective" for Ngak-wang-bel-den. Ngak-wang-bel-den and Jam-yang-shay-ba agree that the perspective in which something is real must be an awareness that apprehends it as real and the perspective in which something is unreal must be an awareness that apprehends it as unreal. However, for Ngak-wang-bel-den, the awareness in relation to whose perspective something is unreal is not necessarily the awareness that actually apprehends it as unreal; it is the awareness whose understanding contradicts or discredits that object's being real. All concealer-truths are falsities, deceptively appearing one way and existing another. Since "being a falsity" and "being a phenomenon that does not exist as it appears" are concealer-truths, they are realized by conventional valid cognizers. This means that all concealer-truths are unreal *in* the perspective of conventional valid cognizers. However, they are not necessarily unreal in relation to the perspective of conventional valid cognizers. Conventional valid cognizers can contradict a reflection's existing in accordance with its appearance as a face, but cannot contradict a face's existing in accordance with its appearance as inherently existent. A conventional valid cognizer can realize that a face does not exist as it appears only in reliance upon, or in relation to, a realization of emptiness which, through realizing the opposite of inherent existence, contradicts the existence of face in accordance with its appearance.

Ngak-wang-bel-den does not need to uphold Jam-yang-shay-ba's distinction between the general meaning of "worldly perspective" and the "worldly perspective in this context."[20] In either case, the worldly perspective is the perspective of conventional valid cognition. Whether something is real or unreal in relation to a conventional valid cognizer is determined by whether a conventional valid cognizer can realize it as unreal without being directed toward suchness or relying on ultimate analysis. That is, when a conventional valid cognizer can realize something as unreal without relying on a realization of emptiness, it is unreal in relation to conventional valid cognition. When a conventional valid cognizer cannot realize something as unreal without relying on a realization of emptiness, then it is real in relation to conventional valid cognition because, while there are some special conventional valid cognizers that can realize that a face is unreal, they do so only in dependence upon a previous ultimate valid cognition.[21]

NGAK-WANG-BEL-DEN INTERPRETS THE TRADITION

Ngak-wang-bel-den claims that Tsong-ka-pa supports the "in/in relation to" distinction. He writes:[22]

> Aside from the distinction of real and unreal in relation to the worldly perspective, not even a single syllable of the distinction of real and unreal in the worldly perspective occurs in the texts of the great Foremost Master [Tsong-ka-pa].

For example, Tsong-ka-pa's *Illumination of the Thought* says:[23]

> The positing of a conventional object—apprehended by [any of] the six consciousnesses that without such impairment—as real and the positing of an object that is the opposite as unreal is done *in relation only to* the worldly consciousness.

and Tsong-ka-pa's *Intermediate Exposition of the Stages of the Path* says:[24]

> Furthermore, [Prāsaṅgikas] posit real and unreal conventionalities *in relation to* just worldly or conventional valid cognizers not *in relation to* a reasoning consciousness that accords with a Superior's perception.

However, Kay-drup clearly uses the phrase "real and unreal *in* the worldly perspective" to explain Candrakīrti's twofold division of concealer-truths. In order to account for this in a manner that is respectful of Kay-drup, Ngak-wang-bel-den argues that Kay-drup is speaking hypothetically:[25]

> This [statement by Kay-drup] explains, as a branch of his analysis of extreme positions, that if one *were* to posit real and unreal in the worldly perspective, they would be posited in this way. It is not like the meaning of real and unreal in relation to the worldly perspective in this context.

While a close examination of the context of Kay-drup's commentary on Candrakīrti's division does not support the contention that Kay-drup is speaking hypothetically, this claim allows Ngak-wang-bel-den to refute what Kay-drup said without refuting Kay-drup.

Ngak-wang-bel-den also tries to avoid contradicting Jam-yang-shay-ba. He reminds us that Jam-yang-shay-ba's *Great Exposition of Tenets* explains that there are two ways an object can be real or true in the worldly perspective:[26]

> One way to posit form and so forth as real in the worldly perspective is by way of a concordance (*mthun pa*) between their mode of appearance and their mode of subsistence in the worldly perspective; another way is to posit them as "real or true" insofar as there exists an object that is consistent with their appearance in the worldly perspective or which is the basis of their appearance. Even Mādhyamikas assert [some things as "real or true"] in this [latter] way.

Ngak-wang-bel-den points out that it is impossible to make sense of this section in Jam-yang-shay-ba's textbook on Mādhyamika unless one realizes that Jam-yang-shay-ba uses the phrase "real in the worldly perspective" in these two very different ways. He writes:[27]

> [Tsong-ka-pa's] *Great Exposition of Tenets* states that there are two disparate ways to posit something as real in the perspective of the world. [Jam-yang-shay-ba's] textbook on Mādhyamika, without clearly saying that there are two disparate ways to posit something as real, states both of these. Therefore, the assertions of those of inferior intelligence, mixing the two, are only a mass of contradiction.

Note, however, that Jam-yang-shay-ba hedges his statement of the second meaning by including the words "real or true" in quotation marks. This could be construed to mean that while there are two senses in which things are *called* real or true, the former is to be taken as the general meaning. Furthermore, the very fact that Jam-yang-shay-ba talks about two ways in which something can be real *in* the worldly perspective proves that he has not made a terminological distinction between "real in relation to the world" and "real in the perspective of the world." In his textbook on Mādhyamika Jam-yang-shay-ba insists that the worldly perspective for which and in relation to which form and so forth are real is not the conventional valid cognizer that fails to realize them as unreal, but a consciousness conceiving true existence that apprehends them as real. Operating without Ngak-wang-bel-den's terminological refinements, Jam-yang-shay-ba emphasizes the refutation of inherent existence conventionally and maintains coherence with Kay-drup by deciding (despite occurrences, which he enumerates, of the other usage in several Mādhyamika treatises) that here, in the context of Candrakīrti's stanza subdividing concealer-truths, "real in the perspective of the world" and "real in relation to the world" both indicate misapprehension by worldly ignorance rather than certification by worldly valid cognition.

OTHER GE-LUK-BA AUTHORS

As noted above, Jang-gya holds that there is a single class of consciousnesses, conventional valid cognizers not directed toward suchness, that represent the worldly perspective in relation to which Candrakīrti divides concealer-truths into real and unreal.[28] While similar to Ngak-wang-bel-den in this regard, Jang-gya does not make the "in/in relation to" distinction. When asserting that a concealer-truth such as a form, which appears to be inherently existent, is real in the perspective of a conventional valid cognizer not directed toward suchness, how can Jang-gya avoid admitting inherent existence conventionally? Jang-gya answers that when Prāsaṅgikas say that form is real in the worldly perspective, "real" does not have its usual meaning. He writes:[29]

> In the sentences, "Prāsaṅgikas do not assert being real even conventionally in their own system," and "Prāsaṅgikas assert the features of being real and being unreal in the worldly perspective," the former "real" and the later "real" are one in name but different in meaning. This is because the former "real" means inherent existence and the latter "real" must be posited as similar to truth in the sense that when someone who definitely stole something says, "I stole it," one posits this as the truth and when he says, "I did not steal it," one posits this as wrong.

This interpretation is undoubtedly based on the explanation of Jam-yang-shay-ba's *Great Exposition of Tenets* that there are two ways that something can be real in the worldly perspective; it is also comparable to the distinction Jam-yang-shay-ba and Jay-dzun-ba make between "truth" and "true." Nevertheless, in taking this approach Jang-gya must agree that the worldly perspective in which a concealer-truth is real need not be a consciousness conceiving true existence. This contradicts statements by Kay-drup and statements by Jam-yang-shay-ba (in his textbook on Mādhyamika); it also contradicts the later views of Ngak-wang-bel-den.

Paṇ-chen Sö-nam-drak-ba and Jang-gya agree that Candrakīrti posits concealer-truths as real or unreal in relation to the perspective of conventional valid cognizers. However, it is interesting to see how differently they respond to the apparently contradictory evidence of this passage from Kay-drup's *Thousand Doses*:[30]

> Therefore, "There is a division into real and unreal in the worldly perspective" means that an ordinary, innate, worldly awareness makes a division into real and unreal. It is not at all the case that worldly conventional valid cognizers make a division into real and unreal because it shows irrationality to propound, "While asserting this as an ob-

> ject established by valid cognition, I do not assert it in my own system." This is also because the worldly awareness in the perspective—that is, mode of apprehension—of which form and so forth are established as real is a consciousness conceiving true existence; thus, it is not suitable to be a conventional valid cognizer.

As we have seen, Jam-yang-shay-ba generally agrees with this passage and builds his interpretation upon it inasmuch as he posits a consciousness conceiving true existence as the worldly perspective in Candrakīrti's phrase, "true from only the worldly viewpoint." Ngak-wang-bel-den disagrees, claiming that this passage is not an interpretation of Candrakīrti's division of concealer-truths because Candrakīrti divides real and unreal in relation to the worldly perspective, not in the worldly perspective. However, Ngak-wang-bel-den and Jam-yang-shay-ba both agree with Kay-drup in asserting that if a concealer-truth is real in the perspective of an awareness, then that awareness must be a consciousness conceiving true existence. Jang-gya, however, disagrees.

Jang-gya's main response to Kay-drup is to point out that there are two ways that something can be real. When Candrakīrti divides concealer-truths into real and unreal, he is referring to the "real" that is like the truth of the thief's statement, "I stole it." Since Kay-drup explains that the mind apprehending a concealer-truth as real has to be a consciousness conceiving true existence, Jang-gya's argument definitely implies that Kay-drup has misinterpreted Candrakīrti. However, not only does Jang-gya avoid explicitly criticizing Kay-drup, he searches for an accommodation. Jang-gya writes:[31]

> Even the statement in Kay-drup's *Thousand Doses* that real and unreal are not posited in the perspective of a conventional valid cognizer is good if we take it to mean that real and unreal are not posited in the perspective of a mere conventional valid cognizer, but must [be posited in the perspective] of a conventional valid cognizer not directed toward suchness.

In order to establish himself in harmony with Kay-drup, Jang-gya temporarily overlooks the portion of Kay-drup's statement that reads, "...the worldly awareness in the perspective—that is, mode of apprehension—of which form and so forth are established as real is a consciousness conceiving true existence."

In contrast, Paṇ-chen Sö-nam-drak-ba gives a straightforward refutation of Kay-drup.[32] He criticizes Kay-drup's assertion that an ordinary, innate awareness makes the division into real and unreal. As Jam-yang-shay-ba also points out, this overlooks the non-innate conventional valid cognizers that cognize the unreality of the coarse self of persons, the principal as imputed by Sāṃkhyas, and so forth. More significantly, Paṇ-chen Sö-nam-drak-ba objects to Kay-drup's apparent assertion that the worldly perspective in which Candrakīrti posits form and so forth as real is a consciousness conceiving true existence. Jam-yang-shay-ba agrees with this statement, Ngak-wang-bel-den claims that it does not represent Kay-drup's own position, and Jang-gya disagrees tactfully, without refuting Kay-drup. By comparison, Paṇ-chen Sö-nam-drak-ba is blunt and unequivocal in his evaluation of this passage:

> This [text] is explained to require interpretation at this point (*re zhig drang don*) because, although real and unreal are posited in relation to conventional valid cognizers, conventional valid cognizers do not necessarily posit real and unreal.

Conventional valid cognizers do not posit real and unreal and unreal concealer-truths because if they were to posit a concealer-truth as real it would have to be inherently existent. Nevertheless, since the division of concealer-truths into real and unreal in relation to the worldly perspective is itself a concealer-truth, it must be posited by a conventional valid cognizer. Also, since the "worldly perspective" is a conventional valid cognizer, we must conclude that while conventional valid cognizers do not posit concealer-truths as real and unreal in general, they do posit them as real and unreal in relation to conventional valid cognizers.

In saying that Kay-drup's commentary requires interpretation at this point, Paṇ-chen is pointing out that while Candrakīrti makes the division of real and unreal in relation to the worldly perspective, he never says that the consciousnesses that comprise that perspective must themselves posit or apprehend concealer-truths as real. Therefore, there is no reason to insist that the worldly perspective include wrong consciousnesses. Paṇ-chen Sö-nam-drak-ba, like Jang-gya and others who preceded Ngak-wang-bel-den, never explicitly differentiates the meaning of "in the perspective" from the meaning of "in relation to the perspective." However, unlike Jang-gya (who uses the phrase "in the perspective" where Ngak-wang-bel-den would require "in relation to the perspective"), Paṇ-chen's phraseology is consistent with Ngak-wang-bel-den's much later interpretation. Not only does Paṇ-chen Sö-nam-drak-ba differentiate what a conventional valid cognizer posits from what is posited in relation to it, but he consistently explains Candrakīrti's division of concealer-truths using the phrases "in relation to the worldly perspective" and "in relation to conventional valid cognition." Ngak-wang-bel-den's familiarity with the Lo-sel-ling textbooks probably contributed to his insight into the potential significance of the terminological distinction between "real in the worldly perspective" and "real in relation to the worldly perspective."

Jay-dzun Chö-gyi-gyel-tsen also comments on the division of concealer-truths exclusively in terms of what is real and unreal *in relation to* the worldly perspective.[33] He does use the phrase "in the perspective" in other contexts (e.g., his etymology of concealer-truth and his explanation of Buddha's way of knowing),[34] but, like Paṇ-chen Sö-nam-drak-ba, his usage is consistent with the distinctions Ngak-wang-bel-den was to outline a few centuries later. Although he never specifically defines the worldly consciousness in relation to which concealer-truths are posited as real or unreal, Jay-dzun Chö-gyi-gyel-tsen explains that a concealer-truth's being real or unreal in relation to the world is determined by whether or not a conventional valid cognizer in the continuum of a person who has not realized emptiness can realize that it does not exist as it appears.[35]

Alone among the authors we have discussed, Jay-dzun Chö-gyi-gyel-tsen never even mentions the controversial views of Kay-drup on this issue. It should be noted that Kay-drup was the older brother of Jay-dzun Chö-gyi-gyel-tsen's namesake, the scholar Ba-so Chö-gyi-gyel-tsen (1402-1473). Ba-so Chö-gyi-gyel-tsen was the revered teacher of Jay-dzun Chö-gyi-gyel-tsen's parents, who were important patrons of the Ge-luk-ba order.[36]

THE WORLDLY PERSPECTIVE

Ngak-wang-bel-den explains that persons who have realized emptiness, even Superiors, do not apprehend a form as a falsity each time they apprehend a form.[37] Even Superiors have ordinary conventional valid cognizers, such as eye consciousnesses apprehending form, that are included among the consciousnesses of the worldly perspective. Also, Superiors have conventional valid cognizers not directed toward suchness that realize the coarse selflessness of persons and so forth. Therefore, the worldly perspective—a conventional valid cognizer not directed toward suchness—exists in the continuums of both those who have not realized emptiness and in the continuums of Superiors and others who have realized emptiness. Although Candrakīrti says that forms are not real in relation to Superiors, Tsong-ka-pa's *Intermediate Exposition of the Stages of the Path* explains that this means "not in relation to a reasoning consciousness that accords with a Superior's perception," i.e., a mind realizing emptiness.[38]

This explanation does not contradict Jay-dzun Chö-gyi-gyel-tsen's definition of real in the worldly perspective as that which a person who has not realized emptiness is unable realize as not existing as it appears. If one were to interpret Jay-dzun Chö-gyi-gyel-tsen to mean that the worldly perspective occurs only among those who have not yet realized emptiness, then there would be a contradiction. However, Jay-dzun Chö-gyi-gyel-tsen does not say that those who have realized emptiness cannot still have the worldly perspective. His point appears to be that prior to the realization of emptiness *all* conventional valid cognizers are included in the worldly perspective; after realization of emptiness some are and some are not.

It could be argued that when persons who have not previously realized emptiness investigate whether phenomena inherently exist, they develop inferential conventional valid cognizers that are "directed toward emptiness" insofar as they are generated as part of a process intended to culminate in the realization of emptiness. For example, a person meditating on emptiness might take to mind the syllogism, "The body is not inherently produced because of not being produced from self, from inherently existent others, from both, or causelessly." In order to generate an ultimate valid cognizer realizing the body's emptiness of inherent production, that person must first generate a conventional valid cognizer establishing that those reasons entail that the body is not inherently produced. He or she must then generate a conventional valid cognizer realizing that the body is not produced from self. Should such conventional valid cognizers be considered conventional valid cognizers directed toward suchness?

Since such conventional valid cognizers exist in the continuums of persons who have not realized emptiness, they must be part of the worldly perspective as Jay-dzun Chö-gyi-gyel-tsen explains it. Except in quoting Tsong-ka-pa, Jay-dzun Chö-gyi-gyel-tsen avoids the phrase "not directed toward suchness." Perhaps the reason for this is that he feels that the worldly perspective includes certain conventional valid cognizers that are directed toward suchness in the way explained above. Besides Jay-dzun Chö-gyi-gyel-tsen, I have not found a Ge-luk-ba author who directly addresses the question of whether persons who have not yet realized emptiness can have conventional valid cognizers directed toward emptiness or conventional valid cognizers that are beyond the worldly perspective. However, since Tsong-ka-pa's *Illumination of the Thought* says:[39]

> The word "just" indicates that just a conventional valid cognizer is sufficient to posit those consciousnesses as mistaken—without relying on a reasoning consciousness,

and Ngak-wang-bel-den states, "It is suitable to make a division into real and unreal in relation to the mere perspective of conventional consciousnesses without relying on reasoning consciousnesses," it seems that "directed toward suchness" means relying on a preceding realization of emptiness.[40] Furthermore, it seems logical to exclude from the worldly perspective only those conventional valid cognizers that are able to realize forms and so forth as unreal in that they do not exist in accordance with their appearance as inherently existent. Since the capacity for such realization arises from the refutation of inherent existence, one must realize the emptiness that is the opposite of inherent existence before one can have a conventional valid cognizer that is not part of the worldly perspective.

Thus, there is no contradiction between (1) identifying the worldly perspective in this context as a conventional valid cognizer not directed toward suchness and (2) dividing concealer-truths into real and unreal in relation to just conventional valid cognition. If "directed toward suchness" means "relying on a previous ultimate valid cognition," then the phrase "not directed toward suchness" can be regarded as redundant when the words "in relation to *just* conventional valid cognizers" are present. The word "just" precludes the need to rely on a previous realization of emptiness. Therefore, the meaning of the division of concealer-truths into real or unreal in relation to just the worldly perspective is that they are divided according to whether a conventional valid cognizer, without relying on a previous realization of emptiness, can realize that they do not exist as they appear.

CONCLUSION

In this chapter, we see the Ge-luk-ba textbook writers confronting the threat of internal contradiction on two fronts. First, there is the danger, pointed out by Kay-drup, of internal contradiction in the doctrine itself. Candrakīrti allows that pillars and pots and ethical distinctions are "real for the world." If the Ge-luk-bas identify that "world" as some form of valid cognition, then they give authoritative confirmation to the reality, i.e., the existence in accordance with appearance, of conventional phenomena. It becomes impossible to turn around and coherently claim that conventional phenomena do not exist as they appear. Jam-yang-shay-ba introduces one set of very fine distinctions to solve this problem, and Ngak-wang-bel-den introduces another set of fine distinctions for the same purpose.

Second, each author has to face the problem of how to handle conflicting passages in the works of revered teachers in their tradition. Of the two early authors, Jay-dzun Chö-gyi-gyel-tsen avoids the problem by stating his own opinion without testing it against, or even mentioning, the contrary opinion of Kay-drup. The burden of either creating a reconciling exegesis or attributing error to Kay-drup is left to the teacher who uses Jay-dzun-ba's text. Paṇ-chen's method is to quote the key passage from Kay-drup's *Thousand Doses* and state that it "requires interpretation," without offering any alternative reading. Some contemporary Ge-luk-ba teachers find Paṇ-chen's approach uncomfortably confrontational. Those using Paṇ-chen Sö-nam-drak-ba's textbook find it difficult to gloss over the conflict between Paṇ-chen and Kay-drup. Feeling forced to "choose sides," Gen Lo-sang-gya-tso, principal of the School of Dialectics in Dharamsala, faults Paṇ-chen for this attack on one of Tsong-ka-pa's spiritual sons.

Compared to Jay-dzun-ba and Paṇ-chen Sö-nam-drak-ba, later Ge-luk-ba authors show a greater tendency to build up bridges between their own theses and the words of the traditional authorities. Jam-yang-shay-ba stays in line with Kay-drup just as far as he possibly can. Even when Kay-drup's position seems to contradict a passage by Tsong-ka-pa, Jam-yang-shay-ba keeps Tsong-ka-pa and Kay-drup in harmony by devising a clever new reading of Tsong-ka-pa. Unlike Jam-yang-shay-ba, Jang-gya actually disagrees with Kay-drup; still, he is similar to Jam-yang-shay-ba in that he cites the passage whence the conflict arises and patches together a reconciling exegesis. Ngak-wang-bel-den proposes an entirely different answer to the doctrinal problem, but keeps up the "pure tradition" façade by offering his innovation as though it were the real meaning to be found by any intelligent reader in the works of Jam-yang-shay-ba and Kay-drup.

9 *Divisions of Ultimate Truths*

TWENTY TYPES OF EMPTINESS

The *Twenty-five Thousand Stanza Perfection of Wisdom Sūtra* sets forth twenty types of emptiness:[1]

(1) Emptiness of the internal (*nang stong pa nyid, adhyātmaśūnyatā*). This is the emptiness of sense and mental consciousnesses.[2]

(2) Emptiness of the external (*phyi stong pa nyid, bahirdhāśūnyatā*). This is the emptiness of the forms, sounds, odors, tastes, objects of touch, and phenomena that are respectively the objects of the eye, ear, nose, tongue, body, and mental consciousnesses. Although consciousnesses can be objects of other consciousnesses, Kensur Padma-gyel-tsen limits this to the emptiness of objects that are not included in the continuum of a sentient being and insists that emptiness of internal and emptiness of the external are mutually exclusive.

(3) Emptiness of the internal and external (*phyi nang stong pa nyid, adhyātmabahirdhāśūnyatā*). This is the emptiness of the loci of the sense powers, i.e., the orb of the eye, etc.[3]

(4) Emptiness of emptiness (*stong pa nyid stong pa nyid, śūnyatāśūnyatā*). Candrakīrti's *Supplement Commentary* explains that Buddha taught the emptiness of emptiness in order to overcome the misconceptions of persons conceiving emptiness to be inherently existent.[4]

(5) Emptiness of the great (*chen po stong pa nyid, mahāśūnyatā*). This is the emptiness of the ten directions (eight compass points,

as well as up and down).

(6) Emptiness of the ultimate (*don dam pa stong pa nyid, paramārthaśūnyatā*). This is the emptiness of nirvāṇa.

(7) Emptiness of products (*'dus byas stong pa nyid, saṃskṛtaśūnyatā*).

(8) Emptiness of non-products (*'dus ma byas stong pa nyid, asaṃskṛtaśūnyatā*).

(9) Emptiness of what has passed beyond extremes (*mtha las 'das pa stong pa nyid, atyantaśūnyatā*). This is the emptiness of what has passed beyond the extremes of permanence and annihilation.[5]

(10) Emptiness of what is beginningless and endless (*thog pa dang tha ma med pa stong pa nyid, anavarāgraśūnyatā*). This is the emptiness of cyclic existence.

(11) Emptiness of the unrepudiated (*dor ba med pa stong pa nyid, anavakāraśūnyatā*). According to Gyel-tsap's *Ornament for the Essence*, the bases of this emptiness are "unrepudiated giving, etc."—that is, practices that are not given up on the Mahāyāna paths.[6]

(12) Emptiness of nature (*rang bzhin stong pa nyid, prakṛtiśūnyatā*). This is the emptiness of the emptinesses that are the final nature of phenomena.

(13) Emptiness of all phenomena (*chos thams cad stong pa nyid, sarvadharmaśūnyatā*).

(14) Emptiness of definition (*rang gi mtshan nyid stong pa nyid, svalakṣaṇaśūnyatā*). This is the emptiness of the definitions of all phenomena.

(15) Emptiness of the inapprehensible (*mi dmigs pa stong pa nyid, anupalambhanaśūnyatā*). This is the emptiness of the past, present, and future. They are called "inapprehensible" because they are not inherently apprehensible as the cessation, presence, and non-production of phenomena.

(16) Emptiness of inherent existence of non-things (*dngos po med pa'i ngo bo nyid stong pa nyid, abhāvasvabhāvaśūnyatā*). Since functioning things are not inherently existent, they are not inherently existent as compounded phenomena. Therefore, they are called "non-things" in this context; their emptiness of being inherently compounded is the sixteenth emptiness.[7]

(17) Emptiness of things (*dngos po stong pa nyid, bhāvaśūnyatā*). This refers to the emptiness of the five aggregates.

(18) Emptiness of non-things (*dngos med stong pa nyid, abhāvaśūnyatā*). This is the emptiness of inherent existence of non-

products, such as non-product space and nirvāṇa.

(19) Emptiness of the self-nature (*rang bzhin stong pa nyid, svabhāvaśūnyatā*). This is the emptiness of the nature of phenomena; thus it is an emptiness of emptiness.[8] Here, the basis of emptiness is emptiness considered as the immanent, the innermost reality of all conventional phenomena.

(20) Emptiness of other-nature (*gzhan gyi dngos pa stong pa nyid, parabhāvaśūnyatā*). This is another name for the emptiness of emptiness. Here, the basis of emptiness is emptiness considered as the supreme and perfect, the limit of reality (*yang dag pa'i mtha', bhūtakoṭi*) completely surpassing cyclic existence.[9]

This first sixteen of these twenty are sometimes given separately as "the sixteen emptinesses," while the last four appear separately as "the four emptinesses."[10] Some texts give a list of eighteen emptinesses, omitting the last two.[11] The most condensed division of emptinesses is a division into two: selflessness of phenomena and selflessness of persons. Candrakīrti's *Supplement* states:[12]

> Regarding this selflessness, in order to liberate migrators,
> [Buddha] stated two types by dividing phenomena and persons.

All of these emptinesses are non-affirming negatives that are mere absences of inherent existence. Fifteen of the twenty are emptinesses posited in relation to concealer-truths, while the other five (#4, #6, #12, #19, and #20) are emptinesses of ultimate truths.[13] Among the latter, the emptiness of the ultimate (#6) is the emptiness of a particular type of ultimate truth, nirvāṇa, while the other four pertain to all ultimate truths. Ngak-wang-bel-den relates that the emptiness of emptiness (#4) is explained by Buddha for the sake of eliminating the conception that emptiness truly exists because of being established by a reasoning consciousness comprehending reality. Emptiness of the nature (*rang bzhin stong pa nyid, prakṛtiśūnyatā*) (#12) and emptiness of self-nature (*rang bzhin stong pa nyid, svabhāvaśūnyatā*) (#19) are both emptinesses of emptiness that are explained by Buddha in order to eliminate the conception that emptiness is truly existent because of being established as the nature, or mode of subsistence, of phenomena. According to Ngak-wang-bel-den, there is no redundancy because the twelfth is part of the extensive division of emptinesses into sixteen, while the nineteenth is part of the intermediate, four-fold division.[14]

Regarding the twentieth emptiness, Candrakīrti's *Supplement*

Commentary explains that "other" (*gzhan, para*) can mean "supreme" (*mchog*), "other," or "farther side" (*pha rol*).[15] In the first sense, emptiness is an "other-nature" because it is the supreme or highest reality. In the second sense, the non-conceptual meditative equipoise is called "other" because it transcends the world. Since emptiness is realized by that consciousness as the nature, it is called an "other-nature." In the third sense, emptiness is an entity of the farther side because it extends beyond cyclic existence to a nirvāṇa that is the exhaustion of cyclic existence. It is therefore called the "limit of reality" (*yang dag pa'i mtha', bhūtakoṭi*) and as such it is immutable. Therefore, Tsong-ka-pa's *Illumination of the Thought*[16] explains that Buddha taught the emptiness of emptiness using the name "emptiness of the other-nature" both in order to eliminate the idea that emptiness is truly existent because of being permanent and in order to eliminate the idea that emptiness is truly existent because of being posited by non-conceptual meditative equipoise.

ACTUAL AND CONCORDANT ULTIMATES

Ultimate truths can also be divided into actual ultimates (*don dam dngos*) and concordant ultimates (*mthun pa'i don dam*) or into metaphoric (*rnam grangs pa'i don dam*) and non-metaphoric ultimates (*rnam grangs ma yin pa'i don dam*). Elizabeth Napper explores the intricacies of this terminology in *Dependent-Arising and Emptiness*.[17] The following paragraphs are a condensed recapitulation of her summary of Ngak-wang-bel-den's usage.

Subjective ultimates (*yul can don dam*) are minds that realize emptiness. The non-conceptual wisdom of meditative equipoise is an actual subjective ultimate, and is also known as a non-metaphoric subjective ultimate. An inferential realization of emptiness is a concordant subjective ultimate, also known as a metaphoric subjective ultimate. Since these consciousnesses are not emptinesses, actual subjective ultimates and concordant subjective ultimates are considered imputed ultimate truths (*don dam btags pa ba*), rather than actual ultimate truths.

Actual objective ultimates (*yul don dam dngos*) are emptinesses of inherent existence—that is, actual ultimate truths. Concordant, or metaphoric, objective ultimates are of two types: (1) emptinesses that are the objects of inferences and (2) illusion-like composites of an object and its emptiness. The former are actual ultimate truths (*don dam dngos*), but they are called concordant objective ultimates because of being objects realized by concordant subjective ultimates. The latter are imputed ultimates (*don dam btags pa ba*) that are cognized in states subsequent to meditative equipoise.

TRUE CESSATIONS ARE ULTIMATE TRUTHS

A true cessation (*'gog bden, nirodhasatya*), the third of the four noble truths, is the complete and final eradication of one or more obstructions (*sgrib, āvarana*) for the continuum of an individual. The meditative equipoise directly realizing emptiness on an uninterrupted path (*bar chad med lam, ānantaryamārga*) acts as the "actual antidote" (*dngos gnyen*) that eradicates the obstructions corresponding to its level. Then, on the path of release (*rnam grol lam, vimuktimārga*), there arises a factor of cessation that is the absence of the obstructions that have just been abandoned. This true cessation is directly realized by the meditative equipoise of that path of release. Subsequent to meditative equipoise, remembering that realization, yogis understand that those obstructions will never again occur in their continuum. Repeated on progressively higher paths, this process culminates, when even the very subtlest obstruction has been abandoned, in the attainment of nirvāṇa—the ultimate true cessation.[18]

Ge-luk-bas hold that in the Prāsaṅgika system, all true cessations (including nirvāṇas) are ultimate truths. There are passages in Candrakīrti's *Commentary on (Nāgārjuna's) "Sixty Stanzas of Reasoning"* that seem to give contrary indications. For example, Candrakīrti writes, "Therefore, a nirvāṇa is only imputed as a concealer-truth," and "Is a nirvāṇa a concealer-truth? It is so." However, Tsong-ka-pa's *Intermediate Exposition of the Stages of the Path* explains:[19]

> Those statements mean that with regard to positing a nirvāṇa or ultimate truth as *existing*, it is posited as merely existent for a conventional consciousness; this system does not assert that a nirvāṇa is a concealer-truth.

As Jam-yang-shay-ba points out, Candrakīrti supports his statement that nirvāṇa is imputed as a concealer-truth with a citation indicating that "if something surpassing nirvāṇa existed, even it would be like a dream or like an illusion."[20] This suggests that Candrakīrti is discussing the manner in which nirvāṇa exists—merely conventionally and like an illusion—rather than actually assigning nirvāṇa to the category of concealer-truths. In fact, Candrakīrti elsewhere specifically states that true cessations are ultimate truths. His *Supplement Commentary* says:[21]

> Truths of suffering, sources, and path are included within concealer-truths. Truths of cessation are entities of ultimate truths.

Also, Candrakīrti makes similar statements even in his *Commentary on (Nāgārjuna's) "Sixty Stanzas of Reasoning"*.[22] The reason that true cessations are considered ultimate truths is that they exist as they appear to the minds of meditative equipoise that directly perceive them.[23]

Is it the case that there are two different classes of ultimate truths, emptinesses and true cessations? Or can true cessations be considered emptinesses? This has been an issue of long-standing controversy within the Ge-luk-ba order, and it remains controversial today. Without pretending to trace the history of this debate, I will lay out some of the arguments on each side.

NIRVĀṆA IS NOT EMPTINESS

Paṇ-chen Sö-nam-drak-ba's *General Meaning Commentary on the Middle Way* and *Disputation and Reply [Regarding] (Candrakīrti's) "Supplement"* explain that true cessations are ultimate truths, but should not be considered real natures (*chos nyid, dharmatā*), suchnesses (*de bzhin nyid, tathatā*), or emptinesses.[24] The scriptural bases for this position include a passage in Nāgārjuna's *Praise for the Sphere of Reality* (*dharmadhātustotra*) that reads:

> Just as the moon is slightly visible on the fourteenth day of waning, there is a slight appearance of the Truth Body for those who believe in the supreme vehicle. Just as the waxing crescent moon is seen to increase periodically, those who have entered a ground see [the Truth Body] increase stage by stage. Just as the moon is complete on the fifteenth day of waxing, so on the final ground the Truth Body is complete and clear.[25]

Also, Gyel-tsap's *Ornament for the Essence* (*rnam bshad snying po rgyan*) says:[26]

> In the meditative equipoise of the tenth ground, although there is no distinction [from the Buddha ground] regarding seeing reality, there is a distinction regarding seeing the Truth Body (*chos sku, dharmakāya*).

In this context, the term "Truth Body" must refer to a Buddha's Nature Body (*ngo bo nyid sku, svabhāvikakāya*) which is a factor of purity from all natural and circumstantial defilement—in other words, nirvāṇa. Since even from the first ground a Bodhisattva fully and directly cognizes reality or emptiness, while yet possessing only a partial nirvāṇa, Paṇ-chen Sö-nam-drak-ba and many of his followers have argued that nirvāṇa cannot be identical to emptiness. Kensur Padma-gyel-tsen cites a passage from Tsong-ka-pa's *Intermediate Exposition of the Stages of the Path* as confirming evidence that true cessations and emptinesses are two distinct types of ultimate truth:[27]

> Furthermore, [ultimate truths] are (1) naturally pure nirvāṇas which are emptinesses of inherent existence of phenomena and (2) nirvāṇas which are true cessations—just those which are separations from any of the seeds of the defilements.

There is no scriptural source that clearly states, "nirvāṇa is not emptiness." Those who hold that nirvāṇa is an emptiness can readily construe each of the sources cited here as simply differentiating emptinesses that are true cessations from emptinesses that are not true cessations. Therefore, while there is some scriptural basis for Paṇ-chen Sö-nam-drak-ba's position, it is far from conclusive.

Somewhat more persuasive are the reasoned arguments against classifying nirvāṇa as an emptiness. First, it is usual to think that the object of negation of an emptiness must be inherent existence, and therefore a non-existent. However, if true cessations are emptinesses, then, since afflictions exist and are objects of negation of true cessations, there must be emptinesses that have *existent* objects of negation. While this consequence may seem slightly odd, it is far from damning to the opposing position. Geshe Tsul-tim-gya-tso argues that when the emptiness of a mind on a path of release is posited as a true cessation, there must be existent objects of negation.[28] This has scriptural foundation in Tsong-ka-pa's *Illumination of the Thought*:[29]

> Although an elimination of true existence—the object of negation—with respect to any base is considered an ultimate truth, *it does not necessarily follow that the objects of negation of all ultimate truths do not exist among knowable objects.*

That is, some ultimate truths—i.e., true cessations—include existent phenomena among their objects of negation. While this stops just short of saying that an emptiness can have an existent object of negation, Tsong-ka-pa seems to be taking that last step when he writes, "If the real nature (*chos nyid*) of phenomena can be freed from defilement, then its objects of negation can exist among knowable objects."[30]

Kensur Padma-gyel-tsen expresses a stronger and more fundamental argument against the acceptance of true cessations as emptinesses:[31]

> If a true cessation were the real nature, then it would have to be the final mode of subsistence of the mind [realizing it]. If you accept this, then, since [true cessations] would have to be established as the mode of subsistence of that mind from the beginning, beings seeking release would be released without exertion, without relying on cultivation of the path.

If it were an emptiness, a true cessation would have to be the final nature of the mind in which it exists. How can it just suddenly become the final nature of the mind at a certain point in the mental continuum, without having been the nature of previous minds in that continuum? The real nature is not subject to fluctuation. If, at the time of the path of release, the real nature of the mind is the absence of contamination by the afflictions, then this must always have been the real nature of the mind. If this were so, it would be pointless to make any effort to train in meditation on emptiness because everyone would already have perfect nirvāṇa.

A third argument holds that if true cessations are realities or emptinesses, then they must be emptinesses of inherent existence. Since a yogi negates or abandons *new* objects of negation (afflictions) on each ground, it would follow that, although emptiness is always emptiness of inherent existence, successively higher uninterrupted paths somehow refute previously unrefuted objects of negation.[32] This would imply that some emptinesses are more profound than others.

In rebuttal of this point, it can be stressed that a true cessation must have *two* objects of negation: (1) inherent existence and (2) the objects of abandonment appropriate to its level. The former object of negation is constant, and its absence is the factor of natural purity. The latter object of negation changes and becomes more subtle as a yogi advances to higher paths. As successively subtler obstructions are abandoned, the factor of purity from adventitious stains is gradually improved.

A fourth argument supporting Paṇ-chen Sö-nam-drak-ba's position runs as follows: Since these two objects of negation are quite distinct, the non-affirming negatives that are their opposites must be ascertained sequentially rather than simultaneously.[33] First the uninterrupted path realizes the emptiness of inherent existence, and then the path of release realizes a true cessation, the absence of the objects of abandonment corresponding to that level. Although both are ultimate truths, there is no need to identify true cessations as emptinesses because Bodhisattvas do not realize emptinesses and true cessations simultaneously.

While scriptural passages cited to show that nirvāṇa is not an emptiness are ambiguous at best, there are strong arguments for it in the Lo-sel-ling literature. Consequently, I am inclined to regard Paṇ-chen's position on this issue as the product of his own reasoned analysis of the problem. Paṇ-chen's willingness to go his own way, overlooking conflicting statements in the works of Tsong-ka-pa, Kay-drup, and/or Gyel-tsap, has been mentioned already in chapters one and eight, and will be exemplified again in chapter twelve.

NIRVĀṆA IS AN EMPTINESS

Jam-yang-shay-ba, Jay-dzun Chö-gyi-gyel-tsen, and their followers hold that nirvāṇa is an emptiness. In his *Ocean of Reasoning*, Tsong-ka-pa makes several statements that support this position. For example:

> Accordingly, emptiness is suchness. By meditating on the view of that, one will realize it at the conclusion of that meditation, when the seeds of afflictions have vanished, the *emptiness that is the elimination of elaborations is called* "liberation" and "nirvāṇa."[34]

While this shows that there is a certain kind of emptiness that is called nirvāṇa, there is another passage in the same text that makes Tsong-ka-pa's meaning even clearer:[35]

> Here [in Prāsaṅgika], *the real nature* (*chos nyid, dharmatā*) of a mind which is the basis for [both] the abandonment of the seeds of afflictions and the vanishing of appearances of the aggregates of appropriation *is considered nirvāṇa*. The non-production of subsequent [afflictions and so forth] of similar type through breaking the continuum of causes and conditions for the afflictions and so forth is not considered nirvāṇa...

Thus, a particular type of emptiness, the emptiness of the mind of a yogi who has abandoned afflictions, is nirvāṇa.

This introduces the reasoned argument for identifying true cessations as emptinesses. If they are not emptinesses, they must be some factor that represents the absence or destruction of the afflictions. This suggests that they might be the "pastness" (*'das pa*) of the afflictions because, in the Ge-luk-ba presentation of Prāsaṅgika, the definition of a pastness is:[36]

> a factor of disintegratedness (*zhig pa*) of another functioning thing that has already been produced.

If true cessations were posited as the factor of disintegratedness of previously existent afflictions, by definition they would be the pastness of those afflictions. However, as implied by the phrase "another functioning thing" (*dngos po gzhan*), pastnesses (as well as present objects and futurenesses) are themselves functioning things, impermanent phenomena. Since true cessations are ultimate truths, it would extremely difficult to posit them as impermanent phenomena. Therefore, they cannot be simply the vanishing, cessation, or disintegratedness of the corresponding afflictions.

Tsong-ka-pa also argues that there is a danger in confusing true cessations with the impermanence of the afflictions. His *Ocean of Reasoning* explains the problem:[37]

> *Question:* If nirvāṇa is the vanishing of the afflictions and the mere non-existence of rebirth through the force of actions and afflictions, [why] is it a non-functioning thing? *Answer:* If [nirvāṇa] were thus, then the impermanence of afflictions and birth would be nirvāṇa because the non-existence of afflictions and birth is just that [imperma-

> nence] and, apart from the [non-existence of afflictions and birth, that impermanence] does not exist. Therefore, while the impermanence of those two would be nirvāṇa [as a consequence of your definition of nirvāṇa, nirvāṇa] is not asserted in that way because, if it were, we would be released without need for exertion [on the path].

That is, if nirvāṇa were the impermanence of the afflictions, then anyone who could realize their impermanence would be liberated from cyclic existence without further effort.

Extending this line of reasoning, if nirvāṇa were merely the impermanence of the afflictions or the non-existence of the afflictions upon the interruption of their causes, then it could not be an ultimate truth. It would not represent the negation of the subtlest object of negation, inherent existence, and therefore it would not be the reality of any phenomena. Consequently, it would not fulfill the definition of an ultimate truth as

> an object realized by a reasoning consciousness distinguishing the final [mode of subsistence] (*mthar thug dpyad pa'i rigs shes kyi rnyed don*).

One response to this argument is the claim that the word "final" (*mthar thug*) pertains not only to the final, or ultimate, mode of subsistence, but also to the final, or last, abandonment of the objects to be abandoned at that level.

Still, once true cessations are ultimate truths, they must be permanent phenomena that are realized only in meditative equipoise. Those who say that true cessations are not emptinesses are hard-pressed to find a formula for describing true cessations that meets these criteria. In the face of this difficulty and in light of the passages from the *Ocean of Reasoning* cited above, many of Paṇ-chen Sö-nam-drak-ba's followers add some sort of qualification to their assertion that true cessations are not emptinesses. For example, Gen Lo-sang-gya-tso mentioned the possibility that Paṇ-chen Sö-nam-drak-ba's arguments on this point are intended to represent the perspective of a lower tenet system. Of course, if this were true it would be quite remarkable because Tsong-ka-pa's *Illumination of the Thought*, upon which the Mādhyamika textbooks are based, is a commentary on Candrakīrti's *Supplement*. Accordingly, they should present an unadulterated Prāsaṅgika view—a standard which Paṇ-chen himself enunciates.[38] Geshe Bel-den-drak-ba seemed reluctant to give a thorough defense of Paṇ-chen's position on this issue, and Kensur Padma-gyel-tsen carefully presents both sides of the controversy.[39] The latter scholar finds a scriptural foundation for the two-mindedness of the Lo-sel-ling college, showing that Paṇ-chen Sö-nam-drak-ba appears to identify true cessations as emptinesses in his *Captivation of the Mind: Skill in the Stage of Generation of Guhyasamāja*:[40]

> The truth of the exalted wisdom of meditative equipoise—the basis for the arising of the marvelous qualities of abandonment and realization of the excellent Bodhisattvas—and the [conventional] things that possess the quality [of being empty] are a reality of one taste within the sphere of the mode of subsistence [i.e., emptiness]. The entity of that suchness is the truth of cessation.

Thus Kensur Padma-gyel-tsen concludes that this is a critically important and extremely difficult problem that requires, but as yet lacks, a satisfactory resolution.[41] This is a perfect example of the Ge-luk use of the "ongoing quest" model as the defensive strategy of last resort when faced with an intractable contradiction.

Gen Lo-sang-gya-tso suggests that the problem can be recast as a difficulty not in substance but in terminology. He argues that if a true cessation is understood as the vanishing of the appropriate objects of abandonment in relation to a path of release, then it cannot be an emptiness. However, if it is understood to be the vanishing of those objects in relation to the *real nature* of a path of release, then it is an emptiness. Therefore, he claims that there is no contradiction between the arguments of Paṇ-chen Sö-nam-drak-ba's Mādhyamika textbooks, which take the former approach, and Tsong-ka-pa's statement that "the real nature of the mind" on a path of release is nirvāṇa. Furthermore, he stresses that it is self-contradictory for someone who thinks that true cessations are emptinesses to posit nirvāṇa in relation to the mind rather than positing it in relation to the emptiness of the mind.

There is a good reason for wanting to describe true cessations as properties of the mind: emptiness is constant. As Hopkins writes, "Though the emptiness of the mind is permanent and non-changing, it is said to improve when the mind of which it is a predicate improves."[42] This is the quandary: how can emptiness be non-changing and yet somehow participate in the improvement of the mind? What is needed is a way to describe purification in terms of the ultimate reality of the mind without implying that reality itself is actually susceptible to change. The best such formulation is summed up by Kensur Padma-gyel-tsen:[43]

> It follows that a true cessation is a real nature (*chos nyid*) because (1) the extinguishment of the afflictions in the element of reality (*nyon mongs chos dbyings su zad pa*) through the power of an antidote is a true cessation and (2) that [extinguishment] is a real nature.

This also could be translated, "...the extinguishment of the afflictions as the element of reality..." Emptiness itself remains constant as a new factor of purity merges with it.

Gen Lo-sang-gya-tso offered an example that may be helpful in conceptualizing true cessations. A drinking glass is clear and reflects light. When it is filled with murky water, the glass itself remains clear by nature, but loses its reflectiveness. Similarly, when one has not abandoned the afflictions, the mind has a clear nature of emptiness, but, marred by circumstantial afflictions, it does not have a purified, enlightened, or reflecting nature. Like a glass of water from which impurities are gradually being removed, the always present clarity of the mind's emptiness is fused with a partial reflecting nature as afflictions are abandoned on the Superior paths. Like clarity in the glass, emptiness is always with the mind; like reflectiveness in the glass, purity from afflictions emerges gradually. The mind of a Buddha is like a glass full of perfectly clear water. The key point that gives this example its value is that to whatsoever extent the reflective factor is present, it is indistinguishable from the factor of clarity.

Another helpful analogy can be drawn from the passage in Nāgārjuna's *Praise for the Sphere of Reality* cited above, comparing the gradual appearance of the Truth Body to the waxing of the moon. Just as one sees the very same moon on the first day of waxing as one does on the day of the full moon, the emptiness realized on the first ground is the same as the emptiness realized on the Buddha ground. A gradual enhancement takes place as the shadows (afflictions) are gradually eliminated. Still, the underlying object—the moon, emptiness—remains the same.

I asked His Holiness, Tenzin Gyatso, the present Dalai Lama, to comment on this issue. He gave this example: Suppose a table (the mind) is basically clean (empty of inherent existence). If one pours oil (the afflictions) on it and then wipes it away, there is nothing left but a clean table. Reasoning that, in a similar way, the factor of purity from the circumstantial stains of the afflictions must be rooted in the natural purity which is the absence of inherent existence in the mind, he stated that true cessations are emptinesses.

It is his opinion that the validity of this position is established mainly through reasoning and reflection, and not merely through the citation of scriptural evidence.

10 *Realizing the Two Truths*

In preceding chapters we have examined the meanings and subdivisions of the two truths. Hereafter, we will deal with questions of how and by whom the two truths are understood. This chapter will focus on the manner in which the two truths are realized by sentient beings trapped within cyclic existence. In later chapters, we will investigate the perspectives of those who have attained liberation.

THE IMPORTANCE OF UNDERSTANDING THE TWO TRUTHS

Although the two truths are discussed and defined in other tenet systems, they are of especial importance in the exposition of Mādhyamika doctrine. In his *Treatise on the Middle Way*, Nāgārjuna declares that[1]

> Doctrines taught by the Buddha
> Rely wholly on the two truths:
> Worldly conventional truths
> And truths that are ultimate.

Consequently, comprehension of the two truths enables one to understand the sūtras, progress on the path and attain Buddhahood. Jñānagarbha's *Distinguishing the Two Truths* says:[2]

> Those who know the divisions of the two truths
> Are not obscured regarding the Conqueror's word.
> Without exception they amass the collections,
> Just going to full perfection.

In order to become a Buddha, a Bodhisattva must complete the collection of merit and the collection of wisdom. The collection of wisdom is amassed through eons of training in meditative equipoise on ultimate truth, the profound emptiness. At the end of the path, it gives rise to a Buddha's Truth Body (*chos sku, dharmakāya*). The collection of merit is amassed through training in compassion and a vast variety of merit-producing activities it gives rise to a Buddha's Form Body (*gzugs sku, rupakāya*). These practices require full conviction that, although devoid of inherent reality, sentient beings and moral effects of actions do exist in a conventional way, as concealer-truths. Therefore, Jam-yang-shay-ba writes:[3]

> The are benefits in knowing the two truths because [the Bodhisattva], moving the broad wings of the two collections, is propelled by the force of the winds of excellent wishes to the end of the ocean of a Conqueror's qualities. [The broad wings of the two collections are:] (1) skill in illusion-like merit and the vast [varieties of phenomena] which, although all phenomena are ultimately inexpressible, are conventionally mere names and mere terms, and (2) skill in maintaining space-like meditative equipoise on the mode of subsistence which is such that although merely nominal causes and effects and so forth arise individually and unerringly, they are not to be conceived as ultimately existent (*don dam par zhen pa med pa*).

On the other hand, it is impossible to progress if the two truths are not understood. Nāgārjuna's *Treatise on the Middle Way* states:[4]

> Those who do not know the division of these two truths
> Do not know the profound suchness in Buddha's teaching.

and Candrakīrti's *Supplement* states:[5]

> Those who do not know the division of the two truths
> Are drawn into bad paths by their wrong conceptions.

Jam-yang-shay-ba explains that it is impossible to attain liberation without understanding ultimate truths because one must realize emptiness in order to attain even a path of preparation (*sbyor lam, prayogamārga*).[6] Also, if one attempts to understand emptiness without also developing the ability to posit conventionalities, the result will be a warped perspective and a bad rebirth.

REALIZING CONCEALER-TRUTHS

It is easy to naïvely suppose that we already understand concealer-truths. Emptiness may be beyond our ken, yet certainly we know tables, chairs, and so forth. Every object of knowledge must be either a concealer-truth or an ultimate truth. Therefore, if we do not know the latter, we must know the former insofar as we know anything at all. The objects we perceive every day, as objects realized by conventional valid cognizers, do fulfill the definition of a concealer-truth.

For these reasons, there can be no dispute as to whether the various ordinary objects with which we are familiar are concealer-truths. Unquestionably, they are. However, if chairs are concealer-truths and we know chairs, do we therefore understand concealer-truths? We know a particular concealer-truth—that is, something that is an instance of concealer-truth. Still, we have no understanding of these objects as concealer-truths. In order to really understand concealer-truths, it is necessary to grasp the meaning of concealer-truth and associate it with an object to which that meaning is appropriate. Tsong-ka-pa's *Ocean of Reasoning* says:[7]

> Although pot, cloth, and so forth are concealer-truths, when the mind establishes them it does not necessarily establish the meaning of concealer-truth.

In his *Illumination of the Thought*, Tsong-ka-pa explains this point using a magic show as an example.[8] Some spectators may see an illusory appearance of a horse without recognizing it as an illusion. Similarly, all of the ordinary objects that we see are concealer-truths, but we do not know them as such.

How, then, can an understanding of concealer-truths be achieved? Tsong-ka-pa's *Illumination of the Thought* describes the process:[9]

> The finding of pots and so forth which are illustrations of concealer-truths does indeed occur among those who have not found the view of the middle way; however, in order to find with valid cognition that something *is* a

> concealer-truth, one definitely must have first found the view of the middle way. This is because if something is established as a concealer-truth, it must be established as a falsity, and in order actually to establish that something is a falsity, it is necessary first to refute with valid cognition that it is truly existent.

Spectators at a magic show can recognize an illusory horse as an illusion if he first sees the pebble or stick that is the actual basis of that appearance. They will then realize that the deceptive power of the magician's spell is obstructing the appearance of the pebble or stick and causing a horse to appear instead. Likewise, Tsong-ka-pa holds that one must first realize emptiness, the real nature of an object, before one can cognize that object as a concealer-truth. The sequence is clear: First one realizes emptiness by refuting inherent existence. Then one realizes that phenomena lacking inherent existence are falsities because they appear to be inherently or truly existent, but in fact are not. Only then can one realize that they are concealer-truths.

It is somewhat counter-intuitive to suggest that realization of emptiness precedes the understanding of conventionalities. Moreover, Candrakīrti's *Supplement* states:[10]

> Conventional truths are the method;
> Ultimate truths are [results] arisen from method.

What sense does it make to say that the result must be realized before the method? Accordingly, some Ge-luk-bas, such as Jay-dzun Chö-gyi-gyel-tsen, hold that concealer-truths are realized prior to ultimate truths.[11] However, all agree that in order to realize that a particular concealer-truth, such as a table, is a concealer-truth, it is necessary first to refute true existence.

Why should it be essential to comprehend something as a falsity in order to comprehend it as a concealer-truth? Jam-yang-shay-ba finds an answer in another passage from *Illumination of the Thought*—a passage wherein Tsong-ka-pa gives the meaning of the the term "concealer-truth":[12]

> When one sees that when a pot and so forth are posited as truths in the phrase "concealer-truths," then, from between being posited for an awareness and being posited in fact, pot and so forth are not posited as truths in fact; rather, they are posited as truths merely for the perspec-

> tive of the consciousness conceiving true existence—the concealer. At that time, one must see that if that distinction is not enforced, [pot and so forth] are not established as truths but are falsities [instead].

This passage is relevant in discussing the sequence of realization because it seems to connect the meanings of "falsity" and "concealer-truth" by way of the etymology of the term "concealer-truth." Jam-yang-shay-ba concludes, "[I]n order to realize something as a concealer-truth, one must realize that it is a truth merely for ignorance and in order to do that, one must refute true existence."[13] Combining this with Tsong-ka-pa's statement that realization of an object as a falsity occurs prior to realization of it as a concealer-truth but after refutation of true existence, we obtain the following sequence:

(1) realization of an object's emptiness of true existence,
(2) realization of the object as a falsity insofar as it appears to be truly existent, but in fact is not truly existent
(3) realization that the object is a truth merely for ignorance,
(4) realization that the object is a concealer-truth.

REALIZATION VIA DEFINITION

Kensur Padma-gyel-tsen quarrels with part of this interpretation when he writes:[14]

> From within the division of the two truths, as for the way that concealer-truths are established, some texts use "true in theperspective of a consciousness conceiving true ignorance and false in the measure of its subsistence." However, if [the way that concealer-truths are established] is posited in relation to an understanding of the *definition* of a concealer-truth, instead of merely its etymology, then only [realizing the definition]—"that with regard to which a valid cognizer distinguishing conventionalities becomes a valid cognizer distinguishing conventionalities"—is enough to establish [a concealer-truth].

As explained in chapter five, the etymological meaning of concealer-truth is "truth for the perspective of the concealing ignorant consciousness." This is broader than the actual meaning of concealer-truth because even ultimate truths are truths in the perspective of the ignorance conceiving true existence. Kensur Padma-gyel-tsen implies that Jam-yang-shay-ba is guilty of an inaccuracy in positing the comprehension of concealer-truths in terms of the etymology rather than the definition.

Indeed, it is a general principle of Ge-luk-ba epistemology that realization of a definiendum does not precede realization of its definition.[15] For example, one cannot know color until one has known its definition, that which is suitable as a hue. Therefore, Kensur Padma-gyel-tsen makes a good point in arguing that an understanding of the definition of concealer-truth must figure in the realization of concealer-truth. In Jam-yang-shay-ba's defense, it should be noted that even Tsong-ka-pa's *Illumination of the Thought* and *Ocean of Reasoning* do not explicitly mention the definition of concealer-truth in the context of their discussions of the process of realizing that a particular object is a concealer-truth.

Moreover, in both Jam-yang-shay-ba's and Tsong-ka-pa's writing, there is a key difference between the *etymology* of "concealer-truth" and the *descriptions of the realization process.* Jam-yang-shay-ba says, "[I]n order to realize that something is a concealer-truth, one must realize that it is a truth *merely* for ignorance. . ." Referring to the passage from *Illumination of the Thought* (cited above) on which this is based, we find that the word "merely" eliminates the object's being a truth in fact.[16] This is different from realizing concealer-truth by way of its etymology because the etymology, lacking the word "merely," does not exclude the possibility of its referent being a truth in fact.

How is it to be known that the object is not a truth in fact? The measure of factuality here can only be establishment by valid cognition. Thus, understanding that something is not a truth in fact means understanding that it is not established as a truth by valid cognition. Accordingly, a realization that an object is a truth *merely* for ignorance implies some understanding of the way it is ascertained by valid cognition. One must not only understand that it is a truth for ignorance, but also understand that it is not a truth for valid cognition. Thus, one must understand the object in question to be a deceptive object for a conventional valid cognizer—thereby associating it with the definition of concealer-truth. My point is that, contrary to Kensur Padma-gyel-tsen's argument, "to realize that something is a truth merely for ignorance and not a truth in fact" probably does involve realizing not only the etymology of concealer-truth, but the definition as well.

Among Ge-luk-bas, it is apparently only Tsong-ka-pa who insists upon including the words like "false" and "deceptive" in his definitions of concealer-truth. The inclusion of such words makes it easier to see how the definition is involved in the realization process and why one must refute true existence before realizing the meaning of concealer-truth. Kensur Padma-gyel-tsen, like most Ge-luk-bas, omits the word "deceptive" from his definition—yet he insists upon the role of definitions in the realization process. If, in order to realize that a table is a concealer-truth, one need only realize that it is an object found by a conventional valid cognizer,[17] then why is it necessary to realize emptiness before realizing that a table is a concealer-truth? Do ordinary students of this topic not already know that a table is something found by conventional valid cognition? Scholars to whom I put this question insist that it is impossible to understand fully what it means for something to be found by *conventional* valid cognition without first refuting true existence.[18]

REALIZING ULTIMATE TRUTHS

Setting aside such complex speculations, the crucial point upon which Ge-luk-bas agree is that practitioners must realize emptiness before they can realize that an object *is* a concealer-truth. In order to understand deceptive appearances *as* deceptive appearances, it is necessary to penetrate reality. Therefore, the initial realization of ultimate truth must precede the initial realization of ordinary phenomena as concealer-truths.

Without contradicting this conclusion, Kensur Padma-gyel-tsen shows that the issue of when ultimate truths are realized is not entirely clear-cut:[19]

> When [an awareness] realizes, for example, the absence of true existence in a sprout—an instance of an ultimate truth—that awareness establishes with valid cognition an ultimate truth. However, it does not necessarily establish that the base, [the absence of true existence of a sprout,] is an ultimate truth.

The mind realizing the emptiness of a sprout merely refutes the true existence of the sprout; it does not think about whether this absence of true existence is an ultimate truth. Above, we argued that the realization of an instance of a concealer-truth does not necessarily involve an understanding of the meaning of concealer-truth. In a sense, it is thus possible to construct a comparison between realization of emptiness in the process of understanding ultimate truth and realization of a sprout, for example, in the process of understanding concealer-truth. Each realization entails the establishment by valid cognition of an instance of one of the two truths, but neither requires the explicit identification of its object *as* one of the two truths.

Still, we should not conclude that the realization of emptiness is no more a realization of the meaning of ultimate truth than the realization of a sprout is a realization of the meaning of concealer-truth. The mind realizing emptiness is a reasoning consciousness that finds the final reality, a non-deceptive object. Reflection upon this realization immediately leads to the identification of the experienced object, emptiness, as an ultimate truth. This identification requires no further effort or elaborate reasoning. It is only necessary to remember what has just been experienced and associate it with the previous knowledge that "ultimate truth" is the name for a non-deceptive object found by an ultimate valid cognizer. Quite dissimilarly, the realization of a sprout by a person who has never realized emptiness is merely an ascertainment of an instance of concealer-truth, and conveys none of the sense of falseness that is essential to the meaning of concealer-truth.

Consequently, Kensur Padma-gyel-tsen holds that the realization of the absence of true existence in a sprout is a realization of ultimate truth.[20] As an example, he gives the case of someone who realizes a bulbous, splay-based vessel. Even before applying the word "pot" to this object, that person has realized a pot. On the other hand, an ordinary realization of a sprout cannot be posited as a realization of concealer-truth. In that case, the mind not only fails to apply the term "concealer-truth" to the sprout, it does not even get at the meaning of concealer-truth. This is exemplified by the spectators at a magic show who see illusions without recognizing them as such.

DO ULTIMATE TRUTHS APPEAR TO THOSE WHO HAVE IGNORANCE?

Candrakīrti's *Supplement Commentary* states that ultimate truths are established through being the objects of the wisdom consciousnesses of Superiors and that concealer-truths are established through being the objects of consciousnesses of ordinary beings.[21] Tsong-ka-pa's *Illumination of the Thought* explains that this means that the *main* apprehenders of concealer-truths are ordinary beings and the main apprehenders of ultimate truths are Superiors.[22] While the meaning of concealer-truth is not realized by persons who have not realized emptiness, instances of concealer-truths, such as pot, are mainly realized by persons who have yet to realize emptiness directly. By introducing the qualifying word "main," Tsong-ka-pa shows that learner Superiors who are not in meditative equipoise and Buddha Superiors can also realize concealer-truths. Conversely, ultimate truths, although they are mainly realized by Superiors, are also realized by ordinary beings via inference.

The notion that ordinary beings can realize emptiness has to be reconciled with a statement from Candrakīrti's *Supplement Commentary*, "The nature [i.e., emptiness] does not appear in any way (*rnam pa thams cad du*) to those possessing ignorance (*ma rig pa dang ldan pa rnams*)."[23] In fact, taken at face value, this seems even to contradict realization of emptiness by Superiors on the first through seventh grounds. In his *Illumination of the Thought*, Tsong-ka-pa gives this interpretation:[24]

> [That statement by Candrakīrti is made] in consideration that [emptiness] does not appear to consciousnesses that are polluted with ignorance (*ma rig pas bslad pa'i shes pa*) since he asserts that Superiors [on the first through seventh grounds], who have not [fully] abandoned ignorance, [nevertheless] do directly realize suchness. Also, because a Learner Superior's exalted wisdom subsequent to meditative equipoise and a common being's viewing consciousness of suchness are polluted with ignorance and its latencies (*bag chags, vāsanā*), [emptiness] does not directly (*mngon sum du*) appear [to those consciousnesses]. However, it must be asserted that, in general, ultimate truth does appear [to those consciousnesses].

Anyone who has not completely abandoned ignorance must still possess it. However, since there must be Superiors who directly realize emptiness before they have abandoned all ignorance, Tsong-ka-pa interprets Candrakīrti's phrase "those possessing ignorance" to refer to consciousnesses that are polluted by ignorance. Even when ignorant consciousnesses conceiving of inherent existence have been completely abandoned, pollution by the latencies of ignorance remains in any consciousness to which an object appears to be inherently existent. Tsong-ka-pa's *Illumination of the Thought* says:[25]

> As long as the Buddha ground has not been attained, there are no consciousnesses—aside from the non-conceptual exalted wisdom of a Superior's meditative equipoise—that are not polluted by the latencies of ignorance.

Also, there are both Superiors and ordinary beings who have conceptual consciousnesses that explicitly realize emptiness by way of a generic image (*don spyi, arthasāmānya*). Since it must be said that ultimate truth appears to those consciousnesses, Tsong-ka-pa takes Candrakīrti to mean that emptiness does not *directly* appear to consciousnesses polluted by ignorance.[26]

An unfortunate complication in this interpretation is that in the Prāsaṅgika system conceptuality (*rtog pa, kalpanā*) and direct perception (*mngon sum, pratyakṣa*) are not mutually exclusive. Following the initial moment of an inferential realization of emptiness, subsequent valid cognizers in that sequence are direct valid cognizers (*mngon sum tshad ma*) realizing emptiness, even though they are conceptual consciousnesses. Unlike the initial inferential realization, they do not rely on a logical mark; instead, they rely upon the power of that preceding inference.[27] Such conceptual minds are mistaken consciousnesses, polluted by ignorance, yet at the same time they are direct valid cognizers realizing emptiness. Thus Geshe Tsul-tim-gya-tso is led to write that even in the light of Tsong-ka-pa's interpretation, difficult qualms remain about the meaning of this passage from Candrakīrti's *Supplement Commentary*.[28] I think that the word "directly" as used by Tsong-ka-pa in this context must mean "in a manner devoid of all dualistic appearance." Only a Superior's meditative equipoise, a consciousness not polluted by ignorance or its latencies, can see emptiness in this way.

Geshe Bel-den-drak-ba finds further problems. He assumes that since ignorance is a consciousness, "those possessing ignorance" must be persons. Following Tsong-ka-pa's interpretation, "persons possessing ignorance" must be understood to mean "persons possessing consciousnesses that are polluted by ignorance." However, since a Bodhisattva in meditative equipoise on the path of seeing, for example, has not yet abandoned all ignorance, it must be said that in general such a Bodhisattva possesses consciousnesses polluted by ignorance. Geshe Bel-den-drak-ba explains that the Losel-ling tradition therefore differentiates persons who possess ignorance (*ma rig pa dang ldan*) from persons in whom ignorance exists (*ma rig pa yod pa*). Just as one might be susceptible to anger in general without being angry at a particular moment, Superiors in meditative equipoise possess consciousnesses polluted by ignorance although such consciousnesses do not exist in them at that time. Having made this distinction, it is then necessary to interpret the statement that emptiness does not appear to those possessing ignorance to mean that emptiness does not directly appear to those in whom consciousnesses polluted by ignorance exist.[29]

Go-mang scholars cannot resolve this difficulty in the same way because Jam-yang-shay-ba's assertions about non-manifest minds differ from those of most Lo-sel-ling scholars. The latter generally hold that when Learner Superiors are in non-conceptual meditative equipoise on emptiness, no conventional awarenesses exist in their continuums at that time. Jam-yang-shay-ba holds that various non-manifest consciousnesses, including an altruistic aspiration to attain enlightenment, exist during meditative equipoise.[30] Therefore, according to Jam-yang-shay-ba's system, emptiness does appear in a non-dualistic manner to persons in whom there exist consciousnesses polluted by ignorance. This is because when emptiness appears to a Bodhisattva in meditative equipoise, various non-manifest mistaken consciousnesses simultaneously exist in that Bodhisattva's continuum.

It seems that the best way to escape this difficulty within the context of Go-mang assertions is to reject the premise that "those possessing ignorance" are persons. Tsong-ka-pa says, "[Candrakīrti's statement] is in consideration that [emptiness] does not appear to consciousnesses that are polluted with ignorance (*ma rig pas bslad pa'i shes pa*). . . ." If we take this simply to mean that those possessing ignorance are *consciousnesses* that "possess" ignorance in the sense that they are polluted by it, the problem raised by Geshe Bel-den-drak-ba may be averted.

11 Mere Conventionalities

ARE REFLECTIONS CONCEALER-TRUTHS?

Candrakīrti's *Supplement* says:[1]

> The Subduer said that an obscuring [consciousness]
> is the concealer (*kun rdzob, saṃvṛti*)
> Because it obstructs the nature and that the fabrications
> It perceives as true are concealer-truths.
> Things that are fabrications [are said] to be [mere]
> conventionalities (*kun rdzob, saṃvṛti*).

In his commentary on this, Candrakīrti states, "That [nature, i.e., emptiness,] and whatever is false even conventionally are not concealer-truths."[2] Commenting on this passage, Jayānanda, the author of the only extant Indian commentary on Candrakīrti's *Supplement*, argues that because they are "false even conventionally," reflections, echoes, and so forth are are neither concealer-truths nor ultimate truths; rather, they are "mere conventionalities" (*kun rdzob tsam, saṃvṛtimātra*).[3] In Tsong-ka-pa's view, Jayānanda's assertion that reflections are neither concealer-truths nor ultimate truths violates the principle that the two truths must stand as a dichotomy of all objects of knowledge. However, in order to refute Jayānanda, Tsong-ka-pa must explain what Candrakīrti means by the statement that whatever is false even conventionally is not a concealer-truth. In his *Illumination of the Thought*, Tsong-ka-pa argues that, since mature worldly persons do not have an ignorant consciousness misconceiving a reflection of a face to be a face, for mature persons a reflection is not a truth for that coarse type of concealing ignorance. He continues:[4]

> Therefore, [Candrakīrti's] statement that a reflection is not a concealer-truth is in consideration that with respect to a reflection of a face, for instance, its being a face is false for a conventional [consciousness] of worldly [persons] trained in language (*brda la byang*) and hence is not a "concealer-truth" in relation to that.

Nevertheless, a reflection must be a concealer-truth in the usual sense as defined by Candrakīrti in his statement that "objects of perceivers of falsities are concealer-truths."[5] Reflections are falsities because they appear to be inherently existent and in fact are not inherently existent. They are truths in the perspective of the concealing ignorance that conceives them to be inherently existent. Referring to Jayānanda, Tsong-ka-pa concludes:[6]

> Therefore, the statement that objects such as reflections which even ordinary worldly consciousnesses understand to be mistaken are not concealer-truths but are mere conventionalities [when in fact they are both] appears to be the talk of those who have not formed an understanding of the precise enumeration of the two truths, truth and falsity relative to the world, and truth and falsity that are posited by Mādhyamikas.

Candrakīrti's *Supplement Commentary* continues, "On the one hand, concealer-truths are posited through the force of afflictive ignorance that is included within the limbs of cyclic existence."[7] Tsong-ka-pa is careful to explain that Candrakīrti's statement that concealer-truths are posited through the force of ignorance means that concealer-truths such as a pot are posited *as truths* in the perspective of the concealing ignorance. It does not mean that a consciousness conceiving true existence posits the very *existence* of pots and so forth because Candrakīrti asserts that what is posited by a consciousness conceiving true existence does not exist even conventionally.[8] In this passage, Candrakīrti's point is that pot and so forth are posited as concealer-truths because they are truths in the perspective of a particular type of ignorance: afflictive ignorance that is at the root of cyclic existence, the ignorance that is the first in the twelve links of dependent-origination.[9]

HOW THE THREE PERSONS SEE CONCEALER-TRUTHS

If conventional phenomena are posited as "concealer-truths" on account of being misperceived as truths by afflictive ignorance, then how are they viewed by those who have abandoned afflictive ignorance? Candrakīrti's *Supplement Commentary* states:[10]

> On the one hand, concealer-truths are posited through the force of afflictive ignorance that is included within the limbs of cyclic existence. On the other hand, for the Hearers, Solitary Realizers, and Bodhisattvas who have abandoned afflictive ignorance and who see compositional phenomena as just being like the existence of reflections and so forth, those have a fabricated nature and are not truths because they have no conceit of true existence. For children, [compositional phenomena] are deceivers; for others, they are mere conventionalities because of being dependent-arisings, like illusions and so forth.

Following some remarks on the perspective of Buddha Superiors (which will be discussed in chapter twelve), Candrakīrti concludes, "In that way, the Supramundane Victor spoke of concealer-truths and mere conventionalities."[11] Jayānanda's interpretation is that forms and so forth are not concealer-truths in the perspective of Hearers, Solitary Realizers and Bodhisattvas who have abandoned afflictive ignorance. Instead, for them forms and so forth are mere conventionalities, like reflections.[12]

Tsong-ka-pa again rejects Jayānanda's approach, holding that forms and so forth are both concealer-truths and mere conventionalities in the perspective of sentient beings who have abandoned afflictive ignorance. Since (1) Hearer Foe Destroyers, (2) Solitary Realizers Foe Destroyers, and (3) Bodhisattvas on the eighth, ninth, and tenth grounds (referred to as "the three persons" for the sake of brevity) have abandoned all consciousnesses conceiving true existence, they no longer see conventional phenomena as *truths*. However, this in no way establishes that they do not see forms and so forth as *concealer-truths*. Tsong-ka-pa's *Ocean of Reasoning* says:[13]

> Those who have abandoned the concealer which is afflictive ignorance do not have the concealing [consciousness] conceiving true existence in whose perspective [pheno-

> mena] are posited as truths. This proves that compositional phenomena are not truths in their perspective; it does not prove that compositional phenomena are not concealer-truths in their perspective. . . . [T]he word "mere" [in the term "mere conventionality"] eliminates truth; how would it eliminate concealer-truth?

In fact, the refutation of true existence and the realization of an object as a falsity are prerequisite to and conducive to the apprehension of that object as a concealer-truth—as discussed above in chapter ten. Accordingly, Tsong-ka-pa argues that if Candrakīrti had been attempting to show that the three persons do not see conventional phenomena as concealer-truths, it would be ridiculous for him to justify this by reason of their abandonment of consciousnesses conceiving true existence.[14]

Imagine the following response to Tsong-ka-pa's argument: Although it is true that one must refute true existence before fully understanding what it means for something to be a concealer-truth, upon extinguishing all afflictive ignorance one no longer views phenomena as concealer-truths. This is because the comprehension of a phenomenon as a concealer-truth involves the apprehension of it as a truth in the perspective of the concealing ignorance; where such ignorance no longer exists, phenomena are no longer understood in those terms.

In rebuttal, Jam-yang-shay-ba follows Tsong-ka-pa in contending that there is no need to misapprehend something as a truth in order to understand that it is misapprehended as a truth by ignorance.[15] Those who have extinguished afflictive ignorance are well able to realize that forms and so forth are truths in the perspective of the ignorant consciousnesses of *other* persons. They can also remember how phenomena formerly appeared to their own ignorant consciousnesses. Accordingly, they *can* identify forms and so forth as concealer-truths.

Although quite persuasive, this logic apparently runs counter to the logic of Tsong-ka-pa's interpretation of Candrakīrti's statement that whatever is false even conventionally (e.g., a reflection of a face) is not a "concealer-truth." As explained above, Tsong-ka-pa understands Candrakīrti to mean that for mature worldly persons, a reflection of a face is not a truth for a concealing ignorance that conceives a reflection, etc., to be a face. Thus, Tsong-ka-pa holds that in that context Candrakīrti is using the term "concealer-truth" in an unusual way, wherein the concealing ignorance is a coarse type of ignorance instead of a consciousness conceiving inherent existence. My point here is that the principles Tsong-ka-pa uses to decide that a reflection is not a coarse concealer-truth in the perspective of mature worldly beings are apparently different from the principles he uses to maintain that forms, etc. *are* concealer-truths in the perspective of the three persons. Just as the three persons can understand that, unlike themselves, ignorant beings misapprehend forms, etc., as truly existent, so language-trained worldly persons understand that, unlike themselves, very young children misapprehend a reflection of a face as a face. Tsong-ka-pa claims that (1) Foe Destroyers see forms as concealer-truths—even though they lack the concealing ignorance—while (2) language-trained persons do not see reflections, etc., as coarse concealer-truths *because* they lack the concealing ignorance (i.e., a consciousness conceiving a reflection to be a face) in relation to which reflections are called (coarse) "concealer-truths." If the logic Tsong-ka-pa applies to Candrakīrti's statement that "whatever is false even conventionally is not a concealer-truth," *were* carried over to the discussion of the three persons, it would seem to justify Jayānanda's position that forms and so forth are not concealer-truths for the three persons because the three persons have abandoned the concealing ignorance.

However, Tsong-ka-pa indicates that "concealer-truth" does not have its usual meaning in the context of Candrakīrti's statement that "whatever is false even conventionally is not a concealer-truth," and he thereby avoids any explicit internal contradiction. Nonetheless, there is an uncomfortable and unexplained inconsistency. Jam-yang-shay-ba recognizes the problem and circumvents it by setting forth general criteria by which it may be determined whether a phenomenon is a concealer-truth in the perspective of a particular person.[16] With some adaptation, Jam-yang-shay-ba's formula states that an object is a concealer-truth in the perspective of a person if: (1) that person has an awareness conceiving the object to exist as it appears, or (2) that person can realize that the object is a concealer-truth. Here are some examples: A reflection of a face is a "concealer-truth" in the perspective of a very young child because such a child has an awareness conceiving that the reflection exists as it appears. A reflection of a face is not a concealer-truth in the perspective of a worldly, language-trained person because such a person neither imagines that a reflection exists just as it appears (since he or she knows that it is not a face), nor recognizes it as a concealer-truth (since he or she does not realize its emptiness of true existence). A table is a concealer-truth in the perspective of a Foe Destroyer because a Foe Destroyer does realize that a table is a concealer-truth.

By setting up one general definition of what it means for something to be a concealer-truth in someone's perspective, Jam-yang-shay-ba's approach tends to blur the distinction between the general meaning of concealer-truth and the special meaning Tsong-ka-pa gives it in his interpretation of Candrakīrti's statement that "whatever exists even conventionally is not a concealer-truth." However, he provides an avenue for reconciling the logic of Tsong-ka-pa's remarks in that context with his assertion that forms, etc. are concealer-truths in the perspective of the three persons.

WHAT ARE MERE CONVENTIONALITIES?

Candrakīrti definitely makes a distinction between concealer-truths and mere conventionalities. Having first explained that *concealer-truths* are posited by afflictive ignorance, he goes on to say that compositional phenomena are *mere conventionalities* for those who have abandoned afflictive ignorance. This distinction is reinforced by Candrakīrti's concluding remark, "In that way, the Supramundane Victors (*bcom ldan 'das*) spoke of concealer-truths and mere conventionalities."

Jam-yang-shay-ba acknowledges that Candrakīrti makes this distinction, but follows Tsong-ka-pa in asserting that the three persons can comprehend compositional phenomena both as concealer-truths and as mere conventionalities. According to Jam-yang-shay-ba, phenomena are designated "mere conventionalities" (*kun rdzob tsam, saṃvṛtimātra*) in order to show that they are only conventionally existent (*kun rdzob tu yod*).[17] He cites the *Meeting of the Father and Son Sūtra*:[18]

> Phenomena which do not have entityness (*ngo bo nyid*) lack actuality (*dngos po*) [that is, inherent existence] . . . . That which is invalid in [each of] the three times does not have name, character, signs, or designation except for mere names, mere terms, mere conventions (*tha snyad tsam*), mere conventionalities (*kun rdzob tsam*), and mere designations [given to them] because they are perceived by sentient beings.

Based on this and another passage from the same sūtra, Jam-yang-shay-ba argues that even emptinesses are mere conventionalities (*kun rdzob tsam, saṃvṛtimātra*) because, lacking inherent or ultimate existence, they exist in a merely conventional way.[19] The advantage of this approach is that Jam-yang-shay-ba can justify Candrakīrti's distinction by explaining that Buddha "spoke of concealer-truths in order to teach one of the two truths and spoke of mere conventionalities in order to teach that although all phenomena lack true existence, they do exist as mere conventionalities."[20] Jam-yang-shay-ba must therefore hold that "conventionality" (a synonym of concealer-truth) and "mere conventionality" (which includes all phenomena) are not coextensive. While it may be awkward to assert that "mere conventionality" is a broader term than "conventionality," Jam-yang-shay-ba's interpretation finds support in Candrakīrti's statement (cited above) that for the three persons compositional phenomena are mere conventionalities "because of being dependent-arisings." If being a dependent-arising proves that something is a mere conventionality, then even emptiness must be a mere conventionality.

It seems more natural, however, to assume that mere conventionalities must be conventionalities, and that mere conventionality and concealer-truth are therefore mutually inclusive. In support of this assumption, it can be noted that Candrakīrti specifically states that the three persons see *compositional phenomena* (*'dus byas kyi chos, saṃskṛtadharma*) as mere conventionalities; he does not say that they see emptinesses in that way. Also, since Tsong-ka-pa says that the word "mere" eliminates *truth*, it is possible to argue that mere conventionalities are necessarily falsities, phenomena that do not exist as they appear. However, inasmuch as compositional phenomena, the particular subjects to which Candrakīrti here refers, are phenomena that deceptively appear to be inherently existent, there was no need for Tsong-ka-pa to differentiate "truth" (*bden pa*) from "truly existent" (*bden par yod*) at this point. In the case of conventional phenomena, a conception that they are truths is necessarily an ignorant consciousness conceiving true existence. The distinction becomes significant only when Jam-yang-shay-ba raises the issue of whether emptinesses are mere conventionalities. Jam-yang-shay-ba can claim that when Tsong-ka-pa states that the word "mere" in "mere conventionality" eliminates "truth," he means that *true existence* is eliminated. Thus, to see a phenomenon as a mere conventionality is to recognize that it exists only conventionally, and does not truly exist or ultimately exist.

Jam-yang-shay-ba concludes his discussion of mere conventionalities by stating:[21]

> Since it appears that the term "mere conventionality" has caused many of our own [Ge-luk-ba order] as well as others to have wrong ideas, I have uprooted a hundred wrong ideas simultaneously.

Although no one explains the precise meaning of *kun rdzob tsam* as clearly as Jam-yang-shay-ba, I have not found any clear statement of the "wrong views" to which he refers in the writings of Paṇ-chen Sö-nam-drak-ba or Jay-dzun Chö-gyi-gyel-tsen. Jay-dzun Chö-gyi-gyel-tsen says that in the perspective of the three persons, forms and so forth are mere conventionalities "and not truly existent" (*bden grub min*).[22] Paṇ-chen Sö-nam-drak-ba is somewhat more vague, saying merely that form is a mere conventionality because the three persons see it as such rather than apprehending it as a truth (*bden par mi 'dzin*).[23] However, neither scholar states that conventionality (*kun rdzob*) or concealer-truth (*kun rdzob bden pa*) is equivalent to mere conventionality (*kun rdzob tsam*), nor do they give any other clear contradiction of Jam-yang-shay-ba's position that even emptinesses are mere conventionalities. Among later Ge-luk-ba scholars, it seems that neither the eighteenth-century Mongolian scholar, Jang-gya, nor the twentieth-century Go-mang scholar, Geshe Tsul-tim-gya-tso, meet this point head on. Kensur Padma-gyel-tsen, a twentieth-century Lo-sel-ling abbot, is in harmony with Jam-yang-shay-ba when he suggests that "mere conventionality" means mere imputation by thought (*rtog pas btags tsam*).[24]

12 *Omniscience*

Having discussed the way that the two truths are perceived by common beings (in chapter ten) and Foe Destroyers (in chapter eleven), we now turn to the perspective of a Buddha. As mentioned earlier, Ge-luk-bas often refer to a Buddha's mind as "inconceivable" (*bsam gyis mi khyab pa, acintya*). Faced with the task of describing the inconceivable, Ge-luk-bas forge ahead in their usual way, making every effort to produce a coherent, rational account of a Buddha's subjectivity.

A BUDDHA'S MODE OF COGNITION IS UNIQUE

Bodhisattvas on the eighth, ninth, and tenth grounds have completely abandoned all afflictive obstructions (*nyon sgrib, kleśāvaraṇa*) from their roots. They are therefore free from cyclic existence. Nevertheless, motivated by compassion, they continue their practice and amass the merit and wisdom needed to attain the full powers of a Buddha. Also, while they have abandoned consciousnesses conceiving true existence and the other afflictions along with their seeds, latencies of the previously existent afflictions remain—like a subtle residual odor in a container from which an aromatic substance has been removed. These latencies are obstructions to omniscience (*shes sgrib, jñānāvaraṇa*). When the final uninterrupted path of the tenth ground Bodhisattva eliminates the last and subtlest of these obstructions, Buddhahood is attained.

Prior to attaining Buddhahood, Superiors realize ultimate truths and concealer-truths in alternation. During periods of non-conceptual meditative equipoise (*mnyam bzhag, samāhita*) on emptiness they cognize only emptiness and do not see other phenomena; in states subsequent to meditative equipoise (*rjes thob, pṛṣṭhalabdha*), conventionalities appear to them. Since emptiness is seen by way of a vanishing of non-dualistic appearance (*gnyis snang nub tshul gyis*) and conventionalities are seen dualistically, sentient beings cannot simultaneously have explicit and direct cognition of both truths individually. However, when the last obstructions are abandoned, all of the concealer-truths that are the bases of emptinesses clearly appear from within a continuous state of non-conceptual realization of emptiness. Tsong-ka-pa's *Illumination of the Thought* explains:[1]

> As long as the latencies of mistaken dualistic appearance are not extinguished, direct comprehension of the mode (*ji lta ba*) [i.e., emptiness] and direct comprehension of the varieties (*ji snyed pa*) [i.e., conventional phenomena] cannot be produced as one entity. Therefore, since the comprehensions of meditative equipoise and subsequent attainment must alternate, comprehension of those two [mode and varieties] in relation to a single moment of exalted wisdom cannot occur. When the latencies of mistakeness are all abandoned, one continuously generates the two exalted wisdoms as a single entity in relation to every moment of exalted wisdom.

Every instant, all of a Buddha's consciousnesses non-conceptually realize all emptinesses by way of a vanishing of dualistic appearance and simultaneously non-conceptually realize all concealer-truths by way of an association with dualistic appearance. According to Jam-yang-shay-ba, it is because of this unique ability to maintain non-conceptual cognition of all phenomena—both ultimate truths and concealer-truths—without mixing individual objects into a composite, that a Buddha's mode of cognition is called "inconceivable."[2] It is for the same reason that Tsong-ka-pa, when defining the two truths as objects found by two different kinds of valid cognizers, treats a Buddha's mode of cognition as an exception.

The fifteenth-century Sa-gya scholar and critic of Tsong-ka-pa, Dak-tsang, takes a completely different view. He asserts that a Buddha is, in effect, an after-effect or epiphenomenon of previous practice by a Bodhisattva and that Buddhas do not have consciousnesses that know ultimate truths and concealer-truths. Jayānanda, the author of the only extant Indian commentary on Candrakīrti's *Supplement*, states that mere conventionalities do not appear to Buddhas, thus implying that Buddhas know only ultimate truths. Arguing against these views, Ge-luk-bas cite several Indian sources as evidence that Buddhas have consciousnesses that know all phenomena. Candrakīrti's *Supplement*:[3]

> Omniscient exalted wisdom is asserted
> To have the character of direct perception.

Just as Candrakīrti speaks of a Buddha as omniscient, so Aśvagoṣa praises Buddha in a similar way:[4]

> Only your exalted wisdom
> Pervades all objects of knowledge.

Jñānagarbha's *Commentary on "Distinguishing the Two Truths"* says:[5]

> Even one moment of [a Buddha's] cognition
> Encompasses the sphere of objects of knowledge.

A Buddha's cognition of the mode of being of phenomena is the culmination of a Bodhisattva's practice of meditative equipoise on emptiness, and a Buddha's cognition of the varieties is the culmination of a Bodhisattva's meditations on illusion-like conventional phenomena in states attained subsequent to meditative equipoise. However, a Buddha's wisdom cognizing the mode is an omniscient mind, and it therefore must also realize all concealer-truths; likewise, a Buddha's wisdom cognizing the varieties knows both truths simultaneously. Thus, it is impossible to divide up a Buddha's consciousnesses according to the type of object they observe because every moment of every consciousness is perfectly omniscient. Nevertheless, omniscient consciousnesses realize each object in a manner appropriate to that object. Concealer-truths are always understood in association with dualistic appearance, and ultimate truths are known by way of the vanishing of dualistic appearance. Therefore, every one of a Buddha's consciousnesses must simultaneously possess dualistic appearance with regard to all concealer-truths and not possess dualistic appearance with regard to the emptinesses that are the final natures of those concealer-truths.

HOW A BUDDHA KNOWS ULTIMATE TRUTHS

Candrakīrti's *Supplement* says:[6]

> One with pure eyes sees the nature—suchness—
> Of falling hairs and so forth in the place
> Where these unreal entities are imputed through the force
> Of eye disease. Know that suchness is similar here.

Candrakīrti's *Supplement Commentary* elaborates:[7]

> Someone with eye disease, due to that disease, sees something that seems troublesome—falling hairs, etc., in a vessel, such as a drinking horn, that he holds in his hand. Because of this, wishing to eliminate them, he is put to the trouble of turning the vessel over again and again. Noticing this, wondering what he is doing, and approaching him, someone without eye disease does not observe the aspects of the falling hairs—even though he looks directly at the object [seen by the one with eye disease as having] falling hairs. Nor does he imagine qualities that depend on those falling hairs, such as being or not being functioning things, being or not being falling hairs, or being azure. The one with eye disease reveals his idea, [asking] the one without eye disease, "Do you see falling hairs?" Then, since [the one without eye disease] wants to eliminate this projection by the one with eye disease, he speaks to the one with eye disease words of straightforward negation: "There are no falling hairs here." Even in so doing, the speaker does not overextend his denial of those falling hairs. The one without eye disease sees the suchness of the falling hairs; the other does not.
>
> Similarly, the entities of the aggregates, elements, sense-spheres, and so forth that are observed by those who, through being damaged by the eye disease of ignorance, do not see suchness, are the conventional entities of those [phenomena]. Their ultimate truth is that which Supramundane Victor Buddhas, who are free from the predispositions of ignorance, see through the nature of those very aggregates and so forth, in the way that one who does not have eye disease sees falling hairs.
>
> *Question:* Would not a nature with an aspect like that be quite impossible to see? Thus, how do they see it?

Answer: True. However, they see [it] by way of not seeing.

Candrakīrti says that Buddhas see the emptiness of the aggregates in the way that a person without eye disease views falling hairs. When persons with good vision understand that the suchness, or real nature, of hairs in a vessel is non-existence, they see that reality without seeing such hairs. Similarly, when Buddhas realize the real nature of the aggregates as emptiness of inherent existence, they see emptiness by way of not seeing the aggregates.

Someone could argue that by giving the answer "True" at the end of this passage, Candrakīrti admits that emptinesses are impossible to see and therefore cannot be objects of knowledge.[8] However, this interpretation is unacceptable because of the arguments given in chapter two. For example, it would imply that Buddha taught emptiness without knowing it. Tsong-ka-pa's *Illumination of the Thought* explains that Candrakīrti means, "Yes, it is true that Buddhas do not see emptiness by way of dualistic appearance."[9] However, they do see emptiness by way of a vanishing of dualistic appearance. When all dualistic appearance is gone, concealer-truths cannot appear. Thus, Buddhas see emptiness in a manner free from any contact with the conventional phenomena that are the bases of emptiness. Candrakīrti's *Supplement Commentary* states:[10]

> Without knowing produced things, they take the nature alone in direct perception (*mngon sum du mdzad*). Therefore, because they understand just that, they are called "Buddhas."

Tsong-ka-pa cites a similar example from the *Condensed Perfection of Wisdom Sūtra*.[11] This sūtra says that the meaning of Buddha's teaching that suchness is seen without seeing forms or consciousness can be understood by reflecting on the meaning of the verbal convention "seeing space." Just as one "sees space" by not seeing obstructive objects, emptiness is seen by way of not seeing conventionalities. Therefore, "seeing by way of not seeing" is not a contradiction or a paradox because that which is seen (emptiness) and that which is not seen (conventionalities) are different. Thus the Ge-luk-bas adhere to the view that emptiness is knowable and Buddha Superiors are persons who have consciousnesses knowing emptiness.

The idea that ultimate reality is known in a negative way, through elimination of contact with anything else, is found in many religious traditions. In addition to the well-known *neti, neti* passage in the *Bṛhadāraṇyaka Upaniṣad*,[12] there are several particularly suggestive passages in the anonymous classic of Christian mysticism, *The Cloud of Unknowing*. At one point, *The Cloud of Unknowing* quotes pseudo-Dionysius:[13] "The most godlike knowledge of God is that which is known by unknowing." In context, it is clear that for the author of *The Cloud* this does not imply some paradox such as "one knows God by way of not knowing God." Rather, it means that the spiritual faculties see God most perfectly within the suspension of the ordinary faculties.

While emptiness is directly realized within the vanishing of dualistic conventional appearances for the perspective realizing it, the Ge-luk-ba tradition stresses that one does not achieve this direct realization merely by withdrawing from or refuting conventional reality. It is essential first to identify the object of negation—inherent existence—and then to refute it using reasoning. The inferential realization of emptiness thus attained is a necessary precursor to the direct realization that works as the "actual antidote" (*dngos gnyen*) to the root of cyclic existence. Although mistaken conventional appearances and conceptual consciousnesses are not found on the Buddha ground, they are necessary tools at the outset. If one sets out to realize emptiness by stopping conceptuality or withdrawing from ordinary conventional appearances, at best one will succeed only in temporarily suppressing the manifest forms of afflictions. Therefore, when it said that one sees emptiness by way of not seeing conventionalities, Ge-luk-bas understand this only as a description of the manner in which the ultimate truth is directly realized; they do *not* take it as the prescribed method used to attain that direct realization.

HOW A BUDDHA KNOWS CONCEALER-TRUTHS

That Buddhas see ultimate truth by way of not seeing concealer-truths might seem to imply that, because they continuously realize ultimate truths, they must never see concealer-truths. Jayānanda apparently holds this view. He argues that Buddhas, having eliminated all obstructions to the perception of suchness, no longer see mere conventionalities. However, this leads to some difficult consequences. Thurman points to the problem:[14]

> The further issue as to whether a Buddha can ever "get drunk" [i.e., see falsities] is more complicated than it seems, since, although all his instinctual habits of distorted perception are gone, Buddhist scholars would not wish to say that he is incapable of seeing the world as imagined by those who still suffer under misknowledge; else how could he interact with them through compassion and assist their own enlightenments?

To push the same problem in a slightly different direction: Since Buddhas are perfectly enlightened, they see things exactly as they are, and if they see no conventional phenomena at all, then conventional phenomena must be utterly non-existent. For example, if Buddhas did not see sentient beings, then it would follow that sentient beings do not at all exist. In that case, whom would a Buddha teach? And who would practice in order to become a Buddha? In fact, even Buddhas are conventionalities, and if conventionalities did not exist there would be no Buddhas or Buddhism. Jam-yang-shay-ba cites *The King of Meditative Stabilizations Sūtra* (*Samādhirājasūtra*) in support of the view that Buddha Superiors see conventionalities:[15]

> [Buddhas] know well the behavior of all sentient beings.
> Their clear knowledge operates with regard to all
> phenomena.

Buddhas can know all conventionalities and at the same time know emptiness by way of not knowing conventionalities because they are able to use two different modes of cognition simultaneously. Each omniscient consciousness knows emptiness by way of the vanishing of dualistic appearance and conventionalities, while simultaneously knowing all conventionalities in association with dualistic appearance.

However, this answer seems to imply that a Buddha's mind still possesses a factor of "drunkenness," or mistaken dualistic appearance. Among sentient beings, the only non-mistaken consciousnesses are those of Superiors in direct non-conceptual meditative equipoise on emptiness. Whenever sentient beings apprehend concealer-truths, they apprehend them with mistaken consciousness. Even among Foe Destroyers and pure ground Bodhisattvas, the appearance of ordinary conventionalities is a latency of previously abandoned ignorance. Therefore, it might be argued that

Buddhas cannot see conventionalities because they have no mistakeness, imperfection, or impurity. Or else, they must have some imperfection on account of their seeing ordinary conventionalities.[16]

Of course, Ge-luk-bas maintain that it is precisely because Buddhas are perfect that they must know everything that exists—including *all* conventionalities.[17] However, in order to answer this qualm more fully, we should first distinguish pure and impure conventionalities. Most conventionalities are impure phenomena that appear under the influence of ignorance or its latencies. Tsong-ka-pa's *Illumination of the Thought* explains how a Buddha sees such objects:[18]

> It is not that a Buddha's knowledge of the varieties [of phenomena] perceives the aggregates, etc. through being polluted by the latencies of ignorance. However, what appears to other persons' consciousnesses, which are polluted by ignorance, must appear to a Buddha.

And Tsong-ka-pa's *Ocean of Reasoning* says,[19]

> When objects polluted by latencies of ignorance appear to a Buddha's exalted wisdom knowing the varieties, they appear to a Buddha only from the viewpoint of their appearing to persons who have pollution by ignorance. They do not appear to a Buddha from his or her own perspective without relying on such an appearance to others.

Jam-yang-shay-ba gives the example of two persons, one with jaundice and one without.[20] When the one with jaundice describes a white conch shell as having a golden color, the other person does not see any gold appearance from his own perspective. He can nevertheless imagine the gold appearance that is appearing to the sick person. As long as he does not consent to the accuracy of such an appearance, he does not err in worldly terms. Analogously, Buddhas see impure conventionalities not as their own appearances (*rang snang*), but only by way of the appearance of such conventionalities to minds polluted by ignorance. Unlike the healthy person in the example, Buddhas do not merely imagine what other persons are seeing. Their clairvoyant powers enable them to directly know all conventionalities. Still, this knowledge of ordinary objects arises via the appearance of such objects to ignorant persons.

Also, there are certain pure conventionalities, such as the major and minor marks of a Buddha's Supreme Emanation Body (*mchog *gi sprul sku, paramanirmāṇakāya*) and a Buddha's omniscient mind itself, that are free from pollution by the latencies of ignorance.[21] They are known by a Buddha's wisdom not only because they appear to minds affected by ignorance, but also as spontaneous effects of a Buddha's eons of practice as a Bodhisattva.

When a concealer-truth appears to a non-conceptual awareness that explicitly realizes it, it must appear in association with dualistic appearance. This holds true regardless of whether the person involved is a Buddha or an ordinary sentient being. However, when sentient beings—including Foe Destroyers and pure ground Bodhisattvas—see a concealer-truth, the latencies of their own ignorance cause the object to appear to be inherently existent. Buddhas, on the other hand, do not have any appearance of inherent existence from their own side. They see the appearances of inherent existence that arise within the minds of sentient beings, but see them only through the force of their appearance to those sentient beings. Therefore, while Buddhas do have dualistic appearance of pure and impure conventionalities, they have no error or imperfection because all phenomena appear to them exactly as they are, without any superimposed appearance of inherent existence.

If all phenomena appear to a Buddha just as they are, then conventionalities must exist just as they appear to a Buddha. This raises a qualm: If conventionalities that appear to a Buddha must *exist as they appear*, then they must be truths; therefore, they should not be called falsities or concealer-truths. Jam-yang-shay-ba's response is that concealer-truths do exist as they appear to a Buddha, but (in general) they do not exist as they appear.[22] The manner in which phenomena appear to a Buddha is exceptional. When it is said that a pot is a falsity because it does not exist as it appears, the appearance referred to is not the appearance of a pot to a Buddha's wisdom. If a Buddha's mode of cognition were not isolated as an exception, then (as explained in chapter six) new definitions of many phenomena would be needed.

HOW A BUDDHA KNOWS HIS/HER OWN MIND

Within the Ge-luk fold, scholars discussing a Buddha's mode of cognition generally agree on the points outlined so far. However, when it is asked how an omniscient mind understands *itself*, even Tsong-ka-pa and his principal disciples—Kay-drup and Gyel-tsap—give different answers. Tsong-ka-pa does not actually describe the way in which omniscience knows itself, but he sets down the ground rules for later discussions in his *Illumination of the Thought*:[23]

> As for the second, [the way that a Buddha knows concealer-truths], since it is not suitable to posit implicit realization (*zhugs rtogs*)—that is, realizing something without its appearing—for Buddhas, [Buddhas] must know [concealer-truths] through appearance.

Explicit realizations occur when an object is known via its appearance to the mind. For example, when a direct valid cognizer explicitly realizes a pot, the aspect of the pot dawns upon the mind, and the pot is thereby cognized. An object's "aspect" (*rnam pa, ākāra*) is a very precise image that is nevertheless distinct from the object itself.[24] When a direct valid cognizer explicitly realizes a pot, ascertainment of the pot arises in conformity with the aspect of pot that is appearing. At the very time that pot is directly and explicitly realized, the same person may understand the presence of something capable of holding water. Without conscious reflection on the ability to hold water, this aspect does not appear. However, when persons who already know that a pot can hold water explicitly cognize a pot, they *implicitly* realize the presence of something that can hold water. Tsong-ka-pa clearly states that it is wrong to speak of such implicit realization when describing how a Buddha knows objects; a Buddha knows every object explicitly, by way of its appearance to her or his mind.

Tsong-ka-pa continues his description of the way a Buddha knows concealer-truths:[25]

> Therefore, [a Buddha] must know them by way of subject and object appearing dualistically in the perspective of the exalted wisdom knowing the varieties.

In meditative equipoise directly realizing emptiness, the sense of subject and object as different vanishes. At that time, yogis experience the emptiness that is the ultimate nature of all phenomena, including their own minds. They do not realize their own minds or any other concealer-truth,[26] and thus it can be said that all dualistic distinctions vanish. The experience of directly cognizing emptiness is compared to pouring fresh water into fresh water. A Buddha, while maintaining this non-dualistic realization of emptiness, also sees all concealer-truths. A Buddha's realizations must be explicit, and thus the aspects of conventionalities must appear. Since conventionalities are of multivariate aspect, this entails dualistic appearance.

In his depiction of this amazing intelligence, Tsong-ka-pa does not directly address the question of how omniscience knows itself. The problem that remains is this: Since a Buddha's mind exists, it is an object of knowledge. A Buddha must know his or her own mind because a Buddha knows all objects of knowledge. Since it is a consciousness, a Buddha's mind must be a positive phenomenon (*sgrub pa, vidhi*); hence, it cannot be an emptiness or an ultimate truth. Therefore, a Buddha's mind is a concealer-truth. Tsong-ka-pa says that a Buddha knows concealer-truths in the manner of subject and object appearing dualistically. Accordingly, an omniscient consciousness must know itself by way of dualistic appearance of subject and object. This implies a sense of difference between subject and object. However, in this case, the subject and the object are the very same omniscient consciousness. Since anything is the same as itself, how can a perfect mind see itself as different from itself?

THE INTERPRETATIONS OF GYEL-TSAP AND KAY-DRUP

In his *Explanation of (Śāntideva's) "Engaging in the Bodhisattva Deeds"*, Gyel-tsap presents his solution to this problem.[27] He argues that if an omniscient mind appeared to itself, it would have to appear either as the same as itself or as different from itself. Since a Buddha makes no errors, if a Buddha were to see his or her mind as different from itself, then it would have to *be* different from itself. On the other hand, if an omniscient mind were to appear to itself non-dualistically, like water poured into water, then it would be an ultimate truth because only ultimate truths explicitly appear to direct valid cognizers in a non-dualistic manner.[28] Therefore, whether or not we choose to call it "implicit realization" (*zhugs rtogs*), an omniscient mind must realize itself without appearing to itself. What about Tsong-ka-pa's statement that implicit realization is not appropriate on the Buddha ground? Gyel-tsap suggests that this be understood to mean that a Buddha does not have realizations that are implicit to other explicit realizations. In the example of implicit realization given above, realization of the ability to hold water occurs implicit to the realization of pot. According to Gyel-tsap's interpretations, a Buddha's cognition of her or his own mind is not implicit in this sense because it is never secondary to the cognition of other objects. Still, omniscience must know itself implicitly in the sense that it knows itself without appearing to itself.

In his *Thousand Doses*, Kay-drup presents the problem in a similar way, but gives a different solution.[29] He sees the quandary as follows: If a Buddha's mind does not know itself, the scriptures stating that a Buddha knows all phenomena would be in error. If it does know itself, it must do so either implicitly or explicitly. The former is contradicted by Tsong-ka-pa's statement that Buddhas do not have implicit knowledge. If omniscience knows itself directly, it must either appear dualistically or non-dualistically. If it knew itself dualistically, then it would have to be a mistaken consciousness because it would have mistaken appearance of itself as different from itself. Therefore, Kay-drup concludes that dualistic realization cannot be the answer.[30] The only remaining possibility is that a Buddha's mind must explicitly know itself by way of a vanishing of dualistic appearance. However, if this position is adopted, there are several difficult problems that must be resolved. The first is that any object explicitly realized by a direct perceiver by way of a vanishing of dualistic appearance should be an ultimate truth. Kay-drup suggests that a Buddha's exalted wisdom must be considered an exception to this principle because it is a concealer-truth and it knows itself non-dualistically—that is, it knows itself as one with itself.[31]

The second problem is that explicit cognition implies that knowledge arises through the appearance of an aspect. When we say that an object appears to a mind, we normally mean that an aspect or image of the object rises in the mind. This aspect is in all ways similar to the object, but it is a likeness of the object and not the object itself. Therefore, the following argument can be made: If an omniscient mind knows itself in an aspectual likeness of itself, then, since that mind is non-mistaken, it must *be* like itself. To say that something is "like" something implies that there are two different things that can be compared. Kay-drup agrees that it is absurd to say that an omniscient mind is like itself. He comes to the startling conclusion that when an omniscient mind explicitly knows itself, there is no arising of an aspect (*rnam pa 'char ba*). That is, in the case of omniscient self-comprehension, explicit knowledge does not involve the appearance of an aspect.

The third difficulty with Kay-drup's interpretation is that a mind that knows itself through the vanishing of dualistic appearance would seem to be a self-consciousness (*rang rig, svasaṃvedana*)—but Prāsaṅgikas refute self-consciousness. The assertion or non-assertion of self-consciousness is a key doctrinal point used by Tibetan doxographers to organize Indian Buddhism into four tenet systems, Vaibhāṣika, Sautrāntika, Cittamātra, and Mādhyamika, each of which has various subdivisions. Cittamātra, the Reason-Following branch of Sautrāntika, and the Yogācāra-Svātantrika branch of Mādhyamika assert self-consciousness, while Vaibhāṣika, Sautrāntika-Svātantrika-Mādhyamika, and Prāsaṅgika-Mādhyamika refute self-consciousness. Systems that posit self-consciousness do so in order to account for the memory of the subjective side of previous experience.[32] Since it is possible to remember the subjective dimension of earlier experiences, and not just its objective content, it is argued that there must be a type of consciousness that "knows the knower" at the same time that the knower is apprehending an object. For example, when one remembers having seen something blue, one remembers not only blue, but also the experiencer of blue, the consciousness apprehending blue. While the eye consciousness apprehending blue takes on the aspect of that external apprehended object, the self-consciousness takes on the aspect of the apprehending awareness. Thus, Pur-bu-jok's *Greater Path of Reasoning* defines self-consciousness in Sautrāntika as[33]

> that which has the aspect of the apprehender (*'dzin rnam, grāhaka-ākāra*).

Self-consciousnesses are necessarily direct perceivers (*mngon sum, pratyakṣa*), and considering them as such, Pur-bu-jok gives another definition:[34]

> that which, being free from conceptuality and non-mistaken, has the aspect of the apprehender.

Self-consciousnesses are one entity, indivisible and simultaneous, with the apprehending consciousness that they observe. Thus, when they take on the aspect of the apprehending awareness, they directly observe themselves. That is, a self-consciousness accompanying an eye consciousness apprehending blue must apprehend not only the eye consciousness, but itself as well. Since they are apprehenders, and since they are generated in the aspect of the apprehending, or subjective, side of an experiential moment, they necessarily apprehend themselves. Thus they are "self-consciousnesses," consciousnesses which serve as their own objects. They directly and non-mistakenly perceive themselves in a non-dualistic manner, that is, without any appearance of subject and object as different.

Prāsaṅgika assert that self-consciousness is absurd because agent and object cannot be identical. If the knowing agent and the known object could be exactly the same, then a knife could cut itself, a finger could touch itself, and so forth; also, darkness could obscure itself, and therefore, darkness could not be seen. Also, if a consciousness could set itself up as a knower without depending on something else as the known, then this would point to its being an autonomous, i.e., inherently existent, knower. Refuting inherent existence, Prāsaṅgikas accordingly argue that self-consciousness is impossible. This seems to contradict Kay-drup's assertion that a Buddha's omniscience knows itself explicitly and non-dualistically, and although Kay-drup raises this problem, he provides no clear solution. However, he does make one telling argument: If an omniscient mind knows itself at all, the problem of object and agent becoming identical remains—regardless of how one describes the mode of cognition.[35]

LATER INTERPRETATIONS

To reiterate, Gyel-tsap asserts that omniscience knows itself without appearing to itself, in a manner that might be called implicit but is not the type of implicit realization ruled out by Tsong-ka-pa. Kay-drup asserts that omniscience knows itself explicitly, but without the rising of an aspect and without dualistic appearance. The former scholar contradicts Tsong-ka-pa's statement that a Buddha's mind knows all concealer-truths through their appearance to it; the latter scholar contradicts Tsong-ka-pa's statement that a Buddha knows concealer-truths in the manner of object and subject appearing dualistically. Hence, it is not surprising to find that both interpretations draw criticism from later Ge-luk-bas.

Paṇ-chen Sö-nam-drak-ba and Jay-dzun Chö-gyi-gyel-tsen summarize and refute the views of both Kay-drup and Gyel-tsap on this issue.[36] Gyel-tsap's argument is that since a Buddha's mind is a concealer-truth, if it appeared to itself it would have to appear dualistically. The resulting appearance of subject and object as different would be mistaken because a Buddha's mind is one with itself. Since Buddhas are not in any way mistaken, a Buddha must know his or her own mind without appearance. Kay-drup sees the same problem, but escapes by asserting that a Buddha's self-comprehension is non-dualistic. Paṇ-chen Sö-nam-drak-ba's response to both interpretations is that the dualistic appearance associated with the direct perception of a concealer-truth does not have to involve a sense of difference.[37] The very appearance of conventional phenomena is one of the meanings of dualistic appearance.[38] If the presence of dualistic appearance were to hinge only upon subject and object appearing as different, then a perfectly non-mistaken omniscient consciousness could have a vanishing of dualistic appearance only with regard to itself because it is the only thing that is exactly the same as itself; it would have dualistic appearance with regard to everything else, including emptiness. Therefore, Paṇ-chen Sö-nam-drak-ba holds that an omniscient mind does appear to itself, and appears in association with a dualistic appearance, taking "dualistic appearance" simply to mean the appearance of a conventionality.

Paṇ-chen Sö-nam-drak-ba states that Kay-drup's approach is "not good" and that Gyel-tsap's writings require interpretation (*drang don*) on this issue.[39] He concludes his discussion with an apologetic poem:[40]

> Although it is improper in two ways for me
> To fling consequences at Gyel-tsap,
> I offer them with the idea of proving
> That this is the thought of [Tsong-ka-pa's] *Explanation.*
> Yet, since there is a single continuum of knowledge
> Between the Conqueror and Gyel-tsap
> I confess that I debate in error
> With a mere appearance, a painting of a lama.

Paṇ-chen Sö-nam-drak-ba insists on interpreting the tradition according to his own lights and he is never afraid to state openly that his conclusions contradict what he finds in the books of his predecessors. However, he wants to be sure that the reader does not mistake his independent spirit for irreverence. Accordingly, he apologizes for debating with a teacher of authentic wisdom who is no longer present to defend his system.

Jam-yang-shay-ba reiterates and amplifies Paṇ-chen Sö-nam-drak-ba's arguments on these points and adds several refutations of his own. He is careful never to say that Gyel-tsap and Kay-drup are wrong, but he does say that their books should not be taken literally on this issue.[41] Although gentler in tone, this is not substantively different from Paṇ-chen Sö-nam-drak-ba's statement that their works require interpretation at this point. However, unlike Paṇ-chen Sö-nam-drak-ba, Jam-yang-shay-ba also devises an apologetic reconstruction of Gyel-tsap's (supposed) actual intention: Gyel-tsap says that it is illogical for an omniscient mind to appear to itself, but, according to Jam-yang-shay-ba, he really means that it does not appear to itself as a whole that is separate from its parts.[42] By making this statement at the beginning of his discussion, Jam-yang-shay-ba distances the revered Gyel-tsap from the rough debate that follows.

As for his statement that Kay-drup's *Thousand Doses* cannot be read literally at this point, Jam-yang-shay-ba softens the blow in several ways.[43] Any implied deficiency is attributed to the *book*, and not its author. In fact, Jam-yang-shay-ba chooses this context to refer to Kay-drup as "omniscient" (*kun mkhyen*). Moreover, he here reiterates his allegiance to an ideal he had enunciated earlier: One should seek to construct a system that accords with Kay-drup's *Thousand Doses*.[44] As noted in chapter eight, the most convoluted aspects of Jam-yang-shay-ba's explanation of the two truths seem to derive from his close reliance upon Kay-drup.[45] Even if he does not always completely live up to this ideal, Jam-yang-shay-ba (unlike Paṇ-chen Sö-nam-drak-ba) clearly feels a need to minimize any sense of contradiction between his positions and those taken by Kay-drup and Gyel-tsap.

Jang-gya is even more determined in his apologetic. He recognizes apparent differences among the statements of Tsong-ka-pa, Kay-drup, and Gyel-tsap on this point. However, he insists that the three should be regarded as united in terms of the idea that they were aiming to convey. Counter-punching at Paṇ-chen Sö-nam-drak-ba without naming him, Jang-gya stresses that it is wrong for any scholar to imagine that his understanding of Tsong-ka-pa's teaching surpasses that of Kay-drup; those who refute Kay-drup disparage him unjustly.[46] Considering these remarks along with those of Jam-yang-shay-ba, it would appear that the tendency of later generations of Ge-luk-bas was gradually to invest Tsong-ka-pa's "spiritual sons" with greater charismatic authority.

JAM-YANG SHAY-BA'S OWN POSITION

The heart of Jam-yang-shay-ba's position on omniscient self-cognition is found in one brief passage:[47]

> Someone says, "It follows that the exalted wisdom of a Buddha appears to itself by way of an association with dualistic appearance with respect to itself because (1) the exalted wisdom of a Buddha appears to itself, and (2) it does not appear by way of a vanishing of dualistic appearance." Some respond, "Those reasons do not entail that consequence," but [my answer] is just, "I accept the consequence."

Like Paṇ-chen Sö-nam-drak-ba, Jam-yang-shay-ba is able to accept that an omniscient mind knows itself via dualistic appearance because dualistic appearance in self-cognition does not require that the consciousness appear as different from itself. Paṇ-chen Sö-nam-drak-ba says that this is because dualistic appearance can mean any conventional appearance. Jam-yang-shay-ba does not question this, but feels a need for further clarification. If a perfect, omniscient mind knows itself through a conventional appearance as one with itself, where is the element of dualism? If there is no sense of subject/object difference, what are the *two* factors that cause this appearance to be designated "dualistic"?

Jam-yang-shay-ba provides an answer: When an omniscient mind knows itself by way of dualistic appearance, it realizes itself "by way of an association with an appearance that it has parts."[48] In Prāsaṅgika, all impermanent phenomena—including all consciousnesses—have parts. Even if not physically divisible, they are susceptible to division by the mind.[49] Also, an omniscience appears to itself along with a multiplicity of dualistic factors—such as its impermanence, its being a consciousness, and so forth—that are one entity with it.[50] Therefore, the appearance of conventionalities does involve dualistic appearances other than the appearance of difference between subject and object.

As for Gyel-tsap's notion that an omniscience can explicitly know itself without the appearance of an aspect, Jam-yang-shay-ba is quick to cite Tsong-ka-pa's *Illumination of the Thought*:[51]

> Candrakīrti's *Commentary on (Nāgārjuna's) "Sixty Stanzas of Reasoning"* clearly explains that [for a Buddha] to know (*mkhyen*) [something] without [that object's] aspect appearing is not the system of this [Mādhyamika school].

Explicit knowledge without the appearance of an aspect would have to be an "aspectless meeting" of knower and known such as is asserted in Vaibhāṣika.[52] In Mādhyamika, explicit realization requires the appearance of an aspect. How can this be reconciled with the argument that if an omniscient mind unerringly knew itself by way of an aspectual likeness, it would have to be similar to itself? Jam-yang-shay-ba suggests that an aspect may not have to be an aspect of similarity or likeness.[53] Through the appearance of an aspectual image a Buddha's mind knows itself not as similar to itself (which would be absurd), but as identical to itself.

Finally, Jam-yang-shay-ba attempts to solve the problem of agent and object becoming one.[54] He argues that an omniscient mind knowing itself is both the knowing agent and the object known, but that the agent and object are not precisely identical because they can be conceptually isolated within that single entity. This is similar to the relationship between an omniscient mind knowing the mode of being of phenomena and an omniscient mind knowing the varieties. An omniscient mind knows all objects, but it sees ultimate truths by way of not seeing concealer-truths, without dualistic appearance, and it sees concealer-truths in association with dualistic appearance. Thus, we can conceptually isolate omniscience knowing the mode from omniscience knowing the varieties. By analogy, Jam-yang-shay-ba argues that in knowing itself, a single omniscient mind can play two roles—agent and object—without mixing them together.

It is difficult to see where this argument will leave the Prāsaṅgika refutation of self-consciousness. Jam-yang-shay-ba's approach may suggest that, unlike Gyel-tsap and Kay-drup, he tends to regard the refutation of self-consciousness as a refutation of inherently existent self-cognition. No consciousness can know itself by itself because that would point to an inherently existent knower—something that, through its own intrinsic nature, functions as a knower. Thus, like the assertion of "production from other" (*gzhan skye*), the assertion of self-consciousness is, for non-Prāsaṅgikas, inextricably bound up with the conception of inherent existence. However, perhaps a Prāsaṅgika can hold that, in merely conventional terms, a consciousness can know itself.[55]

POSITING OMNISCIENCE AS A FALSITY

Through such explanations of how an omniscient mind knows itself in a dualistic manner, Jam-yang-shay-ba and the other textbook authors escape the conclusion that an omniscient mind is an ultimate truth. However, there is another quite different difficulty that threatens to push Ge-luk-bas into a similar corner. As Jam-yang-shay-ba himself points out, something's existing just as it appears to the direct perceiver explicitly realizing it does *not* necessarily entail that it is a truth—because an omniscient mind can be directly realized only by itself or another omniscient mind, and everything appears to that mind just as it is.[56] Therefore, since an omniscient mind exists as it appears to the direct valid cognizer realizing it (that is, it exists as it appears to itself), it would (absurdly) be a truth (and thus an ultimate truth) if this criterion were applied to it. This represents yet another case in which the workings of the Buddha ground give rise to exceptional difficulties in the Ge-luk-ba presentation. Geshe Ngak-wang-pun-tsok's *Medicinal Ear of Corn* lays out the problem this way:[57]

> A Wisdom Truth Body (*ye shes chos sku, jñānadharmakāya*), for example, must be either an ultimate or a conventionality. If it were the former, it would actually have to be asserted as a permanent phenomenon, and thus this is not correct [because it is a consciousness, and thus necessarily impermanent]. If it is the latter, [a conventionality], it must either be established as it appears to the awareness directly realizing it, or not. If it were so established, it would [absurdly] follow that it is a non-deceptive truth, thus contradicting its being a deceptive conventional phenomena. If it is not established [as it appears to the awareness directly realizing it], then that awareness must either be among Buddhas or among sentient beings. If it were a Buddha's, one would have to assert that a Buddha has a mistaken appearance. If it is a sentient being's, does this not contradict the statements that the Wisdom Truth Body is in the province of the direct perceivers that are unique to Buddhas? Tsong-ka-pa did not make this very clear, and thus it appears to be extraordinarily difficult to give an answer.

Here, the case of a Buddha's mind creates an exception and a problem not as a knower, but as an object known; thus, the situation cannot be saved by arguing, as Jam-yang-shay-ba does elsewhere, that a Buddha's unique mode of cognition need not be factored into the formulation of conventional definitions. Geshe Bel-den-drak-ba readily admitted that he had no convincing answer to this problem.

Ngak-wang-bel-den provides a possible solution.[58] He argues that the mind in relation to which deceptiveness or non-deceptiveness of an object is determined is not necessarily a mind directly realizing (*mngon sum du rtogs*) the object, but a mind to which the object is directly appearing (*mngon sum du snang*). Of course, a Buddha's Wisdom Truth Body, the subtle potencies that enable actions to produce specific effects, and so forth directly appear to a Buddha, and a Buddha directly realizes them just as they are. Although sentient beings cannot directly *realize* such phenomena, it is still possible for these phenomena to *appear* directly to them. Ngak-wang-bel-den explains that Buddha's omniscience is an appearing object of the yogic direct perceiver of an advanced Bodhisattva directly realizing the impermanence of that omniscient mind.[59] When a yogi directly realizes the impermanence of an omniscient mind, the omniscient mind itself must also appear because an impermanent thing is one indivisible substantial entity with its impermanence. When an omniscient mind appears to the yogic direct perceiver directly realizing its impermanence, it falsely appears to be inherently existent. Therefore, Ngak-wang-bel-den holds that deceptiveness is posited when something does not exist as it appears to a mind to which it directly appears. He cites Tsong-ka-pa's *Intermediate Exposition of the Stages of the Path*:[60]

> As explained in Candrakīrti's *Commentary on (Nāgārjuna's) "Sixty Stanzas of Reasoning,"* nirvāṇa is an ultimate truth; thus, for the perspective of the mind directly seeing (*mngon sum du mthong*) it, there is no deceptive appearance regarding its lack of inherent existence. As for other, composite phenomena, in the perspective of the mind to which they directly appear (*mngon sum du snang*) there is deceptive appearance regarding their lack of inherent existence.

For Ngak-wang-bel-den, the important point is that Tsong-ka-pa does not use the word *realize* (*rtogs*). However, unlike Ngak-wang-bel-den's influential "in the perspective/in relation to the perspective" distinction, this idea has not found currency in the teachings of modern Ge-luk-bas.

BUDDHAS AND CONCEALER-TRUTHS

Returning to the issue of how a Buddha sees impure conventionalities, consider these qualms: How can Ge-luk-bas claim that forms and so forth are validly established (*tshad mas grub ba*) existents, and yet hold that a Buddha's perfect mind sees them *only* through the force of their appearance to minds polluted by ignorance? If ordinary tables and chairs are validly established, why do Buddhas not have them as their own appearances? As quoted above, Tsong-ka-pa's *Ocean of Reasoning* says,[61]

> When objects polluted by predispositions of ignorance appear to a Buddha's exalted wisdom knowing the varieties, they appear to a Buddha *only* from the viewpoint of their appearing to persons who have pollution by ignorance. They do not appear to a Buddha from her/his own perspective without relying on such an appearance to others.

Surely this assertion that Buddhas see impure conventionalities *only* via their appearance to sentient beings tends to undercut the ontological validity of ordinary conventional reality.

Furthermore, note that there is no person—either sentient being or Buddha—for whose own perspective (*rang snang*) impure conventionalities appear without at the same time being somehow associated with an appearance of inherent existence. It seems that the appearance of impure conventionalities is necessarily associated with the appearance of inherent existence. When an ordinary person sees a table, the table appears to be inherently existent. When a pure ground Bodhisattva sees the table, there is still a mistaken appearance of inherent existence, albeit an appearance that the Bodhisattva knows as mistaken. Even when Buddhas see a table, they see it by way of its appearance to sentient beings, and since the table necessarily appears as inherently existent to sentient beings, that mistaken appearance appears to Buddhas as well. This tends to raise doubts about the Ge-luk-ba claim that inherent existence and existence can be separated.

To pose the problem another way: Since Buddhas see everything exactly as it is, and since everything lacks inherent existence, it follows that Buddhas must see tables, etc., without any appearance of inherent existence. However, this seems contradictory because when tables appear to sentient beings, they necessarily appear as inherently existent, and Tsong-ka-pa explains that Buddhas see tables only in reliance upon their appearance to sentient beings.

It is not clear that there are complete answers available for all of these qualms. However, there are certainly some important points that can be made. It is critical to remember that conventionalities are of two types, pure and impure. Buddhas see all conventionalities. Those that are pure they see as their own appearances, and those that are impure they see as the appearances of sentient beings. That Tsong-ka-pa does allow that Buddhas can see pure conventionalities without relying on their appearance to sentient beings suggests that it is because impure conventionalities are impure, and *not simply because they are conventionalities*, that Buddhas seem them only via their appearance to sentient beings. Since a Buddha's mind can see some conventionalities even as his or her own appearances, conventionalities in general are not invalidated, discredited, or contradicted by the wisdom of a perfected mind. On the contrary, even impure conventionalities are known by a Buddha, and if a Buddha knows something it must exist.

Thus, the question of whether Buddhas cognize a phenomenon as their own appearance or cognize it only via its appearance to sentient beings is linked, not to the ontological validity of the object in question, but to the basis for the phenomenon's having come into (or remaining in) existence. The impure conventionalities of our world, while validly established, come into existence in dependence upon the afflicted actions of sentient beings. Our world is the moral fruition of certain of our past actions, and whether virtuous or non-virtuous, all of those actions were tainted by their association with ignorant consciousnesses that misconceived agent, action, and object as inherently existent. Dissimilarly, the pure conventionalities that are among Buddhas' own appearances arise from their completion of the collections of merit and wisdom through the practice of the six perfections. Having come into existence, pure conventionalities and impure conventionalities have the same ontological status as objects established by conventional valid cognition.

In many ways this approach is satisfying, but some doubt may remain about the status of the mental continuums of sentient beings—and sentient beings themselves. They are surely not the pure results of a Bodhisattva's practice; they must be impure conventionalities. Accordingly, although they have existed beginninglessly, it can be said that their existence at any given time is dependent upon earlier actions that were based in ignorance. The question is: If Buddhas see pots and chairs only via their appearance to the minds of sentient beings, then how do they see the minds of sentient beings? It may be said that they know the minds of sentient beings as objects of the clairvoyant consciousnesses of other sentient beings—but then it may be asked how *those* clairvoyant minds come to appear, etc. Still, the Ge-luk-bas can avoid a vicious infinite regression simply by insisting that (1) the omniscience of Buddhas empowers them to know everything that exists, and that (2) all existents (including the minds of sentient beings) that do not appear to them as their own appearances must appear to them via appearance to minds polluted by ignorance.

Regarding the argument that inherent existence and existence cannot be separated because they always seem to appear in association with one another, several points can be made: First, since Buddhas know pure conventionalities as their own appearances, they certainly can see them as distinct from any mistaken appearance of inherent existence.

Second, it seems that Buddhas also must be able to see impure conventionalities without mixing their existence with an appearance of inherent existence because tables, etc. lack inherent existence and Buddhas see all things as they are. Buddhas know tables, etc. in reliance upon their appearance to sentient beings, but this cannot mean that Buddhas see tables, etc. in the same mistaken way that sentient beings see them. It is impossible to imagine how a table appears to a mind that is simultaneously directly realizing the emptiness of the table, but there must a factor within a Buddha's omniscience that is able to see tables, etc. stripped of the appearance of inherent existence. This is not changed by the fact that Buddhas also see that, for the minds of sentient beings, tables have this mistaken appearance. Buddhas are, of course, undeluded by the appearance to their perfected minds of the mistaken appearances of other minds.

Finally, even though it is not until the Buddha ground that the *appearance* of conventionalities is disentangled from the *appearance* of inherent existence, a valid *understanding* of the distinction between existence and inherent existence can be gained even before entering the path of accumulation.

REMARKS

In this chapter we have seen problems explaining how a Buddha's wisdom knows itself, problems explaining how a Buddha's wisdom is a falsity, and problems in explaining how a Buddha sees impure conventionalities only in reliance upon their appearance to others. In chapter six, we saw the problems that a Buddha's mode of cognition brings to the definitions of the two truths. Why is it that Ge-luk-bas encounter so many problems talking about the Buddha ground? It has been said that the Ge-luk system is set up in terms of the basis (*gzhi*), the Sa-gya system in terms of the path (*lam*), and the Nying-ma system in terms of the result (*'bras*). Of course, this is a rough and sweeping generalization. All three systems tell us what there is to work with, how to work with it, and what the end results will be. However, in doing so they each speak from a different perspective, and the predominant Ge-luk-ba approach is to speak in terms that make sense in relation to where we are now. How can this be reconciled with the assertion that a Buddha is the only one who sees things as they are? If a Buddha sees things just as they are, then would it not be best to build a system that, in so far as possible, describes things as a Buddha sees them?

A Ge-luk-ba response begins by insisting that nothing in their presentation of Prāsaṅgika is *contradicted* or discredited by the realizations of Buddhas. For example, Buddhas must realize that, within the realm of worldly convention, a visible form is characterized by being the object of apprehension of an eye consciousness. Reflection on the powers of a Buddha, the Bodies of a Buddha, and so forth is an enormously beneficial source of religious inspiration. However, as Jam-yang-shay-ba points out, if one attempted to make all conventional presentations in terms of what can be fathomed of the inconceivable subjectivity of the Buddha mind, the resulting system would be chaotic.

A Buddha's mind maintains a wisdom consciousness that discriminates every individual conventional phenomenon—without rising from a perfectly non-dualistic wisdom realizing emptiness. No sentient being can have these two wisdoms simultaneously; they must be practiced in alternation. The delicate question is the pedagogical one: Is it best first to give students an affirmation of conventional distinctions? Or is it best to begin by teaching emptiness and non-duality? Since it is very difficult to understand the distinction between existence and inherent existence, a program that begins by teaching emptiness risks throwing out the baby (conventional distinctions such as virtue and non-virtue) with the bath water. As a prophylactic against the extreme of nihilism, the Ge-luk-ba tradition emphasizes from the outset the validity of conventional distinctions. Students are inoculated with Dignāga and Dharmakīrti before being exposed to Nāgārjuna and Candrakīrti. The danger of this choice is spelled out by Hopkins: "Since even Dzong-ka-ba says that no beginner can discriminate between existence and inherent existence, an emphasis on the valid establishment of conventionalities might merely fortify the habitual sense that things exist as they appear."[62] As noted in chapter one, Ge-luk-bas such as Jang-gya and Den-dar-hla-ram-ba (*bstan dar lha ram pa*, b.1759) have addressed this problem, stressing that the refutation of inherent existence cannot proceed from "a full acceptance of these concrete appearances as givens".[63]

A further point is that while Buddhas have no conceptual consciousnesses, the proper use of conceptuality is indispensable on the path. In particular, it is critical to note that cultivation of the view relies upon analysis and that emptiness is therefore necessarily initially realized in a conceptual, inferential manner. When used properly on the path, conceptual consciousnesses bear the seeds of their own eventual destruction. However, if conceptuality is dismissed or overly deprecated at the beginning of practice, it will be impossible to refute inherent existence. To stop conceptuality without first using it to realize emptiness is only to suppress it temporarily. Although correct conceptual thought is superceded on the Buddha ground, it is an invaluable tool at the outset. Conceptuality *per se* is *not* the enemy—it is a sword that must be used before it is eventually dropped.

A Buddha's non-conceptual wisdom can cognize all phenomena individually without blurring them together inappropriately. However, if one sets out to become enlightened simply by emulating a Buddha's non-conceptuality, one may succeed only in dampening one's ability to make discriminations. The language of Ge-luk-ba presentations relies upon and sharpens the ability to use conceptual reasoning consciousnesses to make accurate discriminations. It is a language-system that suffers strain and seems "out of touch" when it is used to describe the personal experiences of advanced yogis and Buddhas, but it has the advantage of addressing us where we stand today. Āryadeva's *Four Hundred* (*Catuḥśatakaśāstrakārikā*) says:[64]

> Just as a barbarian cannot be approached in another language
> So the worldly cannot be approached except with the worldly.

Similarly, Ge-luk-bas claim that their teachings are not only philosophically correct, but also pedagogically sound inasmuch as they are geared to be grasped by, and thereby to benefit, minds enmeshed in conceptuality and a world of conventional distinctions.

Glossary

English	*Tibetan*	*Sanskrit*
abandonment	spangs pa	prahāṇa
able to withstand analysis	dpyad bzod thub pa	
action	las	karma
actual antidote	dngos gnyen	
actuality	dngos po	bhāva
additional category	phung gsum	
affirming negative	ma yin dgag	paryudāsapratiṣedha
affliction	nyon mongs	kleśa
afflictive ignorance	nyon mongs can gyi ma rig pa	kliṣṭāvidya
afflictive obstructions	nyon sgrib	kleśāvaraṇa
aggregate	phung po	skandha
analysis	dbyod pa	vicāra
appearing object	snang yul	pratibhāsaviṣaya
appehender	'dzin pa	grāhaka
apprehension	'dzin pa	grahaṇa
artificial	kun btags	parikalpita
aspect	rnam pa	ākāra
atomic particle	rdul 'phran	paramānu
attachment	sred pa	tṛṣṇā
attribute	khyad chos	
awareness	blo	buddhi
basis	gzhi	ādhāra

basis of division	dbye gzhi	
basis of emptiness	stongs gzhi	śūnyatādhāra
bodhisattva	byang chub sems pa	bodhisattva
Buddha	sangs rgyas	buddha
Buddha Superiors	sangs rgyas 'phag pa	āryabuddha
cause	rgyu	hetu
cessation	'gog pa	nirodha
circumstantial	glo bur	āgantu
Cittamātra	sems tsam pa	cittamātra
clairvoyance	mngon shes	abhijñā
coarse	rags pa	sthūla
cognition	shes pa, blo	jñāna, buddhi
collection of merit	bsod nams kyi tshogs	puṇyasaṃbhara
collection of wisdom	shes rab gyi tshogs	jñānasaṃbhara
common beings	so so skye bo	pṛthagjana
common locus	gzhi mthun	samānādhibaraṇa
compassion	snying rje	karuṇā
compositional phenomena	'dus byas kyi chos	saṃskṛtadharma
concealer-truth	kun rdzob bden pa	saṃvṛtisatya
conception of true existence	bden 'dzin	satyagrāha
conceptual consciousness	rtog pa	kalpanā
concordance	mthun pa	
Conqueror	rgyal ba	jina
consciousness	shes pa	jñāna
consequence	thal 'gyur	prasaṅga
consistent	rjes su mthun pa	
contaminated	sāsrava	zag bcas
continuum	rgyud	saṃtāna
contradictories not abiding together	lhan gcig mi gnas 'gal	*sahānavastāvirodha
contradictory	'gal ba	virodha
convention	tha snyad	vyavahāra
conventional truth	tha snyad bden pa	vyavahārasatya
conventional valid cognizer	tha snyad pa'i tshad ma	*vyāvahārika-pramāṇajṇāna
conventionality	kun rdzob	saṃvṛti
conventionally	kun rdzob tu	saṃvṛtitaḥ
cyclic existence	'khor ba	saṃsāra
deceptive	slu ba	moṣa
deep cause of error	phul gyi 'khrul rgyu	

defilement	dri ma	mala
definition	mtshan nyid	lakṣana
definitive	nges don	nītārtha
dependent-arising	rten 'byung	pratītyasamutpāda
destructedness	zhig pa	
determine, ascertain	nges pa	niścaya
different	tha dad	nānā
direct contradictories	dngos 'gal	
direct perceiver	mngon sum	pratyakṣa
directed	mngon du phyogs pa, blo kha phyogs pa	
distinguish	dpyod pa	
division	dbye ba	vibhāga
dream	rmi lam	svapna
dualistic appearance	gnyis snang	
effect	'bras pu	phala
elaboration	spros pa	prapañca
element of reality	chos kyi dbyings	dharmadhātu
emptiness of other	gzhan stong	paraśūnyatā
emptiness of self	rang stong	svaśūnyatā
emptiness	stong pa nyid	śūnyatā
empty	stong pa	sūnya
entity	ngo bo	vastu
entityness	ngo bo nyid	svabhāvatā
equivalent	don gcig	ekārtha
erroneous	phyin ci log pa	viparyaya
established base	gzhi grub	vastu
ethics	tshul khrims	śīla
etymology	sgra bshad	
exalted knower of the varieties	ji snyed pa gzigs pa'i ye shes	yāvajjñāna
exalted knower of the mode	ji lta ba gzigs pa'i ye shes	yathavajjñāna
exalted wisdom	ye shes	jñāna
exist as it appears	snang ba ltar grub pa	
existence	srid pa	bhava
existent, existence	yod pa	bhava
explicitly	dngos su	
extreme of annihilation	chad mtha'	ucchedānta
extreme of permanence	rtag mtha'	śaśvatānta
eye disease	rab rib	

fabrications	bcos ma	kṛtrima
faith	dad pa	śraddhā
false	rdzun, brdzun pa	
falsity	rdzun pa, brdzun pa	mṛṣā
foe destroyer	dgra bcom pa	arhat
followers of reasoning	rigs pa rjes su 'brangs pa	*nyāyānusārin
Forder	mu steg pa	tīrthika
Form Body	gzugs sku	rupakāya
form	gzugs	rūpa
functioning thing	dngos po	bhāva
futureness	ma 'ongs pa	
Ga-gyu	bka' rgyud	
Ge-luk	dge lugs	
generic image	don spyi	arthasāmānya
geshe	dge bshes	kalyāṇamitra
ground	sa	bhūmi
Hearer	nyan thos	śrāvaka
ignorance	ma rig pa, mi shes pa	avidyā, ajñāna
illusion	sgyu ma	māyā
illusory	sgyu ma ltar	māyāvat
impermanence	mi rtag pa	anitya
impermanent thing	mi rtag pa	bhāva
implicit realization	zhugs rtogs	
impure conventionalities	mi dag pa'i kun rdzob	
in conventional terms	tha snyad du	
inconceivable	bsam gyis mi khyab pa	acintya
incontrovertible	mi slu ba	avisaṃvadin
indirect contradictories	rgyud 'gal	
indispensable	med na mi 'byung	
inference	rjes dpag	anumāna
inherent existence	rang bzhin gyis grub pa	svabhāvasiddha
innate	lhan skyes	sahaja
interdependent	phan tshun brtan pa	parasparasaṃbhavana
intrinsic existence	rang gi mtshan nyid kyis grub pa	svalakṣaṇasiddha
invalidate	gnod	
investigation	rtog pa	vitarka

isolate	ldog pa	vivartana
jaundice		
karma	las	karma
knowable	shes bya	jñeya
lama	bla ma	
latencies	bag chags	vāsanā
Lhasa	hla sa	
liberation	thar pa	mokṣa
liberation	thar pa	vimokṣa/mokṣa
limit of reality	yang dag pa'i mtha'	bhūtakoṭi
Mahāyāna	theg chen	mahāyāna
meditative equipoise	mnyam bzhag	samāhita
meditative stabilization	ting nge 'dzin	samādhi
mere appearance	snang tsam	
mere conventionalities	kun rdzob tsam	saṃvṛtimātra
mere imputation by thought	rtog pas btags tsam	
method	thabs	upaya
migrator	'gro ba	gati
mind	sems	citta
mirage	smig rgyu	marīci
mistaken	'khrul ba	bhrānta
mistaken consciousness	'khrul shes	bhrāntijñāna
mode of appearance	snang tshul	
mode of subsistence	gnas lugs, sdod lugs, gnas tshul	
moment	sgad cig	kṣaṇa
monastic college	grwa tshang	
mutually exclusive contradictories	phan tshun spangs 'gal	anyonyaparihāra
Mādhyamika	dbu ma	mādhyamika
natural existence	rang gi mtshan nyid kyis grub pa	svalakṣaṇasiddhi
Nature Body	ngo bo nyid sku	svabhāvikakāya
nature	rang bzhin	svabhāva, prakṛti
negative phenomenon	dgag pa	pratiṣedha
nescience	mi shes pa	ajñāna
nihilism	med mtha	nāstyanta
nirvāṇa	myang 'das	nirvāṇa
non-affirming negative	med dgag	prasajyapratiśedha

non-conceptual	rtog med	nirvikalpa
non-deceptive	mi slu ba	amoṣa
non-dualistic	gnyis med	advaya
non-existent	med pa	asat
non-functioning thing	dngos med	abhāva
non-reified object	sgro ma brtags pa'i yul	
Nying-ma	rnying ma	
object found	rnyed don	
object of abandonment	spangs bya	
object of apprehension	gzung yul	grāhyaviṣaya
object of engagement	'jug yul	*pravṛttiviṣaya
object of refutation	dgag bya	pratiṣedhya
object	yul/don	viṣaya/artha
object-possessor	yul can	viṣayin
objects of knowledge	shes bya	jñeya
obstruction	sgrib	āvarana
obstructions to liberation	nyon sgrib	kleśāvaraṇa
obstructions to omniscience	shes sgrib	jñeyāvaraṇa
omniscience	rnam mkhyen, kun mkhyen	sarvākārajñāna
one	gcig	eka
order	chos lugs	
ordinary	rang dga' ba	
other-powered phenomenon	gzhan bdang	paratantra
pastness	'das pa	
path	lam	mārga
path of preparation	sbyor lam	prayogamārga
path of release	rnam grol lam	vimuktimārga
permanence	rtag pa	nitya
permanent phenomena	rtag pa	nitya
person	gang zag	pudgala, puruṣa
phenomenon	chos	dharma
polluted by ignorance	ma rig pas bslad pa	
positive phenomenon	sgrub pa	vidhi
precise enumeration	grang nges	

predispositions	bag chags	vāsana
principal	gtso bo	pradhāna
product	byas pa	kṛta
production from other	gzhan skye	
Prāsaṅgika	thal 'gyur pa	prāsaṅgika
pure conventionalities	dag pa'i kun rdzob	
pure ground	dag sa	
quality possessor	chos can	dharmin
real concealer-truth	yang dag kun rdzob bden pa	tathyasaṃvṛtisatya
real nature	chos nyid	dharmatā
real	yang dag	tathya
reality	yand dag pa/de nyid	samyak/tattva
realize	rtogs	adigam
reason	gtan tshigs	hetu
reasoning consciousness	rigs shes	*yuktijñāna
reasoning	rigs pa	yukti
relationship	'brel ba	saṃbandha
requiring interpretation	drang don	neyārtha
result	'bras bu	phala
result from method	thabs byung	upeya
right	yang dag	tathya
Sa-gya	sa skya	
Sautrāntika	mdo sde pa	sautrāntika
seed	sa bon	bīja
self	bdag	ātman
self-consciousness	rang rig	svasaṃvedana, svasaṃvitti
self-sufficient	rang rkya ba	
selflessness	bdag med pa	nairātmya
selflessness of persons	gang zag gi bdag med	pudgalanairātmya
selflessness of phenomena	chos kyi bdag med	dharmanairātmya
sense consciousness	dbang shes	indriyajñāna
sense power	dbang po	indriya
sense-sphere	skye mched	āyatana
sentient being	sems can	sattva
sign	rtags	liṅga
single	gcig	eka

solitary realizer	rang sangs rgyas, rang rgyal	pratyekabuddha, pratyekajina
sound	sgra	śabda
space	nam mkha'	ākāśa
stage of generation	skyes rim	
subject	yul can	viṣayin
subsequent to meditative equipoise	rjes thob	pṛṣṭhalabdha
substantial entity	rdzas	dravya
substratum	khyad gzhi	
subtle	phra ba	sūkśma
suchness	de kho na nyid, de bzhin nyid	tathatā
suffering	sdug bsngal	duḥkha
superficial cause of error	'phral gyi 'khrul rgyu	
superimposition	sgro btags	āropa
Superior	'phag pa	ārya
Supramundane Victor	bcom ldan 'das	bhagavan
Svātantrika	rang rgyud pa	svātantrika
syllogism	sbyor ba	prayoga
Sāṃkhya	grangs can pa	sāṃkhya
sūtra	mdo	sūtra
tantra	rgyud	tantra
Tathāgata	de bzhin bshegs pa	tathāgata
tenet	grub mtha'	siddhānta
term	sgra/brda	śabda/saṃketa
textbook	yig cha	
thoroughly established phenomenon	yongs grub	paraniṣpanna
trained in language	brda la byang	
true	bden	satya
true cessation	'gog bden	nirodhasatya
true existence	bden par yod pa	satyasat
Truth Body	chos sku	dharmakāya
truth	bden pa	satya
truth-for-a-concealer	kun rdzob bden pa	saṃvṛtisatya
two truths	bden gnyis	satyadvaya
ultimate	don dam	paramārtha
ultimate existence	don dam du yod pa	paramārthasiddhi
ultimate truth	don dam bden pa	paramārthasatya

ultimate valid cognizer	don dam pa'i tshad ma	*paramārtha-pramāṇajñāna
unimpaired	gnod pa med pa	
uninterrupted path	bar chad med lam	ānantaryamārga
unreal concealer-truth	log pa'i kun rdzob bden pa	mithyāsaṃvṛtisatya
unreal	log pa	mithyā
valid cognizer	tshad ma	pramāṇa
valid establishment	tshad grub	*pramāṇasiddha
well known to the world	'jig rten la grags pa	lokaprasiddha
Wisdom Truth Body	ye shes chos sku	jñānadharmakāya
wisdom	shes rab	prajñā
world	'jig rten	loka
worldly concealer-truths	'jig rten kun rdzob	lokasaṃvṛtisatya
worldly convention	'jig rten gyi tha snyad	lokavyavahāra
worldly perspective	'jig rten shes ngo	
wrong consciousness	log shes	viparyayajñāna
wrong	log pa/phyin ci log pa	vipraryaya
yogi	rnal 'byor pa	yogi
yogic direct perceiver	rnal 'byor mngon sum	yogipratyakṣa
Yogācāra-Svātantrika-Mādhyamika	rnal 'byor spyod pa'i dbu ma rang rgyud pa	yogācārasvātanri-kamādhyamika
śāstra	bstan bcos	śāstra

Bibliography

This bibliograpy is divided into three sections. The first lists sūtras, arranged alphabetically by English title. The second section contains Sanskrit and Tibetan treatises. The third lists Western language sources. The latter two sections are arranged alphabetically by author's name, except in the case of a single anonymous work which is listed by title.

ABBREVIATIONS

D	s*De dge Tibetan Tripitaka—bsTan hgyur preserved at the Faculty of Letters, University of Tokyo* (Tokyo: 1977ff).
Dharma	*Nying-ma Edition of the sDe-dge bKa'-'gyur and bsTan-'gyur* (Oakland, CA: Dharma Publishing, 1980).
HJAS	*Harvard Journal of Asiatic Studies*
IJ	*Indo-Iranian Journal*
JA	*Journal Asiatique*
JAAR	*Journal of the American Academy of Religion*
JAOS	*Journal of the American Oriental Society*
JIABS	*Journal of the International Association of Buddhist Studies*
JIBS	*Journal of Indian and Buddhist Studies*
JIP	*Journal of Indian Philosophy*
P	*The Tibetan Tripitaka* (Tokyo-Kyoto: Tibetan Tripitaka Research Foundation, 1956)
PEW	*Philosophy East and West*
SP	*Studia Philosophica*
Toh	*Complete Catalogue of the Tibetan Buddhist Canons* edited by Prof. Hakuju Ui and *A Catalogue of the Tohoku University Collection of Tibetan Works on Buddhism* edited by Prof. Yensho Kankura (Sendai, Japan: 1934 and 1953).
TJ	*Tibet Journal*

I. SŪTRAS

Bodhisattva Scriptural Collection
bodhisattvapiṭaka
'phags pa byang chub sems dpa'i sde snod
P760.12, Vol.22-23; Toh 56, Dharma Vol. 15-16
(see *Heap of Jewels Sūtra*)

Chapter Teaching the Three Vows Sūtra
trisambaranirdeśaparivartasūtra
sdom pa gsum bstan pa'i le'u mdo
P760.1, Vol.22
(see *Heap of Jewels Sūtra*)

Cloud of Jewels Sūtra
ratnameghasūtra
dkon mchog sprin gyi mdo
P879, Vol.35

Compendium of Doctrine Sūtra
dharmasaṃgītisūtra
chos yang dag par sdud pa'i mdo
P904, Vol. 36

Condensed Perfection of Wisdom Sūtra
sañcayagāthāprajñāpāramitāsūtra
shes rab kyi pha rol tu phyin pa sdud pa tshigs su bcad pa
P735, Vol. 21
Trans. by E. Conze, *The Perfection of Wisdom in Eight Thousand Lines and its Verse Summary* (Bolinas, CA: Four Seasons Foundation, 1973)

Descent into Laṅkā Sūtra
laṅkāvatārasūtra
lang kar gshegs pa'i mdo
P775, Vol. 29
Trans. by D.T. Suzuki, *The Lankavatara Sutra* (London: Routledge, 1932)

Eighteen Thousand Stanza Perfection of Wisdom Sūtra
aṣṭadaśasāhasrikāprajñāpāramitāsūtra
shes rab kyi pha rol tu phyin pa khri rgyad stong pa'i mdo
P732, Vol. 19-20

Heap of Jewels Sūtra
mahāratnakūṭadharmaparyāyaśatasāhasrikāgranthasūtra
dkon mchog brtsegs pa chen po'i chos kyi rnam grangs le'u stong phrag brgya pa'i mdo
P760, Vol. 22-24
Partially translated in *A Treasury of Mahāyāna Sūtras*, Garma Chang, ed. (University Park, Pennsylvania: Pennsylvania State University Press, 1983)

Heart of Wisdom Sūtra
prajñāhṛdaya/bhagavatīprajñāpāramitāhṛdayasūtra
shes rab snying po/ bcom ldan 'das ma shes rab kyi pha rol tu phyin

pa'i snying po'i mdo
P160, Vol. 6
Sanskrit: in E. Conze, *Thirty Years of Buddhist Studies*, (Oxford: Cassirer, 1967)
Translated by Lopez in *The Heart Sūtra Explained* (Albany: SUNY, 1988); by E. Conze in *Buddhist Texts Throught the Ages* (New York: Harper, 1964); by Geshe Rabten in *Echoes of Voidness*. (London: Wisdom, 1983), etc.

King of Meditative Stabilizations Sūtra
samādhirāja/sarvadharmasvabhavasamatāvipañcatasamādhirājasūtra
ting nge 'dzin rgyal po'i mdo/chos thams cad kyi rang bzhin mnyam pa nyid rnam par spros par ting nge 'dzin gyi rgyal po'i mdo
P795, Vol. 31-32 Toh 127, Dharma Vol. 20
Sanskrit: *Samādhirājasūtram*. P.L. Vaidya, ed. Buddhist Sanskrit Texts, No. 2 (Dharbhanga: Mithila Institute, 1961).
Partial English translation (chapters 8, 19, and 22): K. Regamey, *Three Chapters from the Samādhirājasūtra* (Warsaw: Publications of the Oriental Commission, 1938)

Life Stories
jātakanidāna
skyes pa rabs kyi gleng gzhi
P748, Vol. 21

Meeting of Father and Son Sūtra
pitāputrasamāgamasūtra
yab dang sras mjal ba'i mdo
P760.16, Vol. 23

Questions of King Dhāraṇīśvara Sūtra
dhāraṇīśvararājaparipṛcchsūtra
gzung kyi dbang phyug rgyal pos zhus pa'i mdo
P814, Vol. 32

Sūtra on the Ten Grounds
daśabhūmikasūtra
mdo sde sa bcu pa
P761.31, Vol. 25
Sanskrit: *Daśabhūmikasūtram*. P.L. Vaidya, ed. Buddhist Sanskrit Texts No. 7 (Dharbhanga: Mithila Institute, 1967)
English translation: M. Honda, "An Annotated Translation of the 'Daśabhūmika'," in D. Sinor, ed. *Studies in Southeast and Central Asia*, Satapitaka Series 74 (New Delhi: 1968), pp.115-276 and as chapter 31 of *The Flower Ornament Sūtra* translated by Thomas Cleary (Boston: Shambala, 1984-87)

Sūtra Unravelling the Thought
saṃdhinirmocanasūtra
dgongs pa nges par 'grel pa'i mdo
P774, Vol.29; Toh 106, Dharma Vol.18
Also, in *The Tog Palace MS. of the Tibetan Kanjur* (Leh: Smanrtsis

Shesrig Dpemzod, 1975).
Edited Tibetan text and French translation: Étienne Lamotte, *Saṃdhinirmocanasūtra: l'explication des mystères* (Louvain: Universite de Louvain, 1935); partial English translation: John Powers, "The Saṃdhinirmochana Sūtra," (typescript, 1986).

Teachings of Akṣayamati Sūtra
akṣayamatinirdeśasūtra
blo gros mi zad pas bstan pa'i mdo
P842, Vol. 34

II. TIBETAN AND SANSKRIT TREATISES

A-khu-ching (a khu ching shes rab rgya mtsho, 1803-1875)
Notes on (Candrakīrti's) "Supplement"
bstan bcos chen po dbu ma la 'lug pa'i brjed byang mthar 'dzin tsha gdung sel ba'i zla ba'i 'od/'jug zin
Collected Works, vol. 6; Delhi: Ngawang Sopa, 1973

Āryadeva ('phags pa lha, second to third century, C.E.)
Four Hundred/Treatise of Four Hundred Stanzas
catuḥśatakaśāstrakārikā
bstan bcos bzhi brgya pa zhes bya ba'i tshig le'ur byas pa
Toh 3846; P5246, Vol. 95
Edited Tibetan, Sanskrit fragments, and English translation: Karen Lang, "Āryadeva on the Bodhisattva's Cultivation of Merit and Knowledge" (Ann Arbor: University Microfilms, 1983). Italian translation from the Chinese of the latter half: Giuseppe Tucci, "La versione cinese del Catuḥśataka di Āryadeva, confronta col testo sanscrito et la traduzione tibetana," *Rivista degli Studi Orientalia* 10 (1925), pp.521-67.

Aśvaghoṣa (rta dbyangs, fourth century?)
Cultivation of the Conventional Mind of Enlightenment
saṃvṛtibodhicittabhāvanopadeśavarṇasaṃgraha
kun rdzob byang chub kyi sems bsgom pa'i man ngag yi ger bris pa
D dbu ma Vol. 15; Toh 3911; P5307, Vol. 102

Atiśa (982-1054)
Introduction to the Two Truths
satyadvayāvatāra
bden pa gnyis la 'jug pa
P5298, Vol. 101 and P5380, Vol. 103

Bel-den-chö-jay
(see Ngak-wang-bel-den)

Bel-den-drak-ba (dbal ldan grags pa)
A Good Explanation, A Beautiful Ornament for Faith
legs bshad dad pa'i mdzes rgyan
Mundgod: Drepung Loseling Library, 1979

Bhāvaviveka (legs ldan byed, 500-570?)
Blaze of Reasoning, Commentary on the "Heart of the Middle Way"
madhyamakahṛdayavṛttitarkajvāla
P5256, Vol. 96
Partial translation by S. Iida in *Reason and Emptiness* (Tokyo: Hokuseido, 1980)
Lamp for (Nāgārjuna's) "Wisdom," Commentary on the "Treatise on the Middle Way"
prajñāpradīpamūlamadhyamakavṛtti
P5253, Vol. 95
Partial translation by David Eckel in "A Question of Nihilism" (Ph.D. dissertation, Harvard University, 1980)

Buddhapālita (sang rgyas bskyangs, c.470-540?)
Buddhapālita Commentary on (Nāgārjuna's) "Treatise on the Middle Way"
buddhapālitamūlamadhyamakavṛtti
dbu ma rtsa ba'i 'grel pa buddhapālita
D dbu ma Vol. 1; Toh 3842; P5254
Edited Tibetan edition of chs.1-12: Max Walleser, Bibliotheca Buddhica XVI (Osnabrück: Biblio Verlag, 1970)
English translation of ch.1: Judit Fehér in Louis Ligeti, ed., *Tibetan and Buddhist Studies Commemorating the 200th Anniversary of the Birth of Alexander Csoma de Körös*, Vol.1 (Budapest: Akadémiai Kiado, 1984), pp. 211-40

Candrakīrti (zla ba grags pa, seventh century)
Clear Words, Commentary on (Nāgārjuna's) "Treatise on the Middle Way"
mūlamadhyamakavṛttiprasannapadā
dbu ma rtsa ba'i 'grel pa tshig gsal ba
P5260, Vol. 98
Also, Dharamsala: Tibetan Publishing House, 1968. Sanskrit: *Mūlamadhaymakakārikās de Nāgārjuna avec la Prasannapadā Commentaire de Candrakīrti*. Louis de la Vallée Poussin, ed. Bibliotheca Buddhica IV (Osnabrück: Biblio Verlag, 1970)
Partial English translation: Mervyn Sprung, *Lucid Exposition of the Middle Way* (London: Routledge, 1979 and Boulder: Prajñā Press, 1979). Partial French translation (chs. 2, 3, 4, 11, 23, 24, 26, 28): Jacques May, *Prasannapadā Madhyamakavṛtti, douze chapitres traduits du sanscrit et du tibetain* (Paris: Adrien-Maisonneuve, 1959). Other partial translations by Hopkins (ch. 2) 1974, de Jong (chs. 18-22) 1949, Lamotte (ch. 17), etc.
Commentary on (Nāgārjuna's) "Sixty Stanzas of Reasoning"
yuktiṣaṣṭikāvṛtti
rigs pa drug cu pa'i 'grel pa
D dbu ma Vol. 8; Toh 3864, P5265, Vol. 98
Supplement Commentary/Commentary on the "Supplement to (Nāgārjuna's) "Treatise on the Middle Way"

madhyamakāvatārabhāṣya
dbu ma la 'jug pa'i bshad pa/dbu ma la 'jug pa'i rang 'grel
P5263, Vol. 98
Also: Dharamsala: Council of Religious and Cultural Affairs, 1968
Edited Tibetan: Louis de la Vallée Poussin, *Madhyamakāvatāra par Candrakīrti*. Bibliotheca Buddhica IX (Osnabrück: Verlag, 1970)
French trans. (to 6.165): Louis de la Vallée Poussin, Muséon 8 (1907), 11 (1910), and 12 (1911)

Supplement to (Nāgārjuna's) "Treatise on the Middle Way"
madhaymakāvatāra P5261, P5262, Vol. 98
(see listings under Candrakīrti's *Supplement Commentary*). Also, partial English translation (chs. 1-5) by Hopkins in *Compassion in Tibetan Buddhism* (Valois, NY: Gabriel/Snow Lion, 1980) and (ch. 6) by Batchelor in Geshe Rabten's *Echoes of Voidness* (London: Wisdom, 1983)

Dak-tsang (stag tshang lo tsa ba shes rab rin chen, 1405-?)
Ocean of Good Explanations: An Explanation of "Freedom From Extremes Through Understanding All Tenets"
grub mtha' kun shes nas mtha' bral grub pa zhes bya ba'i bstan bcos rnam par bshad pa legs bshad kyi rgya mtsho
Thimphu: Kun bdzang stobs rgyal, 1976

Den-dar-hla-ram-ba (bstan dar lha ram pa, 1759-?)
Presentation of the Lack of Being One or Many
gcig du bral gyi rnam gzhag legs bshad rgya mtsho las btus pa'i 'khrul spong dbud rtsi'i gzegs ma
Collected Works, Vol. 1 (New Delhi: Lama Guru Deva, 1971)

Drak-ba-shay-drup (co ne rje btsun grags pa bshad sgrub, 1675-1748)
A Combined Word Commentary, General Meaning Commentary, and Analytical Delineation on (Kay-drup Den-ba-tar-gyay's) "Lamp Further Illuminating the Thought of (Candrakīrti's) 'Supplement' "
dbu ma la 'jug pa'i dgongs pa yang gsal sgron me shes bya ba'i tshig 'grel spyi don mtha dpyod zung 'brel du bshad pa
New Delhi: Lha mkhar yongs 'dzin bstan pa rgyal mtshan, 1972.

Dzay-may Lo-sang-bel-den (dze smad blo bzang dpal ldan, b.1927)
Refutation of (Ge-dun-chö-pel's) "Ornament for the Thought of Nāgārjuna"
dbu ma klu sgrub dgongs rgyan gyi dgag pa
Delhi: D. Gyaltsen and K. Legshay, 1972

Fifth Dalai Lama
see Nga-wang-blo-sang-gya-tso

Gen-dun-chö-pel (dge 'dun chos 'phel, 1905?-1951?)
Ornament to Nāgārjuna's Thought, Eloquence Containing the Essence of the Profundities of Mādhyamika

dbu ma'i zab gnad snying por dril ba'i legs bshad klu sgrub dgongs rgyan
Leh: D.T. Tashigang, 1982; also, Gangtok: Sherab Gyaltsen, 1983 and Kalimpong: Mani Printing Works, n.d.

Gen-dun-drup-ba (dge 'dun grub pa, 1391-1474)
A Precious Rosary, An Explanation of the Meaning of the Words of the Root Text of Mādhyamika, (Nāgārjuna's) "Wisdom"
dbu ma'i rtsa ba shes rab kyi ngag don bshad pa rin po che'i phren ba
Sarnath: 1968

Gön-chok-jik-may-wang-bo (dkon chog 'jigs med dbang po, 1728-1791)
Precious Garland of Tenets/Presentation of Tenets, A Precious Garland
grub pa'i mtha'i rnam par bzhag pa rin po che'i phreng ba
Dharmsala: Shes rig par khang, 1969; also, Mundgod: Dre-Gomang Buddhist Cultural Association, 1980
English translations: Sopa and Hopkins in *Practice and Theory of Tibetan Buddhism* (New York: Grove, 1976) and H.V. Guenther in *Buddhist Philosophy in Theory and Practice* (Baltimore: Penguin, 1972)

Gyel-tsap (rgyal tshab dar ma rin chen, 1364-1432)
An Entrance for the Sons of Conquerors, Explanation of (Śāntideva's) "Engaging in the Bodhisattva Deeds"
byang chub sems dpa'i spyod pa la 'jug pa'i rnam bshad rgyal sras
Sarnath: Gelugba Students Welfare Committee, 1973
Ornament for the Essence, Explanation [of Maitreya's "Ornament for Clear Realization" and its Commentaries]
rnam bshad syning po rgyan
Sarnath: Gelugpa Students Welfare Committee, 1980
Precious Garland: A Presentation of the Two Truths and Words of Instruction on the View
bden gnyis kyi rnam bzhag dang lta ba'i 'khrid yig rin po che'i 'phreng ba
Within *dbu ma'i lta khrid phyogs bsdebs* (Sarnath: Gelugpa Students Welfare Committee, 1985)

Khetsun Sangbo
Biographical Dictionary of Tibet and Tibetan Buddhism
Dharamsala: Library of Tibetan Works and Archives, 1975

Haribhadra (seng ge bzang po, late eighth century)
Clear Meaning Commentary
sphuṭārtha
'grel pa don gsal
P5191, Vol.90

Jam-ba-dra-shi (khyung phrug byams pa bkra shis)
Throat Ornament for the Fortunate, A Good Explanation Clarifying Difficulties in (Dzong-ka-ba's) "Illumination of the Thought"

dbu ma la 'jug pa'i rnam bshad dgongs pa rab gsal gyi dka ba'i gnas gsal bar byed pa legs bshad skal bzang mkul rgyan
New Delhi: Lha mkhar yongs 'dzin bstan pa rgyal mtshan, 1974

Jam-yang-chok-lha-ö-ser ('jam dbyang phyogs lha 'od zer, fl. fifteenth century?)
Collected Topics of Ra Dö
rva stod bsdus grva
Dharamsala: Damchoe Sangpo, Library of Tibetan Works and Archives, 1980

Jam-yang-shay-ba ('jam dbyangs bzhad pa, 1648-1721)
Great Exposition of Tenets
grub mtha' chen mo
Musoorie: Dalama, 1962
Great Exposition of the Middle Way/Analysis of (Candrakīrti's) "Supplement to (Nāgārjuna's) 'Treatise on the Middle Way' ", Treasury of Scripture and Reasoning Thoroughly Illuminating the Profound Meaning [of Emptiness], Entrance for the Fortunate
dbu ma chen mo/dbu ma 'jug pa'i mtha' bpyod lung rigs gter mdzod zab don kun gsal skal bzang 'jug ngogs
Collected Works, Vol. 9 (Ta) (New Delhi: Ngawang Gelek Demo, 1972); Also, Buxaduor: Gomang, 1967

Jang-gya Rol-bay-dor-jay (lcang skya rol pa'i rdo rje, 1717-1786)
Presentation of Tenets
grub pa'i mtha'i rnam par bzhag pa gsal bar bshad pa thub bstan lhun po'i mdzes rgyan
Varanasi: Pleasure of Elegant Sayings Press, 1970
English translation (Sautrāntika chapter): Anne Klein in *Knowing, Naming and Negation* (Ithaca: Snow Lion); (Svātantrika chapter): Donald Lopez, "The Svātantrika-Mādhyamika School of Mahāyāna Buddhism" (Ann Arbor: University Microfilms, 1982); (portion of the Prāsaṅgika chapter): Jeffrey Hopkins in *Emptiness Yoga* (Ithaca: Snow Lion, 1987).

Jay-dzun Chö-gyi-gyel-tsen (rje btsun chos kyi rgyal mtshan, 1469-1546)
A Good Explanation Adorning the Throats of the Fortunate: A General Meaning Commentary Clarifying Difficult Points in (Tsong-ka-pa's) "Illumination of the Thought: An Explanation of (Candrakīrti's) 'Supplement to (Nāgārjuna's) "Treatise on the Middle Way" ' "
bstan bcos dbu ma la 'jug pa'i rnam bshad dgongs pa rab gsal gyi dka' gnad gsal bar byed pa'i spyi don legs bshad skal bzang mgul rgyan
New Delhi: lha mkhar yongs 'dzin bstan pa rgyal mtshan, 1973

Jayānanda
Explanation of (Candrakīrti's) "Supplement to (Nāgārjuna's) 'Treatise on the Middle Way' "

mādhyamakāvatāraṭīka
dbu ma la 'jug pa'i grel bshad
P5271, vol. 99

Jñānagarbha (ye shes snying po, eighth century)
Commentary on "Distinguishing the Two Truths"
satyadvayavibhaṅgavṛtti
bden pa gnyis rnam par 'byed pa'i 'grel pa
Toh 3882
Edited Tibetan and English translation in: Malcolm David Eckel, *Jñānagarbha's Commentary on the Distinction Between the Two Truths* (Albany, NY: State University of New York Press, 1987)
Distinguishing the Two Truths
satyadvayavibhaṅgakārikā
bden gnyis rnam 'byed pa'i tshig le'ur byas pa
Toh 3881 (not in P)
Edited Tibetan and English translation in Malcolm David Eckel, *Jñānagarbha's Commentary on the Distinction Between the Two Truths* (Albany, NY: State University of New York Press, 1987)

Kamalaśīla (c.740-795)
Illumination of the Middle Way
madhyamakāloka
dbu ma snang ba
D dbu ma Vol. 12
Toh 3887, P5287, Vol. 101

Kay-drup Den-ba-tar-gyay (mkhas sgrub bstan pa dar rgyas, 1493-1568)
A Lamp for the Clear-Minded, Illuminating the Intention of (Tsong-ka-pa's) "Illumination of the Thought"
bstan bcos chen po dbu ma la 'jug pa'i spyi don rnam bshad dgongs pa rab gsal gyi dgongs pa gsal bar byed pa'i blo gsal sgron me
New Delhi: Lha mkhar yongs 'dzin bstan pa rgyal mtshan, 1972.
Ocean of Reasoning, an Introduction for the Clear Minded: An Analytical Delineation of (Tsong-ka-pa's) "Illumination of the Thought"
rnam bshad dgongs pa rab gsal gyi mtha dpyod rigs pa'i rgya mtsho blo gsal gyi 'jug sgo
New Delhi: Lha mkhar yongs 'dzin bstan pa rgyal mtshan, 1972

Kay-drup Gay-lek-bel-sang-po (mkhas sgrub dge legs dpal bzang po, 1385-1483)
Thousand Doses/Opening the Eyes of the Fortunate, Treatise Brilliantly Clarifying the Profound Emptiness
stong thun chen mo/zab mo stong pa nyid rab tu gsal bar byed pa'i bstan bcos skal bzang mig 'byed
Dharamsala: Shes rig par khang, n.d.
English translation in José Ignacio Cabezón, "The Development of a Buddhist Philosophy of Language and its Culmination in Tibe-

tan Mādhyamika Thought" (Ph.D. dissertation, University of Wisconsin, 1987)

La-wang-gya-tso (lha dbang rgya mtsho)
Sport of Faith: The Marvellous, Amazing Biography of the Foremost Omniscient Paṇ-chen Sö-nam-drak-ba
rje btsun thams cad mkhyen pa bka' 'drin can bsod nams grags pa'i dpal rnam dpyod mchog gi sde'i rnam par thar pa ngo mtshar rmad du byung ba dad pa'i rol rtsed
in *Three Dge-lugs-pa Historical Works* (New Delhi: Ngawang Gelek Demo, 1978)

Lo-der-wang-bo (blo gter dbang po, 1847-1914)
Lamp Illuminating the Thought of Candrakīrti, A Commentary on the "Supplement to the Middle Way"
dbu ma la 'jug pa'i mchan 'grel zla ba'i dgonds pa gsal ba'i sgron me
Delhi: Trayang and Jamyang Samten, 1975

Lo-drö-gya-tso (blo gros rgya mtsho)
A Shining Sun Opening the Eyes of the View of the Profound Path, Illuminating the Meaning of (Jam-yang-shay-ba's) "Great Exposition of the Middle Way"
dbu ma'i mtha' dbyod lung rigs gter mdzod kyi dgongs don gsal bar byed pa'i nyin byed snang ba zab lam lta ba'i mig byed
Delhi: Kesang Thabkhes, 1974

Lo-sang-chö-ying (blo bzang chos byings)
Disputation and Reply Driving Pain from the Heart of One of Inferior Intelligence: A Companion Piece for "A Drop of Camphor"
rtsod lan blo dman snying gi gdung sel ga bur thig pa'i spun zla
Mundgod: Drebung Loseling Library Society, 1985.

Lo-sang-da-yang (blo bzang rta dbyangs, a.k.a. blo bzang rta mgrin, a.k.a., sog yul rta dbyangs 1867-1937)
A Mirror Thoroughly Illuminating the Meaning of the Profound: Annotations on (Paṇ-chen Sö-nam-drak-ba's) "General Meaning of (Nagarjuna's) 'Treatise on the Middle Way'"
dbu ma spyi don gyi mchan 'grel zab don rab gsal sgron me
New Delhi: Tibet House, 1974

Maitreya (byams pa)
Ornament for Clear Realization
abhisamayālaṃkāra
mngon par rtogs pa'i rgyan
P5814, Vol.88
English translation: Conze. *Abhisayamālankāra*, Serie Orientale Roma VI (Rome: Is.M.E.O., 1954)

Nāgārjuna (glu sgrub, first to second century)
Compendium of Sūtra
sūtrasamuccaya

mdo kun las btus pa
Toh 3934, P5330, Vol. 102
Essay on the Mind of Enlightenment
bodhicittavivaraṇa
byang chub sems kyi 'grel ba
P2665 and 2666, Vol.61
Edited Tibetan and Sanskrit fragments with English translation: Chr. Lindtner in *Nagarjuniana*, Indiske Studier 4 (Copenhagen: Akademisk Forlag, 1982)
Praise for the Sphere of Reality
dharmadhātustotra
chos kyi dbyings su bstod pa
P2010, Vol. 46
Sixty Stanzas of Reasoning
yuktiṣaṣṭikākārikā
rigs pa drug cu pa'i tshig le'ur byas pa
P5225; Toh 3825
Edited Tibetan with Sanskrit fragments and English translation: Chr. Lindtner in *Nagarjuniana*, Indiske Studier 4 (Copenhagen: Akademisk Forlag, 1982)
Treatise on the Middle Way/Fundamental Treatise on the Middle Way, Called "Wisdom"
madhyamakaśāstra/prajñānāmamūlamadhyamakakārikā
dbu ma'i bstan bcos/dbu ma rtsa ba'i tshig le'ur byas pa shes rab ces bya ba
P5224, Vol. 95
English translation: in Kalupahana, *The Philosophy of the Middle Way* (Albany, NY: State University of New York, 1986). For a list of other trans. and ed., see Ruegg's *Literature of the Madhyamaka School of Philosophy in India*, pp.126-27.

Nam-ka-gyel-tsen (sgom sde shar pa nam mkha' rgyal mtshan)
Ornament for the Thought of Candrakīrti, a Ford for Those Seeking Liberation: An Explanation of (Candrakīrti's) "Supplement"
bstan bcos chen mo dbu ma la 'jug pa'i rnam bshad thar 'dod 'jug ngogs zla ba'i dgongs rgyan
New Delhi: Lha mkhar yongs 'dzin bstan pa rgyal mtshan, 1974

Ngak-wang-bel-den (ngag dbang dpal ldan, a.k.a. dpal ldan chos rje, b.1797)
Annotations for (Jam-yang-shay-ba's) "Great Exposition of Tenets", Freeing the Knots of the Difficult Points, Precious Jewel of Clear Thought
grub mtha' chen mo'i mchan 'grel dka' gnad mdud grol blo gsal gces nor
Sarnath: Pleasure of Elegant Sayings Printing Press, 1964
Explanation of the Conventional and the Ultimate in the Four Systems of Tenets
grub mtha' bzhi'i lugs kyi kun rdzob dang don dam pa'i don rnam

par bshad pa legs bshad dpyid kyi dpal mo'i glu dbyangs
New Delhi: Guru Deva, 1972
Partial English translation (Vaibhāṣika section): in J. Buescher, "The Buddhist Doctrine of the Two Truths in the Vaibhāṣika and Theravāda Schools" (Ann Arbor, MI: University Microfilms, 1982); (Svātantrika section): Buescher and Hopkins, unpublished.

Joyful Teaching Clarifying the Mind, A Statement of the Modes of Explaining the Middle Way and the Perfection of Wisdom in the Textbooks of the Lo-sel-ling and Dra-shi-go-mang Monastic Colleges
blo gsal gling dang bkra shis sgo mang grwa tshang gi dbu phar gyi yig cha bshad tshul bkod pa blo gsal dga' ston
Collected Works, Vol. 3 (New Delhi: Guru Deva, 1983)

Ngak-wang-lo-sang-gya-tso, the Fifth Dalai Lama (ngag dbang bloo bzang rgya mtsho, 1617-1682)
Sacred Word of Mañjuśrī, Instructions on the Stages of the Path to Enlightenment
byang chub lam gyi rim pa'i 'khrid yig 'jam pa'i dbyangs kyi zhal lung
Thim-phu: Kun-bzang-stobs-rgyal, 1976
Partial English translation: Hopkins, *Practice of Emptiness* (Dharamsala: Library of Tibetan Works and Archives, 1974)

Ngak-wang-pun-tsok (ngag dbang phun tshog)
Medicinal Ear of Corn, A Good Explanation: A Commentary on "A Song of the View, A Medicinal Sprout To Cast Out the Demons [of Extreme Views]"
lta mgur gdung sel sman gyi myu gu'i rnam 'grel bshad sman gyi snye ma
New Delhi: Tibet House, n.d.

Padma-gyel-tsen (padma rgyal mtshan, ?-1985)
An Eye-Opening Golden Wand: Counsel on the Meaning of the Profound [Emptiness]
zab don gdams pa'i mig 'byed gser gyi thur ma
Vol. 2: Mundgod: Drebung Loseling Printing Press, 1985
Vol. 3: Mundgod: Drebung Loseling Printing Press, 1984

Paṇ-chen Sö-nam-drak-ba (paṇ chen sod nams grags pa, 1478-1554)
General Meaning of (Maitreya's) "Ornament for Clear Realization"
par phyin spyi don
Collected Works Vol. "Ga"
Mundgod: Drebung Loseling Library Society, 1982
Lamp Further Illuminating the Meaning of the Profound [Emptiness], Disputation and Reply [Concerning the Meaning of] (Candrakīrti's) "Supplement"
dbu ma la 'jug pa'i brgal lan zab don yang gsal sgron me
Collected Works Vol. "Ja"
Mundgod: Drebung Loseling Library Society, 1985
Lamp Illuminating the Meaning of the Profound [Emptiness], the General Meaning of (Nāgārjuna's) "Treatise on the Middle Way"

dbu ma'i spyi don zab don gsal ba'i sgron me
Collected Works Vol. "Ja"
Mundgod: Drebung Loseling Library Society, 1985

Religious History of the Old and New Ga-dam-ba, a Beautiful Ornament for the Mind
bka' gdams gsar rnying gi chos 'byung yid gyi mdzes rgyan
in *Three Dge-lugs-pa Historical Works* (New Delhi: Ngawang Gelek Demo, 1978)

Prajñāmokśa (shes rab thar pa)
Commentary on (Atiśa's) "Essential Instructions on the Middle Way"
madhyamakopadeśavṛtti
dbu ma'i man ngag ces bya ba'i 'grel pa
D dbu ma Vol. 15; Toh 3931; P5326

Pur-bu-jok Jam-ba-gya-tso (phu bu lcog byams pa rgya mtsho, 1825-1921)
The Lesser Path of Reasoning
The Intermediate Path of Reasoning
The Greater Path of Reasoning
rigs lam chung ngu
rigs lam 'bring
rigs lam che ba
In: *The Presentation of Collected Topics Revealing the Meaning of the Texts on Valid Cognition, the Magical Key to the the Path of Reasoning*
tshad ma'i gzhung don 'byed pa'i bsdus grva'i rnam bzhag rigs lam 'phrul gyi lde mig
Buxa, India: n.p., 1965

Ren-da-wa (red mda' ba gzhon nus blo gros, 1349-1412)
Lamp Illuminating Suchness, An Explanation of (Candrakīrti's) "Supplement to (Nāgārjuna's) 'Treatise on the Middle Way' "
bdu ma la 'jug pa'i rnam bshad de kho na nyid gsal ba'i sgron ma
Delhi: Ngawang Topgay, 1974

Rong-dön (rong ston shes bya kun rig, 1367-1450)
Ascertaining the Definitive Meaning of (Candrakīrti's) "Supplement"
dbu ma la 'jug pa'i rnam bshad nges don rnam nges
New Delhi: Trayang and Jamyang Samten, 1974

Illuminating the Profound Suchness, An Explanation of (Nāgārjuna's) Root Text on the Middle Way
dbu ma'i rtsa ba'i rnam bshad zab mo'i de kho na nyid snang ba
Sarnath: Sakya Students Union, 1975

Sa-kya Paṇḍita (sa skya paṇḍita kun dga' rgyal mtshan, 1182-1251)
Illuminating the Thought of the Subduer
thub pa'i dgongs pa rab tu gsal ba
Translated as *Illuminations* by Geshe Wangyal and Brian Cutillo (Novato, CA: Lotsawa, 1988)

Śāntarakṣita (zhi ba 'tsho, eighth century)
Subcommentary on (Jñānagarbha's) "Differentiation of the Two Truths"
satyadvayavibhaṅgapañjikā
bden pa gnyis rnam par 'byed pa'i dga' 'grel
D dbu ma Vol.12; Toh 3883; P5283, Vol. 100
Partial English translation: M.D. Eckel, in *Jñānagarbha's Commentary on the Distinction Between the Two Truths* (Albany, NY: SUNY Press, 1987)

Śāntideva (zhi ba lha, eighth century)
Compendium of Instructions
śikṣāsamuccayakārikā
bslab pa kun las btus pa'i tshig le'ur byas pa
D dbu ma Vol. 16; Toh 3939; P5335, Vol. 102
English translation: C. Bendall and W.H.D. Rouse, *Śikṣā Samuccaya* (Delhi: Motilal, 1971; rpt. 1981)
Engaging in the Bodhisattva Deeds
bodhisattvacaryāvatāra
byang chub sems dpa'i spyod la 'jug pa
P5272, Vol.99
Sanskrit and Tibetan edition: *Bodhicaryāvatāra*. Vidhushekara Bhattacarya, ed. (Calcutta: The Asiatic Society, 1960)
English translation by Batchelor (Dharamsala: Library of Tibetan Works and Archives, 1979) and Matics (New York: Macmillan, 1970). Contemporary commentary: Geshe Kelsang Gyatso, *Meaningful to Behold* (London: Wisdom, 1980)

Śānti-ba Lo-drö-gyel-tsen (śānti-pa blo gros rgyal mtshan, fifteenth century)
Powerful King: A Treatise Clarifying Difficult Points in (Tsong-ka-pa's) "Illumination of the Thought"
rnam bshad dgongs pa rab gsal gyi dka ba'i gnad gsal bar byed pa'i bstan bcos dbang gi rgyal po
New Delhi: Lha mkhar yongs 'dzin bstan pa rgyal mtshan, 1973

Shay-rap-ö-ser (shes rab 'od zer, 1058-1132)
The Two Truths in Mādhyamika
dbu ma bden gnyis kyi gzhung
Delhi: Yam Lama, Samtin Jansin Lama, 1961

Shen-pen-chö-gyi-nang-wa (gzhan phan chos kyi snang ba, 1871-1927)
Commentary on Candrakīrti's "Supplement to the Middle Way"
Gangtok: Sherab Gyaltsen Lama, 1979

Tsong-ka-pa (tsong kha pa blo bzang grags pa, 1357-1419)
Essence of Good Explanations, Treatise Discriminating What is to be Interpreted and the Definite
drang ba dang nges pa'i don rnam par phye ba'i bstan bcos legs bshad snying po
P6142, Vol. 153

Also, Sarnath: Pleasure of Elegant Sayings Printing Press, 1973
English translation: Robert Thurman, *Tsong Khapa's Speech of Gold in the Essence of True Eloquence* (Princeton: Princeton University Press, 1984)

Great Exposition of the Stages of the Path
lam rim chen mo
P6001, Vol. 152
Also, Dharamsala: Shes rig par khang, n.d.
Partial English translation: Alex Wayman, *Calming the Mind and Discerning the Real* (New York: Columbia University Press, 1978; rpt. New Delhi: Motilal Banarsidass, 1979)

Illumination of the Thought, Extensive Explanation of (Candrakīrti's) "Supplement to (Nāgārjuna's) 'Treatise on the Middle Way' "
dbu ma la 'jug pa'i rgya bshad pa dgongs pa rab gsal
P6143, Vol. 154
Also, Dharamsala: Shes rig par khang, n.d.
English translation (chs.1-5): Hopkins in *Compassion in Tibetan Buddhism* (Valois, NY: Gabriel/Snow Lion, 1980). Also, unpublished translation (portions of ch. 6) by J. Hopkins and Anne Klein

Intermediate Exposition of the Stages of the Path
lam rim 'bring
P6002, Vols.152-53
Also, Dharamsala: Shes rig par khang, n.d. and Mundgod: Ganden Shardzay, n.d.
Partial English translation: Thurman in *The Life and Teachings of Tsong Khapa* (Dharamsala: Library of Tibetan Works and Archives, 1982). Partial English translation: Hopkins, "Special Insight," unpublished.

Ocean of Reasoning, Explanation of (Nāgārjuna's) "Fundamental Treatise on the Middle Way Called 'Wisdom' "
dbu ma rtsa ba'i tshig le'ur byas pa shes rab ces bya ba'i rnam bshad rigs pa'i rgya mtsho
P6153, Vol. 156
Also, Sarnath: Pleasure of Elegant Sayings Press, n.d.
English translation (ch. 2): Hopkins, *Chapter Two of Ocean Of Reasoning by Tsong-ka-pa* (Dharamsala: Library of Tibetan Works and Archives, 1974)

"Words of Instruction on the Middle Way View"
dbu ma'i lta ba'i 'khrid yig bzhugs
Within *dbu ma'i lta khrid phyogs bsdebs* (Sarnath: Gelugpa Students Welfare Committe, 1985)

Tsul-tim-gya-tso (tshul khrims rgya mtsho, twentieth century)
A Timely Mirror Illuminating the Meaning of Difficult Points
dka' gnad kyi don gsal bar byed pa dus kyi me long
Delhi: Guru Deva, 1983

III. OTHER WORKS

Ames, William. "The Notion of *Svabhāva* in the Thought of Candrakīrti." *JIP* 10 (1982): 161-77.

Avedon, John. *Tibet Today*. London: Wisdom Publications, 1988.

Basham, A.L. *The Wonder That Was India*. New York: Grove Press, 1954.

Berger, Peter. *The Sacred Canopy: Elements of a Sociological Theory of Religion*. New York: Doubleday, 1967.

Betty, L. Stafford. "Nāgārjuna's masterpiece—logical, mystical, both, or neither?" *PEW* 33 (1983): 123-38

Bhattacharya, Kamaleswar. "The Dialectical Method of Nāgārjuna." *JIP* 1 (1972): 217-61.

Broido, Michael. "Padma dKar-po on the Two *Satyas*." *JIABS* 8 (1985): 7-59.

__________. "Veridical and Delusive Cognition: Tsong-kha-pa on the Two *Satyas*." *JIP* 16 (1988): 29-63.

Buescher, John. "The Buddhist Doctrine of Two Truths in the Vaibhāṣika and Theravāda Schools." Ann Arbor: University Microfilms, 1982.

Bugault, Guy. "Logic and Dialectics in the *Mādhyamakakārikās*." *JIP* 11 (1983): 7-76.

Cabezón, José Ignacio. "The Development of a Buddhist Philosophy of Language and its Culmination in Tibetan Mādhyamika Thought." Ph.D. dissertation, University of Wisconsin, 1987.

__________. "The Prāsangika's Views on Logic: Tibetan Dge lugs pa Exegesis on the Question of Svatantras." *JIP* 16 (1988): 217-24.

Carroll, Robert P. *When Prophecy Failed*. New York: Seabury, 1979.

Chandra, Lokesh, ed. *Materials for a History of Tibetan Buddhism*. Śatapitaka series, Vol. 28. New Delhi: International Academy of Indian Culture, 1963.

__________. *Tibetan-Sanskrit Dictionary*. Kyoto: Rinsen Book Company, 1982.

Cheng, Hsueh-li. *Empty Logic*. New York: Philosophical Library, 1984.

The Cloud of Unknowing. Translated by Clifton Wolters. Baltimore: Penguin, 1973.

Cohen, Morris R. and Nagel, Ernest. *An Introduction to Logic*. New York: Harcourt, Brace, and World, Inc., 1962.

Collins, Steven. *Selfless Persons*. Cambridge: Cambridge University Press, 1982

Conze, Edward. *Buddhism: Its Essence and Development*. Oxford: Cassirer, 1951; rpt. New York: Harper and Brothers, 1959.

__________. *Buddhist Thought in India*. Ann Arbor: University of Michigan Press, 1967.

__________. *Buddhist Wisdom Books*. London: Allen and Unwin, 1958.

__________. (trans.) *The Large Sūtra on Perfect Wisdom*. Berkeley: University of California Press, 1975.

__________. *Thirty Years of Buddhist Studies*. Oxford: Cassirer, 1967.

Cozort, Daniel. "Unique Tenets of the Middle Way Consequence School." Ph.D. dissertation, University of Virginia, 1989.

Crittenden. "Everyday Reality as Fiction—A Mādhyamika Interpretation." *JIP* 9 (1981): 323-333.

Das, Sarat Chandra. *A Tibetan-English Dictionary*. Delhi: Motilal Banarsidass, reprint 1976.

Daye, Douglas. "Japanese Rationalism, Mādhyamika, and Some Uses of Formalism." *PEW* 24 (1974): 363-68.

__________. "Major Schools of the Mahāyāna: Mādhyamika." *In Buddhism: A Modern Perspective*, edited by Charles Prebish, pp.76-96. University Park and London: Pennsylvania State University Press, 1975.

Dreyfus, Georges B. J. "Definition in Buddhism." Master's thesis, University of Virgina, 1987.

Dowman, Keith. *The Power-Places of Central Tibet*. New York: Routledge and Kegan Paul, 1988.

Eckel, Malcolm David. "Bhāvaviveka and the Early Mādhyamika Theories of Language." *PEW* 28 (1978): 323-37.

__________. Jñānagarbha's *Commentary on the Distinction Between the Two Truths*. Albany, NY: State University of New York Press, 1987.

__________. "A Question of Nihilism: Bhāvaviveka's Response to the Fundamental Problems of Mādhyamika Philosophy." Ph.D. dissertation, Harvard University, 1980.

Fatone, Vicente. *The Philosophy of Nāgārjuna*. Delhi: Motilal, 1981.

Fehér, Judit. "Buddhapālita's *Mūlamadhyamakavṛtti:* Arrival and Spread of Prāsaṅgika-Mādhyamika Literature in Tibet." In *Tibetan and Buddhist Studies Commemorating the 200th Anniversary of the Birth of Alexander Csoma de Körös*, edited by Louis Ligeti, Vol.1, pp.211-40. Budapest: Akadémiai Kiado, 1984.

Fenner, Peter. "A Study of the Relationship Between Analysis (*vicāra*) and Insight (*prajñā*) Based on the *Madhyamakāvatāra*." *JIP* 12 (1984): 139-197.

Festinger, Leon. *When Prophecy Fails*. Minneapolis: University of Minnesota Press, 1956.

Geertz, Clifford. "Religion as a Cultural System." In *Reader in Comparative Religion*, edited by Lessa and Vogt. New York: Harper and Row, 1972.

Gudmunsen, Chris. *Wittgenstein and Buddhism*. London: Macmillan, 1977.

Guenther, Herbert. *Buddhist Philosophy in Theory and Practice*. Baltimore: Penguin, 1971.

Gyatso, Tenzin (bstan 'dzin rgya mtsho, Dalai Lama XIV). *The Buddhism of Tibet of Tibet and The Key to the Middle Way*. Trans. by J. Hopkins and Lati Rinboche. London: Allen and Unwin, 1975

__________. *Kindness, Clarity, and Insight*. Translated and edited by Jeffrey Hopkins; co-edited by Elizabeth Napper. Ithaca: Snow Lion, 1984.

__________. *Opening the Eye of New Awareness.* translated. by D. Lopez and J. Hopkins. London: Wisdom, 1985.

__________. *Transcendent Wisdom: A Commentary on the Ninth Chapter of Shantideva's "Guide to the Bodhisattva's Way of Life."* Translated and edited by B.Alan Wallace. Ithaca: Snow Lion, 1988.

Gyatso, Kelsang. *Meaningful to Behold.* London: Wisdom, 1980.

Hoffman, Helmut. *The Religions of Tibet.* New York: Macmillan, 1961.

Hopkins, Jeffrey, trans. and ed. *Compassion in Tibetan Buddhism* by Tsong-ka-pa and Kensur Lekden. Valois, New York: Gabriel/Snow Lion, 1980.

__________. *Emptiness Yoga.* Ithaca, NY: Snow Lion, 1987.

__________. *Meditation on Emptiness.* London: Wisdom, 1983.

__________., trans. *The Practice of Emptiness* by the Fifth Dalai Lama. Dharmsala: Library of Tibetan Works and Archives, 1974.

__________., trans. *The Precious Garland and the Song of the Four Mindfulnesses* by Nāgārjuna and the Seventh Dalai Lama. New York: Harper and Row, 1975.

__________. "Reflections on Reality: The Nature of Phenomena in the Mind-Only School." Draft, 1990 (typescript).

__________. *The Tantric Distinction.* London: Wisdom, 1984.

Huntington, C.W., Jr. "A 'Nonreferential' View of Language and Conceptual Thought in the Work of Tsoṅ-kha-pa." *PEW* 33 (1983): 326-39.

__________. "The System of the Two Truths in the *Prasannapadā* and the *Madhyamakāvatāra*: A Study in Mādhyamika Soteriology." *JIP* 11 (1983): 77-106.

Hurvitz, Leon. "Chih I (538-597)" *Mélanges chinois et bouddhiques* 12 (1960-62). Louvain: Brussels.

Ichigo, Masamichi. "A Synopsis of the *Madhyamakālaṃkāra* of Śāntarakṣita." *JIP* 20 (1972).

Ichimura, Shohei. "A New Approach to the Intra-Mādhyamika Confrontation Over the Svātantrika and Prāsaṅgika Methods of Refutation." *JIABS* 5 (1982): 41-52.

__________. "A Study on the Mādhyamika Method of Refutation and its Influence on Buddhist Logic." *JIABS* 4 (1981): 87-94.

Iida, Shotaro. "An Introduction to Svātantrika-Mādhyamika." Ann Arbor: University Microfilms, 1968.

__________. "The Nature of Saṃvṛti and the Relationship of Paramārtha to It in Svātantrika-Mādhyamika." In *The Problem of Two Truths in Buddhism and Vedānta*, edited by Mervyn Sprung. Dordrecht: Reidel, 1973.

__________. *Reason and Emptiness.* Tokyo: Hokuseido, 1980.

Iida, Shotaro and Hirabayashi, Jay. "Another Look at the Mādhyamika vs. Yogācāra Controversy Concerning Existence and Non-existence." In *Prajñāpāramitā and Related Systems: Studies in Honor of Edward Conze*, ed. Lewis Lancaster.

Inada, Kenneth. *Nāgārjuna: A translation of his Mūlamadhyamakakārikā with an Introductory Essay.* Tokyo: Hokuseido, 1970.

Jayatilleke, K.N. "The Logic of Four Alternatives." *PEW* 17 (1967): 69-84.
Jones, Richard Hubert. "The Nature and Function of Nāgārjuna's arguments." *PEW* 28 (1978): 485-502.
Jong, Jan W. de. *Cinq chapitres de la Prasannapadā*. Paris: Geuthner, 1949.
__________. "Emptiness." *JIP* 2 (1972): 7-15.
__________. "The Problem of the Absolute in the Madhyamaka School." *JIP* 2 (1972): 1-6.
__________. "Textcritical Notes on the Prasannapadā." *IJ* 20 (1978): 25-29 and 217-52.
Joshi, L.M. *Studies in the Buddhistic Culture of India*. Delhi: Motilal Banarsidass, 1987 reprint of 2nd revised edition, 1977.
Katz, Nathan. "Nāgārjuna and Wittgenstein on Error." In *Buddhist and Western Philosophy* ed. by Nathan Katz, pp. 306-27. New Delhi: Sterling Publishers, 1981
Kajiyama, Yuichi. *Bhāvaviveka and the Prāsaṅgika School*. Navanalanda Mahavihara Research Publication I. Rajgir: Nalanda Press, 1957.
__________. "Later Mādhyamikas on Epistemology and Meditation." In *Mahāyāna Buddhist Meditation: Theory and Practice*, ed. Minoru Kiyota. Honolulu: University of Hawaii Press, 1978.
Kalupahana, David J.. *Buddhist Philosophy*. Honolulu: University of Hawaii Press, 1976.
__________. *Nāgārjuna: The Philosophy of the Middle Way*. Albany, NY: State University of New York Press, 1986.
Karmay, Samten Gyaltsen. *Secret Visions of the Fifth Dalai Lama*. London: Serindia, 1988.
Kitabatake, R. "Two-fold Truth of Bhāvaviveka and Candrakīrti." In *JIBS* 21 (1963): 36-66.
Klein, Anne. *Knowledge and Liberation*. Ithaca, New York: Snow Lion, 1986.
__________. "Mind and Liberation." Ann Arbor: University Microfilms, 1981.
Kuijp, Leonard van der. *Contributions to the Development of Tibetan Buddhist Epistemology*. Wiesbaden: Franz Steiner Verlag, 1983.
Kunst, Arnold. "The Concept of the Principle of Excluded Middle in Buddhism." *Rocznik Orientalistyczny* 21 (1957): 141-47.
La Vallée Poussin, Louis de. "Documents d'Abhidharma: Les deux, les quarte, les trois Vérités." In *Mélanges chinois et bouddhiques* (1937): 159-87.
__________. "Madhyamaka, Mādhyamikas." *Encyclopaedia of Religion and Ethics* edited by James Hastings, Vol. 8. New York: Scribner's Sons, 1916.
__________, trans. *Madhyamakāvatāra*. *Muséon* 8 (1907): 249-317; 11 (1910): 271-358; and 12 (1911): 235-328.
__________. "Nihilism (Buddhist)," *Encyclopaedia of Religon and Ethics* edited by James Hastings. New York: Scribner's Sons, 1916.
__________. *Nirvana*. Paris: Beauchesne, 1925.

__________. "Reflexions sur le Madhyamaka." *Mélanges chinois et bouddhiques* 2 (1932-1933): 4-59.

Lamotte, Étienne, trans. *Le traité de la grande vertu de sagesse*. Louvain: Institut Orientaliste Louvain, 1949-80

Lang, Karen. "Āryadeva on the Bodhisattva's Cultivation of Merit and Knowledge." Ann Arbor: University Microfilms, 1983.

Lati Rinbochay, Denma Lochö Rinbochay, Leah Zahler, and Jeffrey Hopkins. *Meditative States in Tibetan Buddhism*. London: Wisdom, 1983.

Lati Rinbochay and Elizabeth Napper. *Mind in Tibetan Buddhism*. Valois, New York: Gabriel/Snow Lion, 1980.

Lévi-Strauss, Claude. "The Structural Study of Myth." *Journal of American Folklore* 68 (1955): 428-44.

Lindtner, Christian. "Atīśa's Introduction to the Two Truths, and Its Sources." *JIP* 9 (1981): 161-214.

__________. "Buddhapālita on Emptiness [*Buddhapālitamūlamadhyamakavṛtti* XVIII]." *IJ* 23 (1981): 187-217.

__________. *Nagarjuniana*. Indiske Studier 4. Copenhagen: Akademisk Forlag, 1982.

Lipman, Kennard. "A Study of Śāntarakṣita's *Madhyamakālaṃkāra*." Ph.D. Dissertation, University of Saskatchewan, 1979.

Lopez, Donald. *The Heart Sūtra Explained*. Albany: State University of New York Press, 1988.

__________. *A Study of Svātantrika*. Ithaca: Snow Lion, 1987.

__________. "The Svātantrika-Mādhyamika School of Mahāyāna Buddhism." Ann Arbor: University Microfilms, 1982.

Loy, David. "How Not To Criticize Nāgārjuna: A Response to L. Stafford Betty." *PEW* 34 (1984): 437-45.

Magliola, Robert. *Derrida on the Mend*. West Lafayette, Indiana: Purdue University Press, 1984.

Matilal, Bimal Krishna. "A Critique of the Mādhyamika Position." In *The Problem of Two Truths in Buddhism and Vedānta*, edited by Mervyn Sprung. Dordrecht, Holland: D. Reidel, 1973.

__________. *Epistemology, Logic, and Grammar in Indian Philosophical Analysis*. The Hague, Paris: Mouton, 1971.

May, Jacques. "Kant et le Mādhyamika." *IJ* 3 (1959): 102-11.

__________. "On Mādhyamika Philosophy." *JIP* 6 (1978): 233-41.

__________. "La philosophie bouddhique de la vacuité." *SP* 18 (1958): 123-37.

__________. *Prasannapadā Madhyamakavṛtti, douze chapitres traduits du sanscrit et du tibétain*. Paris: Adrien-Maisonneuve, 1959.

__________. "Recherches sur un système de philosphie bouddhique," *Bulletin annuel de la Fondation suisse* 3 (Paris, 1954): 21-43.

McEvilley, Thomas. "Pyrrhonism and Mādhyamika." *PEW* 32 (1982): 3-35.

Mehta, Mahesh. "'Śūnyatā and Dharmatā: the Mādhyamika View of Inner Reality." In *Developments in Buddhist Thought: Canadian Contribu-*

tions to Buddhist Studies. Waterloo, Ontario: Canadian Corporation for Studies in Religion, 1979.

Mimaki, K. "Mādhyamika classification in Tibetan grub mtha." In *Contributions on Tibetan and Buddhist Religion and Philosophy*, edited by E. Steinkeller and H. Tauscher. Vienna: 1983.

Monier-Williams, Sir Monier. *A Sanskrit-English Dictionary*. Delhi: Motilal Banarsidass, reprint 1976.

Murti, T.R.V. *The Central Philosophy of Buddhism*. London: George Allen & Unwin, reprint 1970.

__________. "Saṃvṛti and Paramārtha in Mādhyamika and Advaita Vedānta." In *The Problem of the Two Truths in Buddhism and Vedānta*, edited by M. Sprung. Dordrecht: Reidel, 1973.

Nagatomi, Masatoshi. "Mānasa-Pratyakṣa: A Conundrum in the Buddhist Pramāna System." In *Sanskrit and Indian Studies*. Boston: Reidel, 1980.

Nakamura, Hajime. *Indian Buddhism*. Hirakata City: Kansai University of Foreign Studies Press, 1980.

Napper, Elizabeth Stirling. "Dependent Arising and Emptiness." Ann Arbor: University Microfilms, 1985.

__________. *Dependent Arising and Emptiness*. Boston, Wisdom, 1989.

Nayak, G.C. "The Mādhyamika Attack on Essentialism: A Critical Appraisal." *PEW* 29 (1979): 477-90.

Newland, Guy. *Compassion: A Tibetan Analysis*. London: Wisdom, 1985.

Obermiller, E. *Analysis of the Abhisamayālaṃkāra*. London: Luzac and Co., 1933.

__________. "The Doctrine of the Prajñā-pāramitā as exposed in the *Abhisamayālaṃkāra* of Maitreya." *Acta Orientalia*. Lugduni Batavorum: E.J. Brill, 1932.

Paden, William E. *Religious Worlds: The Comparative Study of Religion*. Boston: Beacon, 1988.

Perdue, Daniel. "Practice and Theory of Philosophical Debate in Tibetan Buddhist Education." Ann Arbor: University Microfilms, 1983.

Potter, Karl H. *Presuppositions of India's Philosophies*. Englewood Cliffs, N.J.: Prentice Hall, 1963.

Proudfoot, Wayne. *Religious Experience*. London: University of California Press, 1985.

Rabten, Geshe. *Echoes of Voidness*. Translated by Stephen Batchelor. London: Wisdom, 1983.

Raju, P.T. *Structural Depths of Indian Thought*. Albany: State University of New York Press, 1985.

Ramanan, K. Venkata. *Nāgārjuna's Philosophy as Presented in the Mahāprajñāpāramitā-Śāstra*. Varanasi: Bharatiya Vidya Prakashan, 1971.

Robinson, Richard. *The Buddhist Religion*. Belmont, CA: Dickenson, 1970.

__________. "Did Nāgārjuna Really Refute All Views?" *PEW* 22 (1972): 325-31.

__________. *Early Mādhyamika in India and China*. Madison: University of Wisconsin Press, 1967.

__________. "Some Logical Aspects of Nāgārjuna's System." *PEW* 6 (1957): 291-308.

Roerich, George N. (trans). *Blue Annals*. Delhi: Motilal Banarsidass, reprint 1979.

Ruegg, David Seyfort. "The Jo naṅ pas: A School of Buddhist Ontologists according to the *Grub mtha' śel gyi me loṅ*." *JAOS* 83 (1963): 73-91

__________. *The Literature of the Madhyamaka School of Philosophy in India*. Wiesbaden: Otto Harrassowitz, 1981.

__________. "On the Knowability and Expressibility of Absolute Reality in Buddhism." *JIBS* 20 (1971): 495-99.

__________. "On the Reception and Early History of the dbu-ma (Madhyamaka) in Tibet." In *Tibetan Studies in Honour of Hugh Richardson*, pp. 277-9. Edited by Michael Aris and Aung San Suu Kyi. New Delhi: Vikas, 1980.

__________. "Towards a chronology of the Madhyamaka School." In *Indological and Buddhist Studies*, edited by L.A. Hercus et al. Canberra: Faculty of Asian Studies, 1982.

__________. "The Uses of the Four Positions of the *Catuṣkoṭi* and the Problem of the Description of Reality in Mahāyāna Buddhism." *JIP* 5 (1977): 1-71.

Sangharakshita. *A Survey of Buddhism*. London: Tharpa, 1987.

Scharfstein, Ben-Ami. *Mystical Experience*. Baltimore: Penguin, 1973.

Schmidt, Roger. *Exploring Religion*. Belmont, CA: Wadsworth, 1988.

Schumann, Hans. *Buddhism*. Wheaton, IL.: Theosophical Publishing, 1973.

Shakapa, W.D. *Tibet: A Political History*. New York: Potala, 1984.

Siderits, Mark. "The Madhyamaka Critique of Epistemology. I and II." *JIP* 8 (1980): 307-35 and 9 (1981): 121-60.

Singh, Jaidev. *An Introduction to Madhyamaka Philosophy*. Delhi: Motilal, 1978.

Snellgrove, David. *Indo-Tibetan Buddhism*. London: Serindia, 1987.

Snellgrove, David and Richardson, Hugh. *A Cultural History of Tibet*. Boulder, CO: Prajñā Press, 1968.

Sopa and Hopkins. *Practice and Theory of Tibetan Buddhism*. New York: Grove, 1976.

Sprung, Mervyn. *Lucid Exposition of the Middle Way*. Boulder: Prajna Press, 1979.

__________. "The Mādhyamika Doctrine as Metaphysic." In *The Problem of Two Truths in Buddhism and Vedanta*, edited by Mervyn Sprung. Boston: D. Reidel Publishing, 1973.

__________. "Nietzsche and Nāgārjuna: The Origin and Issue of Scepticism." In *Revelation in Indian Thought: A Festschrift in Honour of Professor T.R.V. Murti*, edited by Howard Coward and Krishna Sivaraman. Emeryville, CA: Dharma, 1977.

__________. "Non-Cognitive Language in Mādhyamika Buddhism." In *Buddhist Thought and Asian Civilization*. Emeryville CA: Dharma, 1977

Staal, Fritz. *Exploring Mysticism*. Berkeley: University of California Press, 1975.

Stcherbatsky, Theodore. *Buddhist Logic*. New York: Dover, 1962.

__________. *The Conception of Buddhist Nirvāṇa*. Leningrad: Office of the Academy of Sciences of the USSR, 1927; revised reprint Delhi: Motilal, 1977.

Stein, R.A. *Tibetan Civilization*. London: Faber and Faber, 1972.

Streng, Frederick J.. "The Buddhist Doctrine of the Two Truths as Religious Philosophy." *JIP* 1 (1971): 262-71

__________. *Emptiness: A Study in Religious Meaning*. Nashville, New York: Abingdon Press, 1967.

__________. "The Significance of Pratītyasamutpada for Understanding the Relationship Between Saṃvṛti and Paramārtha in Nāgārjuna." In *The Problem of Two Truths in Buddhism and Vedānta*, edited by Mervyn Sprung. Dordrecht: Reidel, 1973.

Swanson, Paul L. *Foundations of T'ien-t'ai Philosophy: The Flowering of Two Truths Theory in Chinese Buddhism*. Berkeley: Asian Humanities Press.

Sweet, Michael. "The Two Truths in *Bodhicaryāvatāra* 9.2" *JIABS* 2 (1979): 79-89.

Tachikawa, Musashi. "A Logical Analysis of the *Mūlamadhyamakakārikā*." *In Sanskrit and Indian Studies*, edited by Nagatomi, et al. Boston: Reidel, 1980.

Takakusu, Junjiro. *The Essentials of Buddhist Philosophy*. Delhi: Motilal, 1975.

Thurman, Robert. "Buddhist Hermeneutics." *JAAR* 46 (1978): 19-40.

__________, ed. *The Life and Teachings of Tsong Khapa*. Dharmsala: Library of Tibetan Works and Archives, 1982.

__________. "Philosophical Nonegocentrism in Wittgenstein and Candrakirti in Their Treatment of the Private Language Problem." *PEW* 30 (1980): 321-37.

__________. *Tsong Khapa's Speech of Gold in the Essence of True Eloquence*. Princeton, N.J.: Princeton University Press, 1984.

Tillemans, T. "The Neither One nor Many Argument for *Śūnyatā* and its Tibetan Interpretations: Background Information and Source Materials," *Étude de Lettres* (1982): 103-28.

Tillich, Paul. *The Dynamics of Faith*. New York: Harper, 1957.

Tola, Fernando and Dragonetti, Carmen. "Nāgārjuna's Conception of 'Voidness' (Śūnyatā)." *JIP* 9 (1981): 273-82.

Tucci, Guiseppe. *The Religions of Tibet*. Translated by G. Samuel. Berkeley: University of California Press, 1980.

Uieyama, K. "Theory of the Two-fold Truth of Śāntarakṣita." *JIBS* 18 (1961): 531-34.

van der Kuijp, L.W.J. "Phya-pa Chos-kyi Seng-ge's Impact on Tibetan Epistemological Theory." *JIP* 5 (1978): 355-69.

van Walt van Praag, Michael C. *The Status of Tibet: History, Rights and Prospects in International Law*. London: Wisdom, 1987.

Wach, Joachim. *Sociology of Religion*. Chicago: University of Chicago, 1971.

Waldo, Ives. "Nāgārjuna and analytic philosophy, Parts I and II." *PEW* 25 (1975): 281-90, and 28 (1978): 287-98.

Wangyal, Geshe. *Door of Liberation*. New York: Maurice Girodius, 1973.

Warder, A.K.. "Is Nāgārjuna a Mahāyānist?." In *The Problem of Two Truths in Buddhism and Vedānta*, edited by Mervyn Sprung. Boston: Reidel, 1973.

Wayman, Alex. *Calming the Mind and Discerning the Real*. New York: Columbia University Press, 1978.

__________. "Contributions to the Mādhyamika School of Buddhism." *JAOS* 89 (1969): 141-56.

__________. "Who Understands the Four Alternatives of the Buddhist texts?" *PEW* 27 (1977): 93-97.

Welbon, Guy Richard. *The Buddhist Nirvāṇa and its Western Interpreters*. Chicago: University of Chicago Press, 1968.

Whitney, William Dwight. *Sanskrit Grammar*. Cambridge, MA: Harvard University, 1973.

Williams, Paul. "A Note on Some Aspects of Mi Bskyod Rdo Rje's Critique of Dge lugs pa Madhyamaka." *JIP* 11 (1983): 125-45.

__________. "Review of *Compassion: A Tibetan Analysis*." *Buddhist Studies Review* 4, no. 2 (1987): 172-75.

__________. "rMa-bya-pa Byang-chub brTson-'grus on Madhyamaka Method" *JIP* 13 (1985): 205-25.

__________. "Silence and Truth—Some Aspects of the Madhyamaka Philosophy of Tibet." *TJ* 7 (1982): 67-80.

__________. "Some Aspects of Language and Construction in the Madhyamaka." *JIP* 8 (1978): 1-45.

__________. "Tsong-kha-pa on *kun-rdzob bden-pa*." In *Tibetan Studies in Honour of Hugh Richardson*, edited by M.Aris and Aung San Suu Kyi. New Delhi: Vikas, 1980.

Wylie, Turrel. "A Standard System of Tibetan Transcription," *HJAS* 22 (1959): 261-7.

Yamaguchi, Susumu. *Index to the Prasannapadā Madhyamakavṛtti*. Kyoto: Heirakuji-Shoten, 1974.

__________. "Traité de Nāgārjuna pour écarter les vaines discussion (Vigrahavyāvartanī) traduit et annoté." *JA* 215 (1929): 1-86.

Notes

NOTE ON TRANSLITERATION

1. Turrel Wylie, ''A Standard System of Tibetan Transcription,'' *Harvard Journal of Asiatic Studies* 22 (1959): 261-67.
2. Jeffrey Hopkins, *Meditation on Emptiness* (London: Wisdom, 1983), pp. 19-21.
3. Ibid, p. 20.

INTRODUCTION

1. I am referring mainly to Elizabeth Napper, *Dependent Arising and Emptiness* (Boston: Wisdom, 1989); Hopkins, *Meditation on Emptiness*; Georges Dreyfus, ''Definition in Buddhism'' (Master's thesis, University of Virginia, 1987); and Robert Thurman, *Tsong Khapa's Speech of Gold in the "Essence of True Eloquence"* (Princeton: Princeton University Press, 1984).
2. *Mūlamadhaymakakārikā* (P5224, Vol. 95), chapter 24, vs.8.
3. D. S. Ruegg, ''On the Reception and Early History of the dbu-ma (Madhyamaka) in Tibet,'' in *Tibetan Studies in Honour of Hugh Richardson*, ed. by Michael Aris and Aung San Suu Kyi (New Delhi: Vikas, 1980), p. 278.
4. The phrase used by Elizabeth Napper in *Dependent Arising and Emptiness*, p. 146.

CHAPTER ONE

1. Robert P. Carroll, *When Prophecy Failed* (New York: Seabury, 1979), p. 124.
2. Claude Lévi-Strauss, ''The Structural Study of Myth,'' *Journal of*

American Folklore 68 (1955): 428-44.

3. Joachim Wach, *Sociology of Religion* (Chicago: University of Chicago, 1971), p. 20.

4. Ibid, p. 22.

5. Leon Festinger, *When Prophecy Fails* (Minneapolis: University of Minnesota Press, 1956).

6. Clifford Geertz, "Religion as a Cultural System," in *Reader in Comparative Religion*, ed. by Lessa and Vogt (New York: Harper and Row, 1972), p. 172.

7. E. H. Johnston, trans., *The Buddhacārita or Acts of the Buddha* (Calcutta: Baptist Mission Press, 1936).

8. Christian Lindtner, "Atīśa's Introduction to the Two Truths, and Its Sources," *Journal of Indian Philosophy* 9 (1981): 161.

9. Louis de la Vallée Poussin, "Documents d'Abhidharma: Les deux, les quarte, les trois Vérités," *Mélanges chinois et bouddhiques* (1937): 159.

10. Festinger, *When Prophecy Fails*, p. 26.

11. Many scholars hold that Buddhism borrowed the ideas of karma and rebirth from the Brahmānic tradition. L.M. Joshi (*Studies in the Buddhistic Culture of India*, Delhi: Motilal Banarsidass, 2nd revised edition, 1977) takes the contrary view that these doctrines derive from the non-Brahmānic or "heterodox" side of Indian culture and found their way into general acceptance largely through Buddhist influence.

12. Vilhelm Trencker, ed., *The Milindapañho* (London: Royal Asiatic Society, 1928), p. 160; also, T.W. Rhys Davids, trans., *The Questions of King Milinda* (Oxford: Clarendon Press, 1890), p. 226.

13. From the translation of Shotaro Iida, "An Introduction to Svātantrika-Mādhyamika" (Ph.D. dissertation, University of Wisconsin, 1968), pp. 264-5.

14. Theodore Stcherbatsky, *Buddhist Logic*, 2 vols. (New York: Dover, 1962), 1: 70

15. Paul Williams, "Tsong-kha-pa on kun-rdzob bden-pa," in *Tibetan Studies in Honour of Hugh Richardson*, ed. by Aris and Aung (New Delhi: Vikas, 1980), p. 239.

16. John Buescher, "The Buddhist Doctrine of Two Truths in the Vaibhāṣika and Theravāda Schools" (Ph.D. dissertation, University of Virginia, 1982), p. 132.

17. Edward Conze, *Buddhism: Its Essence and Development* (Oxford, Bruno Cassirer, 1951; rpt. New York: Harper and Brothers, 1959), pp. 129-30.

18. David Eckel, *Jñānagarbha's "Commentary on the Distinction Between the Two Truths,"* (Albany: State University of New York Press, 1987), p. 48.

19. From well-known traditional authorities (e.g., the *Encyclopedia of Religion and Ethics*, New York: Charles Scribner and Sons, vol.12, p. 293) to current, popular, introductory works (e.g., Roger Schmidt's *Exploring Religion*, Belmont, CA: Wadsworth, 1988), there is clear precedent for applying the word "theology" to systems of doctrine in non-theistic religions.

To limit the use of the word to systematic discussions of a *personal* sacred is to limit the definition of the word to the narrower sense of its etymology.

Mādhyamika is a Buddhist philosophy, and a substantial volume of fascinating material has been produced by scholars comparing its content with Western philosophical systems. Many (although by no means all) of these scholars are careful to add some sort of qualifying paragraph to their comparisons, pointing out that Mādhyamika, unlike the Western system under consideration, is part of a system of religious practice. Reference may be made to "soteriological intent." If Mādhyamika is, after all, a deeply *religious* philosophy, so fundamentally *salvific* in its program, then why not call it a theology? I want to convey the sense that Tsong-ka-pa's Mādhyamika is not something that one may happen to believe or not, without any ramifications for one's life. Traditionally, at least, Mādhyamika philosophy is one dimension of a religious "world" (Berger, *The Sacred Canopy*, 1967 and Paden, *Religious Worlds*, 1988). Lived experience in such a world involves the affective (e.g., a feeling of reverence for the Buddha, his teachings, and one's own guru; a sense of longing for liberation, etc.) and conative (e.g., the five precepts, monastic vows, Bodhisattva vows, etc.) as well as the cognitive (Tillich, *The Dynamics of Faith*, p. 4). This book focuses very narrowly, within the cognitive dimension, on a slice of the Mādhyamika literature used by the Ge-luk-ba elite. This makes the word "theology" all the more important, as a way of hinting at that literature's embeddedness in a context of living religion.

Furthermore, the Ge-luk-ba scholastic tradition is theological in so far as theology claims to be *re-presenting* for a particular generation the shared truths of revelation. "Re-presentation" does not preclude the creativity of individual analysis; there is a strong analytic tradition in Buddhism, and it is particularly strong in Ge-luk-ba. At the same time, it must be remembered that the Ge-luk-ba textbook writers and their readers value reasoning not as a way of finding a *new* truth, but as the ideal means of getting to the heart of a truth and a teaching that has already been received. Nāgārjuna seeks to recover Buddha's intention; Candrakīrti seeks to recover Nāgārjuna's intention; Tsong-ka-pa seeks to recover Candrakīrti's intention; and Jam-yang-shay-ba seeks to recover Tsong-ka-pa's intention, which he takes to be congruent with the intentions of Candrakīrti, Nāgārjuna, and Buddha.

20. Elizabeth Napper, *Dependent Arising and Emptiness* (Boston: Wisdom, 1989); Georges B. J. Dreyfus, "Definition in Buddhism" (Master's thesis, University of Virgina, 1987); Jeffrey Hopkins, *Meditation on Emptiness* (London: Wisdom, 1983); Anne Klein, *Knowledge and Liberation* (Ithaca, New York: Snow Lion, 1986).

21. Dak-tsang (*stag tshang lo tsa ba shes rab rin chen*, 1405-?), *Ocean of Good Explanation: An Explanation of "Freedom From Extremes Through Understanding All Tenets"* (*grub mtha' kun shes nas mtha' bral grub pa zhes bya ba'i bstan bcos rnam par bshad pa legs bshad kyi rgya mtsho*) (Thimphu: Kun bdzang stobs rgyal, 1976), p. 269.2-4; Michael Broido, "Veridical and

Delusive Cognition: Tsong-kha-pa on the Two Satyas'' *Journal of Indian Philosophy* 16 (1988): 29-63.

22. *Great Exposition of the Stages of the Path* (*lam rim chen mo*), f.377b.5-6; translation adapted Napper, *Dependent Arising and Emptiness*, pp. 149-50.

23. Hopkins, *Meditation on Emptiness*, pp. 16-17.

24. This and the following sentence are based on Hopkins, *Meditation on Emptiness*, pp. 545-47, including an extraordinary excerpt from Den-dar-hla-ram-ba's *Presentation of the Lack of Being One or Many*, Collected Works, Vol. 1 (New Delhi: Lama Guru Deva, 1971), p. 425.1ff.

25. One case in which Tsong-ka-pa apparently contradicts himself within his mature work is noted by Hopkins (*Meditation on Emptiness*, pp. 829-30). Discussing the shift in Tsong-ka-pa's interpretation of the problem of a commonly appearing subject (*chos can mthun snang ba*), Hopkins concludes, ''[I]t may be that in the end he did not hold that these two radically different interpretations are both correct.'' I use the phrase ''mature work'' to exclude Tsong-ka-pa's early work, e.g. *Golden Rosary* (*legs shes gser 'phreng*).

26. Tibetan monastic textbooks (*yig cha*) on Mādhyamika are a resource little touched by Western scholars. In *Compassion: A Tibetan Analysis* (London: Wisdom, 1985), I translated and discussed a section from Jay-dzun Chö-gyi-gyel-tsen's Mādhyamika textbook dealing with the opening stanzas of Candrakīrti's *Supplement*. This textbook is *A Good Explanation Adorning the Throats of the Fortunate: A General Meaning Commentary Clarifying Difficult Points in (Tsong-ka-pa's) "Illumination of the Thought: An Explanation of (Candrakīrti's) 'Supplement to (Nāgārjuna's) "Treatise on the Middle Way"' "* (*bstan bcos dbu ma la 'jug pa'i rnam bshad dgongs pa rab gsal gyi dka' gnad gsal bar byed pa'i spyi don legs bshad skal bzang mgul rgyan*) (New Delhi: lha mkhar yongs 'dzin bstan pa rgyal mtshan, 1973). This apparently remains as the only published translation of a significant mass of material on Mādhyamika from the *yig cha* genre. Ge-luk-ba authors of extant textbooks on Mādhyamika include:

(1) Śānti-pa Lo-drö-gyel-tsen (*shānti pa blo gros rgyal mtshan*, fifteenth century), author for the Kyil-kang (*khyil gang*) College of Tra-shi-lun-bo (*bkra shis lhun po*) Monastery;

(2) Kay-drup Den-ba-dar-gyay (*mkhas sgrub bstan pa dar rgyas*, 1493-1568) author for the May (*smad*) College of Se-ra (*se ra*);

(3) Drak-ba-shay-drup (*co ne rje btsun grags pa bshad sgrub*, 1675-1748), author of textbooks for the May College of Se-ra Monastery;

(4) Jay-dzun Chö-gyi-gyel-tsen (*rje brtsun chos kyi rgyal mtshan*, 1469-1546), author for the Jay (*byes*) College of Se-ra Monastery and the Jang-dzay (*byang rtse*) College of Gan-den (*dga' ldan*) Monastery;

(5) Gom-day Nam-ka-gyel-tsen (*sgom sde shar pa nam mkha' rgyal mtshan*, 1532-1592), a student of Jay-dzun Chö-gyi-gyel-tsen, and an author for the Jay College of Se-ra as well as the Jang-dzay College of Gan-den;

(6) Jam-ba-dra-shi (*khyung phrug byams pa bkra shis*, sixteenth century), another student of Jay-dzun Chö-gyi-gyel-tsen, and an author for the Jang-dzay College of Gan-den Monastery;

(7) Paṇ-chen Sö-nam-drak-ba (*paṇ chen bsod nams grags pa*, 1478-1554), author for the Lo-sel-ling College of Dre-bung and the Shar-dzay (*shar rtse*) College of Gan-den;

(8) Jam-yang-shay-ba (*'jam dbyangs bzhad pa*, 1648-1721), author for the Go-mang (*sgo mang*) College of Dre-bung (*'bras spung*) Monastery.
No longer extant are Mādhyamika textbooks by Lo-dö-rin-chen-seng-gay (*blo gros rin chen seng ge*) and Shay-rap-wang-bo (*shes rab dbang po*), both of which were once used in the Jay College of Se-ra. Jam-yang-shay-ba, Paṇ-chen Sö-nam-drak-ba, and Jay-dzun Chö-gyi-gyel-tsen are the best known and most influential of the Ge-luk Mādhyamika textbook authors.

27. Dreyfus, "Definition in Buddhism," pp. 10-12.

28. Robert Thurman, "Buddhist Hermeneutics," *Journal of the American Academy of Religion* 46 (1978), p. 38, supplies Sanskrit as cited in Śāntarakṣita's *Compendium of Principles* (*Tattvasaṃgraha*), D. Shastri, ed., Varanasi: Bauddha Bharati, 1968.

29. Cf. Napper, *Dependent Arising and Emptiness*, p. 14. Napper (*Dependent Arising and Emptiness*, p. 724) and Hopkins (*Meditation on Emptiness*, p. 544) use the word "renegade" to describe Ge-dun-chö-pel (*dge 'dun chos 'phel*, 1905?-1951?), a twentieth-century Ge-luk-ba-educated monk who published a work critical of Tsong-ka-pa, his *Ornament to Nāgārjuna's Thought, Eloquence Containing the Essence of the Profundities of the Middle Way* (*dbu ma'i zab gnad snying por dril ba'i legs bshad klu sgrub dgongs rgyan*). Note also that there is an "official" definition of a Ge-luk-ba that arises in the context of the study of monastic discipline (*'dul ba, vinaya*) and pertains to the status of a vow in the continuum of a vow-holder.

30. As reported by Khetsun Sangbo (*Biographical Dictionary of Tibet and Tibetan Buddhism*, pp. 134-35), Paṇ-chen Sö-nam-drak-ba was born in the year 1478 in Tse-tang (*rtsed thang*). Tse-tang is city southeast of Lhasa which had been a stronghold of the waning Pak-mo-dru-ba (*'phag mo gru pa*), important allies/patrons of the Ge-luk-ba order. (For a brief history and description of the city, see Keith Dowman, *The Power Places of Central Tibet*, (New York: Routledge and Kegan Paul, 1978), p. 174). Originally named Chen-bo-sö-nam-tra-shi (*chen po bsod nams bkra shis*), Paṇ-chen took the name Sö-nam-drak-ba when he left the lay life. He studied first at Sang-pu-nyi-ma-thang (*gsang phu nyi ma thang*), and later in Jay College of Se-ra under the direction of Tön-yö-bel-den (*don yod dbal ldan*). After completing his novitiate under a lama from Ö-na (*'od sna*), he entered the Tantric College of upper Lhasa, eventually becoming a great scholar and teaching in the Tantric College of upper Lhasa for fourteen years.

At age thirty-six, he composed a commentary on stages of generation and completion in Guhyasamāja. He took teachings from Ge-dun-gya-tso (*dge 'dun rgya mtsho*, 1475-1542), the second Dalai Lama. For one year, he was an instructor at the Lo-sel-ling College of Dre-bung, after which he was appointed abbot of the Shar-dzay College of Gan-den. When he was fifty-two, he was appointed the fifteenth Throne-holder of Gan-den. He wrote numerous treatises on dynastic and religious history, tantra, and

Abhidharmakośa, gaining a reputation as a reincarnation of the great Bu-don (*bu ston*, 1290-1364). He gave audiences and teachings in many places, including Ö-na and Se-ra Monastery and performed the ordination ceremony for the third Dalai Lama, the young Sö-nam-gya-tso (*bdod nams rgya mtsho*, 1543-1588). At age seventy-four he went into retirement at Dre-bung; he died there in 1554.

As reported by Khetsun Sangbo (*Biographical Dictionary of Tibet and Tibetan Buddhism*, pp. 52-57), Jay-dzun Chö-gyi-gyel-tsen was born in Tsang (*gtsang*), near Gyang-tse (*rgyal rtse*), in 1469. His parents were nobles who ruled in that area. They were patrons of the Ge-luk-ba order and disciples of Ba-so Chö-gyi-gyel-tsen (*ba so chos kyi rgyal mtshan*)—the brother of Gyel-tsap and an outstanding scholar in his own right. At age six, Jay-dzun Chö-gyi-gyel-tsen was priveleged to be present at an initiation given by Ge-dun-drup-ba (*dge 'dun grub pa*, 1391-1475), the founder of Tra-shi-lun-bo who was later recognized as the first Dalai Lama. The next year he was ordained, taking the name Chö-gyi-gyel-tsen after his mother's teacher, Ba-so Chö-gyi-gyel-tsen.

At age eleven, he entered Tra-shi-lun-bo; soon, he enrolled in Tö-sam-ling (*thos bsam gling*) where he pursued the standard curriculum (collected topics, valid cognition, Perfection of Wisdom, Mādhyamika, monastic discipline, and *Abhidharmakośa*) under Chö-jor-bel-sang (*chos 'byor dbal bzang*). When he was twenty-three or twenty-four, he travelled to central Tibet and continued a life of constant study and debate at Se-ra Monastery under the tutelage of Tön-yö-bel-den (who also taught Paṇ-chen Sö-nam-drak-ba) and Bel-jor-lun-drup (*dbal 'byor lhun grub*). He left Lhasa to visit his former associates at Tra-shi-lun-bo, and to teach for several years at Nar-thang (*snar thang*) and in Rong-jam-chen (*rong byams chen*).

He returned to central Tibet and studied tantra at Dre-bung under Yön-den-gya-tso (*yon dan rgya mtsho*). He also studied tantra and other topics with Ge-dun-gya-tso, the second Dalai Lama. During this period, while listening to another lama's instructions on the view, he began having recurring visions of Tsong-ka-pa and he received instruction from Tsong-ka-pa on various topics. He also had visions of Vajrabhairava and many other guardian deities. Maitreya appeared to him in a dream.

Jay-dzun-ba was invited to Tö-sam-ling, but chose to take a position at Se-ra where for almost thirty years he wrote on a wide range of topics and taught in the Jay College. At age seventy, he was appointed to the abbacy of Se-ra by Ge-dun-gya-tso. Two years later, he placed one of his students in charge of the Jay College, but remained as abbot of Se-ra as a whole until his death in 1544 at age seventy-five. As a teacher, abbot, and author, he had an enormous role in shaping the next generation of Ge-luk-ba scholars. Two of his students later became important abbots, while two others (Jam-ba-dra-shi and Gom-day Nam-ka-gyel-tsen) became authors of monastic textbooks on Mādhyamika for the Jang-dzay College of Gan-den.

31. David Snellgrove and Hugh Richardson, *A Cultural History of Tibet* (Boulder, CO: Prajñā Press, 1968), p. 183.

32. Jam-yang-shay-ba Ngak-wang-dzön-dru (*sngags dbang brtson 'grus*) was a yogi, a polymath, and a prolific author. Lokesh Chandra (*Materials for a History of Tibetan Buddhism*, Śatapitaka series, Vol. 28; New Delhi: International Academy of Indain Culture, 1963,pp. 45-46) reports that he was born in Amdo in 1648 and became a novice monk at age thirteen. At twenty-one, he journeyed to Lhasa and entered the Go-mang College of Dre-bung Monastery. When Jam-yang-shay-ba was twenty-seven, he received full ordination; two years later he entered the Tantric College of lower Lhasa. At age thirty-three, he began two years of retreat, meditating in a cave near Dre-bung. He was appointed abbot of Go-mang at age fifty-three, but retired from that position and returned to Amdo in the year 1710. There he established Dra-shi-kyil (*bkra shis 'khyil*) Monastery and, at the same location, a tantric college. Jam-yang-shay-ba died at the age of seventy-three or seventy-four, in 1721/2.

33. Although he visited Tibet, Ngak-wang-bel-den spent most of his career in the Dra-shi-chö-pel (*bkra shis chos 'phel*) college of Gan-den (*dga' ldan*) Monastery in Urga (later called Ulan Bator). His teachers included Yang-jen-ga-way-lo-drö (fl. eighteenth century). Ngak-wang-bel-den was deeply conversant with the literature of both Go-mang and Lo-sel-ling. Citations of his work herein refer to his *Explanation of the Conventional and Ultimate in the Four Systems of Tenets* (New Delhi: Guru Deva, 1972) except as otherwise noted. He produced an extraordinary body of work, including a unique, non-partisan, comparative study of the positions of Go-mang and Lo-sel-ling on topics pertaining to Mādhyamika and the *Ornament for Clear Realization* (*Abhisamayālaṃkāra*). His *Annotations on (Jam-yang-shay-ba's) Great Exposition of Tenets* is also excellent; Go-mang scholars do not embrace it whole-heartedly because it includes criticisms of Jam-yang-shay-ba. A portion of Ngak-wang-bel-den's book on the four tantra sets is summarized by Daniel Cozort in *Highest Yoga Tantra* (Ithaca, New York: Snow Lion, 1986).

34. The example is borrowed from Jeffrey Hopkins, "Reflections on Reality" (1990, typescript).

35. Jayānanda's *Explanation of (Candrakīrti's) "Supplement to (Nāgārjuna's) 'Treatise on the Middle Way'"* (*Mādhyamakāvatāraṭīka, dbu ma la 'jug pa'i grel bshad*) is P5271, vol. 99.

36. Sang-pu is an important monastery founded at Ne'u-thog in 1073 by Ngok Lek-bay-shay-rap (*rngog legs pa'i shes rab*). The son of a powerful minister, Ngok Lek-bay-shay-rap was an important patron of Atiśa. His nephew was Ngok Lo-den-shay-rap (*rngog blo ldan shes rab*, 1059-1109), the famous translator.

37. For example, we read in the *Blue Annals* that, of the "Eight Mighty Lions" of Cha-ba Chö-gyi-seng-gay (*phya-pa chos kyi seng ge*, 1109-1169), at least two of them—Ma-ja Jang-chup-dzön-dru (*rma bya byang chub brtson 'grus*) and Dzang-nag-ba Dzön-dru-seng-gay (*gtsang nag pa brtson 'grus seng ge*)—studied and "preferred the system of Jayānanda" to Cha-ba's refutations of Candrakīrti. Ma-ja Jang-chup-dzön-dru studied with Jayānanda

and also studied Mādhyamika with Ba-tsap. Thereupon, he "disseminated widely the system of Mādhyamika" that he had learned. Dzang-nag-ba, although one of Cha-ba's foremost disciples and the author of Cha-ba's biography, wrote several works upholding Candrakīrti in the face of Cha-ba's critique and boasted extravagantly of his expertise in Prāsaṅgika. See George N. Roerich, trans., *Blue Annals*, (Delhi: Motilal Banarsiddas, rpt. 1979) pp. 334 and 343; L.W.J. van der Kuijp, "Phya-pa Chos-kyi Seng-ge's Impact on Tibetan Epistemological Theory," *Journal of Indian Philosophy* 5 (1978): 355 and 366.

38. Jeffrey Hopkins, trans. and ed., *Compassion in Tibetan Buddhism* by Tsong-ka-pa and Kensur Lekden (Valois, New York: Gabriel/Snow Lion, 1980), pp. 97, 103, 104, 106, 111, 113, 131, 135, 144, 148, 160, and 209.

39. For example, *Illumination of the Thought, Extensive Explanation of (Candrakīrti's) "Supplement to (Nāgārjuna's) 'Treatise on the Middle Way' "* (*dbu ma la 'jug pa'i rgya bshad pa dgongs pa rab gsal*) (Dharamsala: Shes rig par khang, n.d.), pp. 207.6-208.1.

40. For example, Jayānanda's *Explanation of (Candrakīrti's) "Supplement to (Nāgārjuna's) 'Treatise on the Middle Way' "* (P5271), f.145a3-4.

41. These points will be discussed in chapters three, ten, and twelve.

42. Robert Thurman, trans., *Tsong Khapa's Speech of Gold in the "Essence of True Eloquence"* (Princeton, N.J.: Princeton University Press, 1984), pp. 105-06 and 324-26.

43. For examples, see Newland, *Compassion: A Tibetan Analysis*, pp. 74, 75, 80, 81, 82, 107, and 110.

44. Toh 3881, vs.12; (not in P). Along with the Jñānagarbha's own *Commentary on "Distinguishing the Two Truths"* (*Satyadvayavibhāgavṛtti*), Toh 3882, this work has been edited and translated into English by Malcolm David Eckel in *Jñānagarbha's Commentary on the Distinction Between The Two Truths* (Albany, NY: State University of New York Press, 1987). Verse numbers are given here as they appear in Eckel's edition.

As for the attention that this work may have been given in Tibet prior to Tsong-ka-pa, *The Blue Annals*, p. 332, indicates that Dö-lung Gya-mar (*stod lung rgya dmar*, fl. twelfth century) wrote a subcommentary on it.

45. Toh 3881, vs. 25; in Eckel, ed., *Jñānagarbha's Commentary on the Distinction Between the Two Truths*, p. 178.

46. None of Ngok's own writings are extant intact. Citations from Ngok's *Epistolary Essay, Drop of Ambrosia* are found within Ser-dok Paṇ-chen Śākya-chok-den's (*gser mdog paṇ chen śākya mchog ldan*, 1428-1507) commentary on that work. See *Collected Works of Gser-mdog Pan-chen*, Vol. 24, 320.6-348.6 (Thim-phu, Bhutan: Kunzang Topgey, 1978). In the account given by Kensur Lekden to Jeffrey Hopkins (*Meditation on Emptiness*, p. 535), Ngok Lo-den-shay-rap is reported as a student of Atiśa (982-1054). Their mismatched dates cast serious doubt on this. According to the *Blue Annals*, Ngok Lo-den-shay-rap's uncle and teacher, Ngok Lek-bay-shay-rap (*rngog legs pa'i shes rab*), was an important patron and disciple of Atiśa. A confusion of these two Ngoks in the Hopkins report

is possible; it may also be that Kensur Lekden was referring to an indirect or spiritual connection between Ngok Lo-den-shay-rap and Atiśa.

47. Robert Thurman, *Tsong Khapa's Speech of Gold*, p. 55

48. Hopkins, *Meditation on Emptiness*, p. 406.

49. We do not have a systematic and convincing reconstruction of Ngok's views. Like Thurman and Hopkins in the sources cited, I am trying to imagine Ngok's position largely on the basis of opinions found in much later Ge-luk refutations. We also have the testimony of the *Blue Annals* (p. 349) that Ngok held that ultimate truth cannot be the object of even an "approximate judgement" (*zhen pa, adhyavasāya*), let alone direct perception (*mgnon sum, pratyakṣa*).

50. See the third "wrong position" in chapter two and the section on ultimate existence in chapter four.

51. Gang-ba Shay-u (*gangs pa she'u*) was influenced by Ngok; Khyung Rin-chen-grags-pa was one of Ngok's four principal disciples. These two were the main teachers of Dö-lung Gya-mar. (See *Blue Annals*, p. 326; van der Kuijp, "Phya-pa Chos-kyi Seng-ge's Impact on Tibetan Epistemological Theory," p. 355 and p. 366.) As reported by Napper (Dependent Arising and Emptiness, p. 53), Lo-sang-gön-chok's (*blo bzang dkon mchog*) *Word Commentary on the Root Text of (Jam-yang-shay-ba's) "Tenets"* (pp. 170-72) attributes to Dö-lung Gya-mar the claim that "Mādhyamikas do not have their own position or system." Similar interpretations of Mādhyamika have been offered by a great many contemporary academic scholars. This claim is rejected by Tsong-ka-pa and his successors. See Napper's excellent discussion in *Dependent Arising and Emptiness*, pp. 111-22.

52. *Blue Annals*, p. 332 and p. 475.

53. Ibid, p. 332. Source for the existence of a Dö-lung Gya-mar commentary on Śāntideva's *Bodhisattvacaryāvatāra* (P5272, Vol.99) is Jam-yang-shay-ba's *Great Exposition of the Middle Way/Analysis of (Candrakīrti's) "Supplement to (Nāgārjuna's) 'Treatise on the Middle Way,' " Treasury of Scripture and Reasoning Thoroughly Illuminating the Profound Meaning [of Emptiness], Entrance for the Fortunate* (*dbu ma chen mo/dbu ma 'jug pa'i mtha' bpyod lung rigs gter mdzod zab don kun gsal skal bzang 'jug ngogs*) Collected Works, Vol.9 (Ta) (New Delhi: Ngawang Gelek Demo, 1972), pp. 516-17.

54. *Engaging in the Bodhisattva Deeds* (*Bodhisattvacaryāvatāra*) (P5272, Vol.99); Vidhushekara Bhattacarya, ed., *Bodhicaryāvatāra* (Calcutta: The Asiatic Society, 1960), chapter 9, vs. 2.

55. Jam-yang-shay-ba, *Great Exposition of the Middle Way*, pp. 515-16. This is discussed in chapter two.

56. This information on Cha-ba is based mainly on Roerich's (tr.) *Blue Annals* (especially pp. 332-4, 349, and 475) and van der Kuijp's "Phya-pa Chos-kyi Seng-ge's Impact on Tibetan Epistemological Theory." Cha-ba's works included numerous commentaries, including commentaries on the "Five Treatises" of Maitreya, Dharmakīrti's *Ascertainment of Valid Cognition* (*Pramāṇaviniścaya*), Śāntarakṣita's *Ornament for the Middle Way* (*Madhyamakālaṃkāra*), Kamalaśīla's *Illumination of the Middle Way*

(*Madhyamakāloka*), Śāntideva's *Engaging in the Bodhisattva Deeds* (*Bodhisattvacaryāvatāra*). Cha-ba is also credited with authorship of a tenets (*grub mtha'*) book and of *tshad ma yid kyi mun sel*, the first indigenous Tibetan work on logic and epistemology, inaugurating the important "Collected Topics" (*bsdus grwa*) genre and beginning the popularity of the *thal-phyir* format that became pervasive in many later Ge-luk and Sa-gya texts. In light of Cha-ba's enormous scholarship and influence upon many students, it is interesting that the *Blue Annals* (p. 475) states that he was "learned in the Tibetan language only"—i.e., not in Sanskrit. It appears that none of Cha-ba's works have survived. Some of his epistemology has been reconstructed by van der Kuijp in "Phya-pa Chos-kyi Seng-ge's Impact on Tibetan Epistemological Theory."

57. *Blue Annals*, pp. 332-34 and p. 349. Napper (*Dependent Arising and Emptiness*, p. 52) notes that the Ge-luk-ba scholar A-gya-yong-dzin (*a kya yongs 'dzin*, eighteenth century) includes Cha-ba among "those who negate too much" (Collected Works, vol. 1, 167.6-168.2). Apparently Cha-ba's reification of an absolute negative left too little room, from a Ge-luk perspective, for the operation of the conventional world. Not beyond reason is Thurman's (*Tsong Khapa's Speech of Gold*, p. 56) notion that there may be a vague philosophical kinship between the position of Cha-ba and the later views of Shay-rap-gyel-tsen.

58. *Blue Annals*, p. 334 and pp. 341-44. Napper (*Dependent Arising and Emptiness*, p. 670) notes that Ma-ja's assertions are specifically refuted Tsong-ka-pa's *Great Exposition of the Stages of the Path*. Paul Williams gives an outstanding analysis of Ma-ja's views, along with a possible explanation for the latter confusion of Ma-ja Jang-chup-dzön-dru with Ma-ja Jang-chup-ye-shay, in "rMa-bya-pa Byang-chub brTson-'grus on Madhyamaka Method" *Journal of Indian Philosophy* 13 (1985): 205-25.

59. Napper ("Dependent Arising and Emptiness," Ph.D. dissertation, University of Virginia, 1985, p. 86) gives this information, citing Lo-sang-gön-chok's (*blo bzang dkon mchog*) *Word Commentary on the Root Text of Jam-yang-shay-ba's Tenets*, pp. 170-72. She adds that some of Tang-sak-ba's followers held that while the two truths exist conventionally, this conventional existence does not qualify as existence. From a Ge-luk perspective, this is still a nihilistic extreme. Napper (*Dependent Arising and Emptiness*, p. 52) also notes that the Ge-luk-ba scholar A-gya-yong-dzin (*a kya yongs 'dzin*, eighteenth century; Collected Works, vol. 1, 167.6-168.2) includes Tang-sak-ba among "those who negate too much." Ruegg states that Tang-sak-ba was among those who identified Candrakīrti's doctrine as "a theory of neither being nor non-being" (*yod min med min gyi lta ba*) in "The Jo naṅ pas: A School of Buddhist Ontologists according to the *Grub mtha' śel gyi me loṅ*," *Journal of the American Oriental Society* 83 (1963): 73-91, 89.

60. Jam-yang-shay-ba, *Great Exposition of the Middle Way*, pp. 514-15.

61. Snellgrove and Richardson, *A Cultural History of Tibet*, pp. 179-80 and pp. 196-97; Roerich, trans., *Blue Annals*, pp. 775-77; David Snell-

grove, *Indo-Tibetan Buddhism* (London: Serindia, 1987), pp. 489-90. Ruegg ("The Jo naṅ pas," pp. 77-78) argues that the Jo-nang-ba school was

> proscribed at the time of the Fifth Dalai Lama both because of the unorthodoxy of its teachings and because of some Himālayan and ultramontane connexions which might have tended to sustain local separatist movements in the southwestern areas of Tibet in which they were chiefly established.

62. For example, Tu-gen (*thu'u bkvan blo bzang chos kyi nyi ma*) in his *grub mtha' zhal gyi me long* (as discussed by Ruegg, "The Jo naṅ pas"), Ngak-wang-bel-den, and Gön-chok-den-bay-drön-may (*dkon mchog bstan pa'i sgron me*, 1762-1823) in his *yid dang kun gzhi'i dka' gnad rnam par bshad pa mkhas pa'i 'jug ngogs*, 137.5. The Jo-nang-bas were named at various times as proponents of Mind-Only (*cittamātra*), proponents of views indistinguishable from Mīmāmsā, and crypto-Vedāntins; they were also attacked for attributing a material nature (shape and color) to the *tathāgatagarbha*. While Shay-rap-gyel-tsen was not charged with deriving his position from non-Buddhist sources, he was frequently charged with holding views which are indifferentiable from those of *ātmavāda* systems. However, Ge-luk sources also charge Jo-nang with nihilism. For example, Napper (*Dependent Arising and Emptiness*, p. 52) notes that the Ge-luk-ba scholar A-gya-yong-dzin (*a kya yongs 'dzin*, eighteenth century; Collected Works, vol. 1, 167.6-168.2) includes the Jo-nang-ba Bo-dong Chok-lay-nam-gyel (*bo dong phyogs las rnam rgyal*, 1375-1450? or 1306-1386?) among "those who negate too much." This charge refers to the deprecation of the status of conventional phenomena in the face of an absolutized emptiness. As Tu-gen puts it (grub mtha' zhal gyi me long, f.7a; tr. by Ruegg, "The Jo naṅ pas," p. 85), they fall to *both* extremes, reifiying the ultimate and denying existence to the conventional.

63. For the arguments against the the claim that the two truths are different entities, see chapter four. Sources for this paragraph: Ruegg, "The Jo naṅ pas"; Hopkins, *Meditation on Emptiness*, pp. 415-16; Thurman, *Tsong Khapa's Speech of Gold*, pp. 60-61; Hopkins, "Reflections on Reality" (draft typescript, 1990); and Roerich, trans., *Blue Annals*, pp. 775-77.

64. In a parenthetical addition to his translation of *Blue Annals* (p.1080), Roerich points to Rong-dön as the first to oppose Tsong-ka-pa. Dowman (*Power Places*, p. 85) reports that Rong-dön's refutations of Tsong-ka-pa were "proscribed," meaning that they were forbidden on the premises of Ge-luk-ba monasteries. From a Bön family of Gyel-rong (far in the eastern part of Tibet), Rong-dön came to central Tibet where he excelled in his studies at Sang-pu and elsewhere. His teachers included the Sa-gya scholar Yak-druk Sang-gyay-bel (*g.yag phrug sangs rgyas dpal*), Śri Vanaratna (the "last pandit" to arrive from India), and Sö-nam-sang-bo (*bsod nams bzang po*, 1341-1433). Ta-shi-nam-gyal (*bkra shis rnam rgyal*, 1398-1459) was prominent among his students. Snellgrove and Richardson (*A Cultural History of Tibet*, p. 180) mention that the Sa-gya-ba Ren-da-wa (*red mda' pa*,

1349-1412), teacher and friend of Tsong-ka-pa, studied under Rong-dön even though Rong-dön was more than twenty-five years his junior. In 1435, Rong-dön founded Nālandā (Nalendra) Monastery in Pan-yul (*'phan yul*). Although this monastery declined somewhat after his death, it remained an important center until 1959.

65. As discussed by Williams (review of *Compassion: A Tibetan Analysis*, by Guy Newland, in *Buddhist Studies Review* 4, 1987: 174) and Ruegg ("The Jo naṅ pas," p. 89), Go-ram-ba and Śākya Chok-den launch scathing critiques of Tsong-ka-pa's interpretations of Mādhyamika. Jay-dzun Chö-gyi-gyel-tsen rises to Tsong-ka-pa's defense at several points in his Mādhyamika textbook, *A Good Explanation Adorning the Throats of the Fortunate.*

66. As noted by Napper (*Dependent Arising and Emptiness*, p. 52), A-gya-yong-dzin (*a kya yongs 'dzin*, eighteenth century; *Collected Works*, vol. 1, 167.6-168.2) includes Rong-dön among "those who negate too much." However, Ruegg ("The Jo naṅ pas," p. 89, n.75) says that Rong-dön "was stated to follow the Mādhyamika-Svātantrika doctrine." Śākya Chok-den is faulted by Lo-sang-gön-chok (*blo bzang dkon mchog*; *Word Commentary on the Root Text of [Jam-yang-shay-ba's]* "Tenets," pp. 170-72) for denying that conventional phenomena are established by valid cognition. Tu-gen (*grub mtha' zhal gyi me long*, 85b.3-4; cited by Ruegg, p. 89, n.75) says that Śākya Chok-den at first followed Mādhyamika, then Vijñāvāda, and finally Jo-nang-ba. According to Tu-gen (11a-11b; Ruegg, pp. 89-90), he wrote "many terrible discourses" and "many apparent refutations" motivated by the "demon of passion and hate" against Tsong-ka-pa's system.

67. Dak-tsang's view as reported by Ngak-wang-bel-den's (*ngag dbang dpal ldan*, also known as *dpal ldan chos rje*, b.1797) *Annotations for (Jam-yang-shay-ba's) "Great Exposition of Tenets," Freeing the Knots of the Difficult Points, Precious Jewel of Clear Thought* (*grub mtha' chen mo'i mchan 'grel dka' gnad mdud grol blo gsal gces nor*) (Sarnath: Pleasure of Elegant Sayings Printing Press, 1964). See Hopkins, *Meditation on Emptiness*, pp. 437-38.

68. From his *Presentation of Tenets* (*grub pa'i mtha'i rnam par bzhag pa gsal bar bshad pa thub bstan lhun po'i mdzes rgyan*) (Varanasi: Pleasure of Elegant Sayings Press, 1970), pp. 300-01. Translated by Hopkins in *Emptiness Yoga* (Ithaca: Snow Lion, 1987), p. 483.

69. Hopkins, *Meditation on Emptiness*, pp. 539-40, 573, 576-77, 648.

70. The first passage is from Ngak-wang-bel-den's *Annotations*, *dbu* section, f.9a.7ff as cited by Hopkins, *Meditation on Emptiness*, p. 540. The second is my translation of Dak-tsang's *Ocean of Good Explanation, an Explanation of "Freedom From Extremes Through Understanding All Tenets,"* p. 269.2-4.

71. Michael Broido, "Veridical and Delusive Cognition: Tsong-kha-pa on the Two *Satyas*," *Journal of Indian Philosophy* 16 (1988): 32.

72. As noted by Snellgrove, *Indo-Tibetan Buddhism*, p. 381-82.

73. The clearest evidence and most cogent argument for Tibet's legal

right to sovereign status is found in van Walt van Praag's *The Status of Tibet* (London: Wisdom, 1987).

74. For an account of the conditions of Tibetan oppression up to March 1988, see John F. Avedon's *Tibet Today* (London: Wisdom, 1988).

CHAPTER TWO

1. *Great Exposition of the Middle Way* (*dbu ma chen mo*) Collected Works, Vol. 9 (Ta) (New Delhi: Ngawang Gelek Demo, 1972), p. 520.

2. *Illumination of the Thought* (*dbu ma la 'jug pa'i rgya bshad pa dgongs pa rab gsal*), pp. 195.2-3. Many (though not all) of the translated excerpts from Tsong-ka-pa's *Illumination of the Thought* that will appear herein are borrowed, often with minor adaptations, from an unpublished work-in-progress by Professor Jeffrey Hopkins. They are used with his permission.

3. *Compendium of Instructions* (*Śikṣāsamuccayakārikā*) *dbu ma*, Vol. 16 in *sDe dge Tibetan Tripitaka* (Tokyo: 1977ff), 142b; also, C. Bendall and W.H.D. Rouse, trans., *Śikṣā Samuccaya* (Delhi: Motilal, 1971; rpt. 1981), p. 236.

According to Ngak-wang-bel-den (*Explanation of the Conventional and the Ultimate*, 150.6-7), all proponents of Mahāyāna tenet systems agree that objects of knowledge are the basis of division of the two truths (though Prāsaṅgikas are alone in using this sūtra passage to support that position). Since the Ge-luk-ba identification of the basis of division was not universally accepted, Ngak-wang-bel-den implicitly places many lineages of Tibetan Buddhism "beyond the pale" of Mahāyāna tenets.

4. *Supplement Commentary* (*Madhyamakāvatārabhāṣya*) edited by Louis de la Vallée Poussin, *Madhyamakāvatāra par Candrakīrti*, Bibliotheca Buddhica IX (Osnabrück: Verlag, 1970), pp. 102.16-103.1.

5. Ngak-wang-bel-den, *Explanation of the Conventional and the Ultimate*, p. 152.2-3.

6. For example, see Nathan Katz's diagram, showing conventional truth as a subdivision of truth, on p. 285 in Nakamura Hajime's *Indian Buddhism*. Williams ("Tsong-kha-pa on *kun-rdzob bden-pa*" in *Tibetan Studies in Honour of Hugh Richardson* edited by Aris and Aung, New Delhi: Vikas, 1980, p. 325), de Jong ("The Problem of the Absolute," *Journal of Indian Philosophy* 2: 3), and Ruegg (*The Literature of the Madhyamaka School of Philosophy in India*, Wiesbaden: Otto Harrassowitz, 1981, pp. 3 and 16) are among the many scholars who refer to the conventional and the ultimate as "levels" of truth or reality. In many cases, this view of the two truths as "truth-levels" is, at the same time, an understanding of the two truths as alternative standpoints or perspectives. This latter approach will be discussed below.

7. The contemporary Lo-sel-ling scholar Kensur Yeshay Tupden holds the minority view that, because they do not exist as they appear to the conceptual consciousness (*rtog pa, kalpanā*) apprehending them, even emptinesses are falsities.

8. Ngak-wang-bel-den (*Explanation of the Conventional and the Ultimate*, p. 150.3) says that those who hold that truths are the basis of the division are "obscured even with regard to the words" because they have mistaken the meaning of the word "truth" in the term "concealer-truth."

9. Michael Sweet, "The Two Truths in *Bodhicaryāvatāra* 9.2," *JIABS* 2 (1979): 80

10. *Supplement* (*Madhaymakāvatāra*) (P5261, P5262, Vol. 98). Edited Tibetan: Louis de la Vallée Poussin, *Madhyamakāvatāra par Candrakīrti*. Bibliotheca Buddhica IX (Osnabrück: Verlag, 1970), chapter 6, vs.23.

11. According to the *Blue Annals* (New Delhi: Motilal Banarsidass, 1976, pp. 343-44 and pp. 650-51), Tang-sak-ba wrote several commentaries on Mādhyamika works by Nāgārjuna, Candrakīrti, and Āryadeva. He founded a monastery (Tang-sak) that became an important center of Mādhyamika teaching. It would appear that he flourished in the latter half of the thirteenth century.

12. *Great Exposition of the Middle Way* (*dbu ma chen mo*), pp. 514-15.

13. Hopkins, *Meditation on Emptiness*, p. 411.

14. *Supplement Commentary* (*Madhyamakāvatārabhāṣya*) as edited by Louis de la Vallée Poussin, *Madhyamakāvatāra par Candrakīrti*, p. 103, line 3.

15. A renowned Ga-dam-ba (*bka' gdams pa*) scholar, Ngok translated a large number of works, including Candrakīrti's *Clear Words* and *Supplement*, and authored several works on Mādhyamika. His position is explained as it is related in Gyel-tsap's *An Entrance for the Sons of Conquerors, Explanation of (Śāntideva's) "Engaging in the Bodhisattva Deeds"* (*byang chub sems dpa'i spyod pa la 'jug pa'i rnam bshad rgyal sras*) (Sarnath: Gelugba Students Welfare Committee, 1973), p. 209.9 and reiterated by Jam-yang-shay-ba, *Great Exposition of the Middle Way*, pp. 516-17. It appears that none of Ngok's own writings are extant intact. Citations from Ngok's *Epistolary Essay, Drop of Ambrosia* are found within Ser-dok Paṇ-chen Śākya-chok-den's (*gser mdog paṇ chen śākya mchog ldan*, 1428-1507) commentary on that work. See *Collected Works* of Gser-mdog Pan-chen, Vol. 24 (Thimphu, Bhutan: Kunzang Topgey, 1978) pp. 320.6-348.6.

16. *Great Exposition of the Middle Way*, p. 514.

17. Hopkins, *Meditation on Emptiness*, p. 406.

18. For example, Jam-yang-shay-ba (*Great Exposition of the Middle Way*, pp. 578.5-6) writes,

> [T]he mode of subsistence of form and so forth must be seen by way of not seeing the aggregates and so forth, and the non-establishment of the aggregates and so forth in the perspective of that perception is the suchness of the aggregates and so forth.

However, to call this "the Ge-luk-ba position" is to speak very roughly. Some Lo-sel-ling scholars, including Geshe Bel-den-drak-ba, argue that form's non-existence in the perspective of an uninterrupted path is *not* form's emptiness. The failure of an uninterrupted path to perceive form is, it might be argued, a consequence of remaining obstructions to omniscience. That is, it indicates a deficiency of the *subject's* enlightenment rather than a deficiency of the *object's* ontological status. The unfindability of form under ultimate analysis is not form's emptiness, it is merely a cognitive circumstance of that particular mind. The unfindability of form *as its own nature*, or the unfindability of an inherently existent form, is form's emptiness. In his *Beautiful Ornament for Faith* (*legs shes dad pa'i mdzes rgyan*; Mundgod: Drepung Loseling Library, 1979, p. 86), Geshe Bel-den-drak-ba writes,

> Through searching to see whether forms and so forth ultimately exist, one realizes that they do not. It is not at all the case that one realizes this through searching for forms and so forth among the substrata, forms and so forth.

In other words, if one seeks to determine whether an inherently existent form is present, one must search for an inherently existent form. At the end of one's search, the non-finding of inherently existent form (not the non-finding of form) is the realization of emptiness. In support of his argument, Geshe Bel-den-drak-ba (*Beautiful Ornament for Faith*, p. 86) cites Tsong-ka-pa's *Great Exposition of the Stages of the Path*,

> According to the statement from Candrakīrti's *Commentary on (Āryadeva's) "Four Hundred,"* "Our analysis is a search intent upon the nature," one searches to see whether forms and so forth have a nature of production, cessation, and so forth. Accordingly, one searches to see whether forms and so forth have production and cessation that are established from their own side. That reasoning [of ultimate analysis] does not search for mere production or mere cessation.

In another argument for the same point, Georges Dreyfus (Geshe Sang-gyay-sam-drup) holds that even scholars without deep meditative experience can realize that form is unfindable under analysis. The unfindability of form under analysis is a consequence of form's being empty, but is much coarser and easier to realize than emptiness itself. In order to realize emptiness, yogis must first identify and become thoroughly familiar with the object of negation (inherent existence) as it arises in their personal experience. Dreyfus argues that Tsong-ka-pa emphasizes the importance of first ascertaining the object of negation in one's personal experience because, thereafter, in later phases of one's analysis, one analytically searches for that very object of negation. The unfindability of the object of negation (and not the unfindability of its substratum) is emptiness.

In rebuttal, it might be argued that: (1) the insistence on taking the inherent existence of the object—rather than the object itself—as the object to be sought in analysis implies a belief that the object itself is findable, and thus inherently existent, (2) if one searches for an inherently existent form, at the end of analysis one finds its nature, utter non-existence, instead of emptiness, and (3) taking the object of negation to be the object sought in analysis involves the meditative use of a syllogism with a non-existent subject (e.g., inherently existent form). The use of non-existent subjects is controversial and is restricted by most Ge-luk-ba scholars to cases in which the reason is a non-affirming negative (*med dgag, prasajyapratiśedha*), and thus one could not use the "king of reasonings," dependent-arising (see Hopkins, *Meditation on Emptiness*, pp. 161ff.). According to the present Dalai Lama, the use of non-existent subjects is frowned upon because it does not foster understanding of dependent-arising (oral communication). See Lopez, *A Study in Svātantrika*, pp. 177-79, for a discussion of the problems of non-existent subjects.

I shall not venture further into this controversy here. I regard it as an important and neglected issue that must be reckoned with in future work on the Mādhyamika view.

19. Ngak-wang-bel-den, *Explanation of the Conventional and the Ultimate*, pp. 149.7-150.1.

20. *Engaging in the Bodhisattva Deeds* edited by Bhattacarya, *Bodhicaryāvatāra*, chapter 9, vs.2.

21. *Illumination of the Thought*, p. 197.2-3.

22. *Compendium of Instructions* (*Śikṣāsamuccayakārikā*), 142b; Cf. C. Bendall and W.H.D. Rouse, trans., *Śikṣā Samuccaya*, p. 236. Michael Sweet ("The Two Truths in *Bodhicaryāvatāra* 9.2," p. 83) mistakenly claims that Ge-luk-bas have not reckoned with this sūtra passage. In fact, it is a critical factor in Tsong-ka-pa's interpretation (*Illumination of the Thought*, p. 197.2-3) of *Engaging in the Bodhisattva Deeds* 9.2, and is also cited by Jam-yang-shay-ba (*Great Exposition of the Middle Way*, p. 519).

23. *An Entrance for the Sons of Conquerors, Explanation of (Śāntideva's) "Engaging in the Bodhisattva Deeds"* (*byang chub sems dpa'i spyod pa la 'jug pa'i rnam bshad rgyal sras*) (Sarnath: Gelugba Students Welfare Committee, 1973), p. 210.12-14.

24. *Thousand Doses* (*stong thun chen mo*) (Dharamsala: Shes rig par khang, n.d.), p. 608.3-6; translation of this passage by Kay-drup appears in José Ignacio Cabezón, "The Development of a Buddhist Philosophy of Language and its Culmination in Tibetan Mādhyamika Thought," (Ph.D. dissertation, University of Wisconsin, 1987), pp. 1006-07.

25. *Great Exposition of the Middle Way*, pp. 515-16.

26. *Ocean of Good Explanations: An Explanation of "Freedom From Extremes Through Understanding All Tenets"* (*grub mtha' kun shes nas mtha' bral grub pa zhes bya ba'i bstan bcos rnam par bshad pa legs bshad kyi rgya mtsho*) (Thimphu: Kun bdzang stobs rgyal, 1976), p. 27.2.

27. Ibid, p. 263.2-3.

28. *Great Exposition of the Middle Way*, p. 515.

29. Ibid, p. 515.

30. In his *Illumination of the Profound Suchness, An Explanation of (Nāgārjuna's) "Treatise on the Middle Way"* (Sarnath: Sakya Students Union, 1975), pp. 286-87.

31. Ngak-wang-bel-den, *Explanation of the Conventional and the Ultimate*, p. 151.2-3.

32. Frederick Streng, *Emptiness: A Study in Religious Meaning* (Nashville, New York: Abingdon Press, 1967), p. 39.

33. Ibid, p. 145.

34. Frederick Streng, "The Buddhist Doctrine of the Two Truths as Religious Philosophy," *Journal of Indian Philosophy* 1 (1971): 264.

35. Christian Lindtner, *Nagarjuniana* (Copenhagen: Akademisk Forlag, 1982), p. 276.

36. C.W. Huntington, "The System of the Two Truths in the *Prasannapadā and the Madhyamakāvatāra*: A Study in Mādhyamika Soteriology,' *Journal of Indian Philosophy* 11 (1983): 91 and 95.

37. *Supplement Commentary (Madhyamakāvatārabhāṣya)* as edited by Louis de la Vallée Poussin, *Madhyamakāvatāra par Candrakīrti*, p. 102.12-15.

38. Ibid, p. 102.16-17. Referring to Tsong-ka-pa's citation of this passage in his *Ocean of Reasoning*, Paul Williams ("Silence and Truth—Some Aspects of the Madhyamaka Philosophy of Tibet," *Tibet Journal* 7: 69) writes,

> And Tsong kha pa remarks that the ultimate is the self nature (*bdag gi rang gi ngo bo*) which is found as the distinct referential sphere of an awareness which apprehends the real (*yang dag*).

Michael Broido ("Padma dKar-po on the Two *Satyas*," *Journal of the International Association of Buddhist Studies* 8: 53) points out that Williams seems to have mistaken this passage for an original remark by Tsong-ka-pa. Broido goes on (pp. 53-54) to criticize Williams' paraphrased translation. The Tibetan for this passage reads: *de la don dam pa ni yang dag par gzigs pa rnams kyi ye shes kyi khyad par gyi yul nyid kyis bdag gi ngo bo rnyed pa yin gyi*. Broido (pp. 53-54) writes:

> Though Williams quotes the critical passage with the instrumental particle (*yul nyid kyis*. . .), that instrumental has disappeared in his translation. . . . The general effect of [this and other] changes made by Williams is to make Tsong-kha-pa's text more "objective" than would otherwise be the case. I have not studied Tsong-kha-pa much and if experts say so, I am prepared to accept that the general slant of his thought supports this "objective" interpretation; but this interpretation is not supported by these particular passages.

As for his own interpretation, Broido (p. 22) writes,

> In many contexts this word [*yul*] is correctly translated by "object." But here this will not do, because in the definition of *paramārtha* the *yul* grasps something. . . .

Based on this understanding of *yul* as an agent, he (p. 20) translates Candrakīrti thus:

> As for *paramārtha*, it is a self-nature (*bdag-gi ngo-bo*) grasped by the particular *yul* (*viṣaya*) of those who have a properly cognizing awareness. . .

Assuming that *yul* is the agent(!) of the verb *rnyed* and ignoring the particle *nyid*, Broido (p. 23) argues that *yul* is a non-specific and "non-dualistic" term that, according to context, "specializes to 'subject' or 'object.' "

In a more recent publication ("Veridical and Delusive Cognition: Tsong-kha-pa on the Two Satyas," *Journal of Indian Philosophy* 16: 36-37 and 56), Broido has persisted in this view. Having in the interim read through the two truths sections of *Ocean of Reasoning* and *Illumination of the Thought*, Broido no longer defers to "experts" but quite erroneously insists that Tsong-ka-pa's commentary on this passage supports his view.

Of course, the instrumental case has many other, non-agentive, uses in both Sanskrit and Tibetan. Louis de la Vallée Poussin (*Muséon* 12: 300) translates this passage as follows:

> La véritable est constitiuée par le fait qu'elle est l'objet de cette sorte de savoir qui appartient a ceux qui voient juste.

For La Vallée Poussin, the particle *nyid* (*tva*) is quite important, indicating the fact of being an object. The instrumental indicates not agency, but the means through which the action is accomplished. This translation is more natural and more logical than those of either Williams or Broido. It also suggests that Broido's criticism of Williams for his "objective" reading is unwarranted. There is abundant evidence that ultimate truth is an *object* in the Ge-luk-ba interpretation of Mādhyamika. Since this is the context in which Williams is working, his phrase "referential sphere" is appropriate insofar as it conveys this point. Furthermore, contrary to Broido's assertion, this passage from Candrakīrti's *Supplement* does seem to support that position.

While we have this passage under scrutiny, it is worth noting that in translating Candrakīrti 's phrase *ye shes kyi khyad par gyi yul nyid kyis* Broido and Williams both construe *khyad par* as modifying *yul*. Williams gives us "distinctive [*khyad par*] referential sphere" and Broido offers "particular [*khyad par*] *yul*." This is contrary to the readings of Tsong-ka-pa and La Vallée Poussin. As quoted above, the latter writes, "l'objet de cette sorte de savoir," using *khyad par* to indicate a specific type of wisdom. This is precisely in accord with Tsong-ka-pa's *Illumination of the Thought* (p. 193.2-3) as I would read it:

> Regarding [Candrakīrti 's phrase] "*ye shes kyi khyad par*": [ultimate truth] is not found by just any exalted wisdom of a Superior; rather, it is to be taken as a special type, or a particular type, of exalted wisdom. (*ye shes kyi khyad par zhes pa ni 'phags pa'i ye shes gang yin gyis rnyed pa min par ye shes kyi khyad par te bye brag pa cig la byed*)

In Broido's more recent work ("Veridical and Delusive Cognition," pp. 37 and 57) he discusses this passage, persisting in the view that *khyad par* refers to *yul*.

39. *Supplement Commentary* (*Madhyamakāvatārabhāṣya*) as edited by Louis de la Vallée Poussin, *Madhyamakāvatāra par Candrakīrti*, p. 103.4-7.

40. de Jong, "The Problem of the Absolute in the Madhyamaka School" *Journal of Indian Philosophy* 2 (1972): 1; Lindtner, *Nagarjuniana*, p. 277; Crittenden, "Everyday Reality as Fiction—A Mādhyamika Interpretation," *Journal of Indian Philosophy* 9 (1981): 328.

41. Robert Thurman, *Tsong Khapa's Speech of Gold*, p. 147.

42. Eckel, *Jñānagarbha's Commentary on the Distinction Between the Two Truths*, p. 49.

43. Lindtner, Nagarjuniana, p. 276.

CHAPTER THREE

1. *Illumination of the Thought*, p. 195.4.

2. Candrakīrti cites this passage twice in his *Supplement Commentary, (Madhyamakāvatārabhāṣya*, as edited by Louis de la Vallée Poussin, *Madhyamakāvatāra par Candrakīrti*, at p. 70.6-9 and again at p. 175.9-12. The first citation is ascribed to the *Meeting of the Father and Son Sūtra*, while the second occurs as part of a longer quote ascribed to the *Superior Sūtra of Definite Teaching on Suchness.*

3. *Supplement Commentary* (*Madhyamakāvatārabhāṣya*), p. 71.3-7.

4. *Supplement Commentary* (*Madhyamakāvatārabhāṣya*), p. 71.8-19.

5. This is stated in accordance with Gen Lo-sang-gya-tso's oral explanation that when one ask whether a particular object exists as it appears, the appearance in question is the appearance of that object to the direct perceiver explicitly realizing it. However, a few concealer-truths (e.g., the subtle interrelationships between actions and their effects) are not accessible to realization by direct perceivers in the continuums of sentient beings. We will touch on this problem again in chapters seven and twelve.

6. Ngak-wang-bel-den, *Explanation of the Conventional and the Ultimate*, p. 97.2-4.

7. D.S. Ruegg, "The Uses of the Four Positions of the *Catuṣkoṭi* and the Problem of the Description of Reality in Mahāyāna Buddhism," *Journal of Indian Philosophy* 5 (1977): 5.

The principle of contradiction is: Nothing can be both A and not-A. The principle of the excluded middle is: Anything must be either A or not-A. Together with the principle of identity (If anything is A, it is A), these are the so-called "laws of thought" in Western logic. See Cohen and Nagel, *An Introduction to Logic*, p. 181. F. Staal (1975, p. 39), T.R.V. Murti (*The Central Philosophy of Buddhism*, London: George Allen & Unwin, 1955, reprint 1970, pp. 146-48), E. Conze (1962, p. 220) and Kajiyama Yuichi (*Bhāvaviveka and the Prāsaṅgika School*, Rajgir: Nalanda Press, 1957, p. 293) are among many who have argued that Mādhyamikas reject one or more of these principles. A.L. Basham (*The Wonder That Was India*, New York: Grove Press, 1954, p. 271) makes an even broader claim, writing that "the Aristotelian Law of the Excluded Middle was never strictly applied in Indian thought. . . ," while La Vallée Poussin wrote that "Indians. . .never clearly recognized the principle of contradiction."

8. *Supplement* (*Madhaymakāvatāra*) (P5261, P5262, Vol. 98). Edited Tibetan: Louis de la Vallée Poussin, *Madhyamakāvatāra par Candrakīrti*, chapter 6, verse 23

9. Jam-yang-chok-lha-ö-ser (*'jam dbyang phyogs lha 'od zer*, fl. fifteenth century?), *Collected Topics of Ra Dö* (*rva stod bsdus grva*) (Dharamsala: Damchoe Sangpo, Library of Tibetan Works and Archives, 1980), pp. 92.5-6.

10. Jam-yang-chok-hla-ö-ser's (*Collected Topics of Ra Dö*, p. 93.3) examples are "the crow and the owl" and "the antidote and the object of abandonment." As examples of indirect contradictories, (a subset of mutually exclusive contradictories) he gives "hot and cold" and "the consciousness conceiving of an [inherently existent] self and the wisdom realizing that a [inherently existent] self does not exist." I see no problem in also giving these as examples of contradictories that do not abide together because all contradictories that do not abide together are also mutually exclusive contradictories. In fact, Lopez (*The Heart Sūtra Explained*, Albany: State University of New York Press, 1988, pp. 78 and 205) gives "hot and cold" and "the mistaken belief in self and the wisdom realizing selflessness" as examples of contradictories that do not abide together. He cites another Collected Topics text, by Pur-bu-jok Jam-ba-gya-tso, a tutor of the thirteenth Dalai Lama, as his source. However, it appears that Pur-bu-jok gives only "antidote and object of abandonment" as an example of contradictories not abiding together, while following *Ra Dö* in using the other two examples for indirect contradictories. See *Intermediate Path of Reasoning* (*rigs lam 'bring*) in *The Presentation of Collected Topics Revealing the Meaning of the Texts on Valid Cognition, the Magical Key to the the Path of Reasoning* (*tshad ma'i gzhung don 'byed pa'i bsdus grva'i rnam bzhag rigs lam 'phrul gyi lde mig*) (Buxa, India: n.p., 1965), f.5a.3-4.

The example "light and dark" is given in accordance with the oral teaching of Gen Lo-sang-gya-tso.

11. Lopez, *The Heart Sūtra Explained*, p. 78.

12. *Collected Topics of Ra Dö*, p. 92.7.

13. *Collected Topics of Ra Dö*, pp. 92.7-93.1.

14. Ibid, p. 93.1; Pur-bu-jok's *Intermediate Path of Reasoning*, f.5a.2.

15. Reflection on these definitions raises a qualm about Ngak-wang-belden's (*Explanation of the Conventional and the Ultimate*, p. 97.3) remark, cited above:

> [T]he deceptive and the non-deceptive are mutually exclusive contradictories. Therefore, they pervade all objects of knowledge.

It is clear that there are many mutually exclusive contradictories—blue and yellow, for example—that do *not* pervade all objects of knowledge. In this context, taking his cue from Kamalaśīla, Ngak-wang-bel-den uses the term "mutually exclusive contradictories" to refer specifically to direct contradictories.

16. *Great Exposition of the Middle Way*, pp. 520-521.

17. *Supplement Commentary* (*Madhyamakāvatārabhāṣya*) as edited by Louis de la Vallée Poussin, *Madhyamakāvatāra par Candrakīrti*, pp. 107.19-108.6. Emphasis added.

18. Although "Foe Destroyer" may seem an awkward translation for the familiar term *arhat*, it accords with the etymology of the Tibetan *dgra bcom pa* and, as Hopkins (*Meditation on Emptiness*, p. 872) puts it, "captures the flavor of an oral tradition that frequently refers to this etymology." Arhats are called "Foe Destroyers" because they have overcome the foe which is the afflictions (*nyon mongs, kleśa*), i.e., ignorance, desire, hatred and so forth. As explained by Hopkins (*Meditation on Emptiness*, pp. 871-73), the Tibetan translators were aware of the other etymology of *arhat* as "worthy one," using it to translate the name of the supposed founder of Jainism, Arhat, as "Worthy of Worship" (*mchod 'od*). When referring to Buddhist yogis who have abandoned cyclic existence, they consciously exercised a preference for the etymology of *arhat* as *ari-han*, and the translation "Foe Destroyer" is an attempt to represent that tradition in English.

19. "Mere conventionalities" (*kun rdzob tsam, saṃvṛtimātra*) will be discussed at greater length in chapter eleven.

20. Leon Hurvitz, "Chih I (538-597)," *Mélanges chinois et bouddhiques* 12 (1960): 274.

21. Ibid, pp. 273-274.

22. Ibid, pp. 272-273.

CHAPTER FOUR

1. D.S. Ruegg, *The Literature of the Madhyamaka School of Philosophy in India*, p. 3.

2. An exception to the general consensus on this point, Geshe Bel-den-drak-ba holds that different names do not always imply different isolates. For example, Guy Newland and Guy Martin Newland are one isolate because, even though the names are different, they describe the same object from the same point of view. Guy Newland and the writer of these words are different isolates because they approach the object from different viewpoints.

3. *Intermediate Exposition of the Stages of the Path* (*lam rim 'bring*) (Dharamsala: Shes rig par khang, n.d. and Mundgod: Ganden Shardzay, n.d.), p. 454.1-2.

4. *Sūtra Unravelling the Thought* (*Saṃdhinirmocanasūtra*) (P774, Vol.29) in *The Tog Palace MS. of the Tibetan Kanjur* (Leh: Smanrtsis Shesrig Dpemzod, 1975), p. 26. Previously translated by John Powers, "The Saṃdhinirmochana Sūtra," (typescript, 1986), p. 22.

Svātantrikas claim that the *Sūtra Unravelling of the Thought* teaches that all phenomena are empty of true existence, and they accordingly interpret this passage as a denial of a relationship as truly existent one or truly existent different. (See Ngak-wang-bel-den, *Explanation of the Conventional and the Ultimate*, pp. 156.7 and 102.6.) In the Prāsaṅgika system, the explicit teaching of this sūtra is that some phenomena truly exist and some do not. Among the three natures, other-powered phenomena (*gzhan bdang, paratantra*) and thoroughly established phenomena (*yongs grub, paraniṣpanna*) are presented as truly existent. (See Hopkins, *Meditation on Emptiness*, p. 618.) Therefore, since this sūtra does teach true existence, it cannot be understood to mean that the two truths are free from truly existent sameness of difference. Instead, in the Ge-luk-ba interpretation of Prāsaṅgika, it indicates that the two truths are neither one isolate nor different entities.

5. *Illumination of the Thought*, pp. 195.6-196.1.

6. *Essay on the Mind of Enlightenment* (*Bodhicittavivaraṇa*) (P2665 and P2666, Vol.61). Tibetan ed. by Chr. Lindtner in *Nagarjuniana*, p. 204, vs. 68.

7. Paṇ-chen Sö-nam-drak-ba, *General Meaning of (Nāgārjuna's) "Treatise on the Middle Way"* (*dbu ma'i spyi don*) Collected Works Vol. "Ja" (Mundgod: Drebung Loseling Library Society, 1985), p. 117.7 cites *Heart of Wisdom Sūtra* (*Prajñāhṛdaya*) P160, Vol. 6, p. 166.2.4. Sanskrit edited by Conze is found in *Thirty Years of Buddhist Studies* (Oxford: Cassirer, 1967). For a recent translation with a study of Indian and Tibetan interpretations, see Donald Lopez, *The Heart Sūtra Explained*.

8. *Illumination of the Thought*, p. 192.6.

9. Ibid, p. 196.3.

10. *Great Exposition of the Middle Way*, pp. 522-523.

11. *Illumination of the Thought*, p. 193.1.

12. *Illumination of the Middle Way* (*Madhyamakāloka*), *dbu ma* Vol. 12 in *sDe dge Tibetan Tripitaka* (Tokyo: 1977ff), f.221a.1-2; Tsong-ka-pa refers to this passage in his *Intermediate Exposition* (p.453.2-3). Jam-yang-shay-ba (*Great Exposition of the Middle Way*, p. 524.4-5) cites the passage itself.

13. Hopkins, *Meditation on Emptiness*, p. 415.

14. *Great Exposition of the Middle Way*, pp. 525-26. Ngak-wang-bel-den (*Explanation of the Conventional and the Ultimate*, p. 97) points out that Vaibhāṣikas and Sautrāntikas also assert that the two truths are different entities, although this is not surprising in that their definitions of the two truths are radically different from those found in the Mahāyāna tenet systems. See J. Buescher's "The Buddhist Doctrine of the Two Truths in the Vaibhāṣika and Theravāda Schools" (Ann Arbor: University Microfilms, 1982) and, with regard to Sautrāntika, A. Klein's *Knowledge and Liberation*. It seems that Jam-yang-shay-ba's refutations of the two truths as different entities are not primarily targeted at proponents of Hīnayāna tenet systems, but at the Jo-nang-bas.

Ngak-wang-bel-den also argues that, from the Prāsaṅgika standpoint, even Cittamātrins may be seen as implicitly asserting that the two truths are different entities. Cittamātrins hold that other-powered phenomena (*gzhan dbang, paratantra*) must be truly existent, for if they were not, they would be unable to produce their effects. From a Prāsaṅgika viewpoint, this assertion that emptiness of true existence and the capacity to produce effects are incompatible in a single phenomenon is tantamount to an assertion that the two truths must be different entities.

15. Hopkins, *Meditation on Emptiness*, p. 413. Bracketed numerals added.

16. Atiśa composed his *Quintessential Instructions on the Middle Way* in Tibet, in the middle of the eleventh century, at the request of Ngok Lek-bay-shay-rap (*rngog legs pa'i shes rab*), founder of Sang-pu monastery. Ngok Lek-bay-shay-rap's nephew was Ngok Lo-den-shay-rap, the famous translator. Roerich, trans., *Blue Annals*, pp. 324-325.

17. Ngak-wang-bel-den, *Explanation of the Conventional and the Ultimate*, p. 155.3-4. See *Sūtra Unravelling the Thought* (*Saṃdhinirmocanasūtra*), chapter three, pp. 18-27; translated by John Powers, "The Saṃdhinirmochana Sūtra," (typescript, 1986), pp. 14-22.

18. Hopkins, *Meditation on Emptiness*, p. 413.

19. *Commentary on (Atiśa's) "Quintessential Instructions on the Middle Way"* (*Madhyamakopadeśavṛtti*), *dbu ma* Vol. 15 in *sDe dge Tibetan Tripitaka* (Tokyo: 1977ff), f.119a.1-2. Bracketed material added.

20. Ngak-wang-bel-den, *Explanation of the Conventional and the Ultimate*, pp. 102.3-4 and 156.2.

21. *Great Exposition of the Middle Way*, p. 526.

22. Ngak-wang-bel-den, *Explanation of the Conventional and the Ultimate*, p. 102.

23. *Sūtra Unravelling the Thought* (*Saṃdhinirmocanasūtra*), chapter 3, p. 26.

24. *Great Exposition of the Middle Way*, p. 528, cites *Illumination of the Middle Way* (*Madhyamakāloka*), *dbu ma* Vol. 12 in *sDe dge Tibetan Tripitaka* (Tokyo: 1977ff), f.234b.7.

25. Hopkins, *Meditation on Emptiness*, p. 413 cites *Great Exposition of the Middle Way* (*dbu ma chen mo*) Collected Works, Vol. 9 (Ta), p. 526. Brackets in this quotation indicate that I have added the numbers.

Ngak-wang-bel-den (*Explanation of the Conventional and the Ultimate*, p. 98) presents an argument suggesting that Prāsaṅgikas can find an implicit assertion that the two truths are a single isolate in the tenets of *all* who assert inherent existence. Suppose a table were inherently existent, just as it appears to be. Since inherently existent phenomena should be findable under analysis, a mind analyzing a table and seeking its ultimate nature would find the table itself. Thus the conventional nature of the table and its ultimate nature would be precisely the same.

26. Ngak-wang-bel-den, *Explanation of the Conventional and the Ultimate*, p. 155.4-6. See *Sūtra Unravelling the Thought*, chapter 3, pp. 14-22.

27. Prajñāmokśa, *Commentary on (Atiśa's) "Quintessential Instructions on the Middle Way"* (*Madhyamakopadeśavṛtti*), *dbu ma* Vol. 15 in *sDe dge Tibe-*

tan Tripitaka (Tokyo: 1977ff), ff.118b.7-119a.l.

28. Ngak-wang-bel-den, *Explanation of the Conventional and the Ultimate*, p. 102.

29. I have not been able to locate this work; it appears that it may not be extant.

30. Ngak-wang-bel-den, *Explanation of the Conventional and the Ultimate*, pp. 100.6 and 102.1.

31. Ngak-wang-bel-den (*Explanation of the Conventional and the Ultimate*, p. 98.4-7) writes:

> The scriptures and commentaries state many reasonings refuting that the two truths are one isolate or different entities. These must be known in order to refute the conceived objects of the *innate* awarenesses conceiving (1) that how things mainly appear is their final mode of subsistence and (2) that emptiness of true existence and the ability to perform actions are incompatible (*gzhi mthun du 'du mi rung ba*). The refutations of the reifications of [other] tenet systems are [only] a branch of the refutation of innate [reifying misconceptions].

32. Based on an oral comment by His Holiness the Dalai Lama XIV.

33. *Treatise on the Middle Way* (*Madhyamakaśāstra*) (P5224, Vol. 95) chapter 24, verse 18. Hurvitz ("Chih I (538-597)," p. 274) reports that this stanza is Chih-i's Indian source for a "middle truth" resolving the contradictions between conventional and ultimate reality.

34. *Presentation of Tenets* (*grub pa'i mtha'i rnam par bzhag pa*) (Varanasi: Pleasure of Elegant Sayings Press, 1970), p. 457.7-12.

35. Ngak-wang-bel-den, *Explanation of the Conventional and the Ultimate*, p. 104.5.

36. This opinion was expressed to me orally by Gen Lo-sang-gya-tso and Geshe Bel-den-drak-ba. The latter pointed out that there is more than one acceptable reply to the question "What is the concealer-truth posited in relation to a table?" Table is a concealer-truth posited in relation to table, but so are the existence of table, the impermanence of table, and so forth. Thus, analogously, it is acceptable to posit the existence of emptiness as a concealer-truth posited in relation to the emptiness of a table or in relation to the emptiness of emptiness.

37. Tenzin Gyatso, Dalai Lama XIV, *The Buddhism of Tibet and the Key to the Middle Way*, trans. by Jeffrey Hopkins (London: George Allen & Unwin, 1975), p. 76.

38. In contrast to the Dalai Lama's view, Geshe Sö-nam-rin-chen (according to notes provided by Prof. Daniel Cozort) holds that, when one considers the emptiness of emptiness, the basis of emptiness (*stong gzhi*) is an ultimate truth and not a conventionality.

39. *Illumination of the Thought*, p. 196.1-2.

40. See *Sūtra Unravelling the Thought*, chapter 3, p. 20.

41. *Essay on the Mind of Enlightenment* (*Bodhicittavivaraṇa*) (P2665 and

P2666, Vol.61) Tibetan ed. by Chr. Lindtner in *Nagarjuniana*, p. 202, vs.57. My translation; Lindtner (p.202) also gives the Sanskrit of this verse.

42. Some hold that permanent phenomenon (*rtag pa*) and impermanent phenomenon (*mi rtag pa*) (which are not related as quality-possessor and quality and are mutually exclusive) are related within one entity. However, Geshe Bel-den-drak-ba approved my general claim.

43. The oneness of entity of the two truths is usually explained in terms of a single, specific phenomenon being one entity with its emptiness. Of course table and its emptiness are no more a dichotomy than are table and its redness. However, Geshe Bel-den-drak-ba and Kensur Den-ba-den-dzin explained that the oneness of entity of the two truths means not only that pot and its emptiness are one entity, but that in general ultimate truth and concealer-truth are also related as one entity.

44. Sangharakshita, *A Survey of Buddhism* (London: Tharpa, 1987), p. 294.

45. Conze, *Buddhism: Its Essence and Development*, pp. 129 and 134.

46. David Eckel, *Jñānagarbha's Commentary on the Distinction Between the Two Truths* (Albany: State University of New York Press, 1987), pp. 38 and 43. Regarding Eckel's interpretation of the two truths as subjective perspectives or viewpoints, it is interesting to note that his own translation of Jñānagarbha (ibid, p. 75) says that, regarding the twofold division (see chapter seven) of concealer-truths (*kun rdzob bden pa, saṃvṛtisatya*), that a correct "relative truth" (*yang dag kun rdzob, tathyasaṃvṛti*) is "a mere thing (*dngos tsam, vastumātra*) which is not confused with anything that is imagined and arises dependently" and (p.79) that "Correct and incorrect relative [truth] are similar in appearance, but are distinguished by their ability and inability to produce functions." Since these definitions are clearly framed so as to include objects as well as "perspectives," some explanation from the translator would have been in order.

47. Ibid, p. 64.

48. Ibid, p. 38.

49. Richard Robinson, *Early Mādhyamika in India and China* (Madison: University of Wisconsin Press, 1967.), p. 43.

50. There is nothing that has an *inherently existent* entity, and it is in just this sense that it is said that all things are "entityless" (*ngo bo nyid med pa*).

CHAPTER FIVE

1. *Clear Words* (*Mūlamadhyamakavṛttiprasannapadā*) (P5260, Vol. 98) Sanskrit edited by Louis de la Vallée Poussin, *Mūlamadhaymakakārikās de Nāgārjuna avec la Prasannapadā Commentaire de Candrakīrti*, Bibliotheca Buddhica IV (Osnabrück: Biblio Verlag, 1970), p. 492.10.

2. The word "all" (*samanta*) occurs only in the Sanskrit.

3. *Ocean of Reasoning* (*rigs pa'i rgya mtsho*) (Sarnath: Pleasure of Elegant Sayings Press, n.d.), pp. 402.12-403.2.

4. Mervyn Sprung ("The Mādhyamika Doctrine as Metaphysic," in *The Problem of Two Truths in Buddhism and Vedanta*, edited by Mervyn Sprung, Boston: D. Reidel Publishing, 1973, p. 43) lists nine usages of *saṃvṛti* in the writing of Candrakīrti and Nāgārjuna. However, it seems that several of these nine are actually not distinct meanings, but simply the same general meaning applied in different contexts.

5. *Clear Words* (*Mūlamadhyamakavṛttiprasannapadā*), p. 492.10.

6. *Supplement* (*Madhaymakāvatāra*) in Louis de la Vallée Poussin, *Madhyamakāvatāra par Candrakīrti*, chapter 6 vs.28.

7. *Supplement Commentary* (*Madhyamakāvatārabhāṣya*) as edited by Louis de la Vallée Poussin, *Madhyamakāvatāra par Candrakīrti*, p. 107.5-10.

8. *Intermediate Exposition of the Stages of the Path*, p. 454.6.

9. *Ocean of Reasoning*, pp. 404.1-3.

10. Ibid, p. 405.15-19.

11. T.R.V. Murti, *The Central Philosophy of Buddhism*, p. 244.

12. T.R.V. Murti, "Saṃvṛti and Paramārtha in Mādhyamika and Advaita Vedānta," in *The Problem of Two Truths in Buddhism and Vedānta*, edited by M. Sprung (Dordrecht: Reidel, 1973), p. 13.

13. Such as Gen Lo-sang-gya-tso (oral communication) and Lo-sang-da-yang (*blo bzang rta dbyangs*, 1867-1937) in his *Annotations to (Paṇ-chen Sö-nam-drak-ba's) "General Meaning Commentary on the Middle Way"* (New Delhi: Tibet House, 1974).

14. *Supplement Commentary* (*Madhyamakāvatārabhāṣya*) as edited by Louis de la Vallée Poussin, *Madhyamakāvatāra par Candrakīrti*, p. 102.16-18.

15. T.R.V. Murti, *The Central Philosophy of Buddhism*, p. 244-245.

16. Christian Lindtner, "Atīśa's Introduction to the Two Truths, and Its Sources," *Journal of Indian Philosophy* 9 (1981): 161-162; Mahesh Mehta, "Śūnyatā and Dharmatā: the Mādhyamika View of Inner Reality," in *Developments in Buddhist Thought: Canadian Contributions to Buddhist Studies* (Waterloo, Ontario: Canadian Corporation for Studies in Religion, 1979), p. 36; Sprung, "The Mādhyamika Doctrine as Metaphysic," p. 47 and Bimal Krishna Matilal, "A Critique of the Mādhyamika Position" in *The Problem of Two Truths in Buddhism and Vedānta* edited by Mervyn Sprung, p. 147.

17. Robert Thurman, *Tsong Khapa's Speech of Gold*, p. 55-6. Combining arguments against absolutism with deployment of "absolute" as a translation for *don dam* (*paramārtha*), Thurman arrives at striking expressions such as (p.56), "if the absolute is taken to be too absolute, then the relative ends up being repudiated." Since we say "absolute" precisely to exclude questions of degree, what could it mean to be "just absolute enough"?

18. See Napper's (*Dependent Arising and Emptiness*, pp. 129-131) fine discussion of this point.

19. He writes, "[W]ith respect to a reflection of a face, for instance, its being a face is false for a conventional [consciousness] of worldly [persons] ('jig rten gyi kun rdzob) trained in language." *Illumination of the Thought*,

p. 207.3-4.

20. In contrast, Bhāvaviveka's *Lamp for (Nāgārjuna's) "Wisdom" (Prajñāpradīpa)* P5253, Vol. 95, as trans. by Eckel, "A Question of Nihilism" (Ph.D. dissertation, Harvard University, 1980), p. 271, commenting on *Treatise on the Middle Way (Madhyamakaśāstra)* (P5224, Vol. 95) chapter 24, vs. 8, second half, leaves the distinct impression that *lokasaṃvṛti* refers specifically to linguistic conventions, without reference to their objects.

21. Douglas Daye, "Major Schools of the Mahāyāna: Mādhyamika" in *Buddhism: A Modern Perspective*, edited by Charles Prebish (University Park: Pennsylvania State University Press, 1975), p. 96.

22. Nathan Katz, "Nāgārjuna and Wittgenstein on Error" in *Buddhist and Western Philosophy*, ed. by Nathan Katz (New Delhi: Sterling Publishers, 1981), p. 319.

23. Napper, *Dependent Arising and Emptiness*, p. 93, discussing Chris Gudmunsen, *Wittgenstein and Buddhism* (London: Macmillan, 1977).

24. *Intermediate Exposition of the Stages of the Path*, p. 454.5-6.

25. *Illumination of the Thought*, p. 206.1-2.

26. *Presentation of Tenets (grub pa'i mtha'i rnam par bzhag pa)* (Varanasi: Pleasure of Elegant Sayings Press, 1970), p. 461.17-20.

27. *Great Exposition of the Middle Way*, p. 536) and Ngak-wang-bel-den, *Explanation of the Conventional and the Ultimate*, p. 123.6-7.

28. *Great Exposition of the Stages of the Path (lam rim chen mo)* (Dharamsala: Shes rig par khang, n.d.), p. 841.1-2.

29. Ibid, p. 841.3-4.

30. Ibid, p. 841.5-6.

31. Ibid, p. 842.2-4.

32. *Great Exposition of the Middle Way*, pp. 573-574.

33. Ibid, p. 574.

34. P5787

35. *Clear Words (Mūlamadhyamakavṛttiprasannapadā)*, p. 493.

36. Ibid, p. 492.6.

37. Ibid, p. 493.

38. *Great Exposition of the Middle Way*, p. 542.

39. Ibid, pp. 540-541.

40. Ibid, p. 539 cites *Engaging in the Bodhisattva Deeds (Bodhisattvacaryāvatāra)* (P5272, Vol.99); Bhattacarya, ed., chapter 9 vs. 3.

41. *Great Exposition of the Middle Way*, p. 540.

42. *Supplement (Madhaymakāvatāra)*; edited Tibetan: Louis de la Vallée Poussin, *Madhyamakāvatāra par Candrakīrti*, chapter 6, vs. 25.

43. *Illumination of the Thought*, p. 201.3-4.

44. As related by Jang-gya (*Presentation of Tenets*, 344.14-17); Lopez translates this passage (*A Study of Svātantrika*, Ithaca: Snow Lion, 1987, p. 316) and comments on it (*A Study of Svātantrika*, p. 143). Ngak-wang-bel-den (*Explanation of the Conventional and the Ultimate*) also refers to this point. Tsong-ka-pa's *Essence of the Good Explanations, Treatise Discriminating What*

Is To Be Interpreted and the Definite (*drang ba dang nges pa'i don rnam par phye ba'i bstan bcos legs bshad snying po*) (P6142, Vol. 153; Sarnath: Pleasure of Elegant Sayings Printing Press, 1973) is the starting point for these remarks, though Tsong-ka-pa does not mention these scholars by name in this context. See Robert Thurman, trans., *Tsong Khapa's Speech of Gold*, pp. 147, 281-85 and 367-68.

45. See K. Mimaki, "Mādhyamika Classification in Tibetan *grub mtha*" in *Contributions on Tibetan and Buddhist Religion and Philosophy* edited by E. Steinkeller and H. Tauscher (Vienna: 1983). A good overview of the Prāsaṅgika/Svātantrika argument is presented by Hopkins (*Meditation on Emptiness*); see also Sopa and Hopkins, *Practice and Theory of Tibetan Buddhism* (New York: Grove Press, 1976). A recent publication of interest is José Ignacio Cabezón, "The Prāsaṅgika's Views on Logic: Tibetan Dge lugs pa Exegesis on the Question of Svatantras," *Journal of Indian Philosophy* 16 (1988): 217-24. Valuable are Ichimura Shohei "A New Approach to the Intra-Mādhyamika Confrontation Over the Svātantrika and Prāsaṅgika Methods of Refutation" *Journal of the International Association of Buddhist Studies* 5 (1982): 41-52; S. Iida, *Reason and Emptiness*, (Tokyo: Hokuseido, 1980); and Kajiyama Yuichi, *Bhāvaviveka and the Prāsaṅgika School* (Rajgir: Nalanda Press, 1957); and Eckel, "A Question of Nihihlism" (Ph.D. dissertation, Harvard, 1980). Donald Lopez (*A Study of Svātantrika*) presents a detailed study of Svātantrika as seen by the Ge-luk-bas. Robert Thurman (*Tsong Khapa's Speech of Gold*) translates the *Essence of Good Explanations* and gives his interpretation of Tsong-ka-pa's argument. Pointing to alternative Tibetan readings of the difference between Svātantrika and Prāsaṅgika is T. Tillemans, "The Neither One nor Many Argument for *Śūnyatā* and its Tibetan Interpretations: Background Information and Source Materials," *Étude de Lettres* (1982): 103-28.

46. Bhāvaviveka, *Blaze of Reasoning* (*Tarkajvālā*), P5256, Vol. 96, 27.5.7-28.1.1. See Lopez, *A Study of Svātantrika*, pp. 135-40 and 315; also, Wayman trans., *Calming the Mind and Discerning the Real*, (New York: Columbia University Press, 1978; rpt., Delhi: Motilal Banarsidass, 1979), p. 280.

A complication involved in this definition of ultimate existence is that emptiness exists for the perspective of a consciousness realizing emptiness because emptiness is the object found or realized in the perspective of that awareness. Bhāvaviveka's *Blaze of Reasoning* (P5256, Vol. 96, 27.3.1-4; cited by Lopez, *A Study of Svātantrika*, pp. 199 and 317) says, "[T]he ultimate exists for an [inferential] wisdom that accords with a [direct] realization of the ultimate," and Tsong-ka-pa's *Illumination of the Thought* says, "The ultimate of the first type and [something] established in its perspective exist. . . ." See also Ngak-wang-bel-den's *Explanation of Conventionalities and Ultimates*, pp. 120.3-123.1 and his *Annotations for (Jam-yang-shay-ba's) "Great Exposition of Tenets,"* ff.38a.4-38b.3. The apparent implication of these remarks is that emptiness ultimately exists in the sense that it exists in the perspective of a valid cognizer realizing emptiness. However, inasmuch as it is fundamental to Mādhyamika to assert that all phenomena are merely conventionally existent, Ge-luk-bas cannot admit that emptiness in any way ultimately exists. Jang-gya and Ngak-wang-bel-den resolve this problem by explaining that even though emptiness exists for the perspective of a reasoning consciousness of ultimate analysis, it does not ultimately exist because it does not bear analysis (*dpyad mi bzod*) by such a reasoning consciousness. That is, just as a table is not found by a mind analyzing the final nature of that table, the emptiness of a table is not found by a mind analyzing the final nature of the emptiness of that table.

In effect, these latter authors are saying that when Bhāvaviveka and Tsong-ka-pa hold that "ultimately existent" means existent in the perspective of a reasoning consciousness, "existent in the perspective of" has the special meaning of "being able to bear analysis by." Nothing can bear ultimate analysis and thus nothing is ultimately existent. On the other hand, they also maintain that when Tsong-ka-pa says that there *is* something that exists in the perspective of the ultimate mind to which the term "ultimately existent" refers, "existent in the perspective of" means "being an object found or realized by." It may seem strained to hold that Tsong-ka-pa uses the phrase "existent in the perspective of" in two different ways, without noting the shift, within the context his discussion of this meaning of ultimate existence. However, the alternative conclusions, that Tsong-ka-pa made an error or that Tsong-ka-pa asserts emptiness to be ultimately existent, are unacceptable to Ge-luk-bas.

47. Jang-gya, *Presentation of Tenets*, pp. 344-46. The key passage from *Illumination of the Middle Way* is cited by Jang-gya, *Presentation of Tenets*, p. 371.20-372.10. See Lopez, *A Study of Svātantrika*, pp. 143-46, 316-18. See also Thurman, trans., *Tsong Khapa's Speech of Gold*, pp. 281-85.

48. *Presentation of Tenets*, p. 346.2.

49. Sources on etymologies of don dam: Ngak-wang-bel-den, *Explanation of the Conventional and the Ultimate*, pp. 120.3-123.1; Jang-gya, *Presentation of Tenets*, pp. 342-43, and Lopez, *A Study of Svātantrika*, pp. 135-6, 314-5. See also Robert Thurman, trans., *Tsong Khapa's Speech of Gold*, p. 282; Alex Wayman, trans., *Calming the Mind and Discerning the Real*, p. 280; and Iida, *Reason and Emptiness*, pp. 82-83.

50. *Clear Words* (*Mūlamadhyamakavṛttiprasannapadā*), p. 494.1.

51. Jam-yang-shay-ba, *Great Exposition of the Middle Way*, p. 593; similar passage in Jay-dzun Chö-gyi-gyel-tsen, *A Good Explanation Adorning the Throats of the Fortunate* (*bstan bcos dbu ma la 'jug pa'i rnam bshad dgongs pa rab gsal gyi dka' gnad gsal bar byed pa'i spyi don legs bshad skal bzang mgul rgyan*) (New Delhi: lha mkhar yongs 'dzin bstan pa rgyal mtshan, 1973), p. 411.

52. The emptiness of a table and the emptiness of the emptiness of that table, etc., are of one taste in that each is a mere absence of inherent existence, and they are surely as inseparable as a red table and its redness. However, they are distinct phenomena, distinguishable because their sub-

strata (table in one case and the emptiness of table in the other) are distinct.

CHAPTER SIX

1. *Supplement* (*Madhaymakāvatāra*), edited Tibetan: Louis de la Vallée Poussin, *Madhyamakāvatāra par Candrakīrti*, chapter 6, vs.23.
2. *Illumination of the Thought*, 195.1.
3. *Ocean of Reasoning*, p. 406.3-4. Note that Tsong-ka-pa's definition of concealer-truth, unlike the definitions of later Ge-luk-bas, specifically includes the word "falsity." Tsong-ka-pa makes it perfectly clear that, in order to realize that something is a concealer-truth, one must first see it as a falsity—an understanding which requires the refutation of its true existence. The later tradition agrees that all concealer-truths are falsities, but drops words like "falsity" and "deceptive" from its definitions—perhaps in order to stress their *validity* as objects found by conventional valid cognizers.
4. *Illumination of the Thought*, pp. 194.6-195.1.
5. *Ocean of Reasoning*, p. 406.2-3.
6. Although the word "definition" typically refers to a statement, in Buddhist philosophy a definition (*mtshan nyid, lakṣaṇa*) is the actual property to which a defining statement refers. Thus, as used here, the word "definition" indicates "the characteristic or group of characteristics that allows us to identify a particular phenomenon" (Dreyfus, "Definition in Buddhism," p. 15). The definition (ibid., pp. 19-20) is "the actual mark that must be. . .previously known in order to allow us to understand" the defined object, or definiendum. The significance of this point will emerge in chapter ten.
7. Ngak-wang-bel-den, *Explanation of the Conventional and the Ultimate*, pp. 110.3-4 and 158.2-3.
8. *Presentation of Tenets*, p. 461.7-9.
9. Jang-gya cites this as *'jug pa rang 'grel*, as though it were from Candrakīrti's *Supplement Commentary*, but actually it is from the root text.
10. *Illumination of the Thought*, pp. 506.6-507.2.
11. *Thousand Doses* (*stong thun chen mo*) (Dharamsala: Shes rig par khang, n.d.), pp. 619.6-620.1; cf. Cabezon, "The Development of a Buddhist Philosophy of Language," p. 1028.
12. *Disputation and Reply [Regarding] (Candrakīrti's) "Supplement"* (*dbu ma la 'jug pa'i brgal lan*) Collected Works Vol. "Ja" (Mundgod: Drebung Loseling Library Society, 1985), pp. 273.4-274.1.
13. *A Good Explanation Adorning the Throats of the Fortunate*, p. 375.
14. Ibid, pp. 375-6.
15. Sopa and Hopkins, *Practice and Theory of Tibetan Buddhism*, p. 140.
16. The term "self-consciousness" has a specific and technical meaning in Buddhist epistemology, as will be explained. It is important to keep in mind that self-consciousness is quite different from the introspective reflections practiced on the Buddhist path. Hopkins (*Meditation on Emp-*

tiness, p. 377) reminds us that although the various tenet systems disagree about self-consciousness in this technical sense, all advocate reliance on meditative introspection and moral self-awareness. "In these cases the mind is perceiving a previous moment of the mind or a part of the mind is perceiving the general mind." See the slightly more detailed discussion of self-consciousness in chapter twelve. Sources for the discussion of self-consciousness include Anne Klein, *Knowledge and Liberation*, pp. 73-76; Hopkins, *Meditation on Emptiness*, pp. 373-74 and p. 377; Lati Rinbochay and Elizabeth Napper, *Mind in Tibetan Buddhism* (Valois, N.Y.: Gabriel/Snow Lion, 1980), pp. 19 and 60; Sopa and Hopkins, *Practice and Theory of Tibetan Buddhism*, passim; and Kensur Yeshay Tupden (oral communication).

17. *Great Exposition of the Middle Way*, pp. 545-546.

18. *Ocean of Reasoning*, pp. 420.19-421.2

19. *Disputation and Reply [Regarding] (Candrakīrti's) "Supplement,"* pp. 273.4-274.1.

20. Ngak-wang-bel-den, *Explanation of the Conventional and the Ultimate*, p. 158.7.

21. *Presentation of Tenets*, p. 461.4-11

22. Again, Jang-gya cites this as *'jug pa rang 'grel*, as though it were from Candrakīrti's *Supplement Commentary*, while in fact it is from the root text.

23. *Presentation of Tenets*, p. 468.15-17.

24. *Great Exposition of the Middle Way*, p. 567.2; see also p. 544.6

25. Ibid, p. 591.4-5

26. Ibid, pp. 544.6 and 592.5.

27. *Great Exposition of Tenets* (*grub mtha' chen mo*) (Musoorie: Dalama, 1962), *dbu ma* section, ff.22a.8-22b.4.

28. *Great Exposition of the Middle Way*, p. 592.2-3.

29. Ibid, p. 592.3-4.

30. Ibid, p. 592.4-5.

31. Ibid, pp. 544-545.

32. Ibid, p. 545; *Great Exposition of Tenets*, *dbu ma* section, f.22b.4.

33. *Great Exposition of Tenets*, *dbu ma* section, f. 22b.1-2.

34. *Engaging in the Bodhisattva Deeds* (*Bodhisattvacaryāvatāra*), chapter 9 vs. 2.

35. *Illumination of the Thought*, pp. 196.6-197.2. A translation of this sūtra passage appears in Bendall and Rouse, trans., p. 236.

36. *An Entrance for the Sons of Conquerors, Explanation of (Śāntideva's) "Engaging in the Bodhisattva Deeds"* (*byang chub sems dpa'i spyod pa la 'jug pa'i rnam bshad rgyal sras*) (Sarnath: Gelugba Students Welfare Committee, 1973), p. 210.8-19.

37. Complications arise when we examine the interpretations of later Geluk-bas. According to Jam-yang-shay-ba (*Great Exposition of the Middle Way*, p. 519), the statement in sūtra that the ultimate is not an object of knowledge and the corresponding line in Śāntideva's stanza mean that ultimate truths are the only objects of knowledge that cannot be known by

mistaken awarenesses having dualistic appearance. Paṇ-chen Sö-nam-drak-ba's formulation (*General Meaning of (Nāgārjuna's) "Treatise on the Middle Way,"* 118.4) is slightly different:

> The meaning of both that sūtra and that śāstra is that ultimate truths are not the objects of conceptual awarenesses in the way that they are seen by an exalted wisdom of a Superior's meditative equipoise.

Paṇ-chen Sö-nam-drak-ba's qualification "in the way that they are seen by an exalted wisdom of a Superior's meditative equipoise" seems rather vague because it does not specify what it is about a Superior's mode of realization that conceptual consciousnesses cannot replicate. Yet, Jam-yang-shay-ba's phrase "mistaken awareness having dualistic appearance" is also quite difficult to interpret. Like all Ge-luk-bas, Jam-yang-shay-ba and Paṇ-chen agree that conceptual, inferential consciousnesses can realize emptiness through the medium of a generic image. Consciousnesses realizing emptiness inferentially are mistaken and dualistic because when emptiness appears to them, it appears as inherently existent. This seems to entail the absurdity that emptiness *is* the province of one type of mistaken dualistic consciousness. Perhaps the best way to understand Jan-yang-shay-ba is to interpret his statements within the framework provided by Gyel-tsap. That is, let us suppose that when Jam-yang-shay-ba (*Great Exposition of the Middle Way*, p. 519) says, "...the one [type of] object of knowledge that is not the province of a mistaken awareness having dualistic appearance is the entity of ultimate truth," he assumes that we will know that, in this context, the word "awareness" refers only to direct perception.

Whatever qualifications are attached to the "awareness" in the third line—"The ultimate is not the province of awareness"—should be carried over to the "awareness" in the fourth line—"Awareness is asserted to be a conventionality." For Jam-yang-shay-ba, the fourth line therefore means, "Mistaken direct perceivers having dualistic appearance, together with their objects, are conventionalities." Although Paṇ-chen (*General Meaning of (Nāgārjuna's) "Treatise on the Middle Way,"* p. 118.4-5) says, "It is easy to understand the meaning of the passage teaching concealer-truths," it is actually quite difficult to work out precisely how his qualifications can be carried over to the fourth line.

38. For other examples of definitions of this type in Svātantrika, see Gön-chok-jik-may-wang-bo (*dkon chog 'jigs med dbang po*, 1728-1791), *Precious Garland of Tenets* (*grub pa'i mtha'i rnam par bzhag pa rin po che'i phreng ba*) (Dharamsala: Shes rig par khang, 1969) as trans. by Sopa and Hopkins, *Practice and Theory of Tibetan Buddhism*, p. 124; also, Paṇ-chen Sö-nam-drak-ba's *General Meaning of (Maitreya's) "Ornament for Clear Realization"* (*par phyin spyi don*) Collected Works Vol. "Ga" (Mundgod: Drebung Loseling Library Society, 1982), f.47a.1ff.; also, Ken-sur Padma-gyel-tsen's *An Eye-Opening Golden Wand: Counsel on the Meaning of the Profound* (*zab don gdams pa'i mig 'byed gser gyi thur ma*) Vol. 3: (Mundgod: Drebung Losel-

ing Printing Press, 1984), p. 315ff. It may be that some Ge-luk-bas tend to reserve these definitions for use in Svātantrika (even though Śāntideva is a Prāsaṅgika) for reasons related to the question of what exactly "dualistic appearance" means and how this relates to the Prāsaṅgika refutation of self-consciousness (*rang rig, svasaṃvedana*). Since Prāsaṅgikas do not posit a distinct self-consciousness that witnesses the subjective side of each experience, the fact that we can later remember not only the experienced object but also the experiencing awareness might imply, for some Ge-luk-bas, that every mistaken consciousness ascertains itself implicitly while ascertaining its main object explicitly. (This, of course, opens up the very vexed question of exactly what Ge-luk-ba Prāsaṅgikas mean to refute when they refute self-consciousness. A careful study of that problem lies beyond the purview of this work, but the issue will be touched upon in chapter twelve.) Presumably, such implicit self-ascertainment would be "non-dualistic" in the sense that there would be no sense of subject and object as different—but of course, its object would not be an ultimate truth. This might account for Gyel-tsap's careful insertion of the word "explicit" in his formula. As we shall see, however, the term "dualistic appearance" can have a very much wider range of meanings, and if all of these types of dualistic appearances have vanished for a direct perceiver, then its object of cognition must be an ultimate truth. Lopez, *A Study of Svātantrika*, pp. 194-6 discusses some of these same issues, i.e., self-consciousness and its relationship to the definition of ultimate truth, in terms of a Svātantrika perspective.

Another reason not to posit these definitions in Prāsaṅgika is that (theoretically) each definiendum can have only one definition. See Perdue ("Practice and Theory of Philosophical Debate in Tibetan Buddhist Education," Ph.D. dissertation, University of Virginia, 1983, p. 98) and Dreyfus ("Definition in Buddhism") on this point. Accordingly, Gen Lo-sang-gya-tso told me that Paṇ-chen Sö-nam-drak-ba simply does not posit "dualistic appearance" type definitions of the two truths in Prāsaṅgika. It is not that they are wrong; they have no fault and are theoretically acceptable. It is just that Paṇ-chen Sö-nam-drak-ba uses another set of definitions and, by the very definition of a definiendum, each definiendum can have only one definition.

39. Ngak-wang-bel-den, *Explanation of the Conventional and the Ultimate*, p. 111.4-5.

40. A point made by Ngak-wang-bel-den in his *Annotations for (Jam-yang-shay-ba's) "Great Exposition of Tenets,"* 90b.7-8.

41. *Precious Garland: A Presentation of the Two Truths and Words of Instruction on the View* (*bden gnyis kyi rnam bzhag dang lta ba'i 'khrid yig rin po che'i 'phreng ba*) in *dbu ma'i lta khrid phyogs bsdebs* (Sarnath: Gelugpa Students Welfare Committee, 1985), p. 133.

42. *Great Exposition of the Middle Way*, p. 591.

43. *Ocean of Reasoning*, p. 415.2-8.

44. *Precious Garland: A Presentation of the Two Truths and Words of In-*

struction on the View, p. 134.

45. *Illumination of the Thought*, pp. 223.5-224.1.

46. Jang-gya, *Presentation of Tenets*, pp. 356.9-10; Lopez, *A Study of Svātantrika*, pp. 195 and 329; Kensur Yeshay Tupden (oral communication).

47. *Great Exposition of the Middle Way*, pp. 585 and 596.

48. Ibid, p. 591.

49. *Supplement Commentary* (*Madhyamakāvatārabhāṣya*) as edited by Louis de la Vallée Poussin, *Madhyamakāvatāra par Candrakīrti*, p. 111.11-17.

50. *Annotations for (Jam-yang-shay-ba's) "Great Exposition of Tenets"* (*grub mtha' chen mo'i mchan 'grel*) (Sarnath: Pleasure of Elegant Sayings Printing Press, 1964), f.91a.3-5.

51. *Precious Garland: A Presentation of the Two Truths and Words of Instruction on the View* in *dbu ma'i lta khrid phyogs bsdebs*, p. 133.14-18.

52. *Supplement Commentary* (*Madhyamakāvatārabhāṣya*) as edited by Louis de la Vallée Poussin, *Madhyamakāvatāra par Candrakīrti*, pp. 102.20-103.2.

53. *Illumination of the Thought*, p. 195.1.

CHAPTER SEVEN

1. *Supplement* (*Madhaymakāvatāra*), edited Tibetan: Louis de la Vallée Poussin, *Madhyamakāvatāra par Candrakīrti*, chapter 6, vs. 24.

2. Ibid, chapter 6, vs. 25.

3. *Illumination of the Thought*, p. 199.4-5.

4. My description of superficial ignorance as "non-innate" derives from Tsong-ka-pa's *Illumination of the Thought* (p.202.2), where, in order to exclude ignorance arising from superficial causes, he states, "Here the impairment that is analyzed as to whether or not there is impairment is to be taken as the impairment of innate erroneous apprehension." Kay-drup's *Thousand Doses* (623.3) contributes the word "circumstantial" (*glo bur*). Cabezón's translation ("The Development of a Buddhist Philosophy of Language," p. 1034) gives "adventitious."

5. *Supplement Commentary* (*Madhyamakāvatārabhāṣya*) as edited by Louis de la Vallée Poussin, *Madhyamakāvatāra par Candrakīrti*, p. 104.8-11. "Thorn-apple" is a translation of *da du ra* in Candrakīrti 's *Supplement Commentary* (p.104.8). In a note to his translation, La Vallée Poussin (*Muséon* 11: 301, n.3) states that Max Walleser suggests the Sanskrit reading *dardura*. However, Tsong-ka-pa glosses *da du ra* as *thang phrom*, also spelled *thang khrom*. Das (*A Tibetan-English Dictionary*, Delhi: Motilal Banarsidass, rpt. 1976, p. 568) identifies the latter as *dhūstūra*. The word "fruit" is not in Candrakīrti; it is supplied by Tsong-ka-pa's *Illumination of the Thought*, p. 200.4.

6. *Great Exposition of the Middle Way*, p. 569.

7. The term *pradhāna* appears in the *Śvetāśvatara Upaniṣad* (I, 10). In the Sāṃkhya system it refers to the primary or principal cause of everything. See P.T. Raju, *Structural Depths of Indian Thought* (Albany: State University of New York Press, 1985) pp. 316-17. For a Tibetan Buddhist

presentation of the meaning of *pradhāna* in Sāṃkhya, see Sopa and Hopkins, *The Practice and Theory of Tibetan Buddhism*, pp. 59-60.

8. *Illumination of the Thought*, p. 201.3-4.

9. Ibid, p. 202.3-4.

10. *Great Exposition of the Middle Way*, p. 562.

11. Ibid, p. 570 (artificial) and p. 562 (innate).

12. See Hopkins, *Meditation on Emptiness*, p. 293.

13. *Distinguishing the Two Truths* (*Satyadvayavibhaṅgakārikā*), Tibetan (Toh 3881) edited by Eckel, *Jñānagarbha's Commentary on the Distinction Between the Two Truths*, vs. 12, pp. 79 and 163. This stanza is cited by Jang-gya (*Presentation of Tenets*, p. 359); see Lopez, *A Study of Svātantrika*, p. 333.

14. *Presentation of Tenets*, p. 360; Lopez, *A Study of Svātantrika*, pp. 333-334.

15. Although Ngak-wang-bel-den complains that these definitions are not acceptable even in Svātantrika because they do not include permanent concealer-truths, such as unproduced space, which do not perform functions, it is clear that they represent a traditional Svātantrika understanding of the terms real and unreal concealer-truth.

16. *Supplement Commentary* (*Madhyamakāvatārabhāṣya*) as edited by Louis de la Vallée Poussin, *Madhyamakāvatāra par Candrakīrti*, p. 105.1-4.

17. Michael Sweet, "The Two Truths in Bodhicaryāvatāra 9.2," *Journal of the International Association of Buddhist Studies* 2 (1979): 80.

18. *Illumination of the Thought*, p. 200.2.

19. *Intermediate Exposition of the Stages of the Path*, p. 461.4-5.

20. Ibid, p. 461.

21. Ngak-wang-bel-den, *Explanation of the Conventional and the Ultimate*, p. 179.6.

22. *Great Exposition of the Stages of the Path*, p. 841.1-2.

23. *Intermediate Exposition of the Stages of the Path*, p. 463.1-2.

24. Ngak-wang-bel-den, *Explanation of the Conventional and the Ultimate*, p. 180 cites the *Buddhapālita Commentary on (Nāgārjuna's) "Treatise on the Middle Way"* (*Buddhapālitamūlamadhyamakavṛtti*) (P5254) *sDe dge Tibetan Tripitaka* (Tokyo: 1977ff) *dbu ma* Vol. 1, ff,244b.6-245a.1.

25. The first part of this sentence is based on Tsong-ka-pa's *Intermediate Exposition of the Stages of the Path*, p. 93 and Ngak-wang-bel-den, *Explanation of the Conventional and the Ultimate*, p. 179.5. The reason clause is accurate for Paṇ-chen and Jam-yang-shay-ba, but may not be precise for Jay-dzun Chö-gyi-gyel-tsen who apparently holds that a mind of non-dualistic meditative equipoise on emptiness cognizes itself (a concealer-truth) as well as emptiness.

26. *Great Exposition of the Stages of the Path*, p. 845.4-5.

27. *Great Exposition of the Middle Way*, p. 560. Compare the explanation of Hopkins, *Meditation on Emptiness*, p. 542.

28. *A Good Explanation Adorning the Throats of the Fortunate* (*bstan bcos dbu ma la 'jug pa'i rnam bshad dgongs pa rab gsal gyi dka' gnad gsal bar*

byed pa'i spyi don legs bshad skal bzang mgul rgyan) (New Delhi: lha mkhar yongs 'dzin bstan pa rgyal mtshan, 1973), p. 409.

29. Although these definitions and those below pertaining to real and unreal objective conventionalities are presented in order to define the different types of conventionalities, Jay-dzun-ba omits the word "conventionality" (*kun rdzob*) from the phrases presenting the definienda that are right or real (*yang dag*). This is because he does not accept the legitimacy of the phrase "real conventionality in relation to the world." The intra-Ge-luk-ba controversy on this point, which is more a matter of grammar rather than substance, will be explained later in this chapter.

30. *A Good Explanation Adorning the Throats of the Fortunate*, pp. 409-410.

31. This sentence represents the predominant view of Ge-luk-bas of all colleges today, but does not necessarily agree with a literal reading of Kay-drup's *Thousand Doses* or Jam-yang-shay-ba's Mādhyamika textbook. We will return to this problem below.

32. Jay-dzun Chö-gyi-gyel-tsen, *A Good Explanation Adorning the Throats of the Fortunate*, pp. 382-383.

33. Ibid, pp. 395-398.

34. Jam-yang-shay-ba, *Great Exposition of the Middle Way*, pp. 570.1; Ngak-wang-bel-den, *Explanation of the Conventional and the Ultimate*, p. 183.1-2.

35. Jay-dzun Chö-gyi-gyel-tsen, *A Good Explanation Adorning the Throats of the Fortunate*, pp. 381.6-382.6; Jam-yang-shay-ba, *Great Exposition of the Middle Way*, p. 570.1.

36. According to Geshe Bel-den-drak-ba (oral communication) and Ngak-wang-bel-den's *Joyful Teaching Clarifying the Mind, A Statement of the Modes of Explaining the Middle Way and the Perfection of Wisdom in the Textbooks of the Lo-sel-ling and Dra-shi-go-mang Monastic Colleges* (*blo gsal gling dang bkra shis sgo mang grwa tshang gi dbu phar gyi yig cha bshad tshul bkod pa blo gsal dga' ston*) Collected Works, Vol. 3 (New Delhi: Guru Deva, 1983), p. 469.1; see also Jay-dzun Chö-gyi-gyel-tsen, *A Good Explanation Adorning the Throats of the Fortunate*, p. 404.

37. *An Eye-Opening Golden Wand: Counsel on the Meaning of the Profound* (*zab don gdams pa'i mig 'byed gser gyi thur ma*) Vol. 3: (Mundgod: Drebung Loseling Printing Press, 1984), p. 341.

38. Paṇ-chen Sö-nam-drak-ba, *General Meaning of (Nāgārjuna's) "Treatise on the Middle Way"* (*dbu ma'i spyi don*) Collected Works Vol. "Ja" (Mundgod: Drebung Loseling Library Society, 1985), p. 123.3-5; Jay-dzun Chö-gyi-gyel-tsen, *A Good Explanation Adorning the Throats of the Fortunate*, pp. 412-413.

39. This is an extrapolation from Paṇ-chen Sö-nam-drak-ba's assertions about the Sautrāntika example and is confirmed by Geshe Bel-den-drak-ba (oral communication).

40. According to Geshe Bel-den-drak-ba and Kensur Yeshay Tupden (oral communications). Also, Ngak-wang-bel-den's *Joyful Teaching Clarifying the Mind*, p. 469.2 states that according to Lo-sel-ling,

> Whatever is an established base necessarily has a discordance between its mode of appearance and its mode of subsistence because whatever is an established base necessarily has a discordance between its mode of subsistence and its mode of appearance to the conceptual consciousness apprehending it.

41. According to Geshe Bel-den-drak-ba (oral communication).

42. This is not to say that direct valid cognition is *always* the consciousness in relation to which this determination is made. The question of what mind is referred to when it is said that something does or does not "exist as it appears" is a vexed one, and there are a variety of answers—no one of which seems fully satisfactory. Jeffrey Hopkins reports (oral communication) that Kensur Lekden, a Go-mang scholar and former abbot of the Tantric College of lower Lhasa, held that whether or not something exists as it appears is determined by whether or not it exists as it appears to its uncommon certifying awareness. He considered direct valid cognizers to be the uncommon certifiers of emptiness and impermanent concealer-truths, and inferential valid cognizers to be the uncommon certifiers of permanent concealer-truths. Such a teaching could be understood to imply that permanent phenomena other than emptiness are not realized in direct perception by sentient beings. However, Kensur Den-ba-den-dzin (oral communication) rejects this, explaining that advanced yogis can directly realize uncompounded space and so forth. Kensur Den-ba-den-dzin's own position is that something is a falsity if it does not exist as it appears to an awareness distinguishing a conventionality. For further discussion of this problem in relation to the question of how to posit a Buddha's Wisdom Truth Body (*ye shes chos sku, jñānadharmakāya*) as a falsity, see chapter twelve.

43. According to Geshe Bel-den-drak-ba (oral communication).

44. This may be the position Jay-dzun-ba (*A Good Explanation Adorning the Throats of the Fortunate*, p. 413.4) is suggesting, although he does not state it explicitly.

45. *Illumination of the Thought* (dbu ma la 'jug pa'i rgya bshad pa dgongs pa rab gsal) (Dharamsala: Shes rig par khang, n.d.), p. 202.4-6.

46. *Great Exposition of the Middle Way*, p. 556.

47. Ibid, p. 570.

48. *Supplement* (*Madhaymakāvatāra*), edited Tibetan: Louis de la Vallée Poussin, *Madhyamakāvatāra par Candrakīrti*, chapter 6, vs. 25.

49. See chapter ten.

50. *A Good Explanation Adorning the Throats of the Fortunate*, pp. 409-410.

51. Ngak-wang-bel-den, *Explanation of the Conventional and the Ultimate*, p. 182.5-7.

52. Jang-gya emphasizes this point in his discussion of the definitions of the two truths in Svātantrika. See his *Presentation of Tenets*, pp. 360.3-9; Lopez, *A Study of Svātantrika*, p. 333.

53. *Supplement* (*Madhaymakāvatāra*), edited Tibetan: Louis de la Vallée Poussin, *Madhyamakāvatāra par Candrakīrti*, chapter 6, vs. 23, line 3.

54. Ibid, chapter 6, vs. 26.

55. *Great Exposition of the Middle Way*, p. 568.

56. *Supplement* (*Madhaymakāvatāra*), edited Tibetan: Louis de la Vallée Poussin, *Madhyamakāvatāra par Candrakīrti*, chapter 6, vs. 24.

57. Jay-dzun Chö-gyi-gyel-tsen, *A Good Explanation Adorning the Throats of the Fortunate*, pp. 408-410; Paṇ-chen Sö-nam-drak-ba, *Disputation and Reply [Regarding] (Candrakīrti's) "Supplement,"*, p. 276.2-3.

58. *Intermediate Exposition of the Stages of the Path*, p. 463.1-2.

59. *Presentation of Tenets*, p. 467.12-16.

60. Paṇ-chen Sö-nam-drak-ba, *Disputation and Reply [Regarding] (Candrakīrti's) "Supplement,"*, p. 276.3.

61. *An Eye-Opening Golden Wand*, p. 337.

62. Apparently *'brel* has been substituted for the practically homophonic *bkral* which appears in the just-cited passage from Paṇ-chen Sö-nam-drak-ba's *General Meaning of (Nāgārjuna's) "Treatise on the Middle Way"* (*dbu ma'i spyi don*) Collected Works Vol. "Ja" (Mundgod: Drebung Loseling Library Society, 1985).

63. Gen Lo-sang-gya-tso, a Lo-sel-ling scholar and principal of the Buddhist School of Dialectics, criticized Paṇ-chen Sö-nam-drak-ba both for this and for the relatively harsh treatment Kay-drup receives at Paṇ-chen's hands (oral communication).

64. *Thousand Doses* (*stong thun chen mo*) (Dharamsala: Shes rig par khang, n.d.), p. 623.4-6; Cabezón, "The Development of a Buddhist Philosophy of Language," p. 1035.

65. *Great Exposition of the Middle Way*, p. 554.

66. Ibid, p. 539.

67. Ibid, p. 538.

68. Ngak-wang-bel-den, *Explanation of the Conventional and the Ultimate*, p. 207.

69. *Supplement Commentary* (*Madhyamakāvatārabhāṣya*) as edited by Louis de la Vallée Poussin, *Madhyamakāvatāra par Candrakīrti*, p. 107.9-17.

70. *Intermediate Exposition of the Stages of the Path*, pp. 461.6-462.1.

71. *Illumination of the Thought*, p. 207.3-4.

72. Ibid, p. 207.4-6.

73. I would like to raise a qualm at this point. Just as mature adults are able to realize that young children, etc., have the coarse concealing ignorance that mistakes a reflection as a face, so Foe Destroyers and pure ground Bodhisattvas are able to realize that unliberated sentient beings have the ignorant consciousnesses that mistake phenomena to be inherently existent. If a Foe Destroyer's understanding of how form appears to the ignorant allows us to say that form is a concealer-truth in relation to a Foe Destroyer, then by analogy we should be able to say that a reflection of a face is a concealer-truth in relation to an adult. It seems, however, that this is not asserted. Compare Jam-yang-shay-ba's (*Great Exposition of the Middle Way*, pp. 528-534) related discussion. We will return to this issue in chapter eleven.

74. T.R.V. Murti, "Saṃvṛti and Paramārtha in Mādhyamika and Advaita Vedānta" in *The Problem of the Two Truths in Buddhism and Vedānta*, edited by M. Sprung (Dordrecht: Reidel, 1973), pp. 12-13. Nāgārjuna was charged by critics with *asatkyāti-vāda*, confounding the illusory with the inexistent (P.T. Raju, *Structural Depths of Indian Thought*, p. 568). Murti incorporates this charge into his presentation of Mādhyamika.

CHAPTER EIGHT

1. *Supplement* (*Madhaymakāvatāra*), edited Tibetan: Louis de la Vallée Poussin, *Madhyamakāvatāra par Candrakīrti*, chapter 6, vs. 25.

2. *Supplement Commentary* (*Madhyamakāvatārabhāsya*) as edited by Louis de la Vallée Poussin, *Madhyamakāvatāra par Candrakīrti*, p. 105.1-4.

3. *Illumination of the Thought*, p. 201.4-5.

4. The phrase "in this context" (*skabs 'dir*) is added here because, in general, a wrong consciousness (*log shes*) is any consciousness that is mistaken with regard to its main object of engagement. Some wrong consciousnesses, such as a consciousness conceiving an inherently existent self of persons, are right in relation to the worldly perspective.

5. *Illumination of the Thought*, pp. 200.2-4 and 202.2-4. This latter passage also appears *verbatim* in Tsong-ka-pa's *Ocean of Reasoning*, p. 410.2-6.

6. *Presentation of Tenets*, p. 464.7-12.

7. *Thousand Doses*, p. 622.2-4. Passage translated by Cabezón, "The Development of a Buddhist Philosophy of Language," p. 1032-3.

8. *Great Exposition of the Middle Way*, p. 552.

9. Ibid, p. 553.

10. This chart is based on statements made by Jam-yang-shay-ba in his *Great Exposition of the Middle Way*, pp. 552-54, 559, 567, and 574.

11. A consciousness conceiving true existence with regard to emptiness is also excluded from the worldly perspective for which things are real. This is because consciousnesses conceiving emptiness to be truly existent do not misconceive emptiness as existing as it appears—for emptiness *does* exist as it appears in Jam-yang-shay-ba's system.

12. Since Jam-yang-shay-ba refers to these consciousnesses conceiving true existence as "ordinary, innate, worldly awarenesses," he may also intend to exclude consciousnesses conceiving true existence that arise artificially, under the influence of training in philosophical systems.

13. *Great Exposition of the Middle Way*, p. 559.

14. *Great Exposition of Tenets*, *dbu ma* section, f.27a4-8.

15. *Great Exposition of the Stages of the Path*, p. 828.2-3.

16. *Intermediate Exposition of the Stages of the Path*, p. 463.1-2.

17. *Great Exposition of the Middle Way*, p. 559.

18. Frequent equivalents of *la ltos te* include *la ltos pa'i* and *la ltos nas* all of which I translate as "in relation to;" another equivalent, *shes ngo'i* (Ngak-wang-bel-den, *Explanation of the Conventional and the Ultimate*, p. 208.1) means "of the perspective." Jam-yang-shay-ba uses these terms

without distinction, and several times clearly contradicts Ngak-wang-bel-den's ideas of their meanings. Paṇ-chen Sö-nam-drak-ba's usage, rather remarkably, is generally consistent with Ngak-wang-bel-den's distinctions.

19. Ngak-wang-bel-den, *Explanation of the Conventional and the Ulti-* 180.5-6.

Ibid, pp. 201.6-7 and 203.6-7.

21. Ngak-wang-bel-den refutes (*Explanation of the Conventional and the Ultimate*, pp. 180.5, 203.6-7, 206.1-2) the distinction between what is real in the perspective of a conventional valid cognizer and what is unreal in the perspective of aconventional valid cognizer. This makes sense when one considers only concealer-truths because no concealer-truth can be real in the perspective of a conventional valid cognizer. However, if emptiness is a reality and a truth, then what awareness apprehends it as such? Since ultimate valid cognizers find only emptiness, they do not find "emptiness' being a truth" or "emptiness' existing as it appears." These are concealer-truths, and as such should be realized by conventional valid cognizers. If special conventional valid cognizers can realize that emptiness is real and that form and so forth are unreal, then what fault is there in asserting a division of real and unreal in the perspective of conventional valid cognition? The point to note is that such a division should not be a subdivision of concealer-truths, but of all objects of knowledge. It is, in fact, a reiteration of the division of objects of knowledge into ultimate truths and concealer-truths.

22. Ngak-wang-bel-den, *Explanation of the Conventional and the Ultimate*, p. 205.6-7.

23. *Illumination of the Thought*, p. 201.3-4. Emphasis added.

24. *Intermediate Exposition of the Stages of the Path*, p. 463.1-2. Emphasis added.

25. Ngak-wang-bel-den, *Explanation of the Conventional and the Ultimate*, p. 206.1-2.

26. *Great Exposition of Tenets*, *dbu ma* section, f.27a4-5.

27. Ngak-wang-bel-den, *Explanation of the Conventional and the Ultimate*, pp. 206.2-4.

28. *Presentation of Tenets*, p. 464.7-12.

29. Ibid, p. 465.8-16.

30. *Thousand Doses*, p. 622.2-4. Passage translated by Cabezón, "The Development of a Buddhist Philosophy of Language," p. 1032-3.

31. *Presentation of Tenets*, p. 467.6-10.

32. Paṇ-chen Sö-nam-drak-ba, *General Meaning of (Nāgārjuna's) "Treatise on the Middle Way"* (*dbu ma'i spyi don*) Collected Works Vol. "Ja" (Mundgod: Drebung Loseling Library Society, 1985), p. 120.2ff and Ngak-wang-bel-den, *Joyful Teaching Clarifying the Mind*, p. 276.2ff.

33. *A Good Explanation Adorning the Throats of the Fortunate*, pp. 405.6-410.6.

34. Ibid, pp. 411.6 and 416.5 respectively.

35. *A Good Explanation Adorning the Throats of the Fortunate*,

pp. 409.2-410.1.

36. Information on the life of Jay-dzun Chö-gyi-gyel-tsen is drawn from Khetsun Sangbo, *Biographical Dictionary*, 52-57.

37. Ngak-wang-bel-den, *Explanation of the Conventional and the Ultimate*, p. 209.3.

38. *Intermediate Exposition of the Stages of the Path*, p. 463.1-2.

39. *Illumination of the Thought*, p. 200.2-4.

40. Ngak-wang-bel-den, *Explanation of the Conventional and the Ultimate*, pp. 179.7-180.1.

CHAPTER NINE

1. See Conze's translation, *The Large Sutra on Perfect Wisdom*, 1975, pp. 144-48. Much of the information in this list is from Hopkins, *Meditation on Emptiness*. Candrakīrti discusses the twenty emptinesses at some length in his *Supplement* 6.183-222. They are also a topic in the *Ornament for Clear Realization* (*Abhisamayālaṃkāra*) and related literature. See, for example, Obermiller, *Analysis of the Abhisamayālaṃkāra* (London: Luzac, 1933), pp. 127-41, and Gyel-tsap's *Ornament for the Essence* (*rnam bshad syning po rgyan*) (Sarnath: Gelugpa Students Welfare Committee, 1980), p. 225.17ff. Although there are traditions that sequentially correlate these emptinesses with ascending levels of the Bodhisattva path, Candrakīrti does not make such a presentation.

2. Hopkins (*Meditation on Emptiness*, p. 204) mentions only the five senses, but Conze's translation, *The Large Sutra on Perfect Wisdom*, 1975, p. 144 refers to all six senses; so do Gyel-tsap's *Ornament for the Essence*, p. 225.19 and Kensur Padma-gyel-tsen, *An Eye-Opening Golden Wand*, Vol. 2, p. 259. (Note that according to the publication information appearing on these books, Volume 2 of *An Eye-Opening Golden Wand* was published in 1985, the year after the publication of Volume 3. The dates appear to be correct because the 1984 publication ("Vol. 3") is also described as "Paṇ-chen Bsod-nams-grags-pa Literature Series Volume 12, while the 1985 publication ("Vol. 2") is described as Paṇ-chen Bsod-nams-grags-pa Literature Series Volume 13. I have not seen a Volume 1 of *An Eye-Opening Golden Wand*.)

3. Cf. Kensur Padma-gyel-tsen, *An Eye-Opening Golden Wand*, Vol. 2, p. 265.5. and Conze, *The Large Sutra on Perfect Wisdom*, p. 144, including n.3.

4. *Supplement Commentary* (*Madhyamakāvatārabhāṣya*) as edited by Louis de la Vallée Poussin, *Madhyamakāvatāra par Candrakīrti*, p. 310.9-11. Candrakīrti 's *Supplement* (6.186) and *Supplement Commentary* (310.7-11) describe this as emptiness' own emptiness of being inherently existent. Obermiller (*Analysis of the Abhisamayālaṃkāra*, p. 129) notes that commentators such as Haribhadra and Ārya Vimuktasena have understood "emptiness of emptiness" to mean the emptiness of the wisdom consciousness realizing emptiness.

5. Kensur Padma-gyel-tsen (*An Eye-Opening Golden Wand*, Vol. 2, p. 267) seems to refer to, or at least include, the mind realizing emptiness—a view free from the two extremes. Similarly, Ngak-wang-bel-den (*Explanation of the Conventional and the Ultimate*, p. 185) apparently includes this among the emptinesses whose basis is a concealer-truth.

6. *Ornament for the Essence*, p. 226.10.

7. Hopkins (*Meditation on Emptiness*, p. 205) identifies this with the emptiness of inherently existent non-products. My explanation derives from Kensur Padma-gyel-tsen, *An Eye-Opening Golden Wand*, Vol. 2, p. 274.9-12. Also, Candrakīrti 's *Supplement* (chapter 6, vs. 218) says:

> Since they are arisen from conditions, things lack
> An [inherently existent] entity of being compounded.
> Regarding the [inherently existent entity of] being compounded,
> Emptiness of just that is the emptiness of non-things.

See also Obermiller, *Analysis of the Abhisamayālaṃkāra*, p. 138.

8. It should already be obvious that many of these emptinesses have the same bases and are simply referred to by different names, e.g. #7, #16, and #17 as well as #8 and #18. There are also several different ways of referring to the emptiness of emptiness. Two of these, #12 and #19, even have the same name in Tibetan: *rang bzhin stong pa nyid*. However, they have different names in Sanskrit: *prakṛtiśūnyatā* and *svabhāvaśūnyatā*. Sometimes #19 is called *rang gi stong pa nyid* to distinguish it from #12 and reflect its complementary relationship with #20.

9. As explained in Candrakīrti's *Supplement Commentary* (*Madhyamakāvatārabhāṣya*) as edited by Louis de la Vallée Poussin, *Madhyamakāvatāra par Candrakīrti*, p. 340.4-11. Also seen as *gzhan gyi stong pa nyid* and *gzhan gyi ngo bo stong pa nyid*.

10. See Gyel-tsap's *Ornament of the Essence*, pp. 226.19-227.1 and Candrakīrti's *Supplement* and *Supplement Commentary*, pp. 302.17-303.20. Lists of sixteen emptinesses are also found in Maitreya's *Discrimination of the Middle Way and the Extremes* (P5522; see Pandeya, ed., p. 41) and Dignāga's *Compendium of the Perfection of Wisdom* (P5207, see Tucci, ed., pp. 56-57, 60-61).

11. As reported by Hopkins, *Meditation on Emptiness*, pp. 204-5 and Lopez, *The Heart Sūtra Explained*, p. 210. See also the *Sūtra Unravelling the Thought* 8.109 (Lamotte, ed. and trans., pp. 108-110) and Lamotte's *Le Traité de la grande vertu de sagesse de Nāgārjuna*, pp. 2027-2151. According to Conze (1975, 670), there is a list of eighteen emptinesses that excludes #17 and #20 (instead of #19 and #20) from the list of twenty emptinesses.

12. *Supplement* (*Madhaymakāvatāra*), chapter 6, vs. 179, lines 1-2.

13. Ngak-wang-bel-den, *Explanation of the Conventional and the Ultimate*, p. 184.7.

14. Ibid, p. 185.1.

15. *Supplement Commentary* (*Madhyamakāvatārabhāṣya*) as edited by

Louis de la Vallée Poussin, *Madhyamakāvatāra par Candrakīrti*, p. 340.4-11. See Monier Williams, *A Sanskrit-English Dictionary* (Oxford: Oxford University Press, 1899; rpt. Delhi: Motilal Banarsidass, 1976), p. 586.

16. As cited by Kensur Padma-gyel-tsen, *An Eye-Opening Golden Wand*, Vol. 2, p. 275.

17. Napper, *Dependent Arising and Emptiness*, pp. 429-439.

18. See Hopkins, *Meditation on Emptiness*, pp. 218 and 288.

19. *Intermediate Exposition of the Stages of the Path*, p. 467.3.

20. *Great Exposition of the Middle Way*, p. 577.

21. *Supplement Commentary*, p. 71.3-5.

22. See the citation by Ngak-wang-bel-den, *Explanation of the Conventional and the Ultimate*, pp. 169.4-170.1.

23. According to Ngak-wang-bel-den, *Explanation of the Conventional and the Ultimate*, pp. 169-171 and Kensur Padma-gyel-tsen, *An Eye-Opening Golden Wand*, Vol. 3, p. 142.

24. *An Eye-Opening Golden Wand*, Vol. 3, p. 147.

25. P2010, vol. 46, p. 32, leaf 5, lines 3-5.

26. As cited by Kensur Padma-gyel-tsen, *An Eye-Opening Golden Wand*, Vol. 3, p. 144.

27. *Intermediate Exposition of the Stages of the Path*, pp. 466.6-467.1.

28. Tsul-tim-gya-tso (*tshul khrims rgya mtsho*, twentieth century), *A Timely Mirror Illuminating the Meaning of Difficult Points* (*dka' gnad kyi don gsal bar byed pa dus kyi me long*) (Delhi: Guru Deva, 1983), pp. 370-371.

29. As translated by Hopkins (*Compassion in Tibetan Buddhism*, p. 229) from the end of Tsong-ka-pa's commentary on the fifth chapter of Candrakīrti's *Supplement*.

30. Ibid. Slightly adapted.

31. *An Eye-Opening Golden Wand*, Vol. 3, p. 146.

32. Ibid, p. 146.

33. Ibid.

34. Ibid, p. 143.

35. As cited by Geshe Tsul-tim-gya-tso, *A Timely Mirror*, p. 372.

36. According to Jam-yang-shay-ba, *Great Exposition of the Middle Way*, p. 624.

37. As cited by Geshe Tsul-tim-gya-tso, *A Timely Mirror*, pp. 372-73.

38. Paṇ-chen Sö-nam-drak-ba, *General Meaning of (Nāgārjuna's) "Treatise on the Middle Way"*, p. 126.3.

39. *An Eye-Opening Golden Wand*, Vol. 3, pp. 142-148.

40. As cited by Kesur Padma-gyel-tsen, (*An Eye-Opening Golden Wand*, Vol. 3, p. 147). It would appear, however, that Paṇ-chen wrote this tantric text prior to his composition of the Lo-sel-ling textbooks, cited above, in which he indicates that true cessations are not emptinesses.

41. *An Eye-Opening Golden Wand*, Vol. 3, pp. 147-48.

42. *Meditation on Emptiness*, p. 382.

43. *An Eye-Opening Golden Wand*, Vol. 3, p. 144.

CHAPTER TEN

1. *Treatise on the Middle Way* (*Madhyamakaśāstra*), chapter 24, vs. 8.

2. Eckel, ed., *Jñānagarbha's Commentary on the Distinction Between the Two Truths*, p. 155; cf. Eckel's translation in same volume, p. 70.

3. *Great Exposition of the Middle Way*, pp. 565-66. This represents Jam-yang-shay-ba's commentary on the concluding stanza of the sixth chapter of Candrakīrti's *Supplement* (chapter 6, vs. 226):

> The king of swans extends the broad, white wings of
> conventionalities and suchness.
> Clearing the way for the swans—sentient beings—
> He soars on the winds of virtue
> To the far shore of a Conqueror's qualities.

4. *Treatise on the Middle Way* (*Madhyamakaśāstra*), chapter 24, vs. 9, second half.

5. *Supplement* (*Madhaymakāvatāra*), chapter 6, vs.80, second half.

6. *Great Exposition of the Middle Way*, p. 566.

7. *Ocean of Reasoning*, p. 407.

8. *Illumination of the Thought*, p. 194.5.

9. Ibid, p. 194.3-5.

10. *Supplement* (*Madhaymakāvatāra*), chapter 6, vs.80, first half.

11. Jay-dzun Chö-gyi-gyel-tsen, *A Good Explanation Adorning the Throats of the Fortunate*, pp. 355-6.

12. *Great Exposition of the Middle Way*, pp. 531-32 cites *Illumination of the Thought*, p. 210.4-6.

13. *Great Exposition of the Middle Way*, p. 531.

14. *An Eye-Opening Golden Wand*, Vol. 3, p. 329.

15. See Perdue, "Practice and Theory of Philosophical Debate in Tibetan Buddhist Education," pp. 93-95 and 100; see also the discussion of this and related issues offered by Dreyfus, "Definition in Buddhism," pp. 19-20 and 27-70.

16. *Illumination of the Thought*, p. 210.4-6.

17. For the sake of simplicity in this already complex argument, I am substituting the short definition of concealer-truth for the long version actually given by Kensur Padma-gyel-tsen in the quotation above.

18. Geshe Bel-den-drak-ba is among those who gave this reply.

19. *An Eye-Opening Golden Wand*, Vol. 3, p. 327.

20. Ibid.

21. *Supplement Commentary* (*Madhyamakāvatārabhāṣya*) as edited by Louis de la Vallée Poussin, *Madhyamakāvatāra par Candrakīrti*, pp. 102.16-103.1.

22. *Illumination of the Thought*, p. 194.1-2.

23. *Supplement Commentary* (*Madhyamakāvatārabhāsya*) as edited by Louis de la Vallée Poussin, *Madhyamakāvatāra par Candrakīrti*, p. 107.15-16.

24. *Illumination of the Thought*, p. 208.1-3.

25. Cited by Geshe Tsul-tim-gya-tso, *A Timely Mirror*, p. 376. Note that "pollution by ignorance" is here defined so as to include all mistaken consciousnesses. In another context, where Tsong-ka-pa's *Illumination of the Thought* (p. 202.4-6) states that objects and subjects polluted by ignorance cannot be discredited by ordinary conventional valid cognizers, "pollution by ignorance" refers to actual ignorant consciousnesses and their conceived objects. See the discussion of this in chapter seven.

26. According to Geshe Bel-den-drak-ba, Candrakīrti's phrase *rnam pa thams cad du* is the basis for Tsong-ka-pa's addition of the qualification "directly" (*mngon sum du*). Emptiness does not appear to the ignorant "in all aspects" means that it does not appear directly.

27. See Sopa and Hopkins, *Practice and Theory of Tibetan Buddhism*, p. 139.

28. Geshe Tsul-tim-gya-tso, *A Timely Mirror*, pp. 374-375.

29. There is a problem in translating the terms in this paragraph. The Tibetan verb *yod*, meaning "exist," is often used to express possession. However, the construction *X dang ldan* also means "having X" or "together with X." In this context, I have chosen to use the words "have" and "possess" only for the *dang ldan* construction, while translating *yod* very literally as "exists."

30. According to Ngak-wang-bel-den, *Joyful Teaching Clarifying the Mind*, pp. 461-62.

CHAPTER ELEVEN

1. *Supplement* (*Madhaymakāvatāra*), chapter 6, vs. 28. Tsong-ka-pa's *Illumination of the Thought* (p. 205.5-6) explains that that Candrakīrti is referring to a passage from the *Descent Into Laṅkā Sūtra*:

> The production of things [exists] conventionally (*kun rdzob tu, saṃvṛtitaḥ*);
> Ultimately, it lacks inherent existence.
> That [consciousness] which is mistaken regarding the lack of inherent existence
> Is asserted as the concealer (*kun rdzob, saṃvṛti*) of reality.

2. Supplement Commentary (*Madhyamakāvatārabhāṣya*) as edited by Louis de la Vallée Poussin, *Madhyamakāvatāra par Candrakīrti*, p. 107.16-17.

3. Jayānanda, *Explanation of (Candrakīrti's) "Supplement to (Nāgārjuna's) "Treatise on the Middle Way" (Mādhyamakāvatāraṭīka)* P5271, vol. 99, f.145a.

4. *Illumination of the Thought*, p. 207.3-4.

5. *Supplement* (*Madhaymakāvatāra*), chapter 6, vs. 23.

6. *Illumination of the Thought*, pp. 207.6-208.1 referring to Jayānanda, *Explanation of (Candrakīrti's) "Supplement to (Nāgārjuna's) "Treatise on the Middle Way"* (*Mādhyamakāvatāraṭīka*), vol. 99, f.145a, lines 3-4.

7. *Supplement Commentary* (*Madhyamakāvatārabhāṣya*) as edited by Louis de la Vallée Poussin, *Madhyamakāvatāra par Candrakīrti*, p. 107.17-19.

8. In his *Supplement* (chapter 6, vs. 26) and the section of the *Supplement Commentary* comenting upon that verse.

9. According to Gen Lo-sang-gya-tso, the afflictive ignorance of Superiors who have not attained liberation, having been weakened by the experience of direct realization of emptiness, no longer serves as the root of cyclic existence in their continuums.

10. *Supplement Commentary*, pp. 107.17-108.6.

11. Ibid, p. 108.11-13.

12. Many contemporary scholars share Jayānanda's view that Candrakīrti intended to separate concealer-truths (*saṃvṛtisatya*) and mere conventionalities (*saṃvṛtimātra*). Broido ("Veridical and Delusive Cognition," pp. 30-31) clearly holds this view. Another example is Nakamura Hajime (*Indian Buddhism*, p. 251) who writes that *saṃvṛtimātra* is "not *saṃvṛtisatya* or the truth in this mundane world."

13. *Ocean of Reasoning*, p. 405.

14. *Illumination of the Thought*, p. 210.3-4.

15. *Great Exposition of the Middle Way*, p. 531.

16. Ibid.

17. Ibid, p. 576.

18. As cited by *Great Exposition of the Middle Way*, p. 576.

19. Ibid., p 575. In contrast, Nakamura (*Indian Buddhism*, p. 251) uses one of the other etymologies of *saṃvṛti* (see chapter five) to arrive at the meaning "merely being concealed" for the term *saṃvṛtimātra*.

20. *Great Exposition of the Middle Way*, p. 575.

21. Ibid, p. 576.

22. *A Good Explanation Adorning the Throats of the Fortunate*, pp. 399.5-400.1.

23. *Disputation and Reply [Regarding] (Candrakīrti's) "Supplement,"* p. 280.1

24. *An Eye-Opening Golden Wand*, Vol. 3, p. 351.

CHAPTER TWELVE

1. *Illumination of the Thought*, pp. 222.5-223.1.

2. *Great Exposition of the Middle Way*, p. 584.

3. *Supplement*, chapter 6, vs.214.

4. As cited by Jam-yang-shay-ba in his *Great Exposition of the Middle Way*, p. 581.1.

5. Eckel, ed., *Jñānagarbha's Commentary on the Distinction Betweeen the Two Truths*, p. 188; cf. his translation in same volume, p. 102. At several points, Jñānagarbha's commentary adds additional verses, such as this, which are not part of the root text. This passage is cited by Paṇ-chen Sö-nam-drak-ba's *General Meaning of (Nāgārjuna's) "Treatise on the Middle Way,"* p. 129.2-3.

6. *Supplement*, chapter 6, vs. 29.
7. *Supplement Commentary*, pp. 109.10-110.14.
8. See the debate in Jam-yang-shay-ba, *Great Exposition of the Middle Way*, pp. 577-78; also, see the various refutations of the position that ultimate truth is not an object of knowledge in chapter two.
9. Illumination of the Thought, p. 223.5-6.
10. *Supplement Commentary*, p. 201.17-19. Some other editions (e.g. the Dharamasala edition) erroneously have *reg* for *rig* in this passage.
11. Cited in Tsong-ka-pa's *Illumination of the Thought* (p. 225) and by Jam-yang-shay-ba *Great Exposition of the Middle Way*, p. 579.
12. *Bṛhadāraṇyaka Upaniṣad*, 3.9.26.
13. *The Cloud of Unknowing*, trans. by Clifton Wolters (Baltimore: Penguin, 1973), p. 137.
14. Robert Thurman, trans., *Tsong Khapa's Speech of Gold in the Essence of True Eloquence*, p. 141.
15. *Great Exposition of the Middle Way*, p. 581.
16. Jam-yang-shay-ba (*Great Exposition of the Middle Way*, p. 581) has a hypothetical opponent raise this argument in a debate.
17. Jam-yang-shay-ba, *Great Exposition of the Middle Way*, p. 581.
18. *Illumination of the Thought*, p. 222.3-4.
19. *Ocean of Reasoning*, p. 419.6-9.
20. *Great Exposition of the Middle Way*, p. 581.
21. According to Gen Lo-sang-gya-tso (oral communication) and Geshe Tsul-tim-gya-tso, *A Timely Mirror*, p. 373.
22. *Great Exposition of the Middle Way*, p. 571.
23. *Illumination of the Thought*, p. 222.3.
24. According to Gen Lo-sang-gya-tso (oral communication), when a wisdom consciousness of meditative equipoise directly realizes emptiness, it realizes it through the appearance of the aspect of emptiness. However, it does not realize that aspect, because if it did it would be realizing a concealer-truth. The aspect of emptiness is a likeness, or image, of emptiness and is not itself an emptiness or ultimate truth.
25. *Illumination of the Thought*, p. 222.3.
26. According to the Go-mang and Lo-sel-ling colleges. However, as explained in chapter six, Jay-dzun Chö-gyi-gyel-tsen holds that a mind directly realizing emptiness also realizes itself.
27. *An Entrance for the Sons of Conquerors, Explanation of (Śāntideva's) "Engaging in the Bodhisattva Deeds"* (*byang chub sems dpa'i spyod pa la 'jug pa'i rnam bshad rgyal sras*) (Sarnath: Gelugba Students Welfare Committee, 1973), p. 211.
28. See chapter six.
29. *Thousand Doses*, pp. 645-647. Also, Cabezón, trans., "The Development of a Buddhist Philosophy of Language and its Culmination in Tibetan Mādhyamika Thought," pp. 1070-1075.
30. *Thousand Doses*, p. 647.3
31. Ibid, p. 647.3-5.

32. The term "self-consciousness" has a specific and technical meaning in Buddhist epistemology, as will be explained. It is important to keep in mind that self-consciousness is quite different from the introspective reflections practiced on the Buddhist path. Hopkins (*Meditation on Emptiness*, p. 377) reminds us that although the various tenet systems disagree about self-consciousness in this technical sense, all advocate reliance on meditative introspection and moral self-awareness. "In these cases the mind is perceiving a previous moment of the mind or a part of the mind is perceiving the general mind." For other discussions of self-consciousness one may refer to Cozort, "Unique Tenets of the Middle Way Consequence School," Ph.D. dissertation, University of Virginia, 1989, pp. 132-59; Klein, Knowledge and Liberation, pp. 73-76; Hopkins, Meditation on Emptiness, pp. 373-74 and p. 377; Lati Rinbochay and Elizabeth Napper, Mind in Tibetan Buddhism, pp. 19 and 60; Sopa and Hopkins, Practice and Theory of Tibetan Buddhism, passim; and Cabezón, "The Development of a Buddhist Philosophy of Language," pp. 980-1005. I have relied on these as well as the oral teaching of Kensur Yeshay Tupden.

33. Pur-bu-jok Jam-ba-gya-tso (*phu bu lcog byams pa rgya mtsho*, 1825-1921), *The Greater Path of Reasoning* (*rigs lam che ba*) in *The Presentation of Collected Topics Revealing the Meaning of the Texts on Valid Cognition, the Magical Key to the the Path of Reasoning* (*tshad ma'i gzhung don 'byed pa'i bsdus grva'i rnam bzhag rigs lam 'phrul gyi lde mig*) (Buxa, India: n.p., 1965), f.7b.2.

34. Ibid.

35. *Thousand Doses* (646.2-4); passage translated by Cabezón, "The Development of a Buddhist Philosophy of Language," p. 1071. This point is approvingly raised by Jam-yang-shay-ba, *Great Exposition of the Middle Way*, p. 583.

36. *Disputation and Reply [Regarding] (Candrakīrti's) "Supplement"* (*dbu ma la 'jug pa'i brgal lan*) Collected Works Vol. "Ja" (Mundgod: Drebung Loseling Library Society, 1985), pp. 282.1-284.7; Jay-dzun Chö-gyi-gyel-tsen, *A Good Explanation Adorning the Throats of the Fortunate*, pp. 415-416.

37. I will not give a separate presentation of Jay-dzun-ba's arguments on this issue, which are similar in most aspects to those of Paṇ-chen Sö-nam-drak-ba.

38. See the discussion of dualistic appearance in chapter six.

39. Paṇ-chen Sö-nam-drak-ba, *Disputation and Reply [Regarding] (Candrakīrti's) "Supplement,"*, 1985), p. 283.5 and *General Meaning of (Nāgārjuna's) "Treatise on the Middle Way,"* p. 129.1-2. At this point Paṇ-chen Sö-nam-drak-ba does not use the term "requiring interpretation" (*drang don*) in its technical Prāsaṅgika sense. He simply means that these teachings are not to be taken literally.

40. *Disputation and Reply [Regarding] (Candrakīrti's) "Supplement,"* p. 284.5-7.

41. *Great Exposition of the Middle Way*, p. 582.

42. Ibid.

43. Ibid, p. 583.

44. Ibid, p. 538.

45. For another fascinating example of the complications that arise for Jam-yang-shay-ba and his followers from their strong loyalty to Kay-drup, see Lopez, *A Study of Svātantrika*, pp. 200-203.

46. *Presentation of Tenets*, pp. 470.17-471.3. In the Svātantrika section of the same text, Jang-gya (as translated by Lopez in *A Study of Svātantrika*, p. 330) describes his own exegetical approach:

> If, having arranged the statements of the three—the father [Tsong-ka-pa] and his sons [Gyel-tsap and Kay-drup]—one comes to know a system for dispelling objections, it appears that it will be speech pleasing to scholars. However, it is not suitable to be easily satisfied by those who, from seeing only one portion of the scriptures, discard other portions and do whatever they can to make up their own interpretations.

47. *Great Exposition of the Middle Way*, p. 584.

48. Ibid, p. 585.

49. Indeed, it is said that *all* phenomena have parts. However, there are complex issues involved in the question of whether emptiness has parts. For example, a chair is designated, or imputed, in dependence upon the collection of the parts of a chair; thus, it is said that the basis of imputation of a chair is the collection of its parts. However, the basis of imputation of the emptiness of the chair is not the collection of the emptinesses of the various parts of the chair. That is, one does not take the emptiness of the chair's leg, the emptiness of the chair's seat, and so forth and collect them together in order to form the basis of imputation of the emptiness of the chair. On the contrary, the emptiness of the chair is imputed in dependence upon the mere absence of inherent existence in the chair. Consequently, since emptiness is not imputed in dependence upon a collection of constituent emptinesses, one may wonder whether emptiness has parts in the same sense that a chair has parts.

50. Jay-dzun Chö-gyi-gyel-tsen (*A Good Explanation Adorning the Throats of the Fortunate*, p. 416) also makes this point.

51. *Great Exposition of the Middle Way*, p. 587 cites *Illumination of the Thought*, p. 521.3-4.

52. Jam-yang-shay-ba (*Great Exposition of the Middle Way*, p. 588) makes the point that an aspectless meeting is found only in the tenets of Vaibhāṣika. Also, see Sopa and Hopkins, *Practice and Theory of Tibetan Buddhism*, p. 79.

53. *Great Exposition of the Middle Way*, p. 582.

54. Ibid, p. 583.

55. Candrakīrti holds that production from other should be refuted even conventionally. For Tsong-ka-pa, this means that production from other *that can be found under analysis* (i.e., inherently existent production from other) does not exist even conventionally. (See Hopkins, *Meditation on Emp-*

tiness, pp. 136 and 162.) Since the non-Prāsaṅgika advocates of production from other are all proponents of inherent existence, it follows that they are actually advocating an inherently existent production from other and that Candrakīrti's refutation of production from other is not intended as a denial of the merely conventionally existent production of sprouts, etc., from seeds, etc., that are different entities from them. Tsong-ka-pa's *Great Exposition of the Stages of the Path* (f. 387a.6ff) explicitly makes such arguments regarding production from other; my extension of them to the case of self-consciousness is primarily a matter of conjecture. This does not seem to be the way Tsong-ka-pa is usually understood, and it should be clear that my suggestion that this may be Jam-yang-shay-ba's view is based merely on an *extrapolation* of the reasoning in his discussion of how an omniscient mind cognizes itself. However, if this is correct, it would mean that a statement such as "self-consciousness is refuted even conventionally" could be read as an utter denial of a self-consciousness that is findable under analysis. For someone who refutes inherent existence, it might still be possible to hold that a consciousness can know itself.

56. *Great Exposition of the Middle Way*, p. 571.4-5.

57. Ngak-wang-pun-tsok (*ngag dbang phun tshog*), *Medicinal Ear of Corn, A Good Explanation: A Commentary on "A Song of the View, A Medicinal Sprout To Cast Out the Demons [of Extreme Views]"* (*lta mgur gdung sel sman gyi myu gu'i rnam 'grel bshad sman gyi snye ma*) (New Delhi: Tibet House, n.d.), pp. 106.3-107.2.

58. Ngak-wang-bel-den, *Explanation of the Conventional and the Ultimate*, pp. 171.6-172.3.

59. Ibid, p. 42.5.

60. Ibid, pp. 170.7-171.1. It seems that Ngak-wang-bel-den intends this as a quotation rather than a paraphrase. Unfortunately, although Tsong-ka-pa often cites Candrakīrti's *Commentary on (Nāgārjuna's) "Sixty Stanzas on Reasoning"* when discussing nirvāṇa, I have not located this particular passage either in Tsong-ka-pa's *Intermediate Exposition* or elsewhere.

61. *Ocean of Reasoning*, p. 419.6-9,

62. *Meditation on Emptiness*, p. 544.

63. This passage from Jang-gya's *Song on the Practice of the View* is cited in Den-dar-hla-ram-ba's *Presentation of the Lack of Being One or Many*, Collected Works, Vol. 1 (New Delhi: Lama Guru Deva, 1971), p. 425.1ff. The translation is that of Hopkins, *Meditation on Emptiness*, p. 545. The Ge-luk-ba monk Ge-dun-chö-pel (*dge 'dun chos 'phel*, 1905?-1951?) criticized the Ge-luk-ba pedagogical strategy on the grounds that, despite cautions such as this by Jang-gya, it fosters a reifying extreme.

64. Āryadeva, *Four Hundred/Treatise of Four Hundred Stanzas* (*Catuḥśatakaśāstrakārikā*) (Toh 3846; P5246, Vol. 95), ed. by Karen Lang, "Āryadeva on the Bodhisattva's Cultivation of Merit and Knowledge" (Ann Arbor: University Microfilms, 1983), chapter 8, vs.19. For references to this verse in Ge-luk-ba contexts, see Hopkins, *Meditation on Emptiness*, p. 837 and Hopkins, *Emptiness Yoga*, pp. 51 and 462.

Index